The Resurrection Narratives

The Resurrection Narratives

A Redactional Study

Grant R. Osborne

Baker Book House
Grand Rapids, Michigan 49506

Copyright 1984 by
Baker Book House Company

ISBN: 0-8010-6707-3 (cloth)
      0-8010-6708-1 (paper)

Library of Congress Catalog
Card Number: 84-71236

Printed in the United States of America

Contents

Foreword

Since Evangelical Christians have always insisted on the actual documents of the Bible for their supreme rule of faith and conduct, they have concentrated their attention on exegesis of the actual text of Scripture rather than attempting to expose, for example, a hypothetical historical reconstruction of the sayings of Jesus which might have greater authority than the Gospels.

In recent years biblical scholarship has devoted more attention to what is known as redaction criticism—the study of how authors of Scripture used historical and theological sources of information in order to write their accounts. Clearly this kind of study should be congenial to scholars who take the authority of Scripture seriously. It is precisely this kind of study which is undertaken in this book. Dr. Osborne carefully examines the accounts of the resurrection in the Gospels to see how each evangelist tells the story from his own distinctive theology. Thus the depth and richness of each account can be more fully appreciated. Preachers especially should profit from this new understanding of the resurrection narratives.

At the same time the obvious question cannot be avoided: How much is theological interpretation in the Gospels true and how much actually happened? Dr. Osborne does not ignore these questions but carefully investigates the underlying traditions which show the evangelists were not repeating cunningly devised myths when they proclaimed the resurrection of Jesus.

Dr. Osborne's work is an important contribution to the study of the Gospels. I commend it as a work of high quality scholarship characterized by genuine reverence for the Bible as the Word of God.

I. Howard Marshall

Preface

Redaction criticism is a fairly recent development in the study of the Gospels. It first appeared in the 1950s as a genuine concern for the theological emphasis and creative work of each evangelist. The term "redaction" itself applies to the editing done by biblical writers in producing their finished product. While redaction criticism is the stepchild of form criticism, it differs in its emphasis on Gospel writers as creative theologians rather than mere compilers of tradition. This dichotomy cannot be stressed too much, however, since redaction criticism is very much like tradition criticism, or the study of the development of traditions behind the gospel accounts. Indeed, both studies are necessary for determining whether a particular element within a passage comes from tradition or the writer's own redaction in order to isolate his particular emphasis.

Redaction criticism in many ways is the synthesis of previous methods of criticism. To utilize it properly one must consider the literary forms of passages, parallels to the passage in light of the religious heritage of the New Testament age, and especially the development of traditions behind the synoptic and Johannine accounts. Much has been written about the excesses and abuses of biblical criticism, but not enough has been said about the benefits of utilizing such valuable tools. Perhaps if we lay aside some negative presuppositions we can use these tools in our search for a total perspective on the biblical text.

A redactional approach to the Gospels must utilize two tools, tradition criticism and redaction criticism. Tradition criticism primarily does two things: (1) It separates tradition from redaction, revealing how the evangelist shaped the original tradition to fit his own message (a good example of this separation technique is the identification of omissions and additions Matthew and Luke made to Mark). (2) It seeks to ascertain the tradition behind the "pericope" or individual passages in the Gospels. This study may be highly speculative yet beneficial to any student who seeks greater understanding of the dynamics behind the New Testament and the theology of the early church.

Redaction study takes the results of tradition criticism and applies them: (1) It isolates and studies redactions in light of the theological purpose of each evangelist in the book as a whole, and in pericopes in particular. Redaction criticism thus helps the student to find the true message of the passage itself in light of the writer's interpretation of Jesus' message. (2) It shows how the author wove tradition into his message and proposes a comprehensive interpretation of the book in terms of that message (this is one area where redaction criticism has moved beyond form criticism; form criticism often produces a fragmentized book of isolated sections whereas redaction criticism seeks to understand the whole message as it is woven through its parts).

The redaction critic uses three methods to determine the message of a particular book: (1) tradition study which helps determine the individual emphasis of a writer and his special interests; (2) the external method which compares Matthew or Luke with the Gospel of Mark to see how and where the narrative has been abbreviated or expanded resulting in a different emphasis; and (3) the internal method which shows how the special emphasis of a pericope or passage fits the thematic development of the Gospel[1] as a whole.

Finally, an important by-product of redaction criticism is the isolation of the historical core of a passage in order to pass judgment on its historical reliability. This separation of history and interpretation helps to identify which parts came from the early days of the church and which were individual additions by the writer or later church. This historical reconstruction is most con-

---

1. Although redaction research is best known with regard to the Gospels, it has also been used successfully to study the historical and prophetic works of the Old Testament and indeed would be helpful with any book of the Bible inasmuch as it isolates the theological emphasis of the writer.

troversial, however, and the excesses of some radical redaction critics have caused many evangelicals to doubt the validity of the method as a whole. I believe both the original traditions and later interpretations were the product of eyewitness testimony (see my articles in *JETS* 19, 1976 and 21, 1978). The method properly applied is thus not a threat to a high view of Scripture but instead supports such a position.

The resurrection of Jesus is an excellent subject for redaction analysis. It not only is the theological core of each Gospel (we will later show how each evangelist used the resurrection to summarize his major emphases), but also provokes the most controversy because of the complexities of the narratives themselves. Seeming contradictions abound (as in the empty tomb narratives), and most scholars despair at harmonizing Jesus' appearance stories since each Gospel presents them so differently. I propose four steps to our redaction study of the resurrection.

1. We must first survey previous studies of the resurrection narratives to give us background for our study. We will review the finds of other schools of criticism and see how they have interpreted the narratives, especially noting their proposed solutions to discrepancies in the accounts. Then we will analyze these finds in terms of their success or failure in answering problems.

2. Next, we will study each Gospel account to isolate the redactions and theological emphasis of each evangelist. We will gather linguistic data in each section and compare it with language and concepts in that Gospel as well as the language and concepts of other Gospels. Then we will note the distinctive style and word usage of each evangelist in order to determine his theological purpose and compositional method.

3. Third, we will study the traditions behind the Gospel accounts in order to discover the development and historical worth of each individual pericope. This will be a two-part study involving: (a) the empty tomb narratives, which for the most part are paralleled in all four Gospels; and (b) the appearance narratives, which for the most part are independent traditions without parallels. In both sections we will try to identify the stages of tradition-development and pass judgment on the historical validity of the nucleus of each pericope.

4. In conclusion we will summarize all our findings, both theological and historical, and blend them into a holistic picture of the

resurrection narratives. From this we will identify probable historical events which lay behind resurrection traditions, as well as the historical development of interpreting those events in the theology of the early church. Our study should help us determine whether or not the New Testament interpretations of the events were justified, as well as how those events and interpretations are relevant for faith today.

Abbreviations used in the text are identified in the "Abbreviations" section at the beginning of the book.

Acknowledgments

This work is a complete revision of my doctoral dissertation done under the insight and careful suggestions of my supervisor, Professor I. Howard Marshall. His detailed and thought-provoking critiques of my various chapters certainly improved each one tremendously. I also owe a debt of gratitude to Professor Robin S. Barber who provided valuable advice and sound counsel. I would like to thank both and owe them a great deal for making my time at Aberdeen both profitable and enjoyable.

The many friends and relatives who encouraged me both during my time at Aberdeen and the lengthy time of revision are too numerous to mention, but I would like to thank them all. My greatest expression of love and gratitude belongs to my wife Nancy, whose constant devotion and help have meant more than I can say. In so many ways she has borne the brunt of this work and I would like to dedicate it to her.

In addition, several secretaries have helped a great deal in typing the manuscripts, in putting up with my "hieroglyphic" style of writing, and in their patience with my numerous, often hasty, requests: Sherry Kull, Patty Light, Jan Olander, Mary Dalton, Marty Irwin. I extend my heartfelt gratitude to each of them. Finally, I would like to thank Norbert Schmidt and Scott McKnight who helped with the indices and proofreading.

Abbreviations

AB	The Anchor Bible
ABR	Australian Biblical Review
AufzNT	Aufsätze zum Neuen Testament
BD	Beloved Disciple
BDF	F. Blass and A. Debrunner (tr. . . . Funk), *A Greek Grammar of the New Testament and Other Early Christian Literature*
BibSac	Bibliothecra Sacra
Bib Tod	Bible Today
BibVieChret	Bible et Vie Chrétienne
BJRL	Bulletin of the John Rylands Library
BL (BibLeb)	Bibel und Leben
BNTC	Black New Testament Commentary
BR	Biblical Research
BZ	Biblische Zeitschrift
CBC	Cambridge Bible Commentary
CBQ	Catholic Biblical Quarterly
CD	Karl Barth, *Church Dogmatics*
CGT	Cambridge Greek Testament Commentary
EQ	Evangelical Quarterly
ET	Expository Times
EphThLouv	Ephemerides Theologicae Louvanienses
EvTh	Evangelische Theologie
EW	J. Jeremias, *The Eucharistic Words of Jesus*
Exp	Expositor
GordRev	Gordon Review
HeyJ	Heythrop Journal

HJ (HibJ)	Hibbert Journal
HST	R. Bultmann, *The History of the Synoptic Tradition*
HTR	Harvard Theological Review
ICC	International Critical Commentary
IEJ	Israel Exploration Journal
Interp	Interpretation
JBL	Journal of Biblical Literature
JR (JRel)	Journal of Religion
JETS	Journal of the Evangelical Theological Society
JTS	Journal of Theological Studies
JTSA	Journal of Theology of Southern Africa
KD	Kerygma und Dogma
KKNT	Kritische-exegetische Kommentar zum Neuen Testament (also known as the Meyer Commentary series)
LumVie	Lumiére et Vie
LXX	Septuagint
NCB	New Century Bible
NEB	New English Bible
NIDNTT	New International Dictionary of New Testament Theology, ed. Colin Brown
NovT	Novum Testamentum
NT	New Testament
NTS	New Testament Studies
OT	Old Testament
PhRev	Philosophical Review
Persp	Perspective
PTR	Princeton Theological Review
RB	Revue Biblique
RC	Redaction Criticism
RevB	Revue Biblique
RevExp	Review and Expositor
RHPR	Revue d'Histoire et de Philosophie Religieuses
RSV	Revised Standard Version
RTP	Revue de Théologie et de Philosophie
SB	Strack, H. L. and P. Billerback. *Kommentar zum Neuen Testament aus Talmud und Midrasch*
SBS	Stuttgarter Bibel-Studien, eds. H. Haag et al.
SBT	Studies in Biblical Theology, ed. C. F. D. Moule
Scr	Scripture
SJT	Scottish Journal of Theology

SNT	Supplements to Novum Testamentum
StANT	Studien zum Alten und Neuen Testament, ed. V. Hanys and J. Schmid
StEv	Studia Evangelica
StTh	Studia Theologica
SWJT	Southwestern Journal of Theology
TB	Tyndale Bulletin
TC	Tradition Criticism
TDNT	*Theological Dictionary of the New Testament*, ed. G. Kittel, tr. G. W. Bromiley (Grand Rapids, 1964-).
Theol	Theology
ThDig	Theology Digest
ThSt	Theological Studies
TIM	Bornkam, G. et al. *Tradition and Interpretation in Matthew*
TQ	Theologische Quartalschrift
TZ	Theologische Zeitschrift
VerbDom	Verbum Domini
ZNW (TNTW)	Zeitschrift für die Neutestamentliche Wissenschaft
ZTK	Zeitschrift für Theologie und Kirche

Part One

Historical Survey

1

The Resurrection—The State of the Study

The strengths and shortcomings of former studies of the resurrection narratives can best be seen in a historical survey of the critical schools and their analysis of the resurrection event. These schools of interpretation characterize various periods of New Testament study and give us an excellent overview of the development of biblical criticism since the Renaissance. This approach will also single out solutions which have been offered in the past to reconcile interpretive problems caused by the resurrection narratives. The study might also reveal areas of study which have not been sufficiently covered in the past as well as propose questions which have yet to be answered.

The Forerunners: Rationalism and Myth

Prior to the seventeenth and eighteenth centuries few scholars challenged the historicity of supernatural events in Scripture,[1] especially the resurrection narratives. One of the earliest challengers was Hermann Samuel Reimarus whose major work, *The Aims of*

1. Although most textbooks begin with Reimarus, many today include his predecessors in biblical rationalism. Grossman (pp. 170–77) points out that Reimarus followed the conclusions of Johann Christian Edelmann who published in 1720. Both in turn were probably influenced by the French skeptics of the seventeenth century such as Spinoza, Simon, and Grotius. For this latter insight, I am indebted to my colleague Dr. John Woodbridge.

Jesus and His Disciples,[2] was published posthumously by the philosopher Gottfried Lessing (1774–1778) because of its controversial nature. Reimarus listed ten contradictions in the resurrection narratives which he said were representative of many more. He concluded that they were apologetic errors and on this basis denied that the resurrection occurred. His primary thesis was that the disciples made up the story to promulgate their religion. After Jesus' death his fearful followers hid awhile, then stole his body and used the Jewish doctrine of a suffering and glorified Messiah to promote a new religion. Their goal was political in terms of gaining money and status. As A. Schweitzer (*Quest,* pp. 22–24) much later wrote, the work of Reimarus did not gain much acceptance simply because it sounded too preposterous. How could men who promoted the sound ethics of Christianity and were willing to die for their beliefs ever have sought to deceive a nation?

In 1828 another life of Jesus was published by H. E. G. Paulus who theorized that Jesus merely swooned on the cross. Since crucifixion was such a slow death the man simply lost consciousness from pain. A soldier's sword in his side relieved internal pressure on his vital organs, and much later embalming spices combined with the coolness of the tomb revived him. Finally he was set free from the tomb by an earthquake and later appeared with his disciples.

Two other liberal views of the life of Christ followed the work of Paulus, the first being F. E. D. Schleiermacher's teaching (his notes published posthumously in 1864) and K. A. Hase's published work in 1829. Both Schleiermacher and Hase believed Jesus had some kind of mystical power (evidenced in his healing ministry) which, combined with divine providence, helped to keep him from dying on the cross. He escaped from the tomb and went to Galilee where his privacy could be maintained. Both Strauss (pp. 31–33) and Schweitzer (pp. 54–55, 64–65) refuted this theory because it was so illogical; Jesus' recovery from an arduous crucifixion was too quick and his disciples' faith too sincere to admit feigned death and escape.

David Friedrich Strauss was trained in the Tübingen school of F. C. Baur who applied the dialectic of Hegel to the history of the early church. Strauss applied Hegel's method to the life of Jesus,

---

2. Two translations have been published but only *Reimarus—Fragments* contains the entire text. The other omits the section on the resurrection (par. 10–30).

contrasting the faith of the disciples (thesis), to the facts of Jesus' life (antithesis), and arriving at a synthesis of myths about Jesus. Said Strauss, this was how the disciples produced a glorified Jesus which fit their own beliefs. Consider the resurrection, for example (pp. 371–95). Their Jewish beliefs in a suffering, glorified Messiah led to inspired but subjective visions of the exaltation of Jesus by the Father. Most of these "visions" occurred in Galilee where there was no tomb to dispute the myths which arose. Therefore the resurrection narratives were written in conjunction with Jewish and hellenistic myths rather than the events themselves. Since this theory of myths is still believed today (Bultmann and others), we will consider it further later on.

Although Strauss had many followers, public reaction against him was so negative that he became a bitter man. Ironically, Ernst Renan in 1864 wrote a life of Christ based on Strauss' thesis which was so romanticized that it became a best seller. Renan's story said the body of Christ was removed from the tomb by unknown persons (pp. 295–96), but the love of disciples and imagination of people like Mary Magdalene created beliefs or myths that Jesus was still with them. These beliefs eventually led to the resurrection stories. Paul Schmiedel, a contemporary of Renan, even rejected the idea of objective visions since they implied something supernatural. He said only subjective visions or dreams could account for the inconsistent narratives.

Many scholars[3] spoke out against this extreme rationalism, arguing that the mental and spiritual certainty of the disciples as well as the universal assumption of an empty tomb in the gospels demanded such miracles. Since science itself did not demand subjective hallucinations or dreams as the basis of the resurrection event, why should hallucinations of his post-resurrection appearances (even by five hundred people at one time in 1 Cor. 15:6) be necessary to prove the validity of those events? The weakness of Renan and Schmiedel's thinking was their basic a priori assumption that supernatural events cannot occur. A different presupposition would produce different answers.

History of Religions School

The basic premise of the history of religions school is that all religions draw their tenets from the religious environment of their

3. Such as Nolloth, Orr, Headlam, Thorburn.

age. Therefore Christianity has a genealogical relationship to the pagan religions of its era. Otto Pfleiderer, a major proponent of this school, said the primitive view of Christ's resurrection proving God's approval of Christ's propitiatory death was derived from later hellenistic Jewish-Christian writings (Isa. 53; 4 Macc. 6, 17) and ultimately from Graeco-Roman myths. These, in turn, were based on primitive beliefs regarding the cycle of vegetation (cp. the Isis—Osiris myth, Spring Equinox festival, etc.). Therefore episodes such as the Emmaus incident were legends, not fact (see his *Early Christian Conception*, pp. 134—51).

Wilhelm Bousset (pp. 56—60; see also the article by McCasland) brought this thinking one step further, teaching that the myth of a dying and risen god in pagan literature led to the formulation of such legends as the "third day" motif. According to Persian legend (taken up by Jewish apocalyptics), the soul of the deceased remains in his corpse three days. Hence the resurrection of Christ was purely a spiritual event in the minds of his disciples, the primary impetus being self-persuasion and the visions merely secondary to that. Alfred Loisy (*Birth*, pp. 93—95, 224—25) also argued along these lines, saying the disciples took motifs from pagan mystery religions and applied them to Jesus, thus giving him celestial attributes. The myth of the angel at the tomb arose to disguise the flight of the disciples, and the empty tomb legend was encouraged by the fact that Jesus' body was thrown into a common criminal's grave in the Valley of Hinnom.

Both liberal and conservative scholars have reacted against this movement. Johannes Weiss (pp. 94—98) said pagan myths may have influenced the resurrection story, but certainly were not the basis for resurrection traditions. Hosea 6:2, for instance, as well as pagan myths influenced the third-day motif. The disciples knew the myths but did not necessarily borrow directly from them. Other scholars[4] argued that these mythological parallels were chosen on the basis of an anti-supernatural bias. The resurrection should never be seen against a backdrop of religious parallels, they said, but instead must be accepted as a unique, cosmic act in which the end of history invaded time. This view, said A. D. Nock (pp. 105—108), points out the inability of evolutionary theory to answer all the inconsistencies in content which may disprove

---

4. See Headlam, pp. 252f.; Sasse, pp. 90f.; and Ehrhardt, pp. 197f.

a superficial resemblance. Pagan myths tell about temporary defeat followed by joyous victory through ancient cultic rites; Christianity rejoices in Christ's death as triumph itself. Resurrection is the timeless capstone to that triumph.

The most serious weakness of the history of religions school is found in the parallels themselves since they are analogical rather than genealogical, or similar to but not the basis of Christian beliefs. More importantly, the influence seems to go from Christianity to pagan mysteries rather than vice versa. Two myths, the gnostic redeemer myth and the oriental royal ritual have been examined recently. Carston Colpe (in his influential doctoral dissertation on the redeemer myth) points out there is no evidence for a pre-Christian gnostic redeemer myth; the more probable view is that it originated with Christian gnosticism and was borrowed by the mystery religions. K. H. Rengstorf examines the royal ritual (cited by many history of religions scholars as the source of much resurrection imagery), and concludes it is based on the Jerusalem-Judean enthronement tradition of Psalm 2 rather than on pagan parallels.

In conclusion, the history of religions school contributed much to biblical scholarship in finding literary genre parallels to the resurrection narratives, and we hope to use some of these insights in our examination of the Gospels. However, we reject categorically the assumption that these parallels are genealogical, leading to the creation of resurrection myths by disciples. The church did use literary genres to present historical events in a way which their readers could understand, but they did not make up the stories themselves.

The Modern Critical Movement

Modern criticism emerged after World War I with the collapse of liberal optimism and its quest for the historical Jesus. Modern criticism took shape in the form criticism of Rudolph Bultmann and dialectical theology of Karl Barth, but also includes existential theology as well as the historical school. Its most recent movement, structural analysis, does not as yet have a full-length work on the resurrection narratives. We will interact with their articles in the body of this work.

Form Criticism began with the 1919 publication of Martin Dibelius's *Die Formgeschichte des Evangeliums* (ET *From Tradition to Gospel*, 1934) and Karl Ludwig Schmidt's *Der Rahmen der Geschichte Jesu*, as well as Rudolf Bultmann's *Geschichte der synoptischen Tradition* (ET *The History of the Synoptic Tradition*, 1963). Dibelius, Schmidt, and Bultmann believed that the literary form of an individual pericope or passage was a key to the traditional sources the author used and therefore was proof of its authenticity. These critics, however, exhibited a general unwillingness to accept the historical truth of the Gospel records. Dibelius was the most conservative, content to apply form criticism to the passages themselves, but Bultmann pushed unhesitatingly toward existential theology and its demythologizing hermeneutic. According to Bultmann the Gospels were essentially a collection of myths which portrayed truths about man's existence rather than told about actual historical events. Therefore they had to be reinterpreted so that first-century mythology could be translated into the language of today.

Bultmann believed[5] the resurrection story was simply the disciples' attempt to express the significance of the cross through kerygma. The real Easter event was not the resurrection of Christ but the birth of faith in the redemptive effect of the cross as an act of God. The cross thus became a transcendent, victorious act, the kerygma transforming the cross into a cosmic event via the resurrection myth which itself was dependent on the gnostic redeemer myth. Earlier stories simply said Jesus was alive and was the Messiah. The Emmaus pericope with its strong messianic teaching was the only primitive story, and the empty tomb narrative came later. In fact, early versions of the story lumped the ascension and resurrection into a single event.

Dibelius refused to make such a radical historical judgment.[6] He said that while "tales" or stories (angels, etc.) are included in the narratives, little other legendary material is used, therefore the question of historicity should remain open. The empty tomb tradition might have emerged later and in some circles was not

---

5. See *Kerygma and Myth*, I, pp. 38–42; *Theology of the NT*, I, pp. 292–96; and HST, pp. 288–90. A resumé of form critical presuppositions is found in Wilder, "Variant Traditions," pp. 307f.

6. See *Fresh Approach*, pp. 43–46; *Message*, pp. 180–82; and *Tradition*, pp. 190–270.

known at all, nonetheless it was not a myth; the differences between it and pagan mythology were too great.

Other form critics have reacted in other ways to Bultmann's deemphasis of historicity. Joachim Jeremias (*Theology*, I, pp. 301–311) stresses objective interpretation, the key being the structural difference between the passion narrative (the basic framework) and the resurrection accounts (independent collections). The passion itself, says Jeremias, was an observable event occurring over a short period of time, while the resurrection was a series of Christophanies occurring over a span of many years. The decisive event occurred when the Lord appeared to Peter (a story which was suppressed by radical Palestinians who disliked Peter's universalism and thus never appeared in the Gospels), followed by other events such as Christ's appearance to the five hundred (probably referring to the original Pentecost experience), and culminating in Paul's vision on the way to Damascus. Jeremias argues for an "objective vision" approach to the resurrection (see ch. 8).

C. H. Dodd is even more positive about the historicity of the resurrection. He says in *Founder* (pp. 165–71) that the resurrection is not a belief which the church developed, but a belief which enabled the church to grow. All four Gospels agree that Mary (alone or with others) visited the tomb on the third day and found it empty, but the differences in the accounts probably happened because the apostles didn't know how best to use the data. Dodd in his famous form-critical analysis of the appearance narratives divides them into "concise stories" (a minimum of detail) and "circumstantial tales" (more elaborate accounts). He does not say these "tales" are secondary elaborations however, but merely that they are well-told accounts. The absence of apocalyptic imagery in them, in contrast to pagan theophanies, makes him believe they are embellished records of historical events.

The problem with radical form criticism is its extreme subjectivity. Dodd's work shows us that form criticism itself gives no hard evidence of its ability to prove historicity, nor does the data support Bultmann's use of formal criteria. Forms are merely guides to the development of traditions and nothing more. Perhaps the conclusions of radical critics are based more on presuppositions than on the results of form criticism.

Dialectical Theology is another attempt to divorce the resurrection from history but with radically different conclusions from Bultmann's form criticism. Karl Barth who first seemed to agree with Bultmann (see his work on Romans in the 1920s), later moved well beyond him into dialectical thinking. Both men believed the resurrection did not depend on objective facts such as the empty tomb or post-resurrection appearances, but Barth taught (*Romans*, pp. 30f., 204) that the resurrection happened outside space and time and thus was not a part of history as we know it. As a result the believer must reach beyond history to grasp the resurrection by a leap of faith.

Another theologian of this school, Emil Brunner, said resurrection faith was more than "faith in the cross as a saving event." He said the New Testament was unclear about the literal truth of a physical resurrection, implying it was more than a subjective vision but less than the resuscitation of an actual corpse. Perhaps the best way to explain it is to say the resurrection is an "eschatological event beyond the grasp of language of the space-time continuum."

W. Künneth supported Brunner's views, saying we dare not be concerned about historicity since the fabric of the resurrection lies outside history. Thinking of it historically removes it from its proper sphere and makes it merely another event in the life of man. Resurrection transcends history as a "revelational absolute." The disciples raised it far above the sphere of Old Testament prophetic vision (probably the source of the original events), making it a "wholly other," once-for-all event.

These theologians for the most part affirmed the basic historicity of the resurrection, but later Barth[7] divorced himself from Bultmann's approach and gave greater credence to the "historical character" of the resurrection. He said it was as important as the cross in the New Testament's portrayal of Christ, therefore it must have been an event which occurred in space and time. Still, it can be known only by faith and is therefore not compatible with historical research.

We see two problems in this approach: (1) its extreme subjectivity removes the historical foundation from truth resulting in the little basis for a leap of faith in such a resurrection; and (2) this

---

7. For a discussion of the differences between the early and later Barth in relation to this, see O'Collins, "Karl Barth," pp. 85f.

partial affirmation of historicity comes minus the weight of "historical research." It is, by definition, a contradiction. A leap of faith which has no basis in reason is no different from the "leap" of a Buddhist or Muslim. The resurrection cannot be excluded from the scrutiny of historical research lest the very basis for its reality be destroyed.

Existential Theology developed with Bultmann's application of Heidegger's philosophy of existence to New Testament theology. Bultmann redefined theology when he said "genuine theological statements are statements about existence" (*Kerygma*, p. 107). His view of the resurrection asks the question, "What is the self-understanding implied by the Christian Easter message?" (*Kerygma*, p. 10). The resurrection is not history but a myth with an existential message, not a past event of salvation but a present proclamation which leads to self-understanding. Says Bultmann, the resurrection expresses the true significance of the cross and helps us to accept suffering voluntarily; this is seen in "the concrete act of living" (*Kerygma*, pp. 40f.). Through the "kerygma of the cross and resurrection" as proclaimed word authentic living is attainable. Life overcomes death when "the Risen One encounters man as love, brings him his future, and means for him not death, but life" (*Kerygma*, p. 33).

Paul Tillich[8] goes one step further, reaching beyond the resurrection event to the historian through an utterly existential theology. He denies Bultmann's attempt to study the event historically, saying Jesus cannot be understood in terms of historical knowledge (*Historie*), but rather as the reality expressed in the New Testament portrait of Jesus as the Christ (*Geschichte*). Each New Testament symbol must be translated into modern terms; the resurrection, for instance, simply expressing the eternal root of the "New Being" which is victorious over the boundaries of existence. The cross represents Christ's end to estrangement from the divine unity—his escape from finite existence. Although the resurrection story is mythical its kernel is true, symbolizing Christ's escape from finitude into authentic existence ("New Being"). The ascension is the final step in this escape.

Radical existential theology presents many problems, although

8. Tillich, II, pp. 101–107, 158–62. J. W. D. Smith says Tillich answers Bultmann's inconsistency when Bultmann attempts to demythologize the resurrection while still asserting that God acted "in and through the visionary experience."

most Bible scholars recognize the value of existential theology as a hermeneutical tool if it is regulated by a realistic historiography and kept from degenerating into mere allegory. Its best usage in hermeneutics deals with the application of the message of the text for the needs of the day, known to homileticians as "life-situation preaching."

Barth[9] says Bultmann is an exegete who is controlled by pre-suppositions and notes several weaknesses in his theology: (1) a theological statement which is defined only partially by a Christian's understanding of existence is not necessarily untrue; (2) an event which cannot be historically verified does not mean it did not occur; (3) an event beyond historical research is not neces-sarily a man-made "myth"; (4) the modern world-view should not deny a priori the supernatural; and (5) we should not reject a biblical statement just because someone else's presuppositions demand it.

Oscar Cullmann[10] has a more positive view of the supernatural. He says Bultmann's subjective approach divorces modern man from New Testament faith which is rooted in the death and res-urrection of Christ as actual historical events. Radical critics have too easily decided that Jesus had no prior knowledge of himself as a suffering servant, Cullman says; most New Testament thinking proves otherwise. Paul, for instance, never once considered the resurrection as a mystery or myth but instead as a once-for-all event. Furthermore, nothing in the New Testament gives credence to demythologization or a purely existential approach to the death and resurrection.

Other[11] modern theologians have a less optimistic view of his-tory yet still maintain it was a real event. For instance, they say the disciples and Paul had more than existential encounters; they were given visions from God that Christ was alive. The resurrection may not have been an actual physical event, yet it was more than

9. Barth, *Church Dogmatics*, III.2, pp. 442 – 47; see also IV.2, pp. 296 – 322. Künneth (pp. 44 – 47) adds: (1) it results in a philosophical reinterpretation of the Christian faith which leaves it no longer Christian; (2) it is one-sided, reducing revelation to "truths of reason" and the resurrection to a timeless symbol; (3) one cannot discover "contempor-aneity" without making the crucified and resurrected Christ a salvation – event.

10. Cullmann, *Salvation*, pp. 121, 184 – 90, 259. See also Bruce, *Spreading Flame*, pp. 61 – 68; and Davies, *Invitation*, pp. 495 – 501.

11. See Lampe and MacKinnon, pp. 27 – 60; Goppelt, ch. 2; and Schweizer, *Jesus*, pp. 46 – 51.

just a dream or hallucination since five hundred people experienced it at once. The presence of so few witnesses in the Gospel accounts indicates the evangelists' desire to present truth rather than just proof (unlike later accounts in the Apocrypha which greatly magnified the number of witnesses).

Unfortunately, existential theologians are so impressed by their method that it becomes an absolute test for Christian truth. The problem is they tend to generalize to the point of distortion, failing to realize that even existential truth needs an objective basis. Their conclusions thus often stray far from Christian truths and degenerate into philosophical allegories on existence and its ramifications. The method of existential theology may be valid, but when it is divorced from history it deteriorates into meaninglessness.

The Historical School gathered momentum in Germany in the 1960s. It had been suggested by scholars such as Cullmann and Jeremias, but achieved full expression with the work of Wolfhart Pannenberg and Jürgen Moltmann. Pannenberg (*Jesus*, pp. 63—73) said Christian faith was based on the historicity of the resurrection; the New Testament basis for belief was not in Jesus' words per se but in God's ratification of those words via the resurrection. The apocalyptic was objectified in history, thereby becoming the basis for Christian faith. Without history faith is groundless, therefore the resurrection must be examined from a historical approach before it can be accepted rationally.

Moltmann (*Hope*, pp. 166—82) also said the resurrection was the basis for New Testament faith. It is historically inaccessible only to those who view it from the Hegelian approach; the reality of Easter not only produces faith but is also the fact behind that faith. Scripture thus gives history an eschatological purpose, denying the man-centered cause-effect nexus of the historian to present the resurrection as an ultimate event.[12]

This movement may be a healthy swing away from radical existentialism, yet even this historical approach must not be taken too far. Pannenberg grounds faith in historical knowledge, thus making it dependent on the changeable verities of historical re-

---

12. Of course, neither Pannenberg nor Moltmann deny the results of biblical criticism; both resurrection accounts are replete with additions and contradictions. For Pannenberg, however, the basic core behind the traditions still remains. Moltmann takes a less rational approach but still affirms the basic historical trustworthiness of the event. See the collection of articles in his *Hope and Planning,*

search. The historical acts of God then can be known only through research, not faith, and knowledge is thus the *basis* for faith rather than the *result* of faith. Historical scholars should be commended for their emphasis on the integration of faith and history (revelation indeed is the historical intervention of God from outside the natural sphere), yet while rational research recognizes God's entry into history only faith can fully acknowledge these acts of God. Historians may acknowledge the cross and resurrection as historical events, but only faith can declare "he was put to death for our trespasses and raised for our justification" (Rom. 4:25).

Redaction Criticism

Although redaction criticism is a step-child of form criticism, it is nonetheless important enough to this study to warrant a separate heading. Redaction criticism developed in conjunction with two other movements: (1) the "new quest" for the historical Jesus which seeks to validate historical elements in the Gospels; and (2) tradition criticism which says the Gospel pericopes evolved over a long period of time and included additions made by the early church. Many redaction critics utilize both of these methods as well as that of redaction criticism in sifting through contradictory data in the Gospels to find kernels of fact which might lead to the actual events.

Redaction criticism was first utilized in R. H. Lightfoot's *Locality and Doctrine in the Gospels* (1938). Lightfoot noted the different geographic locations of resurrection appearances in the Gospels and wondered if they were a key to the purpose of the writer. Mark stressed Galilee, 16:7 a late redaction pointing to the parousia in Galilee or the place of redemption. Matthew focused on the resurrection as God's divine stamp of approval on Jesus' earthly mission and impetus for the universal mission of evangelizing the world. Luke ignored the Galilean location and centered on Jerusalem, making the resurrection a complete rather than transitional event, containing within itself the entire redemptive plan of God. John used many of the same details as Luke, but for a different purpose. Doctrinally *John* is much like *Matthew* and *Mark*, its events in Jerusalem pointing beyond themselves to Christ's present activity in the world.

Recently redaction criticism's approach to the resurrection narratives has been criticized for the following reasons: (1) its conclusions tend to reflect the historiographical a priori of the critic yet these presuppositions are seldom clearly stated; (2) its proponents tend to overemphasize either tradition or redaction-study, thereby producing lopsided, often erroneous results; and (3) most redaction critics are too negative about biblical data, and too willing to accept the premise that redaction included creating rather than selecting or rephrasing the facts.

Willi Marxsen's *The Resurrection of Jesus of Nazareth* provides an excellent summary of non-evangelical views. However, he assumes contradictions without explanation and finds conflict everywhere. One wishes he would expand (chapters are often only ten pages long) and prove his contentions. Marxsen's lack of scholarly discussion, questionable historiography, and blatant presuppositional approach make his work difficult to accept even though it includes some good material on theology. Basically he proposes that Easter began with Peter's experience (either a dream or an objective vision), although its historical uncertainty prevents the resurrection from being a basis for faith, which can come only via one's encounter with the "proclamation" of the Easter message.

C. F. Evans in *Resurrection and the New Testament* has the opposite problem. His style (unlike Marxsen) includes long, rambling discourses on problem passages which present many opinions but fail to draw any conclusions. The result is a weak, inconclusive study of crucial passages like Matthew 28:16–20 and Luke 24:13–35. Furthermore, Evans does a poor job of canvassing passages for redactions, apparently believing tradition to be more important. The result is a failure to understand each evangelist in terms of structure or theology.

Redaction research properly includes two disciplines, tradition criticism which studies the authenticity and development of stories, and redaction criticism which traces the use of those stories by individual evangelists. Most redaction studies of the resurrection emphasize tradition criticism and include a negative approach to its historicity. Hans Grass, for instance, in *Ostergeschehen und Osterberichte* provided the first (and in some ways still one of the best) work on the resurrection, yet he too emphasizes the tradition critical approach in dwelling on the actuality of the

Easter event and the development of individual traditions. He says little can be added to the oldest tradition found in 1 Corinthians 15:3−8 and that all other accounts were secondary embellishments by the church. He believes the core of the resurrection event was a series of visions, first to Cephas, then to the disciples who had fled to Galilee after Jesus' crucifixion. These visions were experienced over a period of years and because they had objective content (were truly sent from God), they convinced the disciples that Jesus Christ was risen and alive.

Unfortunately, Grass too easily dismisses Gospel data. Though he is anxious to maintain the core of the event as demonstrable, he too easily assumes the radical thesis that traditions developed later through legendary embellishment.

R. H. Fuller's *The Formation of the Resurrection Narratives* (1972) is another excellent work on tradition criticism, but one which offers better theological insight than Grass. Fuller includes: (1) the use of material from the New Testament Apocrypha as a critical tool, and (2) a better discussion and resulting conclusions concerning the development of the episodes. He suggests several innovative solutions to problems such as the triadic baptismal formula of Matthew 28:19 and the Emmaus story. Still, unfortunately his theological insights are weak, probably because he attempts to do too much in a limited amount of space. His free-and-easy use of evidence and hastily drawn conclusions resulting in improbable theories are disturbing, but so is his use of apocryphal material. He uses the Apocrypa as if it was a parallel to the Gospels with seemingly little regard for the lateness of its origin. For example, his presentation of the ascension categorizes the Gospel of Peter as "primitive kerygma," the Epistle of Barnabas as a later apocalyptic development, and Acts as an even later creation. His dogmatic considerations thus became more important than historical data itself.

Two recent works which examine the resurrection narratives from a critical approach are much more conservative. Ulrich Wilcken's *Resurrection* (German, 1970) takes a Pannenberg school approach to the problem resulting in a close study of tradition units at the expense of adequately assessing the role of the individual evangelists. Wilcken's purpose is to find the historical core behind the narratives, not necessarily to understand them. He discusses New Testament evidence in the first section of his book, concluding that the earliest tradition presented the empty tomb as "the concluding section of the old account of the Passion" (p. 64). Later a short list of appearances (similar to 1 Cor. 15:3–5) was added to this account which then developed into full-fledged stories by the church. Wilcken's work includes some serious deficiencies: (1) it neglects the results of redaction study, simply putting traditions together without regard to context,[13] and (2) his theological core centers on broad themes in the church without consideration of any specific emphasis of the author. On the whole, however, this work includes a better discussion of the problem within the limits of the Pannenberg approach.

John E. Alsup's *The Post-Resurrection Appearance Stories of the Gospel Tradition* (1975) also attempts to get back to the traditional core behind the resurrection accounts. He argues that the appearance stories did not arise out of the kerygmatic preaching of the early church but developed independently. Group appearances were suggested by Old Testament theophanic narratives but also probably reflected some actual experience when the Risen Lord showed himself to his disciples. Alsup will not commit himself any further than this; his conservative approach to tradition criticism is strangely ambiguous regarding historicity.

Xavier Léon-Dufour's *Resurrection and the Message of Easter* (French, 1971) is a well-written work and healthy corrective to tradition critics. This theologian emphasizes the redaction work of the evangelists; his major contribution is an attempt to present the Easter message in today's language. Léon-Dufour closely examines New Testament language, then discusses the hermeneutics of individual authors in a sound presentation of the structure and thought-patterns involved in writing narratives. Unfortunately Léon-Dufour is often more interested in the language of the narratives than in their historicity, resulting in a somewhat weak approach to tradition criticism. His discussion of problem accounts is quite thorough, but his conclusions are poorly based, often as-

---

13. This method was employed by expositors decades ago (e.g., Calvin's *Harmony*) but one cannot detect the literary purposes of the individual evangelists when their narratives are divided and discussed along with the parallel episodes in the other Gospels. The train of thought becomes lost when all the Gospels are thrown together. Redactional study by definition means the study of each evangelist in turn and the editorial work of each within his own context and *Sitz im Leben*.

suming the nonhistoricity of an account without considering any other option (e.g., Matt. 28:11 – 15 and Mark's ending). Still, Léon-Dufour's theological acumen in examining the accounts more than makes up for his weakness.

Another very interesting work is Norman Perrin's *The Resurrection According to Matthew, Mark and Luke* (1977). Perrin is known as one of the most radical tradition critics, but in this book uses the redactional approach to present an illuminating portrayal of the resurrection accounts in light of the theological development of each Gospel. Mark thus contrasts the failure of the disciples with the power of the Risen Christ and the imminence of his parousia in Galilee.

Perrin's radical criticism enters this discussion when he labels the accounts as "myth," defined existentially as "primordial myth" (which relates basic truths of human existence), and "foundation myth" (which describes particular human groups or movements). He says Mark is primordial myth since it deals with all mankind's encounter with the parousia, suffering, death, and triumph over death. Matthew and Luke, on the other hand, are foundation myths because they are concerned with the conflict between Christian and Jewish communities and thus stress Christian origins and power for the present age. Perrin says this distinction is more important than "what really happened" and in his final chapter opts for the "objective vision" theory regarding the historical event. He also says the evangelists were not concerned with problems like this because they only wished to communicate the importance of Jesus Christ to people of their day.

Bede Rigaux's *Dieu l'a ressuscité* (1973) is probably the best as well as most comprehensive new work. Rigaux traces resurrection theology (1) in Judaism, (2) in the teachings of Jesus, (3) in the resurrection formulae in Acts, (4) in the creedal confessions, (5) in hymns of the New Testament and finally discusses the narratives themselves. Like Wilckens he considers the narratives in thematic rather than chronological order. He divides all the accounts into three categories: the empty tomb narratives, personal appearances (labeled "christophanies"), and apostolic appearances. The problem with this kind of study, of course, is that it is not conducive to redactional study and can lead to a distorted view of the evangelists' biblical theology. Another problem which intrudes on this study is Rigaux's Barthian perspective. He writes, for instance, that the certainty of the creeds is not because of apologetic or historical interest but rather because of ecclesiastical concerns. Although the narratives themselves are based on historical fact, these literary and theological motifs cannot demonstrate that fact. Unfortunately Rigaux's conclusions here produce tentative historical decisions as well as weak redactional appraisals.

Scholars of redaction criticism, although lumped together in the same school, often reach different conclusions. Marxsen, Fuller and Léon-Dufour say the Easter event was basically a subjective experience which inspired a triumphant faith in the disciples, and it is this faith which is objective.[14] Grass and Evans believe the visions were objectively valid.[15] Wilckens, Alsup, and Rigaux put more emphasis on the historical reality of Easter, saying the fact that it really happened is proof of God's ratification of Jesus' claims about himself (Wilckens) as well as God's action in the world and man's relationship to him (Rigaux).

Many redaction critics err when they insist on absolute separation between redaction and tradition, feeling that redaction always involves creation rather than using existing tradition. This simply is not true; no writer using a source quotes it verbatim, but rather absorbs it into his own thought processes and adapts it to the structure of his message. Evangelists also worked this way, taking existing traditions and writing them down in such a way that they met the needs of their readers. This kind of redactional activity included both the selection and creative expression of traditional accounts rather than originating stories which never happened.[16] No strict line should be drawn between tradition and

14. Rudolf Pesch in *TQ* (1973) and *Wie kam es zum Osterglauben*, ed. A. Vögtle and R. Pesch (1975) has sparked a vigorous discussion in German circles with his thesis that neither the empty tomb nor the appearances were the basis of the Easter faith. The formula of 1 Corinthians 15:3−5 was intended to legitimate the apostolic witness rather than the resurrection, and the latter has its true foundation in Jesus' life in the expectation that Jesus as eschatological prophet, upon his death, must have a relevance beyond that death. Therefore it is the historical Jesus, not the Christ of faith, which is the basis of the resurrection faith. The extensive reaction to Pesch, mostly negative, has been chronicled for English-speaking students in J. P. Galvin's article in *ThSt* (1977).

15. Günther Bornkamm in *The Future of our Religious Past* (1971), pp. 203f., accepts the presence of legendary accretions but argues that there must have been an objective revelation of the living Christ behind the dramatic change in the hitherto defeated and discouraged disciples. This is also the view of C. F. D. Moule in Cupit and Moule, *Theol* (1972).

16. Three works make this same assertion: I. H. Marshall, *Luke: Historian and Theologian* (1970); R. P. Martin, *Mark—Evangelist and Theologian* (1972); and S. S. Smalley, *John—Evangelist and Theologian* (1978). Each asserts that the evangelists combine history and theology in their works.

redaction; the critic should recognize that a biblical account may be based on a tradition which has been structured to fit the particular theological interpretation of the evangelist even as it remains true to the event itself.

Conclusion

Our survey of literature on the resurrection narratives demonstrates a real need for a new approach which includes some important characteristics: (1) it must be committed to a historical approach to biblical evidence; (2) it must include a balanced combination of tradition and redaction; (3) it must be an unbiased, objective search for the historical possibilities of the Easter event; and (4) it must judiciously apply critical principles to identify tradition and redaction in order to form conclusions about the development of an author's interpretation.

Each critical school wrestled with questions about the resurrection, using the same evidence to arrive at radically different conclusions. This wide variance is due basically to the problem of presuppositions and methodology, two elements of study which are integrally related. We know, for instance, that a slightly different approach to data will produce vastly different conclusions. However we must ask with Bultmann, "Is exegesis without presuppositions possible?"[17] A "knowledge gap" or epistemological barrier plainly separates us from the resurrection and we should thus carefully examine our a priori beliefs before we apply them to the evidence. We must always work toward a conscious interaction between the evidence and our own presuppositions, but we must also be open-minded toward the data even if it convinces us our presuppositions should be revised.

In a recent article, "The Evangelical and Traditions—geschichte,"[18] I examined the close relationship between presuppositions and methodology. I also identified two criteria which must govern tradition—critical research: (1) any interpretation of an evangelist—author must be based on the original words and

---

17. In *Existence and Faith* (1960), pp. 289–96.

18. In JETS 21/2 (June, 1978), pp. 117–30; and in *Studying the New Testament Today*, Vol. V, ed. J. H. Skilton (1979). Examples of the criteria below can be found in the article.

meaning imparted by Jesus (John 14:26, cf. 2 Peter 1:16), (2) the early church did not indulge in the wholesale creation of stories, but rather maintained a continuity between history and theology (Luke 1:1—4; John 19:35, 21:24).

The same article also includes a list of criteria necessary for making tradition—critical decisions:

1. Episodes or sayings not characteristic of either Judaism or the later church may still be regarded as trustworthy.

2. Peculiarities which could not survive in the early church unless they were genuine (i.e., they contrast with later emphases) seem to indicate authenticity.[19]

3. Unintentional signs of history or signs which would not appear out of the ordinary to the author but which clearly belong to the original setting, probably indicate veracity.

4. If there is no satisfactory *Sitz im Leben* ("situation in the life" of the church) for an episode, it is traditional and probably authentic.

5. If a passage includes language and emphases not characteristic of the author, the passage is traditional.

6. Aramaic or Palestinian features usually indicate an early origin.

7. Characteristics which are used in more than one independent tradition (e.g., Mark, Q, the L or M source) usually indicate authenticity.

8. If an episode or saying is consistent with other traditions that have been proven authentic it probably also is trustworthy.

9. A comparison of theology in the episodes with the general theological scene in the epistles may indicate how it later developed in the church age.

Hopefully these criteria will help us make some difficult tradition-decisions. We, of course, should not assume that only obvious redactional passages will indicate the evangelist's theology; tradition-criticism does more than that. Theologically it provides a control for studying the biblical theology of the evangelists in its attempt to identify each writer's distinctive theology. Nontraditional emphases are not the only indicators of theology, how-

19. The use of terms such as *may* or *seem to* does not mean this writer considers them doubtful. Rather, for apologetic purposes we must go on grounds of probability rather than certainty; therefore terms such as *certainly* or *undoubtedly* would be counterproductive.

ever, they are evidence of special emphasis. Tradition-criticism also provides for a systematic approach to answer the charges of scholars who have denied the historical veracity of Gospel accounts. Perhaps one of the best ways we can do this is to use negative criteria in a positive way to authenticate rather than deny the resurrection accounts.[20]

Redaction criticism assumes that the evangelists were more than compilers of tradition; they were also theologians who used tradition to speak to the people of their day (*Sitz im Leben*). The old liberal-conservative debate centers on the function of the evangelists as either historians or theologians, but we believe the evangelists were both theologians as well as historians. The theology of each evangelist guided both his selection and expression of individual traditions but did not allow him to make up stories. His theology thus influenced his choice of stories and how they were written (choice of language), but did not prevent a historical connection with the events themselves.

In fact, the evangelists imposed on themselves two internal controls in using the traditions:

1. Their interpretation of events had to be based on the original deeds and words of Jesus. John 14:26 says "all that (Jesus) said" was brought to the evangelists remembrance, and 2 Peter 1:16 says the early church had absolute assurance that the kerygma did not include "cleverly devised myths."

2. The early church did not create the stories and *logia Jesu* (the "sayings of Jesus") recorded in the Gospels but instead faithfully remained true to the traditions. Any so-called "coloring" of narratives was actually the highlighting of nuances present in the original events rather than re-creation of an existing story. Luke's prologue (1:1–5) stressing the historical accuracy of his presentation reminds us that he "followed all things accurately." John also stresses that his "witness" and "testimony" are "true." Both statements affirm the historical truth as well as accuracy of the Gospel accounts of the resurrection.[21]

20. Many other evangelicals argue that we should deny their presuppositions *and* their methodology. However, in spite of their protestations, I cannot help but think that this is "throwing out the baby with the bath water." The tools do have exegetical value when used with a positive a priori, and academic honesty forbids my wholesale rejection of them (see my earlier critique of the radical critics and their methodology).

21. See my article in *JETS* 21 (1978), pp. 128–30, for a more thorough discussion of these issues.

Part Two

Redaction Study

Mark's Resurrection Narrative

The structure of Mark's resurrection narrative in chapter 16, like the rest of his book, is known for its brevity. Its direct simplicity is even more obvious when we compare Mark's version of the resurrection with the other Gospels as well as Apocryphal books such as the Gospel of Peter or Acts of Pilate (see R. H. Fuller's *Formation of the Resurrection Narratives*, pp. 189—197). Mark omits any description of the event itself and for the most part Jesus' post-resurrection appearances, concentrating more on the women in a series of collages in three different settings. The first picture (vv. 1—4) presents the frustration of the women who have come to Jesus' tomb to anoint his body but don't know how they will move the stone guarding its entrance. Mark's emphasis here seems to relate directly to his writings on the disciples' continuing misunderstanding of Jesus' ministry (vv. 5—7). The second picture contrasts the women's amazement with the angelic message; here Mark emphasizes the solution to the messianic dilemma. The third episode (v. 8) is a startling contrast to the first; initially the women actively seek the Savior, now they flee from his tomb in fearful silence.[1]

The most obvious question about Mark is, of course, where it

---

1. Léon-Dufour, *Resurrection*, p. 135, notes three contrasts: 1) a darkness-light antithesis from the risen sun to the darkness of the tomb; 2) speaking versus silence in verses 3 and 6—7 in contrast to verse 8; and 3) presence versus absence in the women's anticipated sight of Jesus' body in the tomb followed by their terrified flight provoked by its absence. These contrasts are highly speculative, however, and less appropriate to the structural unity of the passage.

ends. If Mark ends his Gospel with verse 8 and the fleeing women, then this structure which emphasizes the misunderstanding of Jesus' followers graphically illustrates his greater theme in the book, or the tremendous difficulties of discipleship and faith. If the real ending to Mark's Gospel is lost, perhaps verses 9–20 offer an important substitute which emphasizes vibrant faith in the Risen Lord and best expresses the author's message of overcoming doubt and despair via the presence of the Risen One.

The Trip to the Tomb, Verses 1–2

The Name List

The Gospel of Mark presents a basic problem with its use of names (15:40, 47; 16:1), a problem which has caused some critics to argue for direct discrepancy and blame Mark for uncritically combining disconnected traditions. Vincent Taylor partially endorses that view, saying Mark probably combined two separate traditions (15:47 and 16:1) in 15:40.[2] Linguistically this is possible:

15:47	16:1	15:40
Mary Magdalene	Mary Magdalene	Mary Magdalene
Mary the mother of Joses	Mary the mother of James	Mary the mother of James the younger and of Joses
	Salome	Salome

The diagram clearly indicates a redactor might have combined two disparate lists into a single grouping. Still, there are other possibilities. Perhaps 15:40 was the prior list and Salome was left out of the 15:47 list because she was not named in the tradition. At any rate, Mark was not so dependent on the tradition that he would duplicate the same list of women each time he wrote about them. Mark's style seems to argue against such wooden repetition anyway; he felt free to rework any tradition. Stylistic variation seems to be a better solution to this problem, with the complete list occuring first (15:40) and variations of that appearing later.

2. Taylor, *Mark* pp. 652–653. Léon-Dufour, pp. 131–132, believes this is apologetic harmonization, but Schenke, (pp. 20–30) says the author knew Mary and her family relationships too well to make such a mistake.

The juxtaposition of this name list in verses 15:47 and 16:1 also supports the view that Mark did not woodenly repeat the names from tradition.[3] Instead he used them in each section for theological emphasis. The key to this emphasis is Mark's use of the verb *thereō* ("looking") in 15:40, 47; and 16:4. Each time the verb is used to suggest positive, progressive force; the women who "look" in each of Mark's three sections on crucifixion, burial, and resurrection are all witnesses[4] of God's work of salvation. The repetition of the list in 15:47 and 16:1 is Mark's connecting link between the passion and resurrection. In fact, the women provide a continuous thread throughout the resurrection narrative to illustrate Mark's discipleship motif. This author's use of women must be historically valid since it is highly unlikely that any New Testament writer would have chosen such a group, choosing rather to write about the disciples themselves who were qualified to be witnesses rather than the women.[5]

The Motive for Coming

Verse 1 says the women came to the tomb to anoint Jesus' body. Both Mark and Luke mention the purchase of spices, Mark specifically noting they would be used for the last rites of anointing. Wilhelm Bousset (*Kyries Christos*, p. 105) said it was not possible for the women even to think of doing such a thing since Jesus had been dead too long; the body would already have begun to decay. Other critics (Fuller, Wilckens, Lohmeyer, and Pesch) agree with Bousset. However, C. E. B. Cranfield (*Mark*, p. 464) and R. E. Brown (*John*, p. 982) argue that the cool, mountainous Jerusalem in early spring would have delayed deterioration of the body. Furthermore, rational, common sense behavior could hardly be expected from these mourners; their desire to minister lovingly to the body of

3. Note neither Matthew nor Luke use Mark's name lists. Matthew may parallel the three lists but inserts the narrative of the guard at the tomb between the last two lists, thereby avoiding any clumsy repetition.

4. On seeing as witness see W. Michaelis, "*horaō*," *TDNT* V, pp. 347f.; and K. Dahn, "See," *NIDNTT, DNTT,* III, p. 518.

5. Many critics say Mark deliberately chose women to stress the enigmatic nature of resurrection faith. However, this ignores the whole development of Mark's discipleship theme; the disciples themselves would have been more than adequate examples for the resurrection account. The change to women then would have been most unlikely, interrupting rather than illustrating the progression of Mark's theme.

Christ would overcome any obstacles such as early decay. Interestingly, the language in this verse is not typical of Mark, perhaps an indication that he is mouthing tradition.

Often we discover both history and redaction in a particular narrative; that is certainly true with this passage. Note that Mark begins and ends his Passion narrative with an anointing scene (14:3 – 9 and 16:1). The earlier passage initially seems to refer only to the burial of Jesus while 16:1 speaks of the empty tomb. Is Mark merely trying to say that the Risen Lord who has broken the power of death no longer needs anointing? Jeremias (ZNW, 1936, pp. 75f.; and *Theology* I, p. 284) believes more is implied here, since the theme of 14:3f. has messianic connotations. In fact, the phrase "poured it over the head" in 14:8 may even be a conscious repetition of 2 Kings 9:6 which tells about the coronation of Jehu. The motive of the women in 16:1 was of course hardly messianic, but redactional purpose is evidenced in the literary connection between 14:3 – 9 and 16:1; a messianic flavor colors the second passage because of the earlier one.

Mark's emphasis on Jesus as Messiah probably achieves highest expression here. Wilhelm Wrede (*Messianic Secret*) proposed in 1901 that Mark concocted the story of a "messianic secret" to explain the disciples' misunderstanding of Jesus' true role until after the resurrection. Through the years Wrede's theory has encountered much opposition, but historically three reasons are given for Jesus' attitude which support the truth of Mark's presentation: (1) the Jews expected a political Messiah who would free them from Roman oppression and introduce the Kingdom Age while Jesus as the suffering servant Messiah refused to become what they demanded (Cullmann and Taylor); (2) Jesus avoided public pressure to act as a wonder-worker and assiduously avoided publicity (Barclay); (3) Jewish messianic figures (e.g., Bar-Cochba) refused to be identified as Messiah until their mission was complete; therefore Jesus refused his title until after his suffering and death (Longenecker and Flusser). The third answer seems especially appropriate to Mark.

Theologically, C. F. D. Moule ("Messianic Secret") notes many passages where Jesus' messiahship is assumed (9:41; 10:47; 11:1f.; 12:35; 13:6, 21; 14:61), and concludes that any secrecy concerning his role centered mostly on his supernatural status as God's son (cf. 1:11, 9:7). Although Jesus' divinity was recognized by the demons who were silenced by it (1:23f., 34; 3:11f.; 4:39; 5:7), the disciples remained oblivious to it.

Jesus as son of God in Mark (a primary theme) becomes public knowledge with the centurion's cry in 15:39; certainly the turning point of the book. He becomes known as Messiah (a secondary theme) with the woman's anointing in chapter 14, and again subtly in chapter 16 with the women's desire to anoint his body. With these two scenes the messianic secret becomes public. Although the anointing in the earlier passage seems to be evidence of the woman's recognition of Jesus as Messiah, the Savior brushes off her interpretation of that office and redefines it in terms of his death, an act which truly signifies entrance into his messianic office. Mark uses 16:1 to emphasize Christ's fulfillment of that role, using words such as *myrizō* in 14:3f. to refer to the "anointing" for death (i.e., the suffering aspect) and *aleiphō* in 16:1, the more common messianic term for "anointing." Jesus' sacrificial death completed his messianic role and therefore anointing was no longer necessary; the empty tomb confirmed that fact.

The Time Notes

The second problem in Mark rises from the placement of events in his narrative which differs so much from the other Gospels. Some critics (Taylor; Black, *Aramaic Approach*, p. 100) believe, for instance, that *lian prōi* ("very early") in verse 2 refers to the period preceding sunrise while *anateilantos ton hēlion* ("when the sun had risen") verse 2 means dawn had already arrived, that second phrase originating from a misunderstanding of the Aramaic *rĕ gah* in the tradition.[6]

How could Mark have made such an obvious error? Jeremias (*Eucharistic Words*, p. 3) and Anderson (*Mark*, p. 354) suggest that when two time notes occur together, the second is given to clarify the first (cp. 1:35, 14:2, 15:42). Therefore the reference to "very early" in the day is further explained by "when the sun had risen," or just after dawn.

Perhaps the time notes are also symbolic, with the dawning of the day suggesting the New Age (Grundmann, Pesch, Léon-

---

6. This difference is reflected in early manuscripts. Codes D uses a present tense *anatellontos* while others omit *lian prōi* (C), *lian* (D W kn etc.) or *prōi* (q).

Dufour). Perhaps they suggest even more; Swete[7] says the time notes state that the women left before sunrise and arrived as dawn arose, thereby giving the impression that events were rapidly moving to a conclusion. Mark's word order supports this; the two notes appear both at the beginning and end of the women's trip to the tomb, thus implying movement in time as well as geography. Mark rapidly moves the reader from the women's evening purchase of spices (v. 1) to their journey just before dawn toward the tomb (v. 2a), then to the sunrise arrival at the tomb (v. 2b) where they are ushered into the timeless reality of the New Age. The sense of rushing time in Mark's terse phrases proves to be a remarkable lead into the crisis-event at the empty tomb.

The Approach to the Tomb, Verses 3—4

Mark's description of the women's arrival at the tomb (vv. 3 and 4) includes some dramatic touches which strengthen the effect of the scene. The poignant question of verse 3 ("who will roll the stone away from the entrance of the tomb?") is such a contrast to the purposeful action of the women that many critics (e.g., Taylor, Schenke, Grundmann) believe the words to be literary and symbolic rather than historical. Mark introduces more color in this verse when he combines the use of the progressive imperfect *elegon* ("were saying") with the reflexive *pros heautous* ("to themselves"), thereby producing a sense of action (cf. 9:10, 11:31, 12:7, 14:4); the women seem to be asking the question as they rush toward the tomb. Still, the traditional origin of this question should not so easily be dismissed. The verse is clearly indicative of Mark's style, and although this question is found only in his Gospel, perhaps the other evangelists omitted it because it did not fit their redactional purposes.

The question itself presents no real historical problems; the passionate mourning indicative of people in Eastern countries probably had these women in such an emotional state that they rushed off to Jesus' tomb without once taking into consideration such practical matters as removing the stone from its entrance. Fur-

7. Swete, pp. 372—373. Taylor, *Mark*, p. 604, claims the distance is much too short. His view is made invalid by nature; rapid sunrises in the east change the sky in minutes from darkness to light. All these events occurred anyway after the Sabbath which ended at dusk Saturday in keeping with legal requirements.

thermore, the basic wording in this question is repeated in other Gospel accounts, thus almost certainly confirming its origin in tradition. Its editorial color in Mark only heightens anticipation for the coming miracle in verse 4.

The traditional origin of verse 4 has been challenged less, probably because of its more general contents (the stone "rolled away"[8] from the empty tomb). The phrase "for (the stone) was very large," however, seems a bit out of place at the end of the verse; several early manuscripts (D 565, etc.) place it at the end of verse 3. Grundmann (p. 322) and Lohmeyer (p. 353) believe the phrase belongs to verse 4 rather than 3 suggesting that the stone which obstructed the women's view prevented them from seeing the tomb was empty until the last moment. Pesch (vol. 2, p. 531) thinks the phrase belongs in verse 3; the stone "which was very large" proves the women needed help, perhaps even that of an angel, to enter the tomb. Either way the description is colorful detail leading the way toward miraculous intervention. Mark's repetition of the word *lithos* (stone) plus the added note on its size certainly stress its insurmountability, probably even symbolizing the power of the grave. Yet even this great stone is "rolled away"; what man cannot do God can![9] Mark's use of the perfect passive *anakekulista* ("rolled away") in verse 4 is a vivid description of the mighty act. The author creates an intense sense of action, moving the reader toward the climax through an economy of words. The women ask the question, look up, and see.[10]

The Events at the Tomb, Verses 5–7

The Angel

Mark uses simple language to describe the angel in verse 5 in anthropomorphic terms, "a young man dressed in a white robe."[11]

---

8. The only word not common to Mark is *sphodra* (once in Mark vs. seven in Matthew). This may well be a Markan rendition of the tradition.

9. G. Herbert, *SJT* (1962), p. 68, is much too allegorical when he says the stone symbolizes the uprooting of the Pharisaic legal system; this would be more indicative of Matthew than Mark.

10. Compare this with the Gospel of Peter and the gloss in the "k" manuscript. Both add detailed descriptions of the resurrection event itself.

11. Lake, *Resurrection*, pp. 240f., believes the "young man" was a youth rather than an angel, and J. H. McIndoe, *ET* 1969, p. 125, believes it was Mark himself. Such a description, however, was often used by Hebrews to describe angels (cf. 2 Macc. 3:26, 33f.; Josephus' Ant. 5:8.2; Gosp. Peter 9; Luke 24:4; Rev. 7:9, 13; 10:1).

This terse description has led some critics (e.g., Taylor, Lightfoot, Grass) to suggest Mark provided his own redaction here rather than using a traditional basis. Although Mark's description is peculiar to his Gospel, his terms are not; many are used elsewhere in the Gospels and only *ekthambeō* ("amazed," v. 5) is exclusively Markan. The language then does not disprove a tradition origin, and neither does Mark's report of an angel. The resurrection accounts universally agree about the presence of angels and the early church undeniably considered them historical. Mark's account, in fact, is the most conservative Gospel account, leading many to believe it is an even more primitive tradition. The evangelists' emphasis is on the message rather than the angel anyway, and if Mark were indulging in free composition here one would expect the opposite emphasis.

His anthropomorphic description prompts several interesting theological considerations. Perhaps the origin of the description is what K. Haacker (Nov T 1970, p. 70f.) calls "experience language" or describing an event the way it appeared to eyewitnesses rather than to others after the fact. This explanation seems likely in light of Mark's emphasis on the women's lack of understanding. Perhaps he wrote this way to emphasize their total failure to comprehend the purpose of the resurrection, God's mighty act of vindicating his Son. Because these women were so unprepared for the affirming revelation of Jesus' true nature, they also totally failed to understand who the person was at the tomb.

All through his Gospel Mark continues to stress the misunderstanding of Jesus' disciples. Even in the post-resurrection revelation of the "messianic secret" Mark's primary messianic emphasis seems to be the disciples' misunderstanding. Their blindness continues to surface (see 6:52; 8:14f., 32; 9:32; 10:35f., as well as the Passion narratives), even to the point of the women not recognizing an angel for what he was. Perrin (*Resurrection*, pp. 27–31) discusses the "changing roles of the disciples and the women in Mark's Gospel," believing that Mark deliberately replaced the disciples with women who also failed Jesus. Thus in Mark all the disciples, even the women, failed to understand and follow the Master.

When the women finally do begin to understand, "fearful awe" (*ekthambeō*) fills their hearts. The angel who is dressed in a "white robe" and "sits on the right side" is symbolic of eschatological glory and power as well as heavenly origin, and the women's fear or "astonishment" is the kind of emotion which is typically provoked by theophanies or divine revelations. G. Bertram says (*TDNT*, III, 6) the term *ekthambeō* is often used "in ancient miracle stories to indicate the accreditation of the miracle by the spectators."

The Message

The angelic message (vv. 6—7) contains important theological insights. A number of Markan elements such as the use of the historic present *legei* ("says," 150 times in his Gospel) and an abrupt style "which derives peculiar life and freshness from the absence of conjunctions in the first five clauses" (Swete, p. 374) present the reader with swift, short phrases which fall on the ears like the staccato bursts of a machine gun. Many critics accept the traditional origin of verse 6 but reject 7, since the transition from verse 6 to 8 is much smoother without 7. Yet verse 7 does include some indications of traditional origin, for instance the phrase "and to Peter" which may indicate the Petrine authority of the early apostolic years.[12] Another phrase, "the Nazarene," is also more meaningful in a traditional context than a later one.

Remembering our theory of tradition and redaction, consider several interpretive notes which indicate Mark's theological accent. In these verses (as in many cases of awe at a theophany) women are first calmed (cp. Luke 1:13, 30; Rev. 1:17), then given a message (Moses, Elijah, etc.). The message begins with a rebuke. Many scholars (Hebert, Lightfoot, Martin) detect a negative shade of meaning in *zēteite*; the women who "seek" Jesus are a direct contrast to the reality of the resurrection which had been predicted three times yet remained unexpected. Mark continues the theme of misunderstanding here. He also effectively uses the literary device of contrast to highlight the stupendous nature of the Easter event; darkness becomes dawn, the anointing is eclipsed by the anointed one, the enclosed tomb becomes the empty tomb; fear ends in joy, and seeking leads to finding.

The dramatic tone of Mark's narrative includes the use of "the Nazarene," a phrase which emphasizes Jesus' humble Galilean

---

12. Fuller and Wilckens question the authenticity of the verse but agree it has a traditional origin.

origin (cf. John 1:46) and prepares the reader for the "Galilee" reference (v. 7). Lohmeyer (p. 354f.) says Mark used this phrase along with "the crucified one" to show how the women's "purposeless act" (anointing Jesus' corpse) was changed into true fulfillment in "the new fact of the resurrection." The combined use of the words "was crucified" and "was raised" may be another example of literary contrast; the women still mourned over the effects of the crucifixion, but God considered the crucifixion as a single past event which included the resurrection. Christ's defeat of death was complete and final.

"He is not here" and "behold the place where they laid him" are special touches meant to draw the reader into the event. The angel and women "look" into the vacant sepulcher. Although some critics might disagree,[13] most detect a strong apologetic tone here. Mark focuses his resurrection account on these two phrases which become the climax of his narrative. Several possible interpretations exist for verse 7:

Since Galilee is the place of divine revelation, the command ("go, tell his disciples and Peter") could refer to the parousia (the second "coming" of Christ) rather than the resurrection. Evidence for this view might be Mark's absence of a Galilee post-resurrection appearance (if the book ends at v. 8); the importance of the parousia in Mark; the gathering together of the elect in Mark 14:27 — 28 (14:28—16:7); and the testimony of Eusebius (Ch. Hist. III, 5) regarding an early oracle to go to Galilee and wait for the parousia (Lohmeyer, Lightfoot, Marxsen, Michaelis, Weeden). Still, any so-called parousia references are much more likely seen as resurrection passages (see Stein, NTS, 1974, p. 445f.), and the oracle mentioned by Eusebius told the women to go to Pella in Transjordan (not Galilee) and to "dwell there," indicating a permanent rather than temporary home (see Fuller, Resurrection, p. 63).

Proagein could mean "lead" rather than "precede" (based on its use in 14:28 following the shepherd metaphor of 14:27). Galilee

---

13. Evans, p. 78, says "There is no particular emphasis on the emptiness of the tomb. The empty tomb interprets the message of the resurrection, not vice versa." A sentence later he adds, "the visit to the tomb is the means by which the resurrection itself is declared, and not a prelude to . . . appearances of the Risen Lord to follow." His conclusion that apologetics only appear in later Gospels when the tomb is compared to appearances, does not follow. The reverse, in fact, is true; apologetics would increase if it stood alone.

might then be theologically symbolic of the mission to go to the Gentiles rather than the place of Christ's appearances (Hoskyns and Evans). Still, Mark 16:7 probably refers to 1 Corinthians 15:3 – 8 where Galilee is not the mission itself but the place from which it originated.

The angel's command might have been given as a contrast to the disobedience of the women in verse 8b, a symbolic reprimand of the Christian community for staying in Jerusalam instead of going to Galilee in obedience to the Lord's command (Schenke). This is, however, a false interpretation of New Testament history. How can we believe the disciples never went back to Galilee— that would make the narratives of Matthew 28 and John 21 totally fictional. Furthermore, Galilee was home to the disciples who would naturally return there.

Verse 7 might simply refer to a resurrection appearance in Galilee similar to that of 1 Corinthians 15:5f. This seems to be the most natural interpretation since Galilee in Mark was the geographical center of Jesus' ministry. Furthermore, the reference to Peter probably directly alludes to Christ's appearance to that disciple recorded in Luke 24:34, John 21:15 – 17, Acts 10:41, and 1 Corinthians 15:5 (Fuller, Stein).

Consider again the theological emphasis of Mark's reference to Galilee. If his Gospel ends with 16:8 the reference becomes extremely important; if the book's real ending containing a Galilee appearance has been lost, then the reference is not so crucial. Martin (p. 72) and Karnetzki (ZNW, 1961, pp. 228f.) believe Mark's theme expands here into a kind of community theology in which Galilee becomes representative of the inauguration of the church and its universal mission. Data in Mark seems to support this; Galilee is used thirteen times, almost always in the context of Jesus' preaching (1:14, 16, 39; 9:30) and its success (1:28, 3:7, 15:40). Both Matthew and Mark contrast the success of Jesus in Galilee with rejection in Jerusalem, but Mark's antithesis is not as strong as Matthew's. Still, Mark does mention Jerusalem ten times as the place where Jesus' enemies publicly opposed his ministry and sought his death (3:22, 7:18, 11:18, 14:18) and where Jesus predicted he would suffer betrayal and death.

Both tradition and redaction are evidenced in the angelic command of verse 7. Mark records this primarily as a directive for Jesus' disciples to prepare for his Galilean appearance, but also, in light of the Jewish practice of refusing women any legal rights as witnesses, the angel probably sent the women after the disciples so they could prepare themselves to be witnesses. Perhaps the best way to understand the verse is as a promise to the disciples via the women. The women must "tell his disciples" about their Risen Lord; a phrase which feeds into Mark's theme of victory in discipleship. Throughout his Gospel the evangelist emphasizes Jesus' call of chosen followers (1:16f.; 2:14; 3:13; 6:7; 10:27f.) and God's special revelation of truth to the elect in "plain" words (8:31, especially v. 32, and 9:7) rather than hidden parables (ch. 4). E. Schweizer comments (*NTS*, 1964, 421f.):

> Recognition of God earnestly begins with the recognition of the hidden God. How could it be understood and believed that God acted here, except in a discipleship in which the disciple follows his master step by step in as concrete and bodily a way as God Himself encounters him in Jesus? This is what the so-called secret of the Messiah means. It is the hiddenness of God in Jesus which, despite all its mighty manifestations is not seen by a blind world, is often totally misunderstood, and opens itself only to the follower who goes himself on the road of Jesus.

Still, despite the plain words of the Master, Jesus' disciples fail to understand God's truth as revealed in his Son (6:52; 8:17f., 32f.; 9:32f.; 10:35f.). Although Mark seems to stress the antinomy here between God's clear revelation versus the disciples' misunderstanding, his true motif emerges later. For this disciple kingdom truths can be known only in light of Jesus' combined death and resurrection when the cross is framed by the empty tomb. The turning point of Mark's discipleship theme is thus found in the resurrection event where defeat and ignorance disappear in glorious affirmation of the Risen Lord. How positive or negative this emphasis is depends largely on one's view concerning the ending of the Gospel. If Mark ends with the fear and distress of the women, this affirmation is merely anticipated and discipleship continues to remain difficult. If, however, Mark has another, more positive ending, then the evangelist's narrative truly demonstrates affirmation in discipleship.

The women are also instructed to "tell Peter," a phrase which suggests the same tradition as that used in Luke 24:34 and 1 Corinthians 15:5, yet more probably is part of the angel-tradition itself. Perhaps the reference would not seem so oblique if the so-called lost ending of Mark included a record of a post-resurrection appearance of Christ to Peter. None of the evangelists record such an event, however, so the command probably does not suggest a personal appearance of the Risen Lord to Peter. The text itself does not demand this appearance either, so the angel's command to "tell the disciples and Peter" probably emphasizes the report rather than any future appearance. Perhaps the phrase is merely his way of recognizing Peter's special need for assurance and reinstatement after denying Christ.

The angel next reminds the women they will see Jesus in Galilee "even as he told you," an obvious reference to the prophecy in 14:28. Is this question a later addition to tradition? Most critics who argue against the authenticity of 16:7 also question 14:28 on the grounds that 14:27 and 29 fit together if verse 28 is removed.[14] This is not necessarily true, however; Mark could just as easily have written 16:7 on the basis of 14:28. Verse 28 fits well with 27 if *proaxō* is translated "I shall lead"; no real discrepancy exists between translating the verb "lead" in 14:28 and "precede" in 16:7. The imagery of 14:27f. is of a shepherd leading his scattered sheep back to safety. That metaphor is not present in chapter 16 so the word reverts back to its more common meaning. The prophecy itself does not change, therefore affording little reason to question its authenticity.

The phrase itself is a natural part of Mark's fulfillment theme. Although this theme of Christ's fulfillment of prophecy is less obvious in Mark than in Matthew or Luke, it is nonetheless important; Mark includes sixty-eight Old Testament references (nineteen of which are direct quotations [Swete]), proving that Jesus fulfills both Old Testament prophecy and his own prophetic statements.

The Reaction of the Women, Verse 8

Critical Views Regarding Verse 8

The meaning of verse 8 (and perhaps Mark's resurrection narrative as a whole) is greatly dependent on the actual ending of the

---

14. See Fuller, Anderson, Pesch et al. Critics generally consider 14:28 more of a redactional insertion than 16:7; viewing 16:7 as a traditional insert based on the same pre-Pauline list as 1 Corinthians 5:5.

Gospel. Most critics today are convinced the evangelist did conclude his book with verse 8, citing several reasons for their
conviction:

1. Mark wished to emphasize the disciples' awe and fear of God
in light of Jesus' victory over death. The appearances were not
recorded because they were too awesome to be put into words;
Mark ends on a note of fear to stress this (Lightfoot, Anderson,
Pesch, et al).

2. He wanted to explain why the story of the empty tomb remained secret for so long. Since the appearances were well known,
Mark merely alluded to them in verse 7 so he could center on the
empty tomb. The silence of the women, not their fear, was his
major emphasis (Creed, Dibelius, Grass, et al).

3. He wanted to emphasize the *Sitz im Leben* of his own time,
or the imminent parousia. The tension between the command in
verse 7 and the fear-induced silence of verse 8 is characteristic of
the messianic secret, looking for its fulfillment in the parousia
(Lohmeyer, Marxsen, Perrin).

4. No extended narratives existed in Mark's day, only lists of
appearances (1 Cor. 15:5f.). Verse 8 is the usual reaction to an angelophany; the silence due to the messianic secret. The proclamation had to come from the disciples but since that had not
happened yet, an angel had to announce as well as command it
(Fuller, Wilckens).

Most critics who endorse verse 8 as the true ending of Mark
believe he stresses his theme of misunderstanding to the end,[15]
using the women as examples of all disciples (then and now) who
must grapple with existential anxiety in matters of faith. Léon-
Dufour (p. 134) says this is "a literary device which enables him
to show not only how the women faced the unfathomable mystery
of God and death, but also how the reader himself confronts the
mystery." Nothing in life can dispel the terror; one can only wait
with the disciples for divine intervention from God through the
personal touch of the Risen One.

The belief that Mark ends with 16:8 is so widely accepted that

---

15. Lane also says (pp. 591–592) Mark thereby maintains his basic presentation of
the miracles. "Fear is the constant reaction to the disclosure of Jesus' transcendent
dignity in the Gospel of Mark (cf. vv. 4:41; 5:15, 33, 36; 6:50; 9:6, 32). In the light of this
pervasive pattern, the silence and fear of the women are an indirect Christological
affirmation."

most modern literature assumes it and probes for implications. Meye says the Gospel's ending must be understood in light of all of verses 1—8. Mark's resurrection narrative stresses fulfilled prophecy or the actualization of what Jesus promised (e.g., 14:28 in 16:7). The women's fear and silence is therefore not the conclusion but rather a necessary reaction to the staggering truth. The appearances were not necessary to teach Mark's point; they were presupposed.

Weeden (pp. 45—51) views Mark's ending from a different perspective, believing that the women's silence meant the disciples never heard the resurrection message and therefore misunderstood it from the beginning. Verse 16:8 thus concludes Mark's polemic against the disciples.

Some scholars stress the importance of Mark's ending as it applies to the church today. Lindemann argues that Mark emphasizes a *theologia crucis* ("theology of the cross"), with the church in all ages experiencing the same silence as the women who are dependent on the witness of verse 7. Tannehill (pp. 83—84) also comments on Mark's recorded dilemma of discipleship. Although Jesus' words have always proven true, the Christian lingers "between failure and unrealized possibility." Jesus' promise, however, overcomes tension, and his presence overrules it.

Catchpole interprets Mark in terms of divine election. In contrast to Weeden, Catchpole believes Mark stresses the authority of the disciples. The silence of the women is symbolic of the masses whose fear is invoked by the epiphany of God. The message of verse 7 is to inform the divinely chosen leaders (disciples or apostles) about the empty tomb; the reaction of the women proves the exclusivity of that message.

Several scholars have attempted to understand Mark 16 via narrative hermeneutics. Daniel and Aline Patte (pp. 55—56, 85—90) have tried a structural exegesis, viewing 16:8 within the context of chapters 15 and 16. They believe the women represent a polemical axis which demonstrates the opposing forces of expectation and reality. They are a part of Jewish or religious society (unlike the soldiers who portray secular society) whose silence demonstrates that humanity "outside of society" cannot comprehend the glory of God and therefore experiences terror. The only solution is to join the transcendent God "in society."

Petersen speaks of "narrative closure," noting how verse 8 seems to interrupt the flow of the expected conclusion regarding the continuance of the kingdom. The incongruity forces the reader himself to solve the puzzle. Petersen believes irony here rather than literal statement directs attention back to verse 7. Even though the women (as did the disciples) seem to "muddle about," Jesus is in the process of fulfilling his promises.

Boomershine provides perhaps the most complete discussion of Mark's conclusion. He presents three kinds of interpretation— holy awe (Lightfoot, Allen), theological polemic (Weeden, Crossan, Kelber), and a conclusion to the messianic secret (Marxsen, Fuller)—arguing that the *gar* clause suggests the negative implications of the women's flight and silence. "Holy awe" thus explains the reason for their actions but does not excuse their erroneous behavior. A polemical approach to the conclusion, however, which includes a highly positive tone encouraging reader identification with (not against) the women as in earlier passages (15:40–41, 47), seems insufficient and the messianic secret is incomplete in its failure to consider the narrative flow. The key, says Boomershine, is to notice how the arrest, trial, and resurrection scenes all have similar structures which lead the reader to identify with the disciple who "makes a radically wrong response." The total effect of verse 8 thus shows the tension between "the scandal of silence and the fear of proclamation" (p. 237). Mark demands that the reader who also has this problem conquer his fear in order to proclaim the reality of the resurrection.

The congruence of these different approaches (Meye, Tannehill, Petersen, Boomershine) offers probably the most likely interpretation of verse 8 as the concluding verse of Mark. Its primary message is discipleship failure which links it to a primary theme in Mark, and its message urges the reader to rely on Jesus' promises (v. 7) rather than his own propensity to fail (v. 8).

But is Mark 16:8 truly the ending of the Gospel? Perhaps we should examine some proposed alternatives before we come to any conclusions regarding Mark's final statement.

The Conclusion of the Book

Arguments for 16:8

Before any alternate hypotheses can be evaluated we should first consider the evidence for verse 8 as the conclusion of the book. Most critics today would say neither the longer nor shorter endings are the original ending of Mark, both on textual and linguistic grounds. The longer ending is missing from Codeces Vaticanus and Sinaiticus as well as the Old Latin codex Bobiensis; Clement of Alexandria and Origen never mention it, and Eusebius and Jerome said it was missing from most of the manuscripts in their possession. Textual evidence thus argues against a longer ending,[16] as also does its style (see further below).

The shorter ending, on the other hand, is found in several Greek manuscripts of the seventh to the ninth centuries (L Y 099 0112), the Old Latin K, and several others. Aland's recent attempt (*Neotestamentica et Semitica*, pp. 157f.) to demonstrate the early origin of the longer ending is unconvincing since it fails to overcome both the weakness of the manuscript evidence and the clumsiness of the ending itself.[17]

The Gospel of Mark thus has three possible endings: (1) the short, deliberate ending of verse 8; (2) a longer ending which was lost or suppressed by the early church (probably before Matthew or Luke used Mark) in one of three ways: accidental mutilation (majority view); deliberate mutilation by an early church which could not accept the original conclusion because of its primitive, undeveloped form (see Grass); or, an unfinished ending (Mark either was too busy or died before he could finish). Most commentators dismiss a suppressed ending as improbable and an unfinished ending as too speculative; since most early manuscripts end with verse 8 and Mark includes good theological reason for ending there, the Gospel thus ends with verse 8.

Arguments for a lost ending

Scholars who advocate a lost ending use two arguments, linguistic and literary. The linguistic approach says Mark could not have grammatically ended his Gospel with *gar*. Several articles, however, (see Lightfoot, Lohmeyer, Cadbury, Kraeling, Ottley, Richardson) have proved that *gar* was frequently used in Scripture to end a sentence or paragraph (e.g., Gen. 18:15, 45:3 LXX). Although

16. See Metzger, *Textual Commentary*, pp. 122–126; and K. Aland in *Neotestamentica et Semitica*, pp. 157–180, and W. R. Farmer, *Contra*.

17. Metzger, *Commentary*, pp. 125–126, says, "The internal evidence . . . is against its being genuine. Besides containing a high percentage of non-Markan words, its rhetorical tone differs totally from the simple style of Mark's Gospel."

Taylor says none of these examples end a book, P. W. van der Hoerst has recently shown how Plotinus concluded his thirty-second treatise with it (Ennead 5:5). Neither Mark nor any other New Testament writer ends a section with *gar*,[18] it is true, yet the linguistic argument saying it thus may never be done seems a weak rationale for the short ending. Boomershine and Bartholomew have shown conclusively how Mark's narrative technique could indeed have led to such an ending, so it would be erroneous to conclude on literary grounds that it had to continue.

The literary approach provides a better argument for a lost conclusion. Fuller (p. 65) says "there would now seem to be no reason why a work of *Kleinliteratur* of the type that Mark's Gospel represents should not have concluded thus," but there are several indications that Mark intended to continue. The command to go to Galilee suggests more,[19] as does the contradiction between verse 7 and verse 8 if the book ends at 8. The usual interpretation says Mark deliberately established the tension between the command to go to the disciples and the women's silence in order to continue his "discipleship failure" theme (scholars here are willing to accept this disobedience as part of Markan redaction).

Still, we must question whether this meshes with the whole development of Mark's Gospel or whether the whole "messianic misunderstanding" and discipleship failure themes look to the resurrection for the time of victorious reversal.

Arguments for 16:8 as the ending do not really fit the pattern of 16:1−8; the victorious atmosphere of the resurrection is discouraged, not encouraged by such a final contrast. As W. L. Knox (*HTR*, 1942, 13f.) and F. F. Bruce (*EQ*, 1945, p. 169f.) argue, this kind of dramatic conclusion does not appear anywhere else in the synoptics or Hellenistic literature; Mark would have violated the rules of ancient storytelling if he had ended such a glorious section on a negative note. G. C. Bilezikian, in contrast (pp. 134−137), argues

18. Matthew ends sections with the "fear" of the officials (11:18) and disciples (4:41), however 16:8 uniquely necessitates the disobedience of the women, thereby negating the power of the resurrection. This does not fit in with the victory motif in this passage.

19. Lightfoot's objection (*Mark*, pp. 93−96) fails to prove its point. Although 16:7 may hint at something Mark never meant to present in his narrative, it is certainly improbable. The reinstatement of Peter and the disciples is clearly stated in verse 7, hinted at in Luke 24:34, and stressed in John 21:15−17.

that Greek tragedy (which he believes Mark emulates) did contain such enigmatic conclusions.

The atmosphere of 16:1—8 does not imply the stuff of Greek tragedy however; another look is needed. C. F. D. Moule (*NTS*, 1955, pp. 58f.) says verse 8 was meant to be a parenthesis between the command in verse 7 and its fulfillment in verse 9. The silence of the woman was thus temporary and natural; in their awestruck amazement they ran straight back to the disciples without speaking to anyone on the way. Their refusal to linger over an exchange of greetings is simply the eastern sign of great haste (cf. 2 Kings 4:29, Luke 10:4).

Furthermore, Mark's Gospel includes several indications of a victory motif seen first in the title of his work in the terms "Messiah" and "Son of God." The second term is especially significant; although "Messiah" is used rarely, "Son of God" is a central concept in Mark. Both titles reflect Mark's purpose in showing Jesus as the victorious Son who has power over nature and the spirit world. Mark also combines humiliation and enthronement in such a way that Jesus' suffering stresses his exaltation. Thus his suffering and passion proleptically anticipate victory in the resurrection where the centurion declares, "Surely this was the Son of God" (15:39). Only unlikely characters such as demons or a blind beggar recognize Jesus for what he is; the Son of God and Messianic King,[20] but all these motifs prepare the reader for a victorious finale in which everyone will know and be convinced.

Mark's emphasis on discipleship is also significant here; much has been written on this theme recently[21] but a few summary statements can be made. First of all, we should note the intimate connection between Christology and discipleship in Mark; although the messianic secret included both Jesus' role as the Son of God as well as Messiah, the first part of the Gospel centers on the misunderstanding of the disciples. The second half, however, focuses on Jesus' Christology as suffering servant. Each passion

20. Although Jesus is called "king" only in the trial scene (15:2, 9, 12) and crucifixion narrative (15:26, 32), several indications show Mark advocated a kingship Christology not only in the triumphal entry (11:1—10), but also in the kingdom passages (9:1; 10:29) which combine the emergence of the kingdom of God with Jesus' appearance. Thus demonic recognition of Jesus (1:24, 34; 5:7) includes definite royal overtones.

21. See Meye, Freyre, Reploh, Stock, Best, and Schmall. McKnight also includes an excellent summary of the data in chapter 1.

prediction in Mark is followed by a section illustrating the disciples' misinterpretation of Jesus and the Master's attempts to teach them about suffering in discipleship. The blindness of the disciples is demonstrated time after time (8:31f.; 9:30f.; 10:24f., 41f.; 14:3f.), until they actually reach the point of unbelief, rejection, and hardness of heart (4:40, 6:52, 8:17, 32).

This motif has produced two major interpretations (McKnight), the polemical and the pastoral. The polemical view (e.g., Weeden, Kelber) says Mark considered the disciples to be his opponents and used them as a literary foil to combat the heretical Christology they espoused. The pastoral view (Reploh, Martin, Best, McKnight) says the disciples were used as examples of the difficulties of discipleship; the reader can easily identify with their misunderstanding and learn from their mistakes.

How does the narrative itself develop the role of the disciples? Very probably the narrative supports the second view in passages which give the disciples a positive role (3:14f., 4:11, 6:7f., 9:37, 10:28). They may be used as literary foils to highlight their ignorance of the messianic secret, but they nonetheless serve a positive purpose. Peter's confession (8:29), for instance, is a step forward to partial, yet incomplete perception (Weeden et al. are forced to view even this as negative). Jesus' constant efforts following this confession to enlighten the disciples certainly encourage rather than discourage the reader to greater faith in discipleship.

Finally, several events in Mark call for a reversal of misunderstanding at the resurrection. The *crux interpretum* (key passage) here is certainly 9:9 where Jesus states that his secret role will be revealed "when the Son of Man should rise from the dead." Surely this statement clearly coincides with Mark's combined Christology—discipleship theme and suggests the solution, i.e., that the Risen Lord will remove blindness from his followers' eyes. Several other texts also promise a future ministry for the disciples after the resurrection (13:10−13, 14:28, 16:7) and one even says their blindness will be removed (10:46−52).[22] Just as the secrecy motif was reversed at 15:39 and 16:1f., so one would expect that the

22. Two redactional additions suggest this; the mention of "disciples" in verse 46 following their lack of understanding in verses 35−45, and the phrase "he followed him on the way" in verse 52 which ends the pericope on a note of discipleship. This plus the section in chapter 8:1−10:52, centering on discipleship imply that the blindness had greater meaning.

disciples' misunderstanding would also be removed at the resurrection.

A Proposal for the Ending

From a linguistic standpoint, traces of Mark's ending may exist in the other synoptic Gospels. Although Luke uses little of Mark's material, Matthew does. Eta Linnemann (ZTK, 1969, pp. 255f.) has attempted to reconstruct the lost ending of Mark from Matthew 28:16–17 and Mark 16:15–20. Although her work has been severely criticized by Aland (ZTK, 1970, pp. 3f.) for what he called "unsound methodology in approaching textual and internal difficulties," his criticism is for the most part directed against her proposed Markan ending. Mark and Matthew 28:16–20 do include similarities in both theme and structure, however; the Galilean setting and great commission are both appropriate to the promise of Mark 16:7. Matthew's enthronement theme meshes nicely with Mark's royal motif, and Matthew's stress on universalism also follows a similar pattern in Mark (e.g., 7:24f., 31f.; 11:17; 13:10; 14:9; 15:39). The major problem with this approach, says Hans-Werner Bartsch, is linguistic. The language of Matthew 28:16–20 is definitely Matthean with absolutely no trace of Mark. Arguments in support of Matthew's usage of a lost Markan ending are therefore thematic rather than linguistic.

A more obvious use of Mark in Matthew is found in Matthew 28:9–10.[23] The passage includes several terms common in Mark's Gospel: idōn (seven times in Mark, six of them redactional); krateō (fifteen of forty-seven New Testament occurrences in Mark, nine of them redactional); the historic present legei also in 16:6; (see also notes on vv. 6–7; the historic present occurs 150 times in Mark, fifty-two with verbs of speaking[24]); mē phobeisthe (also in 16:6; the verb occurs twelve times in Mark, eight of them redac-

---

23. We depend largely on Pryke's study for redactional usage. His work is based on an exhaustive comparison of Mark with the other Gospels as well as an internal examination of favorite themes and terms. It is therefore a valuable tool for studying Mark. Pryke uses "redactional" to mean Mark's coloring of tradition to bring out a particular nuance. This term therefore suggests a favorite Markan term.

24. Nigel Turner in Moulton-Hope-Turner, Grammar, vol. IV: Style, p. 20. On page 35 he notes that Matthew changes seventy-eight historic presents, adding only twenty-three of his own. Therefore probability favors a Markan original here as well.

tional); *apēlthon* (twenty-two times, eleven redactional); *hypagete
... opsontai* (also in 16:7; *hypagein* is a Markan favorite found fifteen
times, eight of them redactional); *ékeî* (eleven times, six redactional). The passage clearly includes a great number of Markan
terms.

Jesus' message in verse 10 of Matthew 28 might also be the perfect sequel to Mark 16:8, illustrating how the awestruck silence of
the women was broken and their fear turned into joy. G. W. Trompf
(*NTS*, 1972, pp. 308f.; and *ABR*, 1973, pp. 15f.) claims the three-fold
emphasis on Galilee in Matthew might also jive with Mark's methodology (e.g., 6:39f., 8:6f., 15:61 for "Christ"; 1:11, 9:7, 12:6 for "beloved," the passion predictions, etc.). He also says no one should
say Mark did not include the appearances because he combined
the resurrection and the parousia. Mark clearly distinguished the
two, says Trompf (5:42; 8:31; 10:34; 14:58; and 8:34f.; 10:29f.; 13:5f.),
saying the messianic secret would cease after the resurrection (9:9)
while a period of evangelization must take place prior to the parousia (13:10, 26; cf. 8:35; 14:9).

It is therefore possible to construct[25] a Markan ending from his
style, hints in his book, and parallels in Matthew. Verse 9 may have
begun with *kai euthus* ("and immediately," Moule) or *alla* ("but,"
Trompf) but *kai idou* ("and behold") perhaps is best (as in Matthew)
in light of Markan terminology; this provides a change of scene as
well as sets the stage for the joy motif. The Risen One now appears
to the women (probably using *hypantaō* since Matthew also uses
it) with a command similar to that of Mark 16:7 (Matt. 28:10 follows
Mark 16:7). Trompf probably correctly assumes that Mark used
adelphois in imitation of the 1 Corinthian list since "James" is mentioned in 15:40 and 16:1, and "Peter" in 16:7. The women now
"grasp" Jesus (note the use of *krateō* in 1:31; 5:41; 9:27) in "great
joy" and run to tell the disciples. Then he appears to the disciples
in Galilee (on the basis of Matt. 14:28 and Mark 16:7 that such an
event was probable). Perhaps the Markan form based on Matthew
28:9 — 10 would read: *Kai idou hypantēsen autais ho Iēsous kai legei,
Chairete. Mē phobeisthe; hypagete eipate tois adelphois mou hina*

---

25. This section utilizes the suggestions of Moule, "Mark," pp. 58 — 59; Cranfield,
pp. 469 — 470; and Trompf, "Resurrection," pp. 321 — 333.

apelthōsin eis tēn Galilaian;[26] *ekei me opsontai.*[27] *Kai euthus kra-*
tousin tēs cheiros autou meta charas megalēs kai edramon apan-
geilai tois adelphois (or *mathētais autou*). ("And behold Jesus met
them and said, 'Greetings. Do not be afraid. Go, tell my brethren
that I depart into Galilee; they will see me there.' And immediately
they grasped his hand with great joy and ran to tell his
brethren/disciples").

We believe Mark probably did produce an ending which is hinted
at in Matthew 28:9−10 and possible 28:16−20. Our proposed ending includes both elements of fear and joy; the women who were
struck silent by the angel's words encounter the Risen Lord, are
revitalized by this presence, and rush off to tell the disciples. Although Matthew's account combines these two elements of fear
and joy, Mark separates them into two events.

If Mark's Gospel originally did include such an ending, how
was it lost? We simply have no satisfactory answers to that question except to say history is made up of contingent improbabili-
ties. Even though we do not have copies of such a lost ending,
that is no basis for denying that it ever existed. Theological explanations of Mark based on a verse 8 conclusion are really just as
improbable, since they are based on modern literary techniques
rather than ancient historiography. They also fail to satisfy the true
intent of the pericope. We believe our proposed lost ending is a
more satisfactory incorporation of the thematic and linguistic
evidence.

The Theological Purpose of Verse 8

If Mark 16:8 is not the conclusion of the Gospel but instead a
verse which sets the stage for Christ's victorious affirmative appearance, more can be said about its intent. Since the verse is not
reproduced in the other Synoptics (just hinted at in Matthew), we
can conclude that it clearly reflects Mark's own theology. Its vocabulary is obviously Markan yet not peculiar to him; its terms
are also found in the other Gospels as well as Paul's epistles. Its

26. Mark (like Matthew) probably deviated slightly from the angel's message here.
27. Matthew and Mark both use *kakei* (three times each), but the only place Matthew
uses it in a corresponding section he replaces it with Mark's *ekei*. Therefore Mark probably uses *ekei* here.

theme which is so similar to that of Matthew 28 seems to indicate that Mark is closely working with tradition.

Very likely the messianic misunderstanding theme reaches a reversal here, especially if we accept the probability of another scene which fulfills the Markan promise of victory. Verse 8 now has an entirely new perspective; its contrast with verse 7 is deliberate and temporary, utilizing the literary device of contrast (as in the rest of the Gospel[28]). Mark's negative elements usually are juxtaposed with positive ones in order to strengthen the impact of positive truth. The extreme fear and silence of the women in verse 8 thus should be preliminary to the vindicating glory of verses 9f. where fear becomes joy and silence blossoms into witness.

Mark thus proclaims the end of messianic misunderstanding. Jesus' refusal to accept his role of Messiah ceases with his death and resurrection. Others may have recognized, even anointed Jesus in this role (14:3 – 9), but Jesus always projected these forward to his coming death when his work would be complete. In Mark the suffering Messiah precedes the Messiah King; Christ alone is the Son of God.

Philip Vielhauer (*Zeit und Geschichte*, ed. Dinkler, pp. 155f.) says Mark includes the enthronement theme (a statement of authority followed by proclamation of kingship and acclamation) with his use of "Son" in three crucial events: the baptism (1:11, proclamation), transfiguration (9:7, kingship), and crucifixion (15:39, acclamation).[29] Although the Davidic royal sonship is not a central theme in Mark, it is sufficiently present (10:47f.; 11:10; 12:35f.) to support the belief that the victorious vindication of the Messiah in Mark includes a royal motif. In 12:35 – 37 Jesus denies that the royal lordship is his primary role; he is first the suffering Messiah. After he has completed his suffering he will become royal Messiah.

Finally we should note that the women's fear and silence in verse 8 continues Mark's discipleship theme. The verb *pheugō* ("flee") is an important Markan expression (five times, three in relation to the disciple's failure—14:50, 52; 16:8) which, combined

---

28. See Jesus' affirmation at his baptism versus the temptation (1:9 – 11, 12 – 13), rejection of officials versus the "witness" of the evil spirits (3:6, 11), Jesus' universal authority versus his importance among his own people (6:1 – 13), and Jesus' revelation of kingdom truths versus the disciples' misunderstanding or *passim*.

29. Martin's argument against Vielhauer (*Mark*, pp. 100 – 102) assumes that the second Gospel ends at verse 8. If that is challenged Vielhauer's thesis becomes more probable.

with the progressive imperfect *eichen* ("was having"), represents a graphic picture of the women who "fled" from the scene with hearts full of *tromos* ("fear") and *ekstasis* ("astonishment"), terms which express human reaction to divine revelation. Their flight and silence (aorists) reflect the act as a whole while the imperfect verb tenses stress the moment-by-moment emotions behind those acts. Mark's use of verbs thus strengthens the impact of defeat which becomes victory via the glorious affirmation which follows. Mark's discipleship pattern reaches full expression as silence and fear are replaced by true understanding of the mission (cp. 6:7 – 13).[30]

Conclusion

Mark's Gospel centers on the hidden revelation of "Jesus Christ the Son of God" (1:1). Jesus' true nature as well as his works and teaching was revealed by God, but this was misinterpreted by the masses, rejected by its leaders, and misunderstood by his own disciples. Although in odd moments and places people caught glimpses of the truth (evil spirits, 1:24, 2:11, 5:7; Peter, 8:19; blind Bartimaeus, 10:47f.; an unknown woman, 14:3f.), Jesus stedfastly refused to acknowledge publicly his messianic role, asking for silence since his time had not yet come. Mark's narrative proceeds into the passion; the pace quickens as leaks threaten the secrecy motif (10:47f., 14:3f.), and tension builds to a climax until the suffering Messiah cries out. The secret is shattered with the centurion's glorious public affirmation, "Surely this was the Son of God!" (15:39). Mark then includes a marvelous transition from the crucifixion to the resurrection; the triumphant turning point (15:39) seemingly pausing as Jesus' dejected followers bury their Master.

The entire Gospel of Mark leads to the resurrection as God's vindication of this suffering Son, and the pericope of chapter 16 climaxes all the themes of the book. The dutiful but ignorant women

---

30. Robert Tannehill (*JRel*, 1977, pp. 386f.) uses structural principles to argue for an "implicit author" who applies the material to his readers. Although we might question his presuppositions (re historiography), we agree Mark addressed this problem to his readers who were to identify with the disciples and repent of their own lack of understanding. We would add, however, that Mark constantly pointed to the presence of the Risen Lord as the key to victory. That is the message and importance of the "lost ending."

(vv. 1 — 2) illustrate the constant misconception of the disciples regarding Jesus, and the contrast between their question ("who will
roll the stone away") and its answer (v. 4) introduces the first glimmer of hope. What is impossible for man is possible with God; the
empty tomb is a stark witness to the misunderstanding of Jesus'
disciples regarding his predictions.

The angel's message also stresses this lack of faith as it bears
witness to the miraculous affirmation of Jesus' predictions. The
women must bring the good news to the disciples. Their own
strength, however, is insufficient; the awesomeness of the event
strikes them dumb (v. 8). Mark's final glimpse of the misunderstanding motif here is perhaps his most vivid contrast. The failure
of all disciples becomes joy and victorious witness with the direct
appearance of the Risen Lord. The missionary task initiated in the
two-by-two sending out of the twelve in 6:7 — 13 fizzled out because of the blindness of the disciples as well as the movement
of passion events, but it finally bursts into motion by the (probable)
appearance of the Risen Lord in Galilee. The suffering Messiah has
completed his work and now reigns as Messiah-King (cf. 11:8 —
10). The resurrection is not only an integral part of Christ's passion
in Mark, but also the culmination and validation of Jesus' death
as the Christ. Mark's movement toward the cross is also movement
toward the empty tomb (8:31; 9:31; 10:34).

What is the *Sitz im Leben* of Mark's Gospel? Mark vividly presents a two-sided portrait of Jesus as both suffering servant as
well as triumphant Son of God. One side is a stark encounter with
Jesus' humanity (1:41; 3:5; 8:12; 10:14 on his emotions and 6:5 — 6,
10:18; 13:32 on his limitations), while the other is a graphic reminder of his divine authority and power (200 of 661 verses are
about miracles). Why does Mark present both sides of the mystery
this way, and why does he use the Gospel genre to do so? The
epistles say little about Jesus' earthly life; is it because they were
problem-oriented rather than biographical, or applications of Jesus'
principles rather than stories about him?

Perhaps the Gospel writers felt threatened by the passage of
time, feeling that traditions about Jesus' life would begin to fade.
Perhaps more permanent records were necessary to keep truth
intact. Is this sufficient rationale for the formulation of the Gospel-
genre? R. S. Barbaur maintains (*ET,* 1968, pp. 323f.) there were other,
over-riding factors such as problems in the church which led

Mark to write down the particular episodes and emphases recorded in his masterpiece.

Many critics believe Mark wrote his Gospel to combat heretical views which had arisen, like Paul wrote epistles to correct the early church. Weeden believes, for instance, that Mark wrote to contrast two opposing Christologies: that of some disciples who ignored the cross and taught a quasi-divine (*theios anēr*) wonderworker in contrast to Mark's own co-workers who stressed the suffering Messiah. Earlier we discussed how Weeden views the disciples: identifying the negative side of Mark's Gospel and stating several problems with a too-positive approach, but failing to recognize Mark's refusal to deny the power and authority of Jesus. The twelve disciples are therefore not denigrated as much as Weeden intimates, especially in the second half of the Gospel. The resurrection narrative is a prime example, where the angel says the disciples will be enlightened in Galilee; their ignorance will be overcome by new understanding and authority (6:7f.).

Schweizer (*Mark*, pp. 380—386) proposes that Mark wrote his Gospel in response to the docetic heresy which plagued the Pauline churches even after his death. The believers in these churches were neglecting the historical Jesus and spiritualizing him into a divine wonder-worker. His death therefore receded into the background. Because of this Mark wrote to stress the humanity of the miracle-worker and to explain the meaning of his work in the passion. Martin (*Mark*, pp. 156f., 163f.) adds Mark taught via "his innovative joining of a Jesus-tradition and passion-narrative; twin elements which made up Pauline preaching. These are the humiliation and enthronement of the Church's Lord" (p. 161). Martin believes Mark's Gospel was written during a time of persecution. Contrary to Martin, we would add that Mark's triumphant conclusion was necessary to finalize his victory motif, not as "props for a weak faith" (as Martin calls the possibility, p. 218) but as assurance that the believer can endure weakness and failure (16:8). Only thus can the reader know the crucified Christ as the triumphant Son of God.

The *Sitz im Leben* of Mark is thus two-fold: (1) a corrective to the docetic tendency in the Pauline church (whether it is post-Pauline is debatable) showing that the Son of God was first the suffering servant, then the Messiah-King; and (2) an assurance to persecuted believers that suffering, doubts, and spiritual failures (like those of the disciples) will in time result in victorious vindication through the Risen Lord.

Arguments for the Longer Ending, Verses 9–20

We have already said the longer ending was probably not part of Mark's original Gospel. Perhaps it was a section detached from a larger work, edited slightly, then tacked on to Mark, but most likely it was not written specifically for Mark. In form it is a summary of the church's teaching on the appearances and thus is appropriate enough, even with its non-Markan style and lack of transition from verse 8 to verse 9.[31]

A comparison of this passage with parallel accounts in the other Gospels however, quickly reveals its eclectic style. Jesus' appearance to Mary Magdalene in verses 9–11, for instance, sounds much like John 20:8–11,[32] although it also uses elements from other contexts such as (1) the exorcism of seven demons from Mary in verse 9 (Luke 8:2); (2) the emphasis on mourning in verse 10 (Gospel of Peter); and (3) the doubt motif in verse 11 (perhaps Luke 24:10–11 but probably a redactional insertion). The appearance to the two travelers in verses 12 and 13 suggests the Emmaus story (Luke 24:13–35) with the added element of the doubt motif. This strange composite of Gospel stories culminates in verse 14 which uses the supper scene setting from Luke 24:36f. but seems to draw its *Sitz im Leben* from a second-century heretical attack on the resurrection. The doubt motif in the first two pericopes concludes with Jesus' strong rebuke in verse 14. Taylor comments (*Mark*, p. 613) this verse uses language which Mark employs to describe men who are hostile to Jesus: *apistia* (6:6) and *sklērokardia* (10:5). In fact, the words are so strong that a later scribe[33] inserted a

31. The lack of *ho Iēsous*, verse 9 (the subject is implied in the verb) indicates it most likely was separated from another work which contained the subject.

32. Although Dodd, *More New Testament Studies*, pp. 18f.; and Fuller, pp. 56, 216n, believe this passage is independent from John 20:8f., this seems highly unlikely in view of the other parallels already attested. Also, the arguments of Farmer for the primitive origin of this passage do not convince, for the eclectic nature is too strong.

33. Found in W and mentioned by Jerome (*Contra Pelagianos* 2:15), this addition is called the "Freer Logion." Schweizer, *Mark*, believes the redactional purpose was to express the theodicy of that early age. See also K. Haacker, *ZNW*, 1972, pp. 125–29, who believes it may have been a part of the original ending but was dropped out due to the theological difficulties in it. This is possible but has little manuscript evidence.

section here which excuses the disciples' lack of faith on the basis of Satan's power in the world. The original writer, however, stressed this unbelief probably as an example to his own generation.

The longer ending proceeds into its own version of the great commission.[34] Verse 15 sounds much like Matthew 28:19, but verse 16a picks up the baptismal motif of Matthew and Acts 2:38, and 16b (probably from John 3:17 – 18) emphasizes the damnation of unbelievers. The "signs" of verses 17 and 18 are characteristic of John but may be borrowed from Acts (cf. 2:43) and the Synoptics in miracles such as casting out demons "in my name" (Mark 3:15; 7:13), speaking in "new tongues" (Acts 2:4; 10:46; 19:6; 1 Cor. 12, 14), handling snakes (Acts 28:2 – 6), and laying hands on the sick (Acts 28:8, James 5:14 – 15). No New Testament parallel to verse 18's drinking poison without after-effects exists (but see Eusebius, H.E. 3:39,9 and the Apocryphal Acts of John 20).

The conclusion of this long ending (vv. 19 – 20) meshes the exaltation motif with the universal mission. The first motif is a rewrite of the ascension narrative (Luke 24:51, Acts 1:9f.) in light of the Psalms 110:1 testimonium and ascension language of 2 Kings 2:11 (Elijah). It stresses the continuing lordship of "the Lord Jesus" especially in connection with verse 20 which emphasizes the spiritual union between Christ and his followers (cf. Heb. 2:3f.; Acts 14:3), the attendant "signs" bearing witness to his authenticity through them.

Dodd[35] compares this conclusion to 1 Corinthians 15, noting both the list of names as well as use of temporal particles such as "afterwards" and "later." He believes this long ending is a free composition of strung-together bits of tradition. Perhaps after it was detached from its original setting Markan phrases were added to make it appear more authentic (evidenced by Markan phrases which appear in odd places such as *prōi* and *prōton* in verse 9, *apangellō* in verse 10, and *kērussō* and *euangelion* in verse 15).[36]

---

34. Cranfield, p. 473, argues against Taylor that the pericopes in Matthew 28 and here were based on Jesus' actual teaching, since the disciples, as in the Gospels, would need time to overcome the natural Jewish bias against the Gentiles.

35. Dodd, *More New Testament Studies*, pp. 32f. Fuller, p. 157, agrees with him and asserts that the presence of Mary rather than Peter and James shows that the list was not an authentication formula, as 1 Corinthians 15, but a preparation for the Great Commission which follows. This would certainly fit the emphasis in the passage.

36. In fact, it is likely that the doubt motif, so central and yet so strange in verses 9 – 14, was the product of the later redactor, since it was not a part of the original episodes.

Perhaps a second-century scribe who was disturbed by Mark's abrupt ending detached this summary from its original setting, adapted it (cf. v. 14), and attached it to Mark.

Another Shorter Ending

This conclusion uses lofty language such as "the sacred and imperishable proclamation of eternal salvation" which is so obviously non-Markan that we can probably attribute it to a much later age when the use of such terminology was common. Swete (p. ci) thinks this ending must have been produced by a Roman Christian because of its strong reference to the westward expansion of apostolic preaching. This ending includes a two-fold purpose; to provide a better conclusion to the Gospel than verse 8 and to emphasize the evangelistic results of the resurrection (as in Matthew and Luke).

3

Matthew's Resurrection Narrative

Matthew uses Mark's basic outline but adds a lot of new material. This provides some exciting opportunities for redaction study even while it creates problems for traditionalists. Unlike Mark, Matthew's resurrection narrative begins with the posting of guards at Jesus' tomb (27:62−66). Some critics (Meier, *Vision*, pp. 204f.) view Matthew 27:51−66 as a prelude to chapter 28 with verses 51−54 forming a transition from the passion narrative to the resurrection. Verses 55−66 are then divided into three sections: the women at the cross (vv. 55−56), the burial of Jesus (vv. 57−61), and the guards at the tomb (vv. 62−66). These sections then prepare the way for chapter 28's fearstruck guards, women at the tomb, and plots of the priests.

Meier's structure seems reasonable enough, but we believe the resurrection account begins with verse 62 rather than 51 or 55. Matthew uses specific resurrection material at verse 62, while verses 51−61 more properly relate to the crucifixion (although they do prepare for the following). The guard episode, however, is directly linked with chapter 28, suggesting Léon-Dufour's (*Easter*, pp. 139−40) diptych-like pattern:

A. The guards are posted at the tomb (27:62−66)

   B. The women go to the tomb (28:1)

A^1. The guards almost die of fright (28:2−4)

   B^1. The women receive the angel's message which is confirmed by Jesus' appearance (28:5−10)

A^2. The guards report the story to the chief priests (28:11−15)

The next section (16–20) is the climax to the entire Gospel which, together with the preceding resurrection account, brings the Book of Matthew to a close.

Léon-Dufour's structure beautifully illustrates the importance of 28:16–20 to the Gospel as a whole, however, we believe he still misses something in its immediate context. Perhaps 28:16–20 is a greater part of the resurrection narrative than even Léon-Dufour suggests. Indeed the structure seems to be more like a triptych, a progressive pattern of three contrasts with each panel portraying the Risen Lord in victory over his enemies, each building on the one before it:

First Panel:
Preparation—the posting of the guard (27:62–66) vs. the approach of the women to the tomb (28:1)

Second Panel:
Reaction—the fear of the guards (vv. 2–4) vs. the joy of the women (vv. 5–10)

Third Panel:
Results—the spread of lies (vv. 11–15) vs. the announcement of truth (vv. 16–20)

This triptych intensifies Matthew's victory motif and brings to a climax his Christology of Jesus as royal king.[1] For Matthew, Jesus' resurrection proves that nothing can obstruct the glory of the Risen Messiah.[2]

First Panel: Preparation

The Guards at the Tomb (27:62–66; 28:4)

In this first section Matthew probably uses a traditional source (part of the M material), redacting it in two ways. First he adapts

---

1. Matthew uses the titles "Son of man," "Son of God," and "Son of David" far more than the other evangelists. Although Kingsbury (*Structure*, chaps. 2–3) argues that "Son of God" is most important, others say "Messiah" is central with two characteristics, sonship and royal kingship. "Kingship" is especially important here; Matthew's emphasis is on Jesus as "lowly king" in his earthly ministry. Only after the passion and resurrection does he become "triumphant king."

2. This has already been demonstrated in 27:51–54 which links the passion and resurrection scenes, providing a "theologia gloriae" which proleptically alludes to the glory inherent in the passion. See the section on Matthew 27:51b–53.

it to fit his apologetic intent; "after the day of preparation," for instance, is inserted in a different place than in Mark (15:42, cp. Mark 27:57). Matthew uses it in connection with the priests' and Pharisees' attempts to guard the tomb (Mark in connection with Jesus' burial), probably intending to stress their illegal activity on the Sabbath. Some critics (Fuller, p. 72; Campenhausen, pp. 63f.) think Matthew uses this phrase purposely to avoid saying "on the Sabbath," but more likely he is repeating Mark's words (15:42) about the Pharisees' legal error with the use of a double-time note.

The tradition itself probably contained reasons for their actions, evidenced by their repetition of Jesus' prophecy, "After three days I will rise again," as well as their strong reference to Jesus as "imposter" or "deceiver." Matthew probably included the episode to counter the very rumor which was plotted here; that Jesus' disciples stole his body in order to tell the world he had risen from the dead. The early church repeated the tradition to offset the falsehood, Matthew giving it even greater authority by including it in his resurrection narrative.

The second reason Matthew included the account was to contrast the posting of the guard with the approach of the women at the tomb. The antithesis is especially apparent in a comparison between 27:66 and 28:1. Note how Matthew contrasts the elaborate attempts of the Pharisees to "make the tomb secure" with the simple desire of the women "to see the sepulcher." The rulers' cumbersome efforts to "seal the stone" and "set the guard" then prepare the reader for the overpowering act of God who will vindicate the simple faith of the women.

Matthew also includes a touch of irony in Pilate's order to the Pharisees to "make the tomb as secure as you know how," even if their willingness to obey makes them break the Sabbath. Pilate himself becomes mediator between the plans of men and the purposes of almighty God.

The Approach of the Women (28:1)

Matthew names only two women, "Mary Magdalene and the other Mary," in his resurrection account (omitting Salome). Although critics like Marxsen and Fuller see a discrepancy in the list, most scholars do not. Matthew may simply have omitted Salome because his readers were unfamiliar with her.

His time notes, however, are more of a problem. One wonders if Matthew decided to use Mark's time notes (cp. 16:1 –2) but failed to differentiate between them. Lohmeyer, Grundmann et al. say Matthew probably tried to correct Mark, making the women's trip to the tomb on Saturday evening rather than Sunday morning. Another possibility exists, however. We could accept the RSV's prepositional use of *opse*, making the phrase "after the Sabbath" rather than "late on the Sabbath." The time-note is thus a general one qualified by the one which follows.[3] This usage is confirmed by the phrase *tē epiphōskousē eis mian sabbatōn*, a temporal dative which translates "at the dawning toward the first day of the week."

This translation meshes nicely with Mark; by omitting the purchase of spices (Mark 16:1), Matthew changes Mark's time note to a general reference. Unlike Mark, however, Matthew does not take time to build a sense of imminent crisis; he has already done so in 27:62 – 66. He now urges the reader into the event itself, stressing supernatural forces more than people. Léon-Dufour comments (p. 142), "the women are playing the part of spectators and hearers and messengers." Unwittingly they set the stage for God's mighty deed.

Matthew also differs from Mark in his account of the women's motive in going to the tomb, changing Mark's "anointing" to a more general "to see the tomb." Fuller says Matthew does this to correct a flaw in Mark's rendering; Joseph of Arimathea had already performed the rite and so the women's act would have been superfluous.

The real reason for the difference, however, is probably theological; Mark's word choice is closely connected with his "messianic misunderstanding" theme while Matthew's interest bypasses the women's motive to focus on the events at the tomb. He rushes the women toward the tomb, using their motive of curiosity to prepare the reader for his developing witness theme. In 27:55 – 56, 61 he has already written about the women who "watched from a distance" as Jesus suffered and died; now the evangelist tells how the women who came "to look at" the tomb become actual witnesses as their eyes are opened to the reality of their Risen Lord. Thus Matthew's witness motif provides continuity between

3. E. Lohse, ("*Sabbaton*" *TDNT*, VII, 20n) says *opse sabbatōn* corresponds to the rabbinic *môtsa'ê shabbath* and means the night from the sabbath to the first day of the week or the first day of the week itself. There is thus no conflict between the two time notes.

the passion and resurrection as well as the burial and empty tomb; both are witnessed by the women.

Second Panel: Reaction

The Events at the Tomb; Fear of the Guard (28:2−4)

The second section of Matthew's resurrection account is almost a straightforward narration of the resurrection event. Although Matthew must have drawn heavily from tradition for this account, he does emphasize certain events such as the earthquake (cp. the *seismos* scenes of 8:24 [the stilling of the storm] and 27:51 [the earthquake, torn veil, and awakening of the dead during the crucifixion]) and supernatural appearance of the angel of the Lord. The earthshaking events of 27:51f. and 28:2f. are typically Matthean, interconnected in their resurrection emphasis. The earlier passage, in fact, was a resurrection tradition inserted in the passion narrative to link it to the later one. Matthew's primary emphasis here is the eschatological vindication of Jesus' death at the dawn of a new age; the earthquake a shattering sign of the triumphant liberation of the Son of God.[4]

Matthew continues to stress the supernatural; the "angel of the Lord" in words typical of this author (cf. 1:20, 24; 2:13, 19) comes down from heaven, rolls back the stone guarding Jesus' tomb, and sits on it. "His appearance was like lightning," Matthew says, "and his clothes were white as snow." Léon-Dufour and Meier say the evangelist borrows this description from Moses' portrait of the awesome God of Sinai (cf. Exod. 19:18, Ps. 114:7) as well as apocalyptic literature (cp. Dan. 10:5−6; Rev. 1:14f., 10:1), and is part of Matthew's fulfillment motif expressing the victory of God.[5] Matthew thus expands Mark's account in order to emphasize the transcendent importance of the resurrection event. Jesus' triumph

---

4. See Acts 16:26; Rev. 6:12, 8:5, 11:13f., and 16:18. Walter, pp. 418−425, notes a pre-Matthean "opening of doors" myth behind the theme, and although we disagree with his tradition-critical conclusions, we prefer this to the thesis of Hutton et al that the earthquake is a symbol of judgment. It most certainly has a positive purpose here. See also Kratz, pp. 64−65, who speaks of it as a deliverance miracle.

5. Rigaux, p. 202, adds that the "sitting" motif borrowed from Mark may also stress victory.

over death in Matthew clearly marks the dawn of the new age in which Yahweh's awesome power reigns.

Many see a mythical element in Matthew's portrayal. One need only compare the Gospel of Peter 8:35—45, however, to see the restraint exercised by Matthew. In that passage the resurrection occurs at night, before the arrival of the women, and two angels descend from heaven to roll away the stone and help the Risen Lord from the tomb, "and two of them sustaining the other, and a cross following them, and the heads of the two reaching to heaven, but that of him who was led of them by the hand over-passing the heavens."

The guards of 27:62—66 who were once passive bystanders now become active "witnesses" in 28:4,[6] their "fear" like that of other participants in theophanies as they recognize the angel for what he really is. Why do the soldiers, not the woman, show this fear? Perhaps the distinction is part of Matthew's apologetic purpose, adding the secular witness to that of the women already recorded in Mark. This secular emphasis in 27:62f., 28:2f., and 28:11f. proves the resurrection's power affects more than just believers. Although unbelievers did not witness the Risen Lord himself, they did "tremble" (seiō, the cognate of seismos) and "become like dead men" (both biblical reactions to a theophany), proving that God himself was present.

Matthew's use of the guard image might have also served another purpose. Perhaps his former occupation as a tax-collector depended on the protection of soldiers. Throughout his work he shows unmistakable interest in the faith of publicans and soldiers (8:5f.; 9:10f.; 11:19; 21:31f.; 27:54; 28:4). Matthew's natural desire to reach out to former associates might have prompted his use of this material in hopes of confronting them with the Gospel. Perhaps 28:4 would be a vivid lesson to them that even men of power fail when faced with the incomparable glory of the Risen One.[7]

6. Although some critics like Léon-Dufour (p. 143) deny that the guards were witnesses, "fear" is the usual reaction of people who were indeed witnesses of the theophany.

7. Although the fear of these soldiers might seem incongruous, it was probably not written to frighten (contrast the deceit of the leaders) as much as instruct. Note, for instance, the Matthean doublet (ephobēthēsan sphodra); Matthew meaning "even the soldiers quaked with fear!" The former passage, in fact, contains some implicit universalism thus preparing for the mission of 28:19.

The Message at the Tomb: Joy of the Women (28:5—10)

The Angelic Message (vv. 5—7)

Matthew uses Mark's narrative in this section for the most part, with some slight, yet significant changes. He replaces Mark's *mē ekthambeisthe* ("do not be alarmed") with *mē phobeisthe hymeis* ("do not fear"), the pronoun "you" giving emphasis to the angel's command and heightening the contrast between the women's joy (v. 8) and the fear of the guards. He also characteristically avoids using the term *ho Nazarēnos* ("The Nazarene," cp. Mark 16:6 as well as Matt. 20:30), possibly because it was considered a derogatory title by his Jewish readers.[8] Meier says (*Vision*, p. 209) Matthew regularly avoids using lofty christological titles anyway, choosing simply "Jesus" (vv. 5, 9, 10, 16, 18) to establish continuity between the earthly Master, crucified Messiah, and Risen Lord.

Kathōs eipen ("as he said") in Mark is replaced in Matthew by a statement which emphasizes the angel's authority as the messenger of God; "Lo, I have told you" (v. 7). Matthew's words more likely refer to general resurrection predictions (16:21; 17:23; 20:18—19) rather than the particular Galilean reference of Mark, probably because of Matthew's strong fulfillment motif which links together Old Testament expectations with Jesus' own prophecy. Matthew adds the imperative *deute* ("come") in verse 6 because the action in this Gospel takes place outside the tomb; the angel urges the women to enter the tomb whereas in Mark they have already entered and are asked to "see the place where they laid him" (Jesus).

Matthew omits Mark's reference to Peter (cp. Mark 16:7), strange in light of Matthew's continued interest in Peter (twenty-three references in his book) and the importance of Peter's denial. Some critics (e.g., Plummer, McNeile, Fuller) say Matthew omitted the phrase because he was unaware of any such appearance to Peter

8. See McNeile (pp. 292, 431), Grundmann (p. 569). This would no longer be true if one accepts a gentile redactor behind the first Gospel (Strecker, Trilling, Pesch, Frankemölle, Nepper-Christiansen et al. For a good summary, see Meier, *Law*, pp. 14—21). Arguments such as Matthew's supposed ignorance of Jewish views do not seem convincing, however; the evidence for a Jewish provenance seems more compelling. An important consideration would be the growing consensus that hellenistic tendencies can be found in Jewish circles; little significant demarcation can be made between Jewish Christian and hellenistic-Jewish Christian. Matthew certainly would fit the latter category.

(McNeile says the reference was added to Mark after Matthew used it), but this is doubtful since Luke 24:34, 1 Corinthians 15:5, and Mark 16:7 all indicate widespread knowledge of the event. Perhaps a better answer is that Matthew's use of "disciples" here is inclusive (cf. Lohmeyer) thus making any specific reference to Peter superfluous. Matthew's emphasis anyway is on Jesus' coming appearance to all the disciples (28:16–20); singling out Peter might only detract from that message.

Verse 7 includes several changes from Mark's account; the phrase *tachu* ("quickly") which is typically Markan is important to Matthew's purpose and thus appears both here and in verse 8, stressing the urgency of getting the message to the disciples. *Egerthē apo tōn nekrōn* ("rise from the dead") is added to stress the reality of the resurrection, with repetition the Semitic stylistic device used to give emphasis. Note Matthew's special use of the emphatic particle *idou* ("behold") twice in the verse. He uses the term often (sixty-two times vs. seven in Mark), especially in crucial passages such as Jesus' birth (six), apocalyptic sermon (four), betrayal (four), and resurrection (six). Its two-fold use in the angel's message contributes to a sense of urgency, compelling the women to action.

The author's use of the authentication formula (*idou eipon hymin*, "Now I have told you") after the message is strange. Many scholars think Matthew used it because he had already used Mark's ending in verse 6, yet he could just as easily have omitted the formula. Lohmeyer says more likely Matthew altered Mark's ending to make room for the self-authentication formula; the angel who is the *shaliach* or envoy from God speaks with divine authority. The women must obey his command, and quickly.

The Reaction of the Women (v. 8)

Matthew's main redaction in verse 8 is his added motifs of joy and obedience. Critics who affirm the short ending (16:8) of Mark say Matthew tried to alter that somber ending with his own additions in 28:8, but that view hardly seems necessary. Two phrases in fact, *charas megales* ("great joy") and *edramon* ("ran") echo Mark's emphasis, with Matthew combining them with his victory theme rather than separating them like Mark. Since Matthew does not stress Mark's misunderstanding theme, his rendering reduces the meaning of the women's fear somewhat to that of the centurion's and guards' fear in 27:54, i.e., man's natural reaction to the presence of God, rather than evidence of a profound lack of understanding.

In Matthew the "joy" of the women actually dominates the verse, clarifying the meaning of their "fear." The angel had already commanded them to "fear not" since Jesus had risen, therefore their "fear" actually included "great joy." Matthew's combined meaning here is a beautiful reminder of the *megalēn sphodra* ("very great") of Jesus' birth narrative when the "overjoyed" Magi rejoiced at the star (2:10).[9] "Joy" is thus a contrast to the quaking of the guards; probably one of the primary emphases of this section.

The First Appearance (vv. 9–10)

We have already said verses 9 and 10 repeat Mark's original conclusions,[10] yet they also include some revisions necessary to Matthew's purposes. His fourth use of *idou* in this pericope stresses the importance of the event. Mark's original last ending probably included the joy motif (when Jesus appeared to the women), but Matthew used it early when the women were actually leaving the tomb. The phrase *mē phobeisthe* ("do not fear") seems somewhat out of place here in light of Matthew's stress on joy; it is probably a repetition of Mark's emphasis.

Two terms in verse 9 are typically Matthean, *proserchomai* ("come," fifty-two times vs. five in Mark and ten in Luke) and *proskuneō* ("worship," thirteen times vs. twice in both the others). The words appear together four times, stressing worship and lordship,[11] and "worship" is also used in the account of the Magi (2:2, 8, 11), temptation (4:9, 10), healed leper (8:1), ruler's daughter (9:18),

9. In another Matthean redaction Christ (in the parable of the talents) twice repeats the eschatological promise, "enter into the joy of your master" (25:21, 23; cp. Luke 19:17, "have authority"). Here is a partial fulfillment of that kingdom promise.

10. Walter (pp. 415–16) argues this is Matthean rather than Markan because it forms a simple doublet of verses 5–7. As such it indicates a growing tendency on the part of the early church to allow the women a separate appearance. He fails, however, to consider the Markan language in these verses (see chap. 2) which is evidence of Matthew's dependence.

11. Matthew significantly never has the disciples say "teacher" or "rabbi" (Mark), but rather "Lord." While this shows respect rather than homage, we must agree with Albright and Mann that "it is hard to escape the conclusion that Matthew deliberately meant his use of *kurios* to indicate a term of majesty, if not divinity." Both the term and homage in Matthew's Gospel look forward to the post-resurrection glory of the Messiah.

Canaanite woman (15:25), and stilling of the storm (14:33). In each
account Matthew presents Jesus as one who is to be worshiped
as Lord. Fuller (*Resurrection*, p. 79) says the author portrays Jesus
as "divine man," but this hardly seems adequate to describe Matthew's hellenistic emphasis (see Holladay) which clearly reveals
Jesus' divine glory as "Son of God." Even the Markan *karteō* ("grasp")
gathers additional meaning in Matthew as it is linked with *autou
tous podas* ("his feet") and made part of the worship pattern.[12]
Tasker explains, "the women were showing their submission to
the Lord in the manner in which subjects in the East were accus-
tomed to render obeisance to a sovereign prince."

The *tote* ("then") beginning verse 10 is Matthean (ninety times vs.
six in Mark), and serves to keep the story moving. Jesus repeats
the angelic command of verse 7, yet slight differences in wording
indicate this is more than mere repetition. One significant addition is *tois adelphois mou* ("my brothers"), a phrase of fellowship
(cp. John 15:15, 20:17) which means a new relationship and implies
forgiveness. The men who were formerly "disciples" (28:7) are now
"brothers" because of the resurrection, the culmination of Matthew's ecclesiology in which the disciples are the binding glue of
the new "church" (16:17−19, 18:15−20). The changed relationship
prepares the way for Jesus' final statement in 28:18−20.

The significance of "Galilee" is even more of a problem in Matthew than in Mark (16:7); here the message is more emphatic: "Tell
my brethren to depart into Galilee, and they will see me there."
Lightfoot and Lohmeyer believe this command in Matthew has a
theological purpose; the author himself was convinced that Jesus
could appear to his disciples only there since it was the place of
divine revelation. Still, although Matthew did consider Galilee to
be important, he also recognized the crucial significance of Jerusalem, Galilaia (Galilee) appearing sixteen times in his Gospel
and *Ierousalēm* (Jerusalem) twelve. While Galilee is the source of
light (4:15f.) and place where Jesus makes his final appearance,

---

12. In Mark this is never used in a worship atmosphere; "they grasped him" is a
mixture of fear and joy. Matthew uses worship here with a sense of messianic kingship
strongly suggested in titles such as "King of the Jews" (2:2; 27:11, 29, 37), "King of Israel"
(27:42) and "King" (21:5; 25:34, 40). Note, however, that the occurrences do not appear
during the ministry proper. Matthew's narration of the triumphal entry emphasizes Jesus
as the "lowly king" thus pointing the way to the death of the Messiah. Only afterward
can he become "triumphant king" (cf. 28:18f.).

Jerusalem is the place of rejection where Jesus is tempted (4:5) and from which he withdraws to minister to the Galileans (4:12). It is the "desolate" city which rejects God's message and messengers (23:37−39), yet we should remember Jesus did appear in its vicinity, after the resurrection.

Since Galilee was the place where Jesus' message was accepted and Jerusalem where it was rejected, Galilee thus became the place for the final act of the redemptive drama where Jesus' glory would be fully revealed. It is likely that scholars read far too much into geographical terms, however, and this may be one such instance. Matthew heightens the suspense, says Léon-Dufour, as the reader awaits "the meeting which such a theophany has foretold and prepared" (*Easter,* p. 146). This is the major thrust of the verse.

Third Panel: Results

The Deceptive Plot (28:11−15)

The next section in Matthew 28 (11−15) seems to interrupt the flow of the narrative, fitting in more naturally with the earlier account of the guards at the tomb. Yet Matthew's alteration here is deliberate, providing not only a contrast to the next section on the great commission[13] but also to the preceding one on the women's exit from the tomb. Their joyful rush toward home is mimicked by the rush of the soldiers to the priests, the message of truth from the Risen One juxtaposed to the deceptive lie of the chief priests. Matthew even uses similar words in the accounts: *poreuomenōn* ("were going") in verse 11 parallels verses 7 and 19; *apēngeilan* ("reported") and *eipate* ("told") in verse 11 are also found in verses 7 and 10 and implied in *mathēteusate* ("make disciples") in verse 19. The style of all three sections is also similar, emphasizing haste, confrontation with evidence, and a commissioned message.[14] Grundmann says the style also parallels Matthew's infancy

---

13. Pesch (*"Ausführungs formel,"* pp. 79f.) says this pericope contrasts the time of lies (v. 15) with the time of obedience (vv. 16−20) in salvation history.

14. Dodd (*Studies,* pp. 11f.) notes five steps in the appearance narratives: the situation (grief), appearance, greeting, recognition, and command, and finds all five in verses 8−10 and 16−20. This pattern can also be seen in verses 11−15: the situation is the soldiers' sense of failure; the appearance paralleled in their report; the recognition contrasted with their reaction; and the command to lie given by the priests.

narrative in which both the animosity and plots of earthly leaders are foiled by God.

The passage increases the apologetic force of the earlier episode of the guards as Matthew details the efforts of the priests and soldiers to spread the very lie (that the disciples had stolen the body) which prompted their elaborate preparations in 27:62–66. The soldiers are witnesses to the empty tomb and resurrection power (Broer, Kratz, and Rigaux *contra* Léon-Dufour), reporting "all that had happened" (*hapanta ta genomena*, likely a reflection of the *ta genomena* of 27:54). The authorities themselves provide a kind of negative assent, never denying the reality of the empty tomb in their efforts to deceive the people with a deliberate lie.[15]

The passage also reminds us of Judas' betrayal; Matthew using *arguria* ("money") twice in verses 12 and 15 as well as in the Judas pericope (26:15, 27:3, 5, 6, 9). The emphasis on betrayal and bribery is, in fact, part of Matthew's greater fulfillment theme, the thirty pieces of silver used to purchase Judas' burial field a direct fulfillment of Jeremiah 32:6f. Perhaps Matthew also parallels the Judas passage to emphasize the continued opposition of Jesus' enemies; the same hate and greed which incited suffering and crucifixion also became passionate opposition against the resurrection message.

Matthew probably has two reasons for telling this story: to reach nonbelievers and to influence believers. His message to nonbelievers is apologetic, telling how rumors about the theft of Jesus' body were deliberate falsehoods. His message to believers is more like a warning which emphasizes the continuing opposition they can expect (cp. John 15:18f.) in proclaiming the resurrection. Oppression is part of Matthew's discipleship motif which includes participation in Christ's suffering. Both messages merge into the victorious theme of God's triumphant power over his enemies whose wicked plots will be overcome.

The Great Commission (28:16–20)[16]

The pericope on the great commission is Matthean in style; it both concludes the resurrection narrative and summarizes the

15. This stresses the absolute truth of the empty tomb which was so obvious that not even Jesus' enemies could deny it. Bonnard says this is the major thrust of the passage.

16. This section repeats somewhat the work of my earlier article, "Great Commission," *JETS* (1976), pp. 73f.

basic message of the Gospel (Michel, Bornkamm et al). Some critics say the section should not be titled "The Great Commission" since it is primarily an epiphany or exaltation story centered around the Risen Christ[17]; however the contents of the passage clearly demonstrate the validity of its traditional title. Certainly Matthew and the early church thought its basic thrust was the universal mission; comments preceding and following verse 19 provide the encouragement as well as power for accomplishing that task. Most scholars recognize two parts in this section, the setting (vv. 16–17) and the message (vv. 18–20). The message section is further divided into three parts: the statement of authority (18), the command to disciple or mission (19–20a), and the promise of Christ's presence (20b).

Is the message of Matthew 28:16–20 from one tradition or a combination of several related traditions? Many critics (e.g., Lohmeyer, Fuller, Zumstein) think Matthew combines more than one tradition in this section since each part is closely connected with Matthean motifs[18] and the command itself is found in different contexts in other Gospels. Furthermore, Matthew often combines Jesus' speeches (which were given on separate occasions) into one (e.g., Matt. 5–7, 10, etc.); why would not he have done so here?

Perhaps better evidence can be found to prove Matthew drew from a single tradition for this account. Some internal indications already suggest the passage was based on the lost Markan ending. Furthermore, a close examination of the three points of the message show they are paralleled in the other Gospels and thus are not purely Matthean. Authority and mission, for instance, are closely linked in Luke and John (cf. John 4), and Jesus' presence is combined with mission in John 20:19f. Some scholars say[19] the three parts combine into a homogeneous whole and would not have circulated independent of each other. Furthermore, Matthew's practice of combining traditions did not extend to phrases.

---

17. Michel (*"Abschluss,"* pp. 22f.) calls it an "enthronement scene," Bornkamm ("Risen," p. 212) a "hidden mystery scene," Lightfoot (*Locality,* p. 72) a "divine investiture," and Lohmeyer (p. 416) a Jewish revelation scene.

18. Lohmeyer believes these traditions were combined in the pre-Matthean period while others think Matthew himself collated them. Hubbard believes only the middle element (the missionary command) is traditional while the other two are Matthean redactions. Lange and most others believe the entire pericope is a Matthean composition.

19. See Strecher (pp. 210f.) and Bishop (pp. 341f.). Zumstein (*Croyant,* pp. 86–90) is representative of many who believe the parallels show only Matthew composed his theological treatise utilizing traditional elements.

Most likely the tradition came to Matthew possibly via Mark, but more likely from his own source as a single whole; he then put it into his own words.

The literary source of the great commission passage is also questionable, hypotheses including the following:

1. Some critics (e.g., Barth, Lohmeyer, Michel, Fuller, Schaberg) say its background is Old Testament prophecies (especially Daniel) which point to the future power and dominion of the Son of man. The passage fulfills Matthew's Son of man emphasis. Schaberg argues that the triadic formula (Father, Son, Holy Spirit) is built on the Daniel 7 triad (Ancient of Days, and like a Son of man, angels). Meier (*Vision*) adds to this the concept of "proleptic parousia"; the Son of man comes to his church during the interim age via its mission and teaching. Léon-Dufour says the passage reflects a "Galilean type" of Christophany which combines Daniel with Psalm 110:1 to stress exalted lordship.

2. Other critics (e.g., Rengstorf, Jeremias, Michel) argue that the Son of man concept is not a part of verse 18 since no eschatological judge is present. The passage instead reflects Psalm 2:8's royal-enthronement pattern of Judaism. This includes authority, proclamation, and acclamation. Jesus is thus the anointed king and appointed Messiah who assumes his rightful throne.

3. Bornkamm and Zumstein say neither proleptic-parousia nor enthronement are the central message of this passage. Instead they believe Matthew stresses the *mystērion* of the mission to the Gentiles which originated from Hellenistic speculations rather than Jewish traditions. Bultmann and Dibelius call this passage both a "cult legend" as well as "Gnostic revelation."

4. Other critics (Trilling, Malina, Frankemölle, Hubbard) think Matthew patterned his work after Old Testament commission stories, Malina and Frankemölle specifically noting the decree of Cyrus in 2 Chronicles which could be expanded into the kind of apostolic proto-commissioning Matthew used in his account.

5. Evans says the passage does not match any single theory; it is instead an original Christian composition meant to stress discipleship, or what it means to be a Christian in the present age.

The basic problem with most of these theories is that they all are opposed to each other. Perhaps if they were seen as complementary components of a whole we might discover the real purpose of this section. Certainly the Son of man background is predominant in verse 18, and the enthronement pattern (not quite accurate in a formal sense) is appropriate to Matthew's royal emphasis or "lowly king" motif.[20] Bornkamm's thesis nicely applies to verses 19–20a and Matthew's summation of universalism theology, and as form critics we would certainly note a commission *Gattung* or form in the section (more likely than an enthronement pattern). Yet even these analyses fail adequately to explain Matthew's theology which includes both christological and ecclesiological overtones. Evans' discipleship theme nicely explains verse 19, yet does not go far enough. Perhaps the best way to evaluate all these hypotheses is to say no single theory adequately explains all the theological implications of the passage. We, like the early believers, are simply overwhelmed by the richness of this passage.

Preamble: The Scene (vv. 16–17)

Verses 16 and 17 include several important elements, one of which is the reference to "eleven" disciples. This reference is used almost exclusively in the Gospels and only four times by Luke. Matthew probably borrowed the term from tradition but used it as a reminder of Judas' betrayal. The third mention of "Galilee" in the passage is probably borrowed from Mark's lost ending, appropriate as it is to both Gospels.

Most important, however, is verse 16's reference, *eis to oros* since "mountains" are especially significant in Matthew (4:8; 5:1, 14; 8:1; 14:23; 15:29; 17:1, 9, 20; 21:1, 21; 24:3, 16; 26:30). Christ was tempted on a mountain top, preached the Sermon on the Mount, and was transfigured on a mountain. Mountains were places of special communication between the Father and the Son. Some critics (Davies, Fuller, Lohmeyer, and Chavasse) say Matthew presents a "new Sinai" motif in which Jesus is viewed as the "new Moses" who proclaims a "new Torah" for the "new Israel." This thesis weakens, however, on closer examination of the Gospel; Matthew includes very little, if any, Moses typology. Bornkamm's analysis seems far more appropriate; Matthew viewed mountains as places of divine revelation.[21]

20. We agree with Kingsbury and Meier that the primary stress is not kingship but sonship, in the passion and resurrection kingship becoming less important than sonship.

21. Whether *oros* stems from tradition or redaction is a difficult question. Its connection here with the next phrase which is distinctly non-Matthean (see chap. 6) may indicate it is traditional, yet there is no reference to such a "designated" command in Matthew. It is doubtful the word would have been included without the whole phrase being a part of the source.

The disciples' worship of their Risen Lord in verse 17 is like the women's worship in verse 9; part of Matthew's contrast between the hatred of the chief priests (vv. 11–15) and the love of Jesus' own. The verse includes an internal antithesis however; "some doubted" is a jarring note to the worship theme. Is it out of place here? Perhaps not; doubt is a central motif in other gospel appearance stories[22] even though it is found only here in Matthew. Critics have suggested many reasons for its presence here. Some say it is a scribal error (W. D. Morris), some that it refers to other disciples who were present with the eleven (McNeile), and some that it means lack of recognition rather than true doubt (Filson). I. P. Ellis (also Bornkamm and Michel) seems much more believable; he suggests verse 17's verb (which appears elsewhere in the New Testament only in 14:3) does not suggest unbelief as much as hesitation or uncertainty. The disciples thus worship but with uncertainty, unclear about Jesus' new role.

Zumstein (*Croyant*, pp. 97, 254f.) and Meier (*Vision*, pp. 211f.) add that the juxtaposition of seeing (*idontes* here fulfilling Jesus' promise of vv. 7 and 10 that "there they will see me"), worship, and doubt remind us of the "little faith" theme of Matthew which is such a big part of his discipleship motif. Hesitation in the midst of worship is a paradox well known to most believers, certainly Matthew's readers would identify with the problem.

The question still remains, however; is the believer's doubt banished by the presence of the Risen Christ? Meier says yes but Zumstein is less sure; doubt in Matthew, he says, is a "present reality" or "necessary distress" which is a natural part of every believer's perseverance in the faith. The believer conquers unbelief only when he incorporates the powerful word of Christ into his life and thus gains strength in the midst of a hostile world. This victorious word is the message of 28:16–20; the promise of Christ's presence and authority in active discipleship.

"Little faith" is a constant struggle which Matthew probably inserts here for two reasons: to contrast with the worship theme and thus emphasize the victorious promise of verses 18f., and to provide a transition to the reassurance of Jesus' words in that

---

22. Dodd ("Appearances," p. 12) says, "the appearance of the Lord does not bring full or immediate conviction to the beholders, who require some form of assurance: the sight of His wounds, contact with His body, or His word of authority." All three assurances are found in John 20.

passage.[23] Thus Matthew assures the believer that even in the midst of uncertainty he can trust in Christ's authoritative reality. In the other Gospels doubt[24] is banished by Christ's physical presence; here it is dispelled by his authoritative word.

The Message (vv. 18–20)

1. *The statement of authority (v. 18).* Verse 18's connection with Daniel 7:14 has always intrigued critics. Vogtle and Trilling say there is no connection since the verses have little linguistic similarity and different perspectives; Matthew's text deals with resurrection while Daniel's concern is the parousia. Meier, however, says ("Salvation History," p. 211) a linguistic parallel does exist between Theodotian's text and the Septuagint (the Greek Old Testament) and that Matthew does hint at a "proleptic parousia" in which Christ's kingdom is realized in the life of the church. The Son of man theme in Matthew is thus closely related to Daniel's imagery.[25] Albright and Mann add (lxx viii–xcix) Matthew consciously weaves into Mark's account the concept of the glory the Son receives from the Father (cf. 10:27; 12:32; 13:41; etc.). Matthew omits the Son of man title probably for two reasons: (1) believers might misunderstand and see only a parousia interpretation, and (2) Christ wanted to teach that the parousia power and glory belonged to him now and could also be given to believers in the interim period between the resurrection and parousia.[26] This second consideration is also an important part of 27:51–54, a passage which prepares the reader for Jesus' final statement.

23. Giblin argues against the combination of both contrast and reassurance here, however, there is no reason why both cannot be present; contrast strengthens reassurance especially in terms of structural development in chapter 28.

24. Howe puts this doubt in the larger context of the doubt motif in the early church but neglects its *Sitz im Leben* in the post-Easter community. There its prominence probably rose due to the delay of the parousia and a corresponding doubt in the Risen One on the part of later disciples.

25. Frankemölle discusses (pp. 61–66) both Vogtle and Trilling and concludes that Matthew has been influenced by Daniel 7:14. The key, he says, is its influence on both 24:30 and 26:64; both show the extent of its influence on Matthew.

26. Kingsbury ("Composition," pp. 580–84) says that the title Son of God rather than Son of man is the predominant Christology here. This is further evidenced by the Son of man Christology which is subsumed under Son of God. We prefer Meier's contention to this, however; the two form an ellipse ("Son" Christology) with two foci in which one cannot predominate over the other.

Several Matthean themes are interwoven in verse 8. *Edothē* ("has been given," also appearing first in Daniel 7:14) is used to describe the resurrection event as the enthronement of the Messiah; the divine passive accenting *exousia* as the "authority" originally given Christ by the Father "within the limits of his earthly calling and commission" (Matt. 11:27, cf. 9:8); and which now is absolutely his (Foerster, *TDNT* II, pp. 568f.). Several critics (Lohmeyer, Michel, Barth, in *TIM*) say Jesus' words mean he has now become eschatological ruler and judge, the passage stressing exaltation rather than resurrection. This emphasis hardly seems necessary however; Matthew stresses exaltation throughout his book.

Christ's authority is universal (note the stress on *pas* ["all"]) and extends to the church as well as universe. *Exousia* ("authority") is a more comprehensive term than "power" (*dynamis*), referring to position as well as function. The kingdom of heaven (a favorite Matthean phrase) is already present in Christ and thus his assertion of authority (v. 18) provides the foundation for the ecclesiological command (vv. 19–20a).

A key term in Jesus' message is *pas* ("all"). It is used in all three parts, binding them together while stressing the universal lordship of Christ. We might even call the verse a kind of "pearl-stringing" midrash which centers on the "all-ness" of Yahweh transferred to the Risen Lord.[27] Christ is seen positionally (all authority), locally (all the earth), individually (every creature), and temporally (always). The concept includes the exaltation theology expressed in passages such as Ephesians 1:21, Colossians 1:15f., and Philippians 2:9f.; absolutely "all" things are under Christ's dominion.

The first phrase of verse 18 incorporates the next three, summing up Jesus' claims to authority made earlier in the Gospel (4:23f.; 7:29; 8:32; 9:6, 35; 10:1; 12:22; 17:18). His authority is in "heaven" as well as on "earth," a sweeping concept which denotes divinity. In verse 20 Matthew's primary stress on the divine nature of Christ reaches full expression; the resurrected Master has all the authority of Yahweh. Albright and Mann (clviii) say the combination of "son and Lord" in Matthew signifies a role which surpasses even the Messianic office: "The accusations that Jesus is usurping and exercising divine authority (ix 3, xxvi 65) are assumed to be true

27. Malina (pp. 97–98) connects this with a Jewish Haggada which says that ten monarchs would rule the world at the Eschaton.

in xi 25 –30. . . . Jesus meant to convey the fact of a unique relationship which he had with God, a relationship, moreover, which
implied deity."

2. *The command to make disciples (vv. 19 –20a).* "On the basis of"
(*oun*) his claim to authority Jesus now issues his command in
verses 19 and 20a. The purpose of the mission is discipleship, with
mathēteuō ("make disciples") found only in the first Gospel (13:52;
27:57 and here) and in Acts 14:21. Matthew's use of the term implies much more than our usual concept of evangelism; the term
means both the call to and process of becoming a disciple. Certainly this is a central theme in Matthew's ecclesiology which implies both imitation and obedience. The disciples must act, suffer,
and walk like Christ, trusting in his authority and presence[28] (see
Bornkamm, "Risen Lord," pp. 218f.).

Panta ta ethnē ("all nations") is the consummation of Matthew's
universalism theme. The concept refers to the interim period between the resurrection and parousia (v. 20; cf. 24:14) and implies
that some time will pass before those closing events. This universal mission motif is part of the exaltation theme; Bornkamm suggests ("Risen Lord," pp. 210 –212) "all the nations" is universal
lordship "elaborated in various ways" by the early church (cf. Phil.
2:9f.; Rom. 14:9; Col. 1:19f.).

Matthew's account here has provoked a measure of debate because of its seeming antithesis with Jesus' exclusive mission to
Gentiles (12:18f.; 13:38; 24:14; 26:13). Lange does an extensive study
of all these passages and concludes (pp. 300 –305) that 28:19a is
directed at the Gentile nations to the explicit exclusion of Israel.
Lange's hypothesis (that Matthew wrote at a time when the church
had separated from Judaism because God had turned away from
the Jewish nation) is ascribed to today by men such as Nepper-
Christensen, van Tilborg, Clark, Walker, Hare, Gaston, Nicklesburg,
Green, and Flusser. Many of these critics stress a salvation-historical approach, saying Matthew divided the history of salvation into
two periods: Jesus' ministry (the Jewish mission, chap. 10) and the
post-resurrection church (the Gentile mission). Matthew's struc-

---

28. Although Matthew does not emphasize the disciples' failure (8:25; 13:16; 14:23;
etc.) he does tell about their deficient faith (14:31; 16:8, 22f.; 17:20, etc.). He thus connects
faith and works, faith resulting in obedience. Even obedience is based on trust, however,
only God can produce a valid work in the disciples.

ture thus contrasts the compassionate offer of Jesus to the Jews
(10:5f.) with the Jew's absolute rejection of that mission (10:16f.)
which provokes God's rejection of Israel (7:21f.; 8:11f.; 15:7f.; 21:42;
23:35f. et al).

We wonder if this approach is somewhat simplistic and misses
the complex interplay of themes in Matthew. The episodes recorded in 10:5f. and 28:19 are found only in Matthew; it is difficult
to conclude that he makes one more important than the other.
Tagawa notes not only the theme of Jewish condemnation in 8:5 –
13, but also the emphasis in 15:21 – 28 that "Jews will participate
in the final salvation, the Gentiles being admitted only as exceptions. In v. 47, vi. 7, 32, and xviii. 17, the Gentiles are mentioned as
those on the way to perdition . . ." (p. 153). Perhaps we should
avoid altogether the concept of a Jewish vs. Gentile mission and
speak rather of the subordination of both to the overall concern
of the universal mission (see also Hubbard, pp. 84f., and Martin,
"Church," pp. 41f.). This does not mean, of course, that we should
ignore passages which speak of God's repudiation of the Jews, but
rather that we keep firmly in mind the traditional idea that though
Israel has been rejected as a nation, individuals within that nation
may still be recipients of redemptive love. Although this view was
proposed well before the birth of modern criticism it is nonetheless valid, neatly appropriating the complex data of Matthew's
Gospel which includes both salvation and judgment for Israel and
links both to the church's mission. Meier's view ("Nations,"pp. 94f.)
thus seems more logical than that of Hare and Harrington ("Gentiles," pp. 359f.), *ethnē* ("nations") in 28:19 including both Jews as
well as Gentiles.

Two participles, "baptizing" and "teaching," describe how disciples are made. The baptismal motif initially seems strange in
this context,[29] yet in combination with teaching beautifully describes both the sacramental and experiential sides of discipleship
which are essential aspects of ecclesiology. Some scholars think
Matthew does not stress baptism here as much as the trinitarian
formula, blending a high Christology into this ecclesiological statement. Although Matthew does not stress baptism (the verb appears seven times vs. twelve in Mark and ten in Luke, and the

---

29. Trilling (p. 40) says the basic command is the "missionary commission" while the
participles provide "community regulations." Meier (*Vision*, pp. 213f.) says the baptismal
element is used to produce high Christology (trinitarian) in Matthew's ecclesiology.

noun twice vs. four times each in the others), its usage in chapter 28 probably comes from tradition as much as its critical importance in the discipling process. This is illustrated for instance, by Matthew's choice of the words, *eis to onoma* ("in the name"). Some critics who recognize the similarity of both *eis* ("into") and *en* ("in") in New Testament times argue that *baptizein en* in Mark 1:5 and *baptizein eis* in 1:9 show that the phrase here in Matthew has a local sense. Others, however, (e.g., Allen and Albright) concentrate on the meaning of the whole phrase rather than its preposition, saying "in the name" refers to the ceremonial rite which makes the name of Jesus, while "into the name" refers to the results of the act or incorporation "into" the fellowship of the godhead. M. Harris ("Prepositions," p. 1209) says the phrase has three possible meanings: (1) it refers to transfer of ownership, like money credited "to the name of" a person; (2) it means the person who is baptized is endowed with all the benefits of salvation in Christ; or (3) it is a Semitic phrase which means "with reference to," implying a "Jesus" or trinitarian baptism rather than a Jewish or John-the-Baptist rite.

This third view seems a bit unlikely since it implies much more than is actually stated in Matthew, but a combination of the first view with that of Allen and Albright makes a lot of sense; the baptized convert becomes the possession of and therefore enters into fellowship with the Trinity in the discipling process. Jesus' words here are thus more than just a liturgical formula; baptism is an experience which transcends any act of obedience or symbolic rite. It is the initiation of the disciple (cp. 1 Peter 3:19, 20) into the rights and obligations of his calling.[30]

The trinitarian formula also summarizes another Matthean theme which began with the baptism of Jesus (3:11, 16f.); that of the Father-Son relationship (11:27; Mark 13:32; 14:36) as well as the Son of man-Spirit connection (12:32). In fact, Matthew's purposes all interconnect here; the baptized disciple now enters into full

30. It is difficult to evaluate the opinion which connects baptism "into the name of" with Matthew's teaching elsewhere about the law. Baptism is regularly considered to be a replacement for circumcision; is it also therefore the initiation rite which designates the true people of God? On the surface this seems to be a reasonable interpretation, however Matthew includes little evidence to support a "replacement" theology. On the whole it seems better to consider baptism from a liturgical standpoint rather than an anti-Jewish one.

fellowship with the Trinity, each member of which is related to the institutionalization of the church. Lange says (pp. 325f.) Matthew's discipleship theme here is the direct result of his emphasis on Jesus' authority; the responsibility of reaching out to others is combined with the secure knowledge and assurance of the divine Trinity, which extends the *exousia* or "authority" to the disciple and comforts (cp. 11:28–30) him/her.

The second step of discipleship is teaching, possibly a reference in verse 20 to the post-baptismal instruction of the early church (Fuller, pp. 88f., thus calls this a later insertion). Matthew's reference here, however, is based on the tradition of Jesus' own teaching ministry which is a central theme in the book. Mark stresses action[31] while Matthew emphasizes teaching in five basic sections which tell about the believer and his relationship to the world. Although many critics accuse Matthew of a "new Torah" theology, this hardly seems to fit his approach to the law. As Guelich says, Matthew views Jesus as the fulfillment of the law which still has validity yet, "at the same time is transcended and set aside by Jesus' own demand for conduct representative of the present age of salvation" (p. 246, cf. 216–66).[32] Today no "new Torah" supersedes the old; instead God makes a radical demand for a changed life.

Panta ("all") in this verse refers to Jesus' whole teaching which stresses the coming of the kingdom of God as well as man's relationship to it in a kind of blended eschatology and ethics. Privilege and responsibility are also part of this second step of discipleship; *entellō* ("command") anchors this "teaching" in Christology (it appears four times in the book, each time stressing Jesus' authority both in teaching the Father's commands as well as issuing his own injunctions). As Meier says (*Visions*, p. 214):

> Because the one and the same Jesus—the one and the same Son of Man—enjoined these commandments during his public ministry, enjoins them now on his church after the resurrection, and will

31. But see France ("Teaching," pp. 101f.) who argues that Mark stressed Jesus' teaching. We do not contradict this; Mark stressed the activity of Jesus' teaching while Matthew emphasized the content itself.

32. See also McConnell, pp. 86–89. Albright (cvi–cxv), Bornkamm ("Risen," p. 224), and Barth (pp. 154–59) use the phrase "new Torah" but say the old system was not replaced but rather transformed by Jesus' teaching.

judge *all* men according to these same commands, lofty ecclesiology, based on high Christology, also means lofty obligations. In morality as well as in mission and cult, Christology grounds the church's life and action.

3. *The promise of his presence (v. 20b)* The last part of verse 20 provides a fitting conclusion for the Gospel of Matthew. It emphasizes the deity of Christ which was also suggested in verses such as 1:23 ("his name shall be called Emmanuel [which means, God with us]"), and 18:20 ("where two or three are gathered in my name, there am I in their midst"). Michel (pp. 18f.) and Fuller (p. 89) see parallels to verse 20b also in passages such as Exodus 3:12; Joshua 1:5 and 9; Gospel of Thomas 77; and Pirke Aboth 3:2; the theme of these verses being God's Shekinah presence and glory among men applied in Matthew to the Risen One's omnipresence among his people. This divine language of comfort (Michel says "divine succor") is given by God to his people throughout the Old Testament and is offered to the church in the New Testament, Jesus' presence providing the power necessary for believers to "obey everything" commanded by God. Then, says Bornkamm (p. 228), "the gospel ends with the 'Immanuel' with which it began (1:23)."

Lange adds (pp. 340ff.) Jesus' promise here is the solution to the problem of the disciples' "little faith," especially in light of his warning in 17:17 that he would not be with them long.[33] Even though Jesus will not be present physically, his power will be available to his disciples so they will be able to carry on his work. His living presence is mediated to the disciples as divine authority which they must appropriate to overcome their lack of faith.

The last phrase of chapter 28, "until the consummation of the ages" beautifully expresses Matthew's theology. *Synteleia* ("end") is used five times in the book (13:39f., 49; 24:3), while only once (Heb. 9:26) elsewhere in the New Testament. The term is apocalyptic, Jesus' words saying the authority he promises to his disciples will be with them every moment (*pasas tas hēmeras* means "all the days" of the interim period) until the new kingdom is ushered in

---

33. See also Léon-Dufour (p. 148) who says Jesus guides his disciples from heaven and therefore "bypasses" doubt via "his sovereign and sufficient word" (cf. John 20:29). This seems to be a better solution than that of Wilckens (p. 49) who says the "little faith" is cured by the mission entrusted to the disciples.

(physically as well as spiritually). The mission itself is thus an integral part of the parousia expectation (cf. 24:14), becoming indeed a "proleptic parousia."[34]

Verse 20b applied to all the years that will pass before Jesus comes again. Until he does, says Matthew, believers are to act out the radical command to "go and make disciples of all nations." This statement provides comfort for his people, for it promises his continued presence during that time. The "church"[35] is the vehicle for that mission, charged with responsibility as well as sustained by Christ's presence until "the very end of the age."

Conclusion

Senior ("Passion," pp. 354 – 56) says Matthew in chapters 26 and 27 sets Jesus' majesty and power against the plots and betrayals of the Jewish leaders, thereby confronting the reader with "a series of stylized tableaux contrasting the Messiah and his enemies." Chapter 28 seems to build on this structure; the contrasting pictures in the three panels of the triptych move to a final, climactic scene in which the reader is assured of the triumphant results of believing in Christ regardless of external opposition or internal doubt. Opposition (27:62 – 66) leads to victory (28:1 – 10) which in turn produces more opposition (28:11 – 15). This is eventually overcome by the all-encompassing authority of the Risen Lord and promise of total victory (28:16 – 20). The characters in this drama (the women and disciples) find fulfillment not in themselves but in the power of God at work in their lives.

Matthew's Gospel is longer than Mark's by at least two sections. The first (27:62 – 66, 28:4, 11 – 15) serves two purposes; it answers the Jewish argument against the empty tomb and reaches out to Matthew's readers (specifically soldiers) by showing how power-

34. Cf. Barth, *TIM*, pp. 136f. Grundmann goes too far when he says the mission is itself "part of his parousia" expectation. Lightfoot (*Locality*, p. 72) more reasonably labels it "a foretaste of the consummation."

35. Matthew alone uses *ekklēsia* in the Gospels (16:18; 18:17), systematically stressing her origins and heritage, e.g., the choice of the twelve (10:2f.; 13:11f.; 16:12f.; 18:18f.; 19:28). He views the church as the inheritor of Israel's mantle (but not the "new Israel"), emphasizing Israel's rejection (see also the discussion of "all nations," v. 19) to underscore the church as God's chosen people.

less both Jewish and Roman forces are against the will of God. In verse 4 (cp. 27:54) the soldiers even become secular witnesses to the supernatural phenomena of the resurrection event.

The second addition (vv. 16 – 20) has a twofold relationship both to the resurrection narrative and the Gospel as a whole. In chapter 28 it serves as a vivid contrast to the guard episode to show the glory and power of the Risen One, especially in light of the evil treachery of the Jewish leaders in verses 11 – 15. Pesch says ("Ausführungsformel," pp. 79f.) verses 16 – 20 are a direct contrast to the lies of verses 11 – 15, assuring the success of Christ's mission.

Matthew's final section summarizes all his themes, combining both apologetic and missionary motifs to answer his opponents as he reaches out for converts. Plummer (p. 424) says Matthew begins and ends his work on an apologetic note, thus answering Jewish opposition with christological doctrine. In chapters 1 – 2, for instance, he answers the charge that a mere man, born of Joseph, could not be divine, while here he opposes the rumor that the disciples stole Jesus' body. All criticism falls silent in the presence of the Risen Lord.

Matthew's Christology also culminates in his resurrection narrative. G. M. Styler ("Stages," pp. 404f.) believes Matthew extends and clarifies Mark's theology, especially with regard to Jesus' kingly authority and divine status. Some critics (e.g., Hill, p. 65) argue that Matthew has a functional rather than ontological approach, but Albright says ontology is expressed via the functional in the New Testament.

In Matthew, for instance, four titles suggest the evangelist's basic Christology (McConnell, pp. 154f.; 179f.; 199f.): suffering servant, Son of man, Messiah, and Son of God (perhaps also "Lord" which appears forty-nine times). These terms can be divided into two groups, one describing Jesus' earthly purpose (suffering servant) and the other his resultant status (Son of man, Messiah, Son of God), with Son of man perhaps belonging to both groups. The first titles culminate in the passion and the second in the resurrection, therefore the second ones appear in chapter 28. Jesus is now kingly Messiah and divine son,[36] the "Lord" who has "all authority." Matthew stresses both promise and fulfillment here, demonstrating

36. We agree with Meier (*Vision*, p. 214) vs. Kingsbury (*Christology*, pp. 58f.) that "Son" in 28:19 cannot strictly be Son of God; verse 18 also stresses a connection with Son of man teaching. The two are rather combined in one comprehensive title.

that Jesus is the fulfillment of all the messianic promises of the Old Testament. He is Messiah, yet more, transcending messiahship to become both Son and Lord.

Matthew's ecclesiology and eschatology are also finalized in 16—20. Says Hill, "Matthew's Christology is inextricably inter-woven with his doctrine of the Church and his eschatology." He believes Matthew divides time into three periods: (1) Jesus' min-istry which finalizes the sacrifice and ritual of the Old Testament and provides a new interpretation of the law; (2) the interim period during which Jesus reigns as exalted Lord and the church reaches out to the nations; and (3) the parousia when Christ's kingdom will be established with finality.[37] The resurrection in Matthew thus concludes the first period, establishes the second, and pro-leptically represents the third. Jesus, the Risen King, now comforts and sustains his followers while the mission expands to believers all over the world in active, obedient discipleship.

Matthew's *Sitz im Leben* probably includes a combination of Jewish and Gentile elements. His strong Jewish flavor and anti-pharisaic emphasis suggest he was writing at a time when the church and synagogue were in strong opposition to each other (Guelich, pp. 26ff.; Goppelt, pp. 23f.), and his universalist emphasis hints at a message to Jewish Christians who were becoming too isolationist.[38] The book was thus written both to refute oppo-nents and to correct dangers in the church. Most of all, however, Matthew wrote to instruct and encourage believers, comforting them with the glorious reality and power of their Risen Lord.

37. In contrast to this, Kingsbury (*Christology*, pp. 31f.) argues there are two epochs, the time of Israel and the time of Jesus. Meier says, however, (*Vision*, pp. 29f.) that Mat-thew emphasizes Christ's death and resurrection as the critical turning-point of salva-tion—history. The age of Israel is thus viewed entirely under the guise of promise-fulfillment with Matthew's emphasis on the three phases as Hill enumerates them. See also Tagawa, pp. 149f.

38. See footnote 8 for a suggestion that the first Gospel was written from a gentile rather than Jewish perspective.

Luke's Resurrection Narrative

Luke's narrative is replete with theology prompted by his emphasis on salvation-history (see Conzelmann and Marshall's clarification in *Luke—Historian*). Several emphases thus dominate this work:

1. The resurrection is important from a soteriological perspective especially evident in the prophecies of verses 17, 26, and 46 which parallel other prophecies in the Gospel (16:21; 17:22f.; 20:18f.). Some critics shy away from a soteriological emphasis here on the basis of *theologia crusis/theolgia gloriae*, saying the passage is actually the denouement of Jesus' suffering prior to his glorification. This may indeed be a denouement yet its very emphasis is redemptive, especially within the context of Luke's salvation theme here and in Acts where the resurrection rather than crucifixion is stressed. The passage represents this change in emphasis and also places Jesus' death and resurrection within the context of God's salvation plan (note the emphatic *dei*, "must," in all three verses of chap. 24). The redemptive link between the passion and resurrection is thus made clear; resurrection is not only the vindication of Jesus' death but also a sign of the new life that results from it. Luke did not "historicize" (Conzelmann) the salvation thrust of the early church and remove the sacred encounter (see below).

2. Luke's narrative is strong in ecclesiology. The resurrection is a transition to the church age as well as conclusion to Jesus' earthly ministry. It thus bridges from Jesus' work to the work of his followers. Chapter 24 begins near Jerusalem (the starting point of the mission) with a series of episodes leading up to the coming

mission. It looks both backward as it clarifies the redemptive significance of Jesus' death, and forward as it prepares for the resurrection message of Acts.

3. Luke clearly stresses the witness theme here which later dominates Acts. Consider, for instance, his emphasis on "two" angels at the tomb, and all the attempts to "witness" to the Eleven who themselves would become "witnesses" (24:48, cf. Acts 1:8). Léon-Dufour (pp. 155–57) states the entire narrative teaches that "only the official disciples are witnesses" who are "formally appointed" by God prior to the worldwide mission thrust of Acts. This view seems somewhat overstated—others besides the Eleven become witnesses too—yet Léon-Dufour's indentification of Luke's witness theme is accurate.[1]

Luke clearly writes in the narrative genre here, placing all events in Jerusalem on the same day and linking them with the use of phrases such as "that same day" (v. 13), "that same hour" (v. 33), "while . . . speaking" (v. 36), and "he led them" (v. 50). These phrases hint at Luke's theology, but they do more. Dillon says (p. 269) Luke deliberately tries to "reconcile and harmonize" his various sources rather than "to validate one at the expense of the other." All the events are laced together into a unified whole; Luke's *"eye-witnesses* become *ministers of the word"* and finalize the introductory message of Luke 1:1. "The Christian preacher's interpretative word will be simply a faithful stewardship of the tradition of Jesus' words," says Dillon. "It is the Easter chapter which establishes this Lukan equation, and it is an ultimate coherence of narrative and sayings tradition which is achieved thereby!" (p. 272).

Luke's narrative structure is basically linear, providing a straightforward development of his message. Each section adds to and clarifies the themes of the previous section, so its structure is quite simple: the empty tomb narrative focuses attention on the glimmers of truth in the angel's message and the women's witness to the disciples, who respond with unbelief and perplexity (Peter). The tension produced by this scene continues into the Emmaus story which describes two men who are also perplexed about the empty tomb and are moving away from Jerusalem. Later they

1. Other theses such as Talbert's view of the physical reality of the Risen Christ as an answer to a docetic heresy or the view that Luke wants to prove the radical continuity between the earthly Jesus and the Risen Christ (with his stress on "alive" etc.) are true of certain sections but are not theological threads which tie together the whole narrative. They will be considered as they arise in the text.

return "to" Jerusalem in triumph where the mission of Acts will begin.

The dialogue of the two men in verses 17–27 is somber, indicative of unenlightened minds who are blinded to the reality of the Risen Christ. The path to understanding leads to the Word (vv. 25–27) and the breaking of bread (vv. 28–31); these "open their eyes" (v. 30) and mouths (v. 34), and evoke enthusiastic witness to the Eleven (v. 34).

The appearance to the Eleven in verses 36–49 which leads to their commissioning as worldwide evangelists reminds us of the doubt theme of verses 12 and 13f.; the disciples are "startled and frightened" by Jesus' appearance. They do "not believe" even when he "shows them his hands and feet." Still, the resurrection has power to overcome all barriers to the mission of the church; three kinds of doubt are countered by three proofs of the Risen Lord which become the foundation of the commissioning in verses 44–49.

The commission itself repeats Luke's primary thrust; the disciples are to be witnesses both of the passion and resurrection (vv. 44–46, cf. vv. 7, 25f.). This work was already described in prophecy (v. 47 is a third complement of the main verb in v. 46), and includes preaching, repentance, and forgiveness (three of Luke's soteriological emphases). The task of the apostles is witnessing (v. 48) which is empowered by the presence of the Holy Spirit (v. 49). These themes naturally lead into the next book, Acts.

The Empty Tomb Narrative, 23:54–24:12

The Journey of the Women, 23:54–24:1

We have already suggested that Luke used his own sources as well as Mark to produce his resurrection narrative,[2] thereby serving his own redactive purposes rather than borrowing them from

2. Marshall, "Resurrection," argues that Luke used Mark as his primary source, yet in his commentary (p. 882) modifies this by saying, "I am now less certain about this verdict, and would leave open the possibility that Luke was following an alternative source."

others. Still, he probably did have access to the earlier Gospels and (even if unconsciously) did interact with them in his account.

The women's motive for bringing spices to the tomb in Luke is similar to that in Mark, yet with a different thrust. Luke does not include a messianic motif here (note the omission of Jesus anointing at Bethany, Mark 14:3 – 9). Taylor says (*Passion*, pp. 102 – 104) Luke probably combined a non-Markan tradition (23:55 – 56) with a Markan one (24:1) here, thus producing a straightforward account minus Mark's sense of haste and rush to the tomb.

Luke refers instead to the passing of time, moving the time note from Mark 15:42 to the beginning of his resurrection narrative (23:54) and highlighting its importance. Luke, in fact, uses four time notes in these verses sandwiched between the burial and resurrection (two in v. 54 and one each in vv. 56b and 24:1), stressing the long duration of this Sabbath. The special use of these notes is clearly Luke's redaction, demonstrating his particular emphasis on time which is theologically important throughout the rest of the narrative.

Sabbatōn appears three times here (23:54, 56; 24:1), showing Luke's emphasis on Jesus' authority over the "Sabbath." He uses Mark's two references on Jesus and the Sabbath (4:31f.; 6:1f.), and adds two more: the healing of the crippled woman (13:10 – 17) and the man with dropsy (14:1 – 4). For this author Sabbath healings are a prelude to the greatest Sabbath miracle of all, the resurrection.

The women who approached the tomb that resurrection morning still observed the Sabbath laws (v. 56b), expecting Jesus (or Lord of the Sabbath) to be "silent" (*hēsuchazō*), ironically even while God was at work raising him.[3] Luke describes the emptiness of these disciples in heart-rending words. We can almost feel time drag as they silently move toward the tomb.

Luke's Sabbath motif is part of his salvation-history theme, with the "same day" theme the unifying thread which binds the episodes together. Ellis says (*Luke*, p. 275) Luke introduces an "eighth-day" theme with Resurrection Sunday a part of the "new creation," but the evangelist's stress in 24:1 is more likely literary rather than theological. The text hardly supports such a theory. Instead the recurring emphasis which binds the narrative together stresses the historical oneness of the event in relation to God's activity.

3. Or was Luke really emphasizing here that Jesus remained in the grave on the Sabbath? This hardly seems likely especially in light of Luke's special emphasis on Sabbath authority and Jesus' activity on the Sabbath.

At the same time it also represents the beginning of the new age in which God reaches down to man personally and individually through his Son. This quality of intimacy increases through the narrative; the women and Peter face the empty tomb (impersonal), Jesus reveals himself in the "breaking of bread" to two travelers on the way to Emmaus (personal), and finally the Risen Lord not only eats but asks to be touched by the disbelieving disciples (intensely personal).

Most scholars agree that salvation history is a major element of Luke's theology, but how that theme should be defined is something else. Conzelmann says it means a "historicizing" of the kerygma (*Theology,* pp. 185–206) and Käsemann proposes it introduces an "early Catholicism" (*New Testament Questions,* pp. 21f.; *Freedom,* pp. 116f.), but these views are too radical. Cullmann is more believable, asserting (*Salvation,* pp. 244f.) this motif from the early church does not replace eschatology but rather clarifies it. Jesus' birth thus not only becomes the "center of time" (Conzelmann), but also ushers into time the power of the kingdom. The church age which stands "between the ages" thus looks forward to the parousia. Marshall correctly qualifies Luke's use of this theme (*Luke—Historian,* pp. 93–102), saying "salvation" is Luke's major focus with salvation-history a sub-theme of that.

In the brief period between the time Jesus died and rose from the grave God's power was at work even though Jesus' followers were unaware of it. Luke's use of the terms *now* (39 times in Luke-Acts vs. three in the others) and *today* (19 times in Luke-Acts vs. nine total in the others), perhaps best describe the impact of the scene where the disciples wait for God to act. Navone says (pp. 182–84) these terms express "the eschatological time of salvation" (cf. 2:11; 3:22; 4:21, etc.), Jesus' death and resurrection becoming a "timeless" present to the church who waits. Here Luke assures her that even in the darkest hour God is already at work.

This section also emphasizes the role of the women as witnesses. Dillon and others (pp. 8–13) call attention to Jesus' *anabasis* ("going up") "from Galilee" and the women who witnessed that; in verse 55 Luke deliberately replaces the names of the women (mentioned in Mark with "the women who had come out with him from Galilee"). The description neatly connects this scene with the anointing in 7:36–50 and the women in the Galilean ministry (8:2–3, cp. 24:10). Dillon says (pp. 12–13) Luke thus expands the role of the women in the burial scene, fusing the burial and empty tomb sequences into a united episode with the women as central characters. "They saw the tomb and how his body was laid" (v. 55b) adds even more to their witness and prepares the reader for Christ's later ascension (24:3, 22−23, 36−43; cf. Talbert, *Gnostics*, pp. 30−31). The stage is set for the progress of God's mighty act in salvation-history.

The Tomb Events, 24:2−3

Mark 16:2−5 and Matthew 28:1−4 are reduced in Luke to a few terse phrases: they come, find the stone rolled away, enter, and find the body gone. Luke's choice of words indicates he is using Mark or a similar tradition here, although he is redacting heavily. The last phrase, especially "Lord Jesus," is the focal point here. Luke also omits Mark's description of the women's concern and builds his narrative slowly to a climax as Easter faith unfolds in the Emmaus story (not in the empty tomb narratives).

Luke's double use of *hueron* here (eighty times in Luke-Acts) stresses the witness theme as the women "verify the fact" of the empty tomb. "They found the stone . . . but did not find the body"; tension builds as the women search for an answer to explain the mystery of the empty tomb.

The solution is hinted at in the phrase "the Lord Jesus" in verse 3.[4] Luke's usage of *kyrios* to describe Jesus is uniquely his; no other gospel writer uses it. In Luke's books the title appears eighteen times, nearly always in a non-Markan context.[5] Here Luke

4. This is one of nine verses (Matt. 27:49; Luke 22:19b−20; 24:3, 6, 12, 36, 40, 51, 52) labeled by Westcott and Hort "western non-interpolations," i.e., passages which contain a phrase or word group present in all except the western group of manuscripts. Since they normally have the "wilder" readings, earlier scholars rejected the authenticity of these readings. However, recent times have seen a re-examination of the problem, due partly to the discovery of p[75] (see Aland, "Papyri," pp. 193f.). Today each passage must be considered as a separate case. The external evidence is quite strong for the inclusion of the phrase here (all but D, several Old Latin manuscripts and Eusebius), and it is likely that Codex Bezae was influenced by verse 23 and *kyrios* omitted as an assimilation to Matthew 27:58 or Mark 15:43 (Snodgrass, "Western," p. 375; and Metzger, *Textual*, p. 183; *contra* Aland, pp. 203f.). Furthermore, the expression is Lukan and is necessary here, providing a transition from Jesus' earthly life to his resurrection glory (so de la Potterie, *"Le titre KYRIOS,"* pp. 121f.).

5. Marshall (*Historian*, p. 166), Rehkopf (*Sunderquelle*, p. 95), Hahn (*Titles*, pp. 94−97), and Schürmann (*Lukasevangelium*, p. 401) all believe Luke took the title from his sources, but Vielhauer, (*Aufsatze*, pp. 154f.) argues it is a Lukan composition. If Vielhauer is right, however, the title should appear in Mark's account as well.

uses the title for the climax of his passion narratives unlike Mark and Matthew who ended their narratives with the centurion's cry (Luke, due to his stress on the righteous sufferer, has the centurion cry, "Surely this man was innocent," 23:47). Luke's description of the passion flows into the burial events with the grief of the crowd, silent witness of the women, and tender action of Joseph culminating in the climactic christological statement: "they did not find the body of the Lord Jesus."

Luke carefully avoids placing the title on the disciples' lips, using it instead in his own editorial comments which consistently attempt to prove that Jesus was not only Lord after the resurrection but also from the moment of his birth[6] (even though the disciples did not believe that until after the resurrection). The title emphasizes Jesus' divine authority; through him God showed himself and his work among men. Luke uses the term to stress that "Jesus is now risen and Lord over death" (Marshall, "Resurrection," p. 67). Franklin (Lord, pp. 49–55) says this is Luke's key christological term, "an expression of commitment" (p. 53). Its usage here adds a strong exaltation aspect to the mystery of the event described in verses 2–3.

Danker (Luke, pp. 41–43) applies 10:1, where the "Master" sends his "servants" to hear his message. Verse 3 thus prepares the reader for the "mission" of the women to the disciples in the following section.

The Angelic Message, 24:4–8

Although Mark and Luke use basically the same subject matter in this section, their wording is so different that it is difficult to determine which sources Luke actually used. Critics differ on this matter but the opinion of Marshall, Dillon, and Liefeld seems most reasonable; Luke uses a combination of tradition and redaction to produce this passage. For instance, Luke has moved the perplexity of the women from the trip to the tomb (Mark 16:3) to the discovery that the tomb was empty. There may be two reasons: (1) Luke does not wish to focus on the journey but rather on the empty tomb

---

6. The only exceptions are Jesus' own use of the title (19:31), the angels' usage (2:11), and Elizabeth's (1:43). Moule (Phenomenon, pp. 57f.; and "Christology," pp. 160f.) notes Luke uses the term because he is faithful to the historical record rather than inserting later views into Jesus' life (contra Conzelmann, Theology, pp. 174n.).

and the angelic message; and (2) the perplexity provides a transition from the tomb to the message. Their confusion, a natural result of discovering the tomb empty, leads easily into the message. As in Mark, the doubt motif is again at work, and the angelic message will also here begin with a chastisement of their lack of understanding. In fact, it is even more explicit than in Mark.

Scholars have traditionally linked the "two men" of verse 4 with the two at the transfiguration (9:30) and ascension (Acts 1:10). Bultmann's view, however, (*HST*, p. 315) that this repetition reflects ancient methods of storytelling and therefore is "a completely popular folk motif . . . resting on the demands of comprehension, or symmetry" is faulty, as is Fuller's assertion (*Resurrection*, pp. 96f.) that this is merely "parousia imagery, and this apocalyptic scenery may be the source of the tradition about the angels." Both of these views are too simplistic, failing to consider adequately the theological meaning and purpose of the imagery.

Morgenthaler is more believable (*Zeugnis*, I, p. 97f.; II, p. 7f; also Liefeld); he says Luke used the phrase "two men" to emphasize a "double witness." Leaney (pp. 71, 167, 291f.) and Manek (pp. 219f.) go too far when they say Moses and Elijah are the "two men" in all three passages, yet the repetition of similar terms in all three passages[7] shows clearly that Luke meant an obvious connection between the passages.[8]

The amazement of the women in Mark becomes "fear" and "bowing to the ground" (a natural Jewish reaction to an angelophany), and even the angel's message is different. Luke omits "do not fear" (Mark 16:6; Matt. 28:5), probably because the women's act of reverence sufficiently emphasizes the divine origin of the mes-

---

7. *Astraptōn* describes both Christ's garment (9:29) and the angels' robes (24:4, cf. 17:24). This term is found only in Luke and Acts and is reserved for divine revelations of God to man. Note also the use of *kai idou* and *andres duo* in all three passages.

8. Dillon provides a good discussion (pp. 22–26) of the transfiguration connection, noting that Luke's unique *exodus* in 9:31 looked forward to the passion-resurrection-ascension as a whole and that he deliberately styled the event as proleptic of the following events. As such he follows Flender, Conzelmann and others in arguing that Luke changes Mark's messianic misunderstanding to a misunderstanding with regard to the passion, contending that "Easter revelation is essentially the unlocking of the mystery of the Messiah's passion" (p. 24). The transfiguration was also a foretaste of resurrection "glory" (24:26) and the ascension (Acts 1:10) the capstone of that "glory." The "two men" were meant to be witnesses of God's startling activity on behalf of "Jesus the Lord" (v. 3). This heavenly witness was twofold, in keeping with Deuteronomic requirements, and so provided a valid, convincing proof of the truth.

sage. He also changes the statement about seeking Jesus to a rhetorical question, "Why do you look for the living among the dead,"
thus making an implied rebuke more obvious. Schubert (p. 167)
says this "noticeably diminishes the interest in the empty tomb as
providing by itself direct or even inferential evidence for the fact
of Jesus' resurrection"; yet he misses Luke's true intention. Luke
considers the empty tomb as historical fact as well as an apologetic tool (cf. v. 12), but in this passage his intent is to contrast the
women's lack of comprehension with the reality of the event. The
question is literary rather than apologetic, a reminder to the women
(and Luke's readers) that they should know better. The word that
is emphasized here is "living," a word which is central both to the
resurrection and Acts. *Zaō* appears nine times in Luke and twelve
times in Acts; it shows that Jesus could not be bound by death
but was Lord over it. Mark and Matthew's vindication theme is
thus replaced here by a lordship Christology.

Luke's most obvious differences from Mark appear in verses 6—
8. Taylor (*Passion*, pp. 107f.) believes this material suggests Luke
used an independent tradition since the only similarity to Mark
is the reference here to Galilee; yet the passage might also be a
combination of Mark, independent tradition, and Luke's redaction. Verse 6a, for instance, is Luke's redaction of Mark while
verse 6b probably came from an independent source. Fuller (p. 98)
believes the whole passage is Luke's composition since all of its
terms are used in Mark and Luke's predictions except *stauroō*
("crucify") which he says is a hellenistic term and therefore Lukan.
This theory is somewhat debatable (*stauroō* is used in a Palestinian setting by Matthew and is not Lukan); nonetheless verse 7 is
a summary of these predictions which seems to support a combination of tradition and redaction.

"He is not here but has arisen"[9] reverses the word order of Mark
to make "has arisen" the climax of this scene (note the use of *alla*
"but," here). All of Luke's short, terse phrases in preceding verses
have led up to this announcement. The angel's message recapitulates Jesus' predictions about his own suffering and death and
results in the specific response of the women, "then they remem-

9. This may be a "western non-interpolation"; Fuller (p. 97) calls it an "assimilation"
to Mark and Matthew. Metzger, however, says (p. 184) the presence of antithetical *alla* is
evidence of Lukan authorship. See also Jeremais (*Words*, p. 149), Aland (p. 205), and
Snodgrass (p. 375).

bered his words" (cp. the disciples' incomprehension in 9:45; 18:34). The motif is like that of Acts 11:16, where Peter says to the believers in Jerusalem that after he witnessed the gentile Pentecost with Cornelius he "remembered" Jesus' statement about Spirit-baptism.

Some critics are quick to note that Luke does not use the empty tomb apologetically; it "is fundamentally inadequate for evoking faith" while it is "the words of Jesus which are the sole basis of faith" (Léon-Dufour, p. 159). Dillon argues that verse 8 continues to express the "hidden and incomprehensible" nature of passion understanding; "if those 'words' (*rhēmata*, v. 8 = 9:45, 18:34) were not comprehended by the disciples when they were uttered, the 'remembrance' of them now cannot be taken to imply faith or understanding unless the shift is explicitly noted" (p. 51). There is more evidence to support this in Luke's use of "Son of Man" in verse 7; the title becomes "Christ" only in Jesus' words of verse 26. Dillon concludes this theme of Christ's hidden status continues until Jesus himself makes it clear.

Yet Dillon may have over-theologized here; both the women and angels become witnesses to the Risen Lord in this passage, and the women's awakening understanding is part of Luke's remembrance theme (see also K. H. Bartels, *NIDNTT*, III, p. 230—47) which also appears in Acts 11:18. The angels' command to "remember" (v. 6) surely implies the women ought to understand what they remember, and verse 8's assurance that they remembered also meant they understood. In answer to Léon-Dufour and Dillon we ought to say Luke's text includes glimpses of truth (v. 3b and here) to suggest the real meaning of the resurrection. The empty tomb is one piece of that puzzle which the women "announce" to the disciples who further advance the misunderstanding theme by refusing to believe (v. 11). Luke's narrative shows how the problem must be overcome in stages, first by the message of the empty tomb and finally by the Risen Lord himself.

The evangelist's use of "Galilee" is significant in verse 6;[10] he

10. Luke shifts the forward-looking utilization out of Galilee as the place of revelation (Mark 16:7, Matt. 28:7) to a backward—looking employment as the place of prediction (here). Many (e.g., Evans, Leaney, Rigaux) believe that "Galilee" is added on the basis of Mark but altered because Luke made Jerusalem the theme of his narrative and so shunted the Galilean appearances aside. This, however, is only partially correct. While Luke does center on Jerusalem and thus does refer to a Galilean appearance, this is insufficient to account for the presence of "Galilee" here.

could easily have omitted the reference entirely. He must have introduced it for a good reason, though. It is further evidence of Luke's witness motif: "Luke stresses the fact that it is the Galilean disciples who are the witnesses of the Jerusalem appearances (Acts 1:11; 13:31)" (Marshall, *Luke—Historian*, p. 155). Although traditionally critics (Simpson, pp. 65f.; Conzelmann, pp. 73f.) say Luke uses Galilee as a symbol of the place of acceptance and Jerusalem as the place of rejection, this view is far too simplistic, however. It ignores the positive role of Jerusalem in both the opening and closing sections of the book. Davies (*Land*, pp. 252–60) shows how Luke's narrative moves from Jerusalem to Galilee to Jerusalem and believes that Luke is "honorably demoting" Jerusalem from the eschatological center of the imminent parousia to stress its position as the "geographic center of Christian beginnings" (p. 260). Galilee thus becomes a place of past witness; not even important enough to mention in Jesus' program for outreach in Acts 1:8.

Although Davies' assessment of Jerusalem seems accurate, his view of Galilee is shortsighted. Perhaps Conzelmann's theological interpretation of Galilee is better, one which Dillon builds on. He says Luke's "Galilee to Jerusalem" format is a "journey in christological understanding" with Galilee a symbol of the "land of miracles" where enthusiasm toward the miracle-maker is dimmed only by his passion and suffering in Jerusalem. The reminder in verse 6 of Galilee thus asks for the kind of discipleship which moves beyond asking for miracles to center on deeper theological commitment based on the passion and resurrection.

Dillon's emphasis on miracle-enthusiasm is a bit overstated;[11] perhaps the best evaluation of the reference to Galilee sees it primarily as the place of "witness." Verse 6 is a reminder of that witness which is clearly stated in verse 7. The "christological journey"

---

11. In Acts the miracle stories deliberately look back to Jesus' ministry and stress continuity (e.g., Acts 8:32–35 = Luke 5:18–26, Acts 8:36–43 = Luke 8:49–56) in the aeons. Therefore, at best the passion understanding clarifies but does not replace the stress on miracles in the Galilean ministry. As all recognize, the key to the problem is the "travel narrative" of 9:51–19:10, which keynotes the christological development from Galilee to Jerusalem. Conzelmann's interpretation (pp. 65–73) of the journey as a symbolic representation of Jesus' "awareness that he must suffer" is correct in its basic appraisal but has certain exegetical weaknesses. As Marshall points out (*Luke—Historian*, pp. 148–53), Luke does not create the motif but borrows it from Mark and expands it along the lines of preaching to the crowds and instructing the disciples (see also Reicke, "Instruction"). In other words, it is part of a broader stress on "salvation."

thus leads to an understanding that salvation is rooted in the passion and resurrection.

Luke emphasizes Jerusalem, then, for two reasons: (1) he uses it as a literary device to maintain continuity between the passion narratives and the opening chapters of Acts, Jerusalem being the center of missionary activity; and (2) he uses it theologically as the place where Jesus triumphs over rejection and extends his hand of forgiveness through the early church. The appearances take place only near or in Jerusalem, bridging the gap between Luke's rejection theme and universal mission motif.[12]

Luke emphasizes another point in this section, the promise-fulfillment theme of verse 7. Schubert (pp. 173–77) believes this is the central idea of Luke's resurrection narrative (in continuity with 2:38f.; 4:14; 7:18f.; 9:22, 31, 43f., 18:31f.) and because it appears in all three pericopes (vv. 7, 25f., 32, 46f.) it binds all of them together. Central as it is, however, the theme still is subordinate to Luke's more important salvation emphasis. Although a clear soteriological emphasis is missing from the passion narrative itself, it is very evident in other scriptural fulfillment passages (9:22, 44; 17:22; 18:31; 22:22; 24:7, 26, 46) which parallel passages in Acts and speak of the suffering Messiah (2:36, 3:13–15, 4:27, 7:52, 10:39).[13]

The salvation theme is also implied by the forceful use of *dei* in prediction passages. This usage is peculiar to Luke (forty-four occurrences in Luke and Acts vs. eight in Matthew, six in Mark, ten

12. Other transition scenes between rejection and outreach include the ascension with its command to go; the selection of the twelfth disciple symbolizing the completion of the remnant for evangelizing the people and Pentecost which empowers the church for the task. See also Rengstorff, "Election," *Issues*, ed. Klassen, pp. 182–87. This is part of Luke's universalism. Several have noted that Luke softens Matthew's harsh attitude toward the Jews by refusing to exclude Israel from salvation (24:47) and stressing those who believe; while the nation is judged, the gospel continues to go to Israel (see Navone, pp. 185–87; Ellis, *Luke*, pp. 16–18; Jerrell, pp. 41–74), and the mission is truly universal (see further on v. 47).

13. Tiede (pp. 97–125) notes how these passages on the necessity of the suffering Messiah prove a corrective to those scholars who deny that Luke has a soteriological purpose in his passion narrative. Dillon's thesis (pp. 39–46) that the passion predictions "bring out the *hiddenness* of the divine plan of which the Son of Man is executor" (p. 42) is unconvincing. It is based on 17:25; however the context is the parousia rather than the passion. The passion emphasis of verse 25 contrasts the suffering and rejection of the Son of man with the glory of that day, thus the "hiddenness" of the passion or resurrection is not a consideration. Although Dillon says the apocalyptic logia in 17:20f. is altered by the insertion of 17:25, we believe that the explanation here better explains its presence.

in John); one which Grundmann says (*TDNT*, II, pp. 23f.) is a spe-cial eschatological term referring to the necessity of God-ordained events. Although Conzelmann says (*Theology*, pp. 154—56) Luke translates Jewish "election" into a type of hellenistic doctrine of "predetermining fate," Marshall disagrees (*Luke—Historian*, pp. 111—15); Luke uses this concept within a Palestinian milieu in his Gospel. His divine "must" simply means that resistance to the eschatological power of God is futile (see Flender, pp. 143f.). Consider, for instance, Gamaliel's warning in Acts 5:39, Peter's de-fense in 11:17, and Jesus' words to Paul in 26:14; redemptive his-tory is both divinely established and inevitable. In Luke and Acts the term means God ordains his plan of salvation which moves through history. The fulfillment motif uses "proof from prophecy" to authenticate Jesus as the Messiah, Luke showing how the Son of man (in all the prophecies until vv. 26, 46) becomes Messiah (vv. 26, 46) through suffering, thereby fulfilling scriptural prophecy.

Three words in verse 7 describe how redemption comes to God's people; Jesus is "delivered," "crucified," and "raised." *Hamartōlōn* (possibly redaction borrowed from Mark 14:1b) emphasizes this theme by describing the men who crucified Jesus, as does the statement that the women "remembered." Michel says (*TDNT*, IV p. 676) "there is a connection between the saving act of God and effective remembering" in the infancy stories (1:54, 72), a theme which is repeated in Luke's parable about Lazarus (16:25) and the story of the thief on the cross.

Just as Luke links salvation with remembering, he also links it with prophetic proof. The women who "remember" can now pro-claim (v. 9) what is proved true by prophecy.

The Women's Report, 24:9—11

Verses 9—11 sound so much like Matthew 28:9—10 that many scholars believe Luke (as well as Matthew) borrowed here from Mark's lost ending.[14] He omits describing the women's emotion

14. Fuller (p. 100) argues against a common source behind Matthew and Luke, stating that the only correspondence is *apangellō*. However, he ignores the similar structure (departure and report) as well as the phrase *apo tou mnemeiou* (see Metzger, p. 184); and Aland, p. 204, for the authenticity of this phrase). However, as stated below, we would agree with Fuller and Dillon, that the whole is a Lukan redaction of his source.

(cp. Mark 16:8; Matt. 28:9), probably because he has already used the fear motif (v. 5). The women simply "return" and "report" the events "to the Eleven and all the rest." Luke's words are plain here, an effective stylistic device which leads into the doubt motif of verse 11. Luke also omits Jesus' appearance at the tomb, perhaps choosing to focus less on the women's need for confirmation than on the disciples' refusal to accept their witness. The dramatic impact of Jesus' first appearance is thus saved for the Emmaus account.

Luke surprisingly interrupts his narrative in verse 10 to list the women by name. Did he hold off until this point to avoid Mark's problem of redundancy? Probably not; Fuller says (p. 95) Luke used his own source for this list (cp. 8:1−3) and his own kind of procedure (cf. Acts 1:13). The list is like that used in Luke 8:2, 3 plus the name, "Mary of James." Joanna appears instead of Salome, probably because of the special source as well as Luke's efforts to reach his readers who knew Joanna but not Salome.

The term *apostles* is used instead of disciples, another deliberate choice which leads naturally into Acts. According to Luke, apostles were uniquely chosen disciples who were called both to receive as well as proclaim the Word. They were also special witnesses of the Risen Christ (1:3, 22; 10:41; 13:30−31). According to Acts 1:21−22 apostles were companions of Jesus and eyewitnesses of his resurrection (cp. 1 Cor. 9:1). ("The Twelve on Israel's Thrones") (pp. 75−112) shows how Luke presents the apostles as the Twelve who serve as vice-regents of Israel's restoration and who thus fade in importance after the Apostolic Council of Acts 15.

It is questionable that Luke limits the term *apostle* to include just the Twelve: nonetheless Jervell's point is certainly valid that the church was not a new Israel replacing the old one and therefore the Twelve had a special ministry as apostles to the restored Israel.

Luke's phrase, "the Eleven and all the rest," further emphasizes this theme. The apostolic core stays together in Jerusalem. Some leave it briefly (vv. 13f.), but return later to report back to the group (vv. 33f.). Dillon says this is both a model of the church as well as transition to the gathering at Pentecost. These "concentric circles—the Twelve, then the other disciples gathered about them, and then a cosmospolitan public hearing the word from within the circle," are Luke's portrait of the gathering process from all nations which constitute the Church.

The church is thus not "new Israel" but "true Israel," heir to both the promise and mandate to evangelize Israel (the righteous remnant theme). The church is not separate from this purpose. The church grows naturally out of the Isaianic promises, and 24:9f. is part of the complex picture combining the mission to Israel with the gathering of the nations.

Doubt is a common feature of resurrection tradition. Luke uses it in verse 11, however, outside of an appearance pericope. Why? Fuller thinks the evangelist uses it here "to preserve the independence of the apostolic witness: apostles cannot come to true faith as a result of third parties. They must see and believe for themselves in order that they can provide first-hand witness" (p. 101). This view is somewhat shaky however, especially in light of Jesus' rebuke concerning doubt in verse 25.

Dillon believes Luke sees doubt here to continue his misunderstanding theme; the disciples continue to misinterpret the passion and fail to recognize the fulfillment of Jesus' own predictions. Dillon's view seems reasonable; Luke's purpose like Mark's (16:8) shows how the human weakness of Jesus' followers can be overcome only through the power of the Risen Christ. Luke's comments generally are not as harsh as Mark's in describing the disciples but in these resurrection predictions he is even more critical than Mark (cf. 9:43f. and 18:32f.).

Verse 11 shows the worst side of the disciples to make the point that they will not believe until Christ appears, proving his living presence both physically (vv. 42—43) as well as spiritually (vv. 45f.). Only the "infallible proof" (Acts 1:3) of the Risen Lord is sufficient to overcome doubt.[15]

Peter's Reaction, 24:12

Verse 12 is quite controversial; many scholars dismiss it as another "western non-interpolation." They say it interrupts the nar-

---

15. This may say something about Luke's *Sitz im Leben*. He lived in a time when the eyewitnesses were to a great extent dead. Therefore, he stressed the similarity of the doubts of his own time to those of the disciples themselves, using what remained of the "witness" apologetic.

rative, is a bad adaptation of John 20:3—10, a poor contrast to Luke 24:24, and contains non-Lukan language (Grass, p. 34; Fuller, pp. 101f.; and Mahoney, pp. 53f.). Today, however, more and more scholars are favoring its authenticity (Jeremias, *EW*, pp. 149f.; Aland, pp. 205f.; Metzger, p. 184; Snodgrass, p. 373; Dillon pp. 59f.), especially since the discovery of p^{75} and further work on the internal dynamics of this chapter.[16]

Verse 12 clarifies the unbelief of the disciples stated in verse 11; the *thaumazōn* ("amazement") of Peter is reminiscent of the combination of amazement and lack of understanding Mark described all through his Gospel. The term also parallels the "amazement" (*exestēsan*) of the travelers who listened to the women's report in verse 11.[17]

Although the empty tomb produces wonder instead of faith, Luke's emphasis on it in verses 12, 22, and 24 and details about it (the "strips of linen lying by themselves") in v. 12 indicate its critical importance to the appearance and presence of the Risen Lord which alone produces faith. The empty tomb is thus the reality which lays the foundation for the first appearance. It may indeed mark a "shift of emphasis to the empty tomb" in the early church (Fuller). As the eyewitnesses began to pass from the scene, the empty tomb began to grow in importance as an objective apologetic alongside the other traditions. As yet it still produced "amazement" rather than faith but was a valid, important step in the correct direction.

Ellis calls Peter "the representative disciple" (p. 180). Luke, however, softens his portrait of Peter, especially in the accounts of Jesus' transfiguration and Peter's denial. The effect is less concen-

---

16. As Grundmann, p. 440; and Marshall, p. 888, state, the seeming contrast with verses 24 and 34 is the likely reason why it was omitted by several scribes. Most today accept a common tradition underlying both Luke and John, perhaps with Luke 24:12 a stage between the 1 Cor. 15:5f. tradition and the John 20:3f. tradition (so Alsup, p. 105) or, more likely, with Luke cognizant of the more complex tradition (Dillon, pp. 64f.). By employing the plural in verse 24, Luke demonstrates his awareness of the more complex tradition. His focus on Peter in verse 12 is a stylistic ploy, designed to draw attention to this concluding verse of the empty tomb narrative.

17. An interesting contrast lies between Dillon, pp. 76f., who sees in this a Lukan "passion secret," i.e., that Luke stressed the hiddenness and mystery of the empty tomb, and Fuller, pp. 106f., who argues that Luke here gives the empty tomb a greater apologetic force than Mark and with him it becomes "the primary cause of Easter faith." I believe that the answer lies between these two poles.

tration on the disciple's faults and more on his leadership.[18] At the tomb Peter is the only disciple who even admits the possible truth of the women's report. He jumps up and runs to the tomb, his action the first step toward faith. The way is thus open for Peter's reinstatement (v. 34) and leadership role in Acts.

The Emmaus Appearance, 24:13–35

The Setting

Amazingly, this beautiful narrative about Jesus' appearance to the Emmaus travelers was neglected by critics until very recently (see Dillon, pp. 69–82). During the past decade however, scholars have produced some excellent literature.

In this long pericope Luke uses two literary devices, a time-framework and geographical journey-sequence. The narrative begins with *en autē tē hōra* ("in this hour," v. 13) and ends with *autē tē hōra* ("this hour," v. 34), continuing the same-day theme already used in 23:54, 56 and 24:1. This theme meshes with the "third-day" motif of verses 7 and 21 as well as the time reference at the beginning introducing the meal scene in verse 29 (an important theological device, says Dillon [p. 85] in preparing for the eucharistic scene which follows).

The travel device or geographical journey sequence is even more obvious in the narrative. It is used especially in verses 13, 15, 17, 28, 32, 33, and 35 and parallels the earlier travel narrative of 9:51–19:10. As Jesus moves into the final stages of his messianic office at Jerusalem, his followers move away from their ministry of witness (from Jerusalem), then back again after their encounter with the Risen Christ (to Jerusalem). The movement away from and toward Jerusalem thus dramatizes the tension which lingered after the discovery of the empty tomb and became joyful anticipation after Christ appeared.

The section opens with two unnamed disciples who are "going"

18. In 9:33 = Mark 9:6 he removes the phrase "they were exceedingly afraid," and in 22:62 = Mark 14:72 he adds two elements, the searching glance of Jesus and the statement that Peter wept "bitterly." In both the effect is to diminish Peter's faults.

(the imperfect periphrastic *ēsan poreuomenoi* dramatically pictures the movement) to Emmaus which is "about seven miles from Jerusalem."[19] The distance note accents Luke's travel theme, as does his combination of dialogue and travel juxtaposing verbs like "talking" (vv. 14, 15), "conversing" (v. 15), and "walking along with" (v. 17). The imagery is a strong dramatic vehicle for Luke's misunderstanding theme; the travelers' repetitious recital of empty tomb events (vv. 22–24) which climaxes in the first half of the narrative and leads into Jesus' revelation of himself all take place within the framework of geographic movement. This device is not merely peripheral, but is crucial to the dialectic behind the entire narrative.

The pattern continues in the second half, although the emphasis shifts now from the travelers to Jesus. Verse 28 which contrasts the "approach" of the men with Jesus' desire to "go further" is resolved in verse 29; here the disciples plead with him to "stay" and he makes the decision to "enter in order to remain with them."

The table scene, of course, is the crucial point of the entire narrative; Jesus' true identity is revealed, even as the men remember how the "Scripture" he taught them on the road made their hearts "burn." The results of this encounter are their rapid return to Jerusalem and witness to the disciples there.

The travel theme in Luke is obviously important, but the question is whether it provides a vehicle for theology (Marshall) or is theological itself (Conzelmann). Although Luke implies that movement to and from Jerusalem has theological significance, this should not be overemphasized. Marshall's view is probably more acceptable than Conzelmann's; Luke's travel theme is an important vehicle for theology but not theological itself.

Tradition, Redaction, and Structure

Most critics find both tradition and redaction in the Emmaus narrative. Some (e.g., Stanton, *Gospels*, II, pp. 308ff.) think Luke

---

19. The mention of the distance to Emmaus is undoubtedly part of his accent on the travel form. The difficulties it causes for the archeological question related to the presence of the ancient village (i.e., is it the Maccabean town *Imwas*, 160 rather than 60 stadia from Jerusalem, or one of the other sites posited from time to time?) are not crucial to our discussion. For bibliography see Wanke, pp. 37f., and for a more recent discussion see Liefeld.

created the whole episode while others (e.g., Grass, p. 36) say he took the whole story from tradition, but most scholars agree with Schubert (p. 174) that a traditional core exists in verses 13, 15b – 16, and 28 – 31 even though Lukan language permeates the whole account. Attempts to separate tradition from redaction in the narrative have proved unnecessary as well as unprofitable, however; tradition is an integral part of, not peripheral to Luke's redactional message.

The passage's structural development is also debatable. Léon-Dufour (pp. 161 – 62) thinks the structure is a chiastic pattern[20] in concentric circles (vv. 13/33; 14/32; 15/31b; 16/31a) with further chiasm in the central dialogue section (17/29; 18 – 21/25 – 27 subdivided into 18/25, 19/25c, 20/26, 21/27; 22 – 23b/24) revolving around 23c ("He is alive"). Although Léon-Dufour's analysis of the two main sections (13 – 16, 31 – 33) can be substantiated linguistically, his more detailed attempts to establish the same for the central narrative section are too contrived. Whether the chiastic core is the resurrection statement of verses 23, 34, the scriptural proof of verse 26, or the discipleship test of verses 28 and 29,[21] the central section seems to be linear rather than chiastic.

Theological Motifs

Luke does not simply repeat a story; his touch is evident in every part. The journey "from" Jeusalem as the place of witness is heavy with defeat while the return "to" the place of witness is bright with victory. The resurrection in Luke is an integral part of God's redemptive plan. Mark and Matthew see it as the vindication and culmination of the passion while Luke views the events together, making the resurrection a transition from the redemptive

20. Similarly Jeanne D'Arc argues that the chiastic core is verse 26 (on the necessity of Jesus' suffering and glory) and B. van Iersel asserts that the critical mode is the test of verses 28 and 29. R. Meynet criticizes D'Arc for ignoring a second chiasm in 30 – 35 and states that the core is Jesus risen and alive (vv. 5, 23, 34).

21. A far less likely but nevertheless interesting approach is the structuralist attempt by X. Thévenot to take a Freudian look at the structure. He believes that Luke calls the reader to enter with the disciples into the world of symbol and there to encounter God. Luke thereby is saying that the linguistic world of metaphor is the answer to the sin of Adam and Eve. It appears to be another fine example of reading modern concerns into the ancient story.

act on the cross to the worldwide mission of the church. All of this is included within the movement to and from Jerusalem. Dillon comments (p. 94), "The church will live a strained existence which combines the *outward* paths of the world mission with the *return* to Jerusalem to embrace the prophetic destiny of the Master."

The dominant theme here is the reality of the resurrection. Every other motif leads to this one, Luke having carefully prepared for it in his resurrection narrative. He even omits the Galilean prediction from the angel's message at the tomb, knowing his account would show how Christ appeared to many under quite different circumstances. The tension created by the disciples who doubted, then wondered about the message of the empty tomb, continues into the Emmaus story where men who walk with Jesus and listen to his teaching still fail to recognize him. The suspense builds until the climax where Christ reveals himself through the Eucharist and Word to the men whose eyes are "opened" so that they recognize him. Liefeld says Luke continues his witness theme here; "Two witnesses bear testimony to the arrival of the Messiah, Simeon and Anna (2:25−38), and the two travelers now testify to this resurrection appearance (24:35)." This secondary theme is a part of Luke's primary theme.

The Nonrecognition vs. Recognition Motif

This motif is commonly thought to be the primary thrust of the Emmaus story (Dodd, Schubert, Wilckens, Wanke). Several scholars have noted the story strongly parallels hellenistic cult legends which tell about the recognition of strangers and thus call Luke's account a legendary creation (Bultmann, Dibelius, Grass, especially Betz). But Marshall ("Resurrection," p. 84) counters this by showing the parallels are more analogical than genealogical; Luke's narration is simply too rich to fit into such a narrow category.

Nonrecognition though, is the major focus of the first half of the narrative. The wayfarers are returning home from Jerusalem and "debating" what happened in the passion and empty tomb. Their confusion is a marked contrast to Jesus in 9:51−19:10, who purposefully sets off toward Jerusalem, his Kingdom purpose firmly in mind.

Dillon comments (p. 145): "This picture-passion instruction framed in a 'journey' is the structure of the central gospel chapters all over again! The unknown Emmaus disciples are being caused to recapitulate the path already charted by the evangelist, evidently because they are put forth as representatives of the vast body of believers gathered about the nucleus of the historic Twelve."

The first critical point in the story comes in verse 16 when Jesus asks the men, "what are you discussing?" Their failure to recognize him is much different from Mary's failure to recognize the "gardener" in John 20:14f.; here the reason for blindness is not sorrow's tears but a God-ordained closing "that they might not recognize him." Marshall says this blindness is like "the similar blinding of the disciples with respect to the prophecies of the passion in 9:45 and 18:34, where it is clearly God who produces the blindness" ("Resurrection," p. 83).[22]

The structural purpose here is difficult to determine even though the message is quite simple. In spite of Jesus' teaching (9:45; 18:34) and message of the empty tomb by the women (24:1–12), the disciples fail to realize the truth, primarily because the divinely chosen moment has not arrived (24:16). That moment of truth comes in two stages, the Word and the Eucharist, both of which focus attention on the real presence of the Risen Christ.

Still, the purpose of this message is not so clear. Did Luke write this narrative to show that only the living presence of the Risen Lord could make faith possible? Then why did he choose a story that was so different from those of the other Gospel writers?

Perhaps a better reason for Luke's choice here is that this recognition scene is a transition to the mission of Acts. The gradual unfolding of revelation thus connects vertically to God's control of salvation-history and horizontally to the church's mission. The next section further demonstrates this point; God permits blindness only until the time is ripe. In the fullness of time eyes are opened via the proclamation of the Word and breaking of bread.

The Interpretive Word

Luke's ecclesiastical emphasis is quite different from Matthew and Mark's christological view of the resurrection. Luke says the

---

22. This revelation of the hidden glory of the Messiah is a key to the entire episode, for the presence of divine passives in verse 31 (their eyes "were opened") and verse 35 (he "was made known" to them) controls the key revelatory points. The latter verb, egnōsthē, also occurs in each of these pivotal passages: in verse 16 they are kept from "recognizing" him (epiginōskein) then in verses 31 and 35 their eyes are opened and they "recognize" him through the "breaking of bread."

event is glorious because of its results (proclamation and fellowship). The living presence of Jesus in the community is what counts, a point which Betz ("Emmaus") stresses when he says the purpose of the story is cultic, to present the "living" Jesus who is recognized and experienced in both language event and the eucharistic fellowship of the church.

The "word" is central to the dialogue of verses 17−27, clearly the longest section of the Emmaus narrative. It is more than a prelude to the eucharistic scene; the first half (vv. 18−24) actually recapitulates the passion and empty tomb within the framework of two themes, redemption and prophetic-Messiah. The misunderstanding of the disciples continues, however, even as they discuss the events they expect an eschatological redeemer rather than a suffering Messiah. In fact, they expect a Messiah who would live out a dual role[23] as Mosaic prophet as well as Davidic King. Their "downcast" looks in verse 18 are evidence of their disappointments as they walk away from Jerusalem.

Jesus meets their sorrow head-on; forcing them to look at "all" the prophets wrote, which included an explicit portrait of the suffering Messiah. Jesus had to become suffering servant-Messiah before he could become the glorious "prophet" of expectation. Salvation had to be won before glory could be realized.

Many scholars (Dupont, Grassi, Wanke, Marshall, Dillon) have noted parallels between this pericope and that of the Ethiopian eunuch in Acts 8:26−39. Both include the same kind of dialogue, feature a search for spiritual understanding with strangers (Jesus and Phillip), and reveal the truth about the suffering Messiah from the Scriptures. The emphasis of both stories is also the same: the Word is essential to God's plan of salvation.

Verse 19's description of Jesus as a "prophet, powerful in word and deed before God and all the people" has prompted some debate. Léon-Dufour (p. 204), Wanke (pp. 60f.), and Johnson (pp. 84f.) say the words are negative, Luke's emphasis here being the dis-

---

23. See Kuhn, "Two Messiahs"; and Braun, "Messianologie." Marshall, *Luke—Historian*, pp. 127f., asserts that Luke combines the role of prophet and Messiah. Actually, this does not conflict with our thesis; both are correct. The roles are indeed combined in the person of Jesus but differentiated in the ongoing process of salvation-history. The suffering Messiah of the passion and the exalted prophet of the resurrection-parousia are interconnected and interdependent; yet the latter comes via the former, and this is Luke's clarification in this scene.

ciples' failure to understand Jesus' true role. Fuller (p. 110) and Dillon (pp. 117f.), however, believe the words are positive, looking to the eschatological prophet. Perhaps both views are correct; Jesus as "prophet mighty in deed" summarizes what he said about himself in 4:18−19 as the fulfillment of Isaiah 61:1−2: "The spirit of the Lord is on me, because he has anointed me to preach good news to the poor. . . ." It also brings to mind verses such as 4:24; 7:16; and 9:7f. where Jesus is thought to be a "great prophet." The Emmaus travelers, however, do not use the words with full understanding, and it is this lack of understanding that Jesus corrects in verse 26.[24] Jesus as prophet could be fully known only through his role as suffering servant since, as Liefeld says, "the term prophet was inadequate . . . an incomplete description of Jesus." Franklin comes closer in his ascription of lordship to the Christology of Luke 24.

The same kind of discussion revolves around verses 20−21a, some critics stressing Jesus' description as "redeemer of Israel" in a positive sense while others note the incomplete understanding of the disciples. Although some scholars differ on the literal meaning of "Israel" here (believing Jews or the church as the "new Israel"), Luke's emphasis here really centers on Jesus' mission. He will not accept the disciples' faulty role of political Messiah to "redeem Israel" the way they expect him to. Instead he will follow God's sovereign plan which includes the way of suffering, death, and resurrection. The same misunderstanding occurs here as in Acts 1:6−8, where the Lord again refuses to accept the role of political Messiah. Luke continues to build to the explanation of

24. Dillon's portrait of the theme (pp. 121−26) has a lot to commend itself. Stephen's speech does connect the Mosaic prototype with suffering and martyrdom (Acts 7:22, 35−36, 51−52) in an obvious parallel with Jesus, and Peter's Pentecost sermon does connect Jesus' miraculous ministry with his rejection and crucifixion by the nation (Acts 2:22, 36). However, while he correctly recognizes the crucial importance of Jesus' interpretive word to Luke's scheme, he erroneously attributes the full-blown understanding to the disciples' statement in verses 19f. The clarification comes in Jesus' corrective teaching of verse 26. Therefore Wanke is also correct that verse 19 centers on misunderstanding and the prophet image must be understood via the suffering servant motif. The disciples (and undoubtedly many of Luke's readers) failed to understand this vital interdependence. Dillon, p. 128, argues that only verse 20 "reflects the travellers' deficient understanding of their Master," since it contains language reminiscent of the passion predictions but without a realization of their significance. However, we believe that this produces an unnecessary dichotomy; it fails to realize how verse 19 is corrected by verses 26f., e.g., verse 27, where Luke significantly has Jesus "beginning with Moses and all the prophets" in his complete explanation of "the things concerning himself."

verses 26f. "Redeem Israel" thereby speaks on two levels: Jesus would not "redeem" in the way they expected but in the way sovereignly chosen by God, through the passion and resurrection.

Verses 21b−24 review what Luke said earlier about the empty tomb, adding the words "but him they did not see" as an inclusion with verse 12 to bring the reader to a state of tension and anticipation which will be alleviated only by Jesus' words in verses 25f. Luke also uses the phrase "third day" in this passage, probably to emphasize the true significance of the resurrection events. Most critics believe he borrowed the phrase more from general Old Testament passages on the Day of Salvation than any single reference to the resurrection.[25]

The definitive word is spoken in verses 25−27. The vocabulary is like that of other passion prediction passages (7, 44), but the reproach of the Risen Christ is even more severe than the angel's words at the tomb. "How foolish you are," says Jesus, "and how slow of heart to believe all that the prophets have spoken!" Dillon (p. 133) says the whole theme of secrecy in Luke comes to climax in this passage where the "purposeful schedule of concealment and disclosure, divinely appointed," concludes with Jesus' "personal gift" of the revelation of himself in all his glory. Dillon is only partially correct, however; Jesus' full revelation comes later in the "breaking of the bread" (vv. 28−31).

Both "third day" (v. 21) and "enter into glory" (v. 26) emphasize resurrection as the fulfillment of prophecy, an emphasis which meshes well with Luke's total view of Jesus' ministry. The event was foreordained by God and foretold by the prophets, and, according to Luke, truly understood only within the context of the sacrificial meaning of his death. The other Gospel writers viewed the cross through the empty tomb, but Luke views the empty tomb through the cross. Christ's post-resurrection "glory" is thus part of the passion and provides a transition to the proclamation of the early church.

Jesus uses the word *all* three times ("all that the prophets have

25. While some, like Gunkel or Bousset, believe that it originated from the mystery religions, the parallels are inexact and the evidence is too late. Also, the argument for Hosea 6:2 cannot go beyond mere possibility, since there is no other evidence for its use in the early church. The same is true of a Jonah analogy, which is probably only part of a larger theme (see Bode, pp. 114−16). Both Hosea 6:2 and Jonah 2:1 belong to a general teaching regarding God's salvation (so Bode, Hooke, Dillon).

spoken," v. 25; "all the prophets," and "all the Scriptures," v. 27), emphasizing the universal or complete message of the passion and resurrection. As Liefeld states, "It shows that the sufferings of Christ as well as his glory, were predicted in the Old Testament, and *all* the Old Testament Scriptures are important."

The Breaking of Bread

This passage includes a dramatic recognition scene. The scene begins with Jesus' "pretending" or "acting as if" *(prospoieomai)* he intends to continue on his way, but his purpose here is surely theatrical; Marshall says *(Luke,* p. 897), "on one level of understanding he intends to stay with them" but on another level he confronts them with the need to invite him in. Perhaps the structural development of the narrative indicates that "only those who desire his (Jesus) company will come to further realization of his identity" (Danker, *New Age,* p. 250). The primary impetus in the recognition drama may be God's (cf. the divine passives in vv. 16, 31, 32 already discussed), but man also needs to act.

The breaking of bread scene (v. 30) reminds us of other "meals" in Luke. Although no single theological emphasis emerges from these eight scenes,[26] the concept of "table fellowship"[27] (sharing and teaching) is evident in all of them. The table scenes also suggest the following emphases: (1) *soteriological;* Jesus symbolizes God's forgiveness and acceptance of sinners through the act of eating and drinking with them (cf. Luke 5:27f.; 15:1f.; 19:1f.; see Marshall, *Luke—Historian,* pp. 138f.); (2) *social;* the "kerygma enters a particular social environment, opens it up to hear the gospel aright and transforms it into a parable of God's new creation" (14:7f.; 22:31f.; see Flender, pp. 80f.); (3) *mission instruction;* Jesus' "instruction concerning his person and mission" to his own disciples invites their participation, or "the Master breaking bread with his

26. There are simple meals (7:36, 11:37, 14:1), a feast (5:29), a miracle (9:16), a cultic celebration (22:14), teaching about a wedding feast (14:8f.) and the eschatological banquet of the last days (12:37, 13:29). This theme is also suggested in the debate with the leaders (15:1) and the Zaccheus incident (19:1f.).

27. We cannot agree with Jeremias, *EW,* pp. 118−22, that the *koinōnia* of Acts 2:42 separates table "fellowship" from the eucharist as one of the four foundations of early Christian worship. Rather, it seems probable that the communal sharing stressed in 2:42−47 is in view.

followers is the Master sharing his mission and destiny with them"
(Luke 9:10f.; 22:24f.; Acts 20:7f.; 27:33f.; see Dillon, pp. 105f.).

One term must be clarified before we evaluate these emphases.
"Breaking of bread" in Luke was a Semitic phrase which meant the
beginning of a meal. The father, or head of the house, broke bread
after the blessing to begin the meal. The Books of Acts says this
phrase was used first to describe the fellowship meal, and later
the cultic celebration of the Eucharist connected with it (Acts 2:42,
46; 20:7; cf. 1 Cor. 11:20). Is the "breaking of bread" in Luke 24:30
like the feeding of the 5,000 (messianic rather than eucharistic), or
like the Eucharist itself? Critics differ widely on the point, but
whatever approach is accepted does not minimize the importance
of Jesus breaking the bread precisely at the moment of recognition
(vv. 31, 35), thus placing it at the critical point of the narrative. In
terms of literary connections, the evidence favors the Luke 9 parallel (see Dillon, pp. 149f.); but as he admits, we cannot rule out
eucharistic theology in the feeding pericope as well. On the whole,
the technical use of the term in Acts suggests that any first-century
reader would connect the term with the Eucharist. Wanke says
(pp. 104f.) that though Luke's account definitely parallels the feeding miracle, it also definitely features the Eucharist in the recognition scene itself.

A social interpretation of this meal scene seems doubtful since
Luke's account does not include a social setting. A soteriological
emphasis seems more likely since Jesus extends fellowship, but
the third interpretation (mission instruction) is the most appropriate due to the structure of the passage. The word and the bread
are the means to mission. Luke wants to show that the presence
of the Lord in teaching and eucharistic fellowship empowers the
church for participation in Jesus' mission to the lost (cf. Luke
19:10). Verse 32 graphically illustrates this point; the disciples' hearts
"burned within" them when Jesus "opened the Scriptures" in the
recognition experience.[28] Mission is the result of this recogni-

---

28. A number of scholars (Danker, Dillon) identify it more closely with the feeding of
the 5,000 in 9:11–17 and therefore find messianic significance rather than eucharistic
force (Dillon sees the eucharistic as secondary but still present); the meal scene is the
revelation of Jesus as the Messiah. Others (Marshall, Jeremias, Dupont, Orlett) see the
eucharist as primary. Jeremias asserts (EW, p. 120n.) that the recognition "in" the breaking
of bread (v. 35) does not mean a characteristic way of performing the act (instrumental
en, "by") but the meaning he imparted to the act itself (temporal en, "during"). Thus he

tion as the disciples rush back to Jerusalem to tell the Eleven about the Risen Christ.[29]

Verses 33—35 tell about that triumphant return "to Jerusalem." Verse 33 combines both temporal ("at that same hour") and geographical ("to Jerusalem") factors. The result of recognition is mission; both are linked with the resurrection and Jerusalem as the starting point for the church's outreach.

Verse 35 stresses the importance of the word and bread in the disciples' recognition of Jesus "on the way." Verse 34 (which reflects v. 12) in this context seems a bit strange, a seeming contradiction to verses 33 and 35 in its implication that the faith of the Eleven rose not from the witness of the Emmaus travelers as much as Jesus' appearance to Peter. Why does Luke insert this information here? Some attempt to get around the problem by reading the statements as questions: "Has the Lord really risen, and has he appeared to Simon?" However, the wording makes that unlikely, and most correctly recognize them to be statements.

Most likely the verse was written to affirm the reality of the resurrection through this bold affirmation from the Eleven, who came to faith *while* the events on the road to Emmaus were taking place. Peter is the key here, Luke using him at crucial junctures (vv. 12, 34) to verify the empty tomb as well as living presence of Christ. Verse 12 sets the tempo of tension as the disciples refuse to believe while verse 34 breaks the tension in a striking announcement of belief which adds force to the reality of the resurrection.

Verse 35 anchors this newborn faith in the presence of the Lord expressed in both the Word and bread. The symbols, in fact, point ahead to church worship; "In the reading of Scripture and at the breaking of bread the Risen Lord will continue to be present, though unseen" (Dillon, pp. 100f.). The primary message here, however, is the awakening of faith. In this context Luke wrote the verse for three probable reasons: (1) Jesus' followers needed to understand the sacrificial meaning of his death (via the Word, vv. 25—27, and the symbolic meal, v. 30) before they could appreciate

---

changed the simple meal into a holy meal. The disciples knew him because he transformed the meal into one like the last supper (22:14f.). Dupont (p. 90f.) states that Jesus actually gave the eucharist to the disciples.

29. We would not go so far as Dillon in positing "the self-image of itinerant Christian missionaries of the early years" (p. 153) behind the entire milieu of the stranger hosted at meal.

the full glory of his resurrection. (2) They needed to be assured that Jesus had forgiven their desertion at the time of his death and the symbolic table fellowship readmitted them "into the old fellowship" (Jeremias, p. 204). (3) This readmittance meant they were to continue Jesus' witness, empowered by the reality of the resurrection.

The Appearance to the Eleven, 24:36—49

The Appearance Itself, vv. 36—43

In these next verses Luke confronts the reader with the physical reality of the resurrection. Although the pericope sounds much like John 20:19—23, the differences in the accounts highlight Luke's redaction. Dodd ("Essay," pp. 17f.) calls this pericope "a piece of controverisal apologetic" which relates Luke's doubt motif to the problems of his day. It is "an example of the 'concise' type of narrative in which apologetic motives have caused everything else to be subordinated to an elaborate presentation."

"While they were speaking these things" provides the transition from the Emmaus story to this one, a temporal link which also appears in John's account. This "same-day" theme creates an atmosphere of tension and suspense; Jesus suddenly "stands" in the midst of the disciples. They respond with fear, as they did earlier when the two angels suddenly "stood" before them.

Jesus greets them with "Peace be with you," the words so much like John 20:19 that most critics think Luke borrowed it from him. Others, however, disagree, for the same reasons elucidated above on v. 12. Some (e.g., Léon-Dufour) who accept its authenticity believe it has no special purpose but was simply inserted woodenly from tradition. Dillon, however, says (p. 187) the message of peace has a distinct purpose in the structure; it even implies a sense of mission since it parallels the "peace" given by the seventy-two in their witness endeavors (10:5f.) and unites "peace-greeting and kingdom-heralding."

Dillon stretches the point a bit; the structural need for the greeting is perhaps enough reason for its usage here.[30] After the disciples affirm belief in the Risen Lord in verse 34 and have that belief corroborated by the witness of the Emmaus travelers in verse 35, Jesus suddenly stands among them. They are "startled" (a Lukan word used only here and 21:9 in the New Testament) and "afraid" (another Lukanism, cp. 24:5, 37; Acts 10:4; 24:25), thinking that they are seeing a ghost.

Jesus meets this fear and doubt head-on in verse 38. He asks why they are troubled and have "questionings" in their minds, "questionings" another Lukan term connoting hostile doubts regarding Jesus' person (2:35; 5:22; 6:8) or foolish strife with little purpose (9:46, 47). Jesus clearly says here that his disciples have disappointed him with their lack of faith. Even after he shows them his hands and feet, verse 41 says they still "disbelieved for joy and wondered."[31] Luke's doubt motif reaches full expression in this passage.

Jesus beautifully condescends to the needs of his disciples who find it so difficult to assimilate the truth. Verses 39 and 40[32] tell how he proves he is not a "spirit"; both sight *(idete)* and touch *(psēlaphēsate)* should convince them. Marshall ("Resurrection," p. 49) says Jesus' imperatives have two purposes here: (1) to prove that he is the same Jesus who was crucified by showing his nail-scarred hands and feet; (2) to prove he is not a spirit by letting his disciples touch the "flesh and bones" of his body. Verses 41b—43 offer even more evidence; Jesus proves he is real by eating a "piece of broiled fish."[33] Luke's narrative thus provides not only a three-

30. Verses 34—36 are a singular set on the reality of the resurrection, opening with the apostolic testimony (v. 34) and corroborating witness (v. 35) already discussed. With the sudden appearance and messianic peace-promise here, the turning point seems to have been reached. Then the jarring reappearance of the doubt motif comes in verse 37, and this deliberately prepares for the true *piece de resistance* in verse 38, the corporeal proof of the resurrection. This seeming contradiction of the peace-promise returns once again to the disbelief of verse 11.

31. Here one notes a diminishing of the doubt theme. The disciples want to believe in the midst of their joy (see further v. 52) but cannot. The result is "wonder" or, as Grundmann says (p. 451), "joyful, bewildered wonder." He adds that "disbelieved for joy" is a perfect Lukan antithesis to 22:45, "sleeping for sorrow."

32. Verse 40 is another "western non-interpolation" often dismissed as an assimilation to John 20:20. However, as Metzger asserts (p. 187) if it had come from there, "copyists would probably have left some trace of its origin by retaining *tēn pleuran* in place of *tous podas.*" See also Aland and Snodgrass.

33. While the patristic period saw this is a eucharistic sense (evidenced in the "and from a honeycomb," added in several old manuscripts, with honey used in the eucharist), this is unlikely here. The apologetic sense is primary.

fold development of doubt but also a threefold answer to that doubt in apologetic proof. Luke may have done this because of his stress on legal witness; a response to the Jewish legal demand for "two or three witnesses."[34]

He may have also included it because of a docetic threat to his church, a heresy which stressed the incorporeality of Jesus' resurrection body. This may be a too-specific rationale, however. Marshall says (Luke, p. 900) the passage "is not concerned to refute docetism in the proper sense of that term, since it is concerned with the nature of the Risen Jesus and not with the nature of the earthly Jesus. Its point is to stress the identity of the Risen One with Jesus and to emphasize the physical reality of the resurrection body." It does seem more likely that the purpose deals not so much with countering false ideas as showing beyond doubt that the Crucified One has become the Risen One.

The entire pericope (vv. 36–49) also includes a strong missionary emphasis, functioning as a bridge between Luke's Gospel and Acts. Verses 36–43 prepare the reader for the mission thrust of verses 44–49, and that section anticipates what will happen in the Book of Acts. Says Hubbard ("Role," p. 198), "the epiphanic commissioning accounts ... occur at decisive places throughout the narrative in such a way that God's hand is continually seen as making possible each new step in the missionary program of the book. Acts is a success story made possible by divine intervention."[35]

34. Talbert (Gnostics, pp. 14, 23f.) shows that this witness theme is primarily a Lukan emphasis and includes many aspects of the resurrection narrative, e.g., the stress on the "Galilean" followers (23:49, 55; 24:6) and the accent on "apostles" (24:10); see also Grundmann, p. 449; Lightfoot, Locality, pp. 86f.; Loisy, Birth, pp. 48f. Käsemann, "Questions," p. 21, calls Luke "the first representative of nascent early Catholicism," which he defines as "nothing but the church's defense mechanism in the face of the threat of a gnostic takeover" (cf. his "Early Catholicism," pp. 206–51). Contra Marshall, "Early Catholicism."

35. Several recent articles (two by Hubbard and one by Mullins) have applied the Old Testament commission formula to 24:36–49 and several in Acts. While certain details are overdone (Hubbard, for instance, often forces evidence to fit his general pattern) certain similarities do seem too striking to be merely chance.

The basic pattern does fit this pericope, although the order is different and verses 36–43 go beyond it to stress primarily the reality of the resurrection, as we have already said. Both Mullins and Hubbard note the recurring pattern: (1) Introduction, which in Luke and Acts usually includes time and/or place along with a reference to standing (v. 36a); the temporal and geographical references, of course, predominate throughout the entire chapter. (2) Reaction and reassurance—interestingly here the startling reversal of the normal pattern (via the presence of the peace-promise before the reaction of fear)

This conclusion is enhanced if we agree that verses 42−43 stress table fellowship. While Dillon (pp. 200f.) sets this in contrast to an "apologetic" thrust of the episode (as stated above), we do not believe that this is so. The table fellowship, like the mission form of the whole narrative, is enhanced and deepened by the stress on the reality of the resurrection. As we stated with regard to the similar theme in verses 28−31, table fellowship in Luke is soteriological, centering upon Jesus' forgiveness and acceptance of those sharing the repast with him. Jesus extends forgiveness to those who are soon to be sent out to extend "forgiveness" to the lost world.[36]

The Commission, vv. 44−49

Verses 44−49 are a combination of tradition and redaction, parts of which seem to be a kerygmatic development of tradition since the form is similar to sermons in Acts. It blends with the "great commission" tradition of verse 47 (like Matt. 28:19 and John 20:21) and "spirit" tradition of verse 49 (like John 20:22), but is not necessarily a free Lukan composition. The form instead probably took shape well before Luke's Gospel. As Benoit says (*Passion*, pp. 277f.), Luke follows the catechetical teaching of the early church "in order to describe a real conversation, but one of which there

appears at first glance to break the pattern; however, that serves to heighten the true "reassurance" which comes by way of the physical proof pattern elucidated above. (3) The "commission" itself (vv. 44−48) concludes with a statement of assurance (p. 49). (4) The conclusion (vv. 50−53) suggests future blessing and power. Themes which are missing include the stress on a voice or vision, the command to rise or stand, and the mention of prayer. It is true, of course, that no single passage contains every element; and the similarities add probability to their thesis, especially when one considers the Old Testament commission form behind it (see Hubbard, *Matthean Redaction*, for a detailed discussion; and for a chart of passages in Luke and Acts in this respect, see his "Role," pp. 190, 193).

36. This is much more likely than the more extended interpretation by Dillon, who expands the table fellowship scene itself to a commission narrative, i.e., "the continuation of Jesus' earthly ministry in the mission of his witnesses" (p. 202). That is extended in verse 47; here Jesus' acceptance of *them* becomes a model and preparation for that mission.

was no shorthand record," describing "only what was probably said" in "the exact terms of catechesis."[37]

Scriptural Fulfillment

Verses 44–46 includes Luke's third recapitulation of passion predictions. A few terms, however, are unique to this passage. Verse 44, for instance, includes the first explicit use of *plērousthai* ("fulfill"); here divine "necessity" (*dei*) is directly connected to the idea of "fulfillment" which "must" occur. This term closely links the ideas of passion, resurrection, and mission which are central to Luke's Gospel as a transition to Acts.[38]

Jesus names "the Law of Moses, the Prophets and the Psalms" in verse 44, specifically reminding the disciples of all the Old Testament prophecies that were written about him and thus had to be fulfilled by him. The fact that this is the only place in the New Testament where a writer felt constrained to mention the psalms alongside the other two sections shows just how much stress Luke gives this theme here. Two types of fulfillment are juxtaposed here—Jesus' words and the Old Testament witness about him— yet the two are synonymous; Jesus' teachings were the fulfillment of the Old Testament.

Now the Master "opens the minds" of his disciples so they can "understand" Scripture, bringing to a climax the doubt motif of 30f. What they understand now is all of the Scriptures in light of Christ's full mission. The "opening" of their "eyes" in verse 32 is

---

37 Rigaux, p. 275, believes that it is primarily Lukan, while Alsup, pp. 182f., argues for mostly tradition. Dillon, pp. 203f., takes a mediating position, asserting that the commission in some form (though reworked by Luke) was traditional (cf. John 20:21f.) but that the trappings (e.g., the prophecy fulfillment saying in vv. 44f.) are Lukan. We would agree more with Marshall and Benoit that the language favors tradition behind the whole. See further on this section in chapter 7.

38. 1 Corinthians 15:3–5 demonstrates how crucial the fulfillment proof was to the primitive church's conception of the resurrection. Dillon (pp. 205f.) points to the connection of *dei* with Isaiah 53:12 in the Last Supper scene (22:37, also Lukan) and its connection with "the global realization of all prophecy" in the "mission directive" of Jesus (22:35). The thematic-conceptual parallels between that passage and this indeed provide a plausible reference point here. In that scene Jesus is preparing the disciples for the difficult conditions and the opposition they are soon to face, using both the mission (v. 35, pointing back to 10:3f.) and his imminent suffering (v. 37 = Isa. 53:12) as examples. Jesus' divinely necessitated suffering and mission which concludes the Last Supper scene now commences the commission here.

thus completed with the "opening" of their "minds" in verse 45. Redemption is now complete; Jesus' disciples are ready for mission.[39]

The Mission Commission

Verses 47–49 includes the word *kēruchthē nai* ("preach") which is the third infinitive complementing *houtōs gegraptai* ("written thus"). The use of the term is significant, meaning that Christ's suffering, resurrection, and mission are all linked to prophetic fulfillment and are therefore combined aspects of the divine plan.[40]

39. The details in verse 46 summarize a final time the kerygma of verses 7 and 26. Only "from the dead" is new as "suffer" is found in both; "Christ" has already appeared in verse 26 as the replacement of "Son of God" in verse 7; and "rise on the third day" repeats verse 7. Since "from the dead" is found so often in Acts (cf. 3:15; 10:41, etc.) it again functions as a transition to the Easter message as crucial to early church kerygma. Kurz's thesis (pp. 180–82) that Luke's argument from scriptural proof to conclusion in verses 27 and 45f. stems from hellenistic laws of rhetoric (especially the Aristotelian enthymeme, a rhethorical form of syllogism proceeding from minor premise to major premise to conclusion) is interesting but inconclusive; (1) he admits that the major and minor premises are reversed in the two passages; (2) the many scholars who point to similarities with Jewish forms of exegesis (see 182n) make it less valid to posit a mainly Hellenistic background; and (3) his arguments that Luke had such training are speculative.

40. Several argue that verse 47 reflects Mark 13:10, deliberately left out of Luke 21:13 (so Hahn, *Mission*, pp. 103f.; Dillon, pp. 208f.; Wilson, *Mission*, p. 47). However, while there is a distinct conceptual link, we doubt that Luke deliberately omitted it in his eschatological discourse in order to include it here. Doublets have not disturbed him elsewhere (e.g., vv. 7, 26, 46 of this chapter alone!) It is more likely that the mission command is based on resurrection tradition (cp. John 20:21f.) but like verse 46 is couched in catechetical language.

Many plausible explanations may be posited to explain the omission, perhaps due to his following a different source in chapter 21 (as Marshall, *Luke*, p. 766 states, only vv. 12, 17 show linguistic affinities with Mark 13), or perhaps because Luke was writing before AD 70. Conzelmann believes Luke desired to separate the mission from the Eschaton, primarily due to Conzelmann's views of salvation history in Luke. Wilson's modification (p. 47) is more plausible, that by failing to stress the connection, Luke removes the obstacle for providing a history of the mission in his second volume.

The link with Old Testament prophecy is manifold, and the New Testament characteristically links the universal mission to Old Testament prophecy (e.g., Acts 2:5, 10:35; Rom. 9:24f., 10:12f.; etc.) drawing on such passages as Isaiah 42:6, 49:6; Joel 2:1 and for beginning in Jerusalem Isaiah 2:2f. par. Micah 4:1f. (see Marshall, *Luke—Historian*, p. 906). However, it may be more a theological theme than specific passages which are in mind here. Hahn and Wilson both link the mission with the Lukan promise/fulfillment emphasis, which Wilson argues (pp. 53f.) provides the framework for Luke's scheme of salvation history. "In this manner Luke makes it clear that the inclusion of the Gentiles is not the result of a mere quirk of history or a whim of God; rather, it is grounded in the eternal will of God and is an integral part of his promises to Israel."

The blend of mission with soteriology in this passage is also significant; Jesus links mission preaching with "repentance and forgiveness of sins." These three elements are a succinct synopsis of Luke's salvation theme; Marshall (*Luke—Historian*, pp. 192 – 95) as well as Navone ("Conversion," pp. 38 – 46) explain what role they play.

1. *Metanoia* ("repentance") is a crucial element in Luke, demonstrated, for instance, in Jesus' words, "I have not come to call the righteous but sinners" (5:32; cf. 13:3f.; 15:7f.; 16:30; 17:3f.). Luke uses the noun and verb for repentance twenty-five times in his two books, the term implying both a negative act (turning from sin in Luke 22:32: Acts 3:26; 8:22f.) as well as positive one (turning to God and taking expression in righteous deeds in Acts 3:19f.; 19:1f., 18; 26:20). Repentance means a change of heart which results in changed behavior.[41]

2. *Aphesis* ("forgiveness of sins") is God's response to repentance and includes acceptance by God. "Forgiveness of sins" is a special Lukan phrase seldom used elsewhere in the New Testament. Luke uses it in his Gospel frequently, building on John the Baptist imagery (1:77; 3:3) to stress the fulfillment of the "baptism of repentance for the forgiveness of sins" in the fact that Jesus forgives (5:17f.), thus "assuming," says Marshall (*Luke—Historian*, p. 138), "the prerogative of God." Luke then uses the term in Acts to show the results of salvation (2:38; 5:31; 10:43; 13:38; 26:18), a stress which was also used in the prophets where God demanded sacrifices from the heart and linked forgiveness with them. Note Jesus' use of Isaiah 61:1f. in his inaugural message (Luke 4:18f.); the idea of forgiveness appears twice. Forgiveness of sins is the goal of mission which is linked eschatologically to prophetic fulfillment (e.g., Acts 10:43).

---

41. With *epistrephō* in several of these passages, Conzelmann (pp. 99f.) equates the two verbs, concluding that Luke changed the religious concept into an ethical code of conduct. Marshall (p. 194) shows he errs because the two are not synonymous in Luke. Rather, the change in behavior results from a change of heart. Navone (pp. 45f.) correctly notes the interplay between the eschatological side of repentance (i.e., its connection with the coming of the Kingdom in the Gospel [3:10f.; 13:3f.; 15:16f.] and with the future parousia in Acts [3:19f.; 10:42; 17:30f.]) and the salvation history stress (i.e., the role of conversion in the church's mission, as men face God through the preaching of the Word [Acts 3:8; 5:32; 15:7f., etc.]). This structure is especially evident in the speeches in Acts, with their recurrent pattern "from the Jesus kerygma to the appeal to repent, then baptism 'in the name of Jesus' (Acts 2, 38; 8, 16), forgiveness bestowed by the power of the 'Name' (Acts 10, 43; 13, 38) and reception of the Holy Spirit (Acts 2, 38; 8, 17; 11, 15)" (Dillon, p. 213).

3. *Keruchtēnai* ("preaching") is to be done *epi tō onomati autou* ("in his name"). In Acts preaching is the first step to conversion, presupposing both hearing and belief resulting from hearing. Marshall (*Luke—Historian*, p. 192) notes the strong link between preaching and hearing in Acts which is the basis for both repentance and forgiveness.

Preaching must be done, says Jesus, "in his name." Conzelmann says (p. 177) this phrase stresses the need for Jesus' presence and power in the church. Dillon says (p. 210) this "name formula" is used in every stage of the Lord's ministry in Luke and Acts and means the extension of Christ's ministry to his followers via mission. That mission moves forward both in "the wondrous ministrations that display his powerful, saving presence, and the suffering which fosters the spread of his message, waxing stronger in the face of mightier opposition." Jesus alone can provide the power and authority to proclaim and perform divine realities: preaching, miracles, and persecution "in his name" means the eschatological sharing of his ministry.

Jesus also specifies preaching must be done "to all nations," *arxamenoi apo Ierousalēm* ("beginning at Jerusalem"). The addition here is purely Lukan (found here and Acts 1:8 in the resurrection narratives), and its purpose is obvious; it emphasizes the origin of the mission.[42] Luke, more than any other evangelist, stresses the evangelization of Israel. He shows how the Jews rejected the Messiah (following synoptic tradition) and how that gave impetus to the mission to the Gentiles,[43] but always he refuses to exclude Israel in the ongoing evangelism program of the church. In fact, he takes special pains to show how both Jews and Gentiles are a part of God's plan. Kodell ("*Laos*," pp. 327f.) does an in-depth study of people in Luke's Jerusalem narrative and concludes that Luke stresses the guilt of the leaders in crucifying

42. As Liefeld points out, there is a link here with prophetic expectation, for Isaiah 42:6; 49:6; 60:3 point to the coming of the gentiles and "may underlie verse 42 here." This is fulfilled in the use of "repent ... forgiven" in Acts 2:38; 10:43; 17:30.

43. Cf. Luke 2:34; 4:16f.; Acts 13:45; 14:2; 28:28; etc. Talbert, *Gnostics*, pp. 441f.; and Ellis, pp. 17 and 59, believe that universalism is the dominant theme of Luke and Acts, but this is undoubtedly exaggerated, for it is subsumed under his salvation theme. For Luke rejection began in Jesus' life and continued via his death to the church, which inherited both this suffering and his mission to borrow the Pauline phrase. With Israel's rejection the mission becomes gentile directed and therefore rejection is the primary force in the transition in salvation history to the universal mission. Luke prepares for this theme throughout his Gospel (cf. 2:30f.; 3:6; 4:16f.; 7:1f.; 9:51f.; 10:30f.; 13:28f.; 17:11f.).

Christ, rather than the guilt of the *laos* ("people"), to whom salvation is still offered. Thus Luke in his Gospel makes Israel's rejection individual rather than corporate.

Jervell's study of this issue notes that Luke's Gospel reaches a turning point in chapters 10—11 and makes "the main point ... that salvation has come to the Gentiles through Israel" (p. 67).[44] Thus part of Luke's purpose in writing was to call the church back to a truly *universal* mission or a ministry to both Jew and Gentile. Jerusalem implies more than just the place of rejection; it has a crucial role in salvation-history as the place where Jesus won redemption. It is not only the place of death but also the place where the church launched its worldwide mission effort.

Verse 48 introduces the witness motif (one of the central themes in Acts) as Jesus tells his disciples, "You are witnesses of these things." "These things" refers to both the reality of the resurrection and the recognition of Jesus as suffering Messiah (the two major themes of the Emmaus account and appearance to the Eleven), but on the surface the statement "you are my witnesses" is a bit out of place. The disciples had not yet begun to evangelize; the universal mission had not started. Was Jesus referring here instead to the sending out of the seventy (10:1—24) which already contained some hints (vv. 12, 13) of the universal mission and therefore would already qualify the disciples as "witnesses"? That would imply a much broader concept of "witness." In this context Dillon says (p. 216) that *toutōn* ("this") in verse 48 refers back to all the elements of verses 46—47; thus the disciples are witnesses not only of the resurrection but also all of Jesus' acts that fulfilled Old Testament prophecy.[45]

---

44. Comparing this with Acts, one concludes that the rejection of Israel's Messiah was individual at the crucifixion, focused in the leaders. It did not become corporate until the nation's rejection at the time of the universal mission. The separation of *laos* from the leaders continues in 3:23; 4:17, 21; 5:12—13, 17f. In 4:27, 6:12, and 12:11 the "people" are misled by the venomous official when the church is persecuted. However, from 15:14 the gentiles are included in the "people" (18:10; 19:4f.; 26:17). The Jewish "people" reject the message of salvation (21:27—36). The Good News will still be proclaimed to them (26:23) but as a "people" they are rejected (28:25—28). The tide turns to corporate rejection and individual conversion.

45. Although we believe Dillon characteristically goes too far in applying it *only* to the opening of the Scriptures, he is certainly correct in arguing that it goes beyond factual data to an eschatological ministry; in effect, this is the mainstay of the thesis behind his title, as "eyewitnesses" become "ministers of the word" (Luke 1:2). Yet here it is a both/and situation, for the disciples "witness" to the fact that Scripture was indeed

Verse 49 contains both a command and a promise, "stay in the city" as well as "I am going to send you what my father has promised." This promise of "power from on high" provides a good transition from Jesus' work on earth to the work of the Holy Spirit in Acts, particularly the coming of the Spirit in Acts 2. Dunn (*Baptism*, p. 47) shows how this promise of the Spirit in Luke and Acts utilizes a term which brings to mind covenant promise of God for his people. The Spirit thus becomes for Luke "the new covenant fulfillment of the ancient covenent promise."

Verse 49 is significantly different from John 20:22 with the difference obviously redactional. Luke looks forward to a future event and thus speaks of it as *epaggelia* ("promise") while John makes it a present event.

Leaney notes (p. 294) that Luke mentions the outpouring of the Spirit here in light of Acts 2:17 which is the fulfillment of Joel 3:1 – 5. Jesus' messianic office and God's gift of the Spirit are thus closely connected, the link being the "witness" concept.[46] Consider, for example, Luke's infancy narratives (1:15, 41, 67; 2:25f.) where the Spirit inspires prophetic witness to Christ's messiahship (cf. 4:1, 14, 17; 10:21, drawn from Mark). In these accounts the "promise" is actualized in the coming of the Messianic Age. Once Jesus has finished his work as Messiah, Joel's prophecy about the Spirit can be fulfilled.[47]

fulfilled in the resurrection as a real event. The apostolic criteria of Acts 1:21 – 22 would support this broader understanding of "witness." In support of a factual interpretation, see Flender, pp. 159f.; Talbert, *Gnostics*, pp. 17f. It is unlikely that one can remove factual content entirely from the "witness" motif, even though a case might be made (as we attempt herein) to broaden the Lukan concept.

46. See Ellis, p. 10; Marshall, *Luke—Historian*, pp. 91f. This is a welcome corrective to the otherwise excellent study of Lampe, "Spirit," pp. 159f., who believes that the theme always presents anointing/endowment with power. However, he reads the development in Acts back into the Gospel; while the anointing function is certainly present, the witness theme may well be primary.

47. In this regard we would note the overstatement of Conzelmann. He dichotomizes the age of Christ from the phenomena Luke utilized to overcome the problem of the delay of the parousia (*Luke*, pp. 95f., 136f.; cf. also Schweizer, *TDNT*, VI, p. 412). Yet the Spirit establishes continuity rather than discontinuity between Jesus' ministry and that of the church. As Flender says (p. 139), "The Spirit-endowed church remains the counterpart of its Lord, not merely the extension of his personality." They are not two distinct ages but the one leads naturally into the other. This does not negate the salvation-historical approach, as Flender so clearly demonstrates. Rather, the Hegelian separation of Luke's eschatology and the relegation of the theme to "early catholicism" are unnecessary. The same Spirit who anointed/empowered Jesus in his ministry (Luke 4:18) also

This "promise" is defined further in verse 49 as *ex hypsous dunamis* ("power from on high"). This link between Spirit and "power" is a familiar one (Luke 1:17, 35; 4:14; Acts 1:8, 6:8, 10:38), as is the phrase "on High," used to describe God. Luke's obvious thrust here within a Jewish context would be to emphasize the outpouring of messianic salvation. Grundmann (*TDNT*, II, pp. 310f.) says this power, grounded in Jesus and poured out via the Spirit, is the power of God expressed in proclamation (Acts 4:33; 6:10) and miracles (Acts 4:7f.; 6:8). He adds, "In the combination of *dunamis* and *pneuma* there is expressed the power with which the Risen Lord is presented to his people as *pneuma*." The purpose of this power is to establish the messianic community, the church, and Luke's stress here is on the divine impetus which alone makes the church and its mission possible.

The Ascension, 24:50—53

The final section of Luke is linked to the resurrection narrative, yet separate from it, and its brief length is little indication of its crucial significance. Some tradition critics thought this section might have been a later addition to Luke (see Conzelmann, *Theology*, pp. 94, 203), but most scholars today accept it as Luke's composition since both the language and event are peculiar to him.[48] Perhaps the best way to view the account is to see it as a combination of tradition and Lukan redaction; an account which O'Toole says (p. 110f.) connects resurrection and ascension with Jesus' exaltation.

empowers the church (Acts 16:7). In connection with 1:78, Grundmann (*Lukas*, p. 453) declares that the *anatolē* from on high (see below) in Jesus' earthly ministry corresponds to the *dunamis* from on high in the history of the church.

48. Lohfink (pp. 147f., 163f.) accepts the whole as a Lukan composition, since both language and event are peculiar to him (see Taylor, *Passion*, p. 115, on the Lukan language). We certainly do not wish to deny the presence of redaction, but rather to argue for the same combination of tradition and Lukan coloring which we have found behind each of the episodes (see chap. 7 for details). A good summary is found in O'Toole's article, which discusses the connection of resurrection and ascension with exaltation in Luke. We would agree with those mentioned (pp. 110f.) who argue that the historical realities point to the validity of the event: "Jesus' appearances had to extend over a number of days and had to come to an end." O'Toole himself notes that Luke would have much less of a problem than modern scholars with the two foci of the resurrection/ascension/exaltation "dilemma."

Luke 24 and Acts 1

Some scholars have called attention to the apparent "contra-dictions" between Luke 24:50−53 and Acts 1:9−11. One of the most obvious differences is the matter of time. The word *kai* ("and") in verse 50 may indicate Jesus ascended to Heaven the same day as his appearance to the disciples, thus combining resurrection, ascension, and exaltation into a single event. Acts 1:3, on the other hand, separates these events by at least forty days. Why do we have this difference?

Some critics have suggested Luke combined different traditions here without noting their differences, yet such careless work hardly seems indicative of the author.[49] Luke stressed the "same day" motif in chapter 24, carefully omitting any specific references to time (cf. vv. 13, 29, 33, 36), while in Acts he used the "forty days" motif, an important concept borrowed probably from Sinai im-agery (Exod. 24:18). C. J. Hemer (*NIDNTT*, 2, p. 696) says this theme has two other possible parallels: forty days meaning "the duration of successive developments of God's redemptive acts" and also the "apocalyptic period of time necessary for a term of instruction" (2 Bar. 76:4; cf. 4 Ezra 14:23).[50] At any rate the difference in time in the two accounts might simply be due to a difference in emphasis.

Other discrepancies between Luke 24 and Acts 1 are not so dif-ficult to understand. In Luke the ascension takes place in Bethany while in Acts it happens on the Mount of Olives. Since both are so close to each other geographically (Bethany is on the mount's eastern side), the discrepancy is minimal. Another difference, Luke 24:23's "eleven and those who were with them," vs. Acts 1:2's "apostles" only is eliminated by the realization that the time ref-

49. In fact, Menoud (*Neotestamentica*, pp. 148f.) changed his earlier position for this very reason. The same-day theme is only implied in verse 50, although the theological stress is certainly intended. To this extent we agree with Dillon's statement (p. 181): "Luke is not primarily interested in our chapter, at least, in the external time-framework of the paschal happenings, but in their inner unity and totality." We disagree, however, that the two accounts are thereby irreconcilable.

50. In this latter vein we might mention that Ezra and Baruch also waited forty days before their ascension (4 Ezr. 16:23, 49; 2 Bar. 76:4; see Wilson, 98n.). With this in mind it is likely that forty days was an apocalyptic figure stemming from Moses and signifying a necessary time for instruction before a direct theophanic act. Wilson, pp. 99−100; and Marshall, *Acts*, p. 57, both add a historical note. The "forty days" dating also provides a link with the date of Pentecost and Acts becomes a necessary transition to that epochal event.

erence in Luke 24:50 is not specific and thus only the disciples could have been present at the ascension.

The accounts also differ in theological emphasis, Luke 24 being more like a doxology with its priestly blessing and worship while Acts 1 seems more ecclesiastical, preparing for the growth of the church (see van Stempvoort, O'Toole). Luke 24 thus is an appropriate conclusion, the triumphant culmination of the Gospel, while Acts 1 is an introduction which provides a christological foundation for the work of the church.[51] The same event is viewed from two vantage points, as an end and a beginning.

Some scholars have seen a discrepancy also between Luke's account of the ascension and other New Testament accounts which include an ascension theology linking exaltation with the resurrection (e.g., 1 Thess. 1:9f.; 1 Cor. 15:3f.; Rom. 1:3f.; Eph. 1:19f.) and implying a heavenly, invisible event rather than an earthly, visible one. This difference is easy to explain; the epistles are doctrinal rather than historical, and theological identification in them does not necessarily imply chronological, historical events. The Gospels, on the other hand, are more historical. The ascension was a part of Jesus' glorification, and as such this theme in time naturally extended to the resurrection. "Resurrection" thus became an all-embracing term in the kerygma (preaching) of the early church.

In addition, Luke specifically does connect exaltation with the resurrection. He adds to Mark's description of the angels at the tomb, writing "dazzling apparel" rather than "white robe," bringing to mind the "dazzling" glory of Jesus on the mount (9:29). He also links resurrection and "glory" in verse 26.[52] Thus Luke does not separate the events of Jesus' exaltation, but presents those events from two perspectives, theological (Luke 24) and historical (Acts 1).

Theological themes. The ascension is theologically significant in Luke's writings, providing a crucial transition between Jesus' ministry and passion as well as the church's birth and growth. It thus

51. Wilson further interprets Acts 1:9−11 (building on Haenchen's view that Luke is combating a false view regarding the "imminent expectation") as a polemic against those who denied a parousia. This (as well as Haenchen's view) seems to be forced. We would see the purpose as salvation-historical, linking the resurrection with the parousia as the foundations for the universal mission. It has a positive rather than negative role.

52. Both Navone (pp. 91f.) and Leaney (pp. 36f.) describe "enter into his glory" as a royal motif. Conzelmann (pp. 203f.) correctly notes here that his glory is thereby no longer a future event looking to the ascension but rather is already present.

serves as the concluding scene of the Gospel as well as opening scene of church history, demonstrating the continuity between Jesus and the church.[53]

The priestly emphasis. This concept is demonstrated in this passage by the use of the *eulogein* ("bless") word group (vv. 50, 51, 53), a Lukan term (seventeen times vs. five each in Mark and Matthew) which also appears in verse 30 in the description of Jesus' priestly prayer. The passage has a decided priestly flavor, especially with Jesus' "lifted-up hands" in verse 50 which reminds us of the priestly benediction in passages like Numbers 6:23f. and Psalm 110.

Ellis (p. 79) thinks the act has a particular messianic significance, saying "It may signify the priestly character of Messiah's present exaltation and of his relationship to believers."[54] In this passage the raised hands of Christ mean the fulfillment of that messianic promise. The priestly blessing thus closes the chapter about the earthly Jesus and at the same time looks forward to his exaltation and glorification. The earthly life and the Risen Lord are linked and become interdependent. This Christology provides the underpinning for the church.[55]

The worship emphasis. There is a strong ecclesiastical flavor in this passage, even if we omit verse 52 as a possible late addition

53. This motif is carried over into Acts, which has a distinct emphasis on this continuity, as in Luke's selection of miracle stories (see Hamblin) and his description of the trial scenes (see O'Toole, "Imitators"), which seek to link the church's experiences with Jesus' ministry and passion.

54. As such it denotes messianic blessing (Luke 9:16); in 19:38, for instance, Luke alone adds the messianic concepts of "peace" and "glory" to the crowd's cry at the triumphal entry. It also has a special place in the infancy narratives, employed prophetically with respect to the messianic nature of the Christ child (1:12, 64; 2:28, 34). The Risen One gives his messianic blessing to his followers. In this light Franklin (pp. 36—41) believes that the ascension has more a christological than an ecclesiological emphasis.

55. A growing number of scholars (van Stempvoort, Lohfink, Dillon, etc.) believe that this deliberately reflects Sir 50:20f. (the high priest Simon's blessing), which has the raising of hands in priestly blessing and congregational worship centering on the "joyful" response. These parallels lead Lohfink and Dillon to interpret Luke's scene in light of Ben Sira s utilization of Simon to conclude his chronicle of the prophet-heroes. Here, of course, special mention would be made of the Enoch and Elijah ascensions. This furthers the theme relating the resurrection to Moses typology and links it to the prophecy/fulfillment pattern already noted in the chapter (see above and Dillon, pp. 221f.). However, we must disagree with Dillon's further thesis (p. 22) that this chronicle of sacred prophetic history has replaced the priestly interpretation already discussed herein. Rather, the two complement one another (see further below, "ascension terminology").

to the account.[56] The theme is enriched by the "great joy," "staying continually at the temple," and "praising God" of the witnesses of the ascension, each contributing to a beautiful Gospel conclusion and transition to the ministry of Acts.

Chara ("joy") is a typically Lukan term, even though its meaning is also conveyed in at least four other word groups and six terms. The word, says Navone (pp. 71f.) "in every case is related to the recognition of the present salvation process and is experienced in the measure that one participates in it." "Great joy" thus condenses the worship theme and applies it to the enriched faith of the disciples. It is a direct response to the doubt theme of verses 11f., 13f., and 36f., and is the outward expression of the results of Christ's teaching in verses 44 −49.

It is also the antithesis of the disciples' incomplete joy of verse 41 which then was mixed with amazement or unbelief but now soars upward in a paeon of praise. "Great joy" is central to Luke's own theology of joy, emphasizing both an eschatological link with the kingdom and the personal participation of the worshiper in that kingdom.[57] In this light verse 52 fulfills the promise of verse 41 and provides a transition to the joyful proclamation in Acts (8:4f.; 13:48f.; 15:3).

"Temple" is another term that is important in the worship theme. This place was important in Luke's infancy stories (2:27, 37, 46), implying, says G. Schrenk (*TDNT*, III, p. 245) that the teaching role of the temple has been superseded by Jesus' "new revelation" (2:30). The temple is the place of Jesus' messianic teaching (20:1; 21:5f.; 37f.; 22:53) as well as rejection (19:44f.; 22:52), but here in Luke it refers primarily to the passion. It is not mentioned between the temptation (4:9) and triumphal entry (19:45) except in one prayer parable (18:10).

Conzelmann says (*Luke*, pp. 75f.) Luke regards temple-events as ecclesiological rather than eschatological, something which applies even to the triumphal entry (19:37f.) and the temple cleansing

56. "Worshiped him" (v. 52), is the final of the several western non-interpolations (see on vv. 3, 12, etc.). As argued above, we believe it is authentic.

57. Both ideas are reflected in the key chapters of Luke's developing schema, chapters 14 −15. In 14:15 −24, the parable of the messianic banquet shows that joy results from the messianic salvation offered; chapter 15 contains three parables which link this joy to one's part in the salvation process. Further, 24:49 presents the entrance of the kingdom in the person of the Spirit, and the disciples thereby participate in the joy of the resurrection (see Navone, pp. 77f.; Reicke, *Luke*, pp. 75f.).

(19:45f.) which lead to the establishment of the messianic com-munity.[58] Acts continues this theme; the temple is the center of apostolic teaching (5:12, 20, 25, 42) where the apostles pray (2:46; 3:1f.) and continue to practice their ceremonial vows (21:26; 24:6f.; 25:8; 26:21). Still, the temple is no longer the center of worship (7:49f.; 17:24) and the "house of prayer" (Luke 19:46) is no longer God's particular dwelling. "Temple" thus has two meanings; it is the place of future teaching but one which Christ's authority now supersedes.

Other terms used in this worship theme are *eulogein* ("bless," see above) and *proskunein* ("worship"), the natural result of priestly blessing (v. 50) but with a somewhat larger emphasis. The atmos-phere of worship permeates the entire 24th chapter of Luke. The women "bow down with their faces to the ground" when they see the angels at the tomb (v. 5), the proclaimed Word and breaking of bread in the Emmaus account are primary acts of worship (vv. 25f., 29f.), and now the disciples "worship" the ascended Christ (v. 52). Reverence and awe dominate Luke's resurrection account. Yet Lohfink (pp. 171f; also Dillon pp. 223f.) makes the point that in other accounts where these emotions are prompted by miraculous works of the earthly Jesus, Luke studiously avoids using the spe-cific term for "worship." Instead, he uses the more neutral descrip-tion, "fell with his face to the ground" (5:12), deliberately saving the specific term for the ascension scene where it effectively sums up the worship theme as a whole.[59]

Worship also permeates the entire Gospel of Luke. The concep-tion of John the Baptist and Jesus was announced in the context of worship (1:8f., 35, 41f., 46f., 64f.), Jesus birth produced awe and wonder (2:9f., 20), his purification ceremony inspired Simon's song of worship (2:28f., 37f.), and his temple visit clarified his priorities

58. However, he goes too far in rejecting the eschatological element in the triumphal entry. While Luke does add that "the disciples" were the ones proclaiming him "king," it goes too far to conclude that eschatology is thereby replaced by a "non-political" Christology. Luke does not "omit" the Davidic lordship but replaces Mark's terminology with the "king" title; the meaning is much the same. Therefore both elements are present and Luke adds (but does not replace) ecclesiology to eschatology. On the "new Israel" theme, see the clarification in the discussion on 24:7 above.

59. Yet they admit the places where such homage does occur (8:41—petition; 17:16—thanksgiving; 5:8, 8:47—fear) and we wonder whether such a terminological switch can truly outweigh the conceptual stress. We can say that Luke has reserved the term for this passage, where it sums up the worship motif, but not that it is a new emphasis.

in life with regard to worship (2:49). Worship also plays a part in the temptation of Christ (4:16f.) and the inauguration of his ministry, and though his ministry was primarily one of confrontation leading to his passion, Jesus did inspire many touching scenes of worship (5:26; 7:16, 37f.; 9:16, 43; 10:39f.; 13:7; 17:15f., 18:43).[60]

The worship theme in Luke expresses itself basically in two ways, through the inward presence of joy and the outward activity of praise. Both expressions are clearly evident in 24:50−53, although the passion narrative provides a special showcase. Jesus' cleansing of the temple (19:45f.) symbolizes the removal of impurities from the "house of prayer," after which his teaching in the temple (21:37) inspires awe and silence (20:26, 40) and focuses on true worship (21:1f.). The Last Supper and prayers in Gethsemane provide a transition to the crucifixion which brings the worship motif to a climax. Worship, in fact, is a central theme in the crucifixion story,[61] evidenced particularly in three of Jesus' sayings which deal with prayer or God's response to prayer (23:34; 40f., 46) and which include the themes of forgiveness, salvation, and commitment. In addition, we might note the omission of nonworship elements: the wine mixed with myrrh, the cry of dereliction, the Elijah incident. As I have concluded elsewhere ("Crucifixion," pp. 90f.), "Luke has removed those scenes which contribute to Mark's atmosphere of horror and replaced them with others which suggest awe and reverence. To Luke, the crucifixion was above all a scene of awesome worship." This emphasis continues into the resurrection scene and ends with the denouement of the ascension.

Ascension typology More fully presented in Acts 1:9−11, the idea is still present here. Some critics see a parallel between *an-*

60. Prayer is certainly one of the major themes in Luke. Not only does Jesus pray extensively, but also prayer is a central tenet in his teaching (6:28; 10:2; 11:1f.; 18:1.; 21:36f.). Navone, p. 118, shows that in all but two instances (10:21f., 41) the prayers are only in Luke and occur at central points of his ministry, e.g., his baptism, selection of the Twelve, Peter's confession, transfiguration, crucifixion. There is a twofold purpose in Luke's prayer theology, sonship and dependence; Jesus' prayers show his unique sonship and dependence on the Father. See also Trites, pp. 168f., who also traces this theme in Acts.

61. While most scholars center on Luke's crucifixion scene as stressing the death of the innocent, righteous martyr (Dibelius, Marshall, etc.), we would argue that worship plays a parallel and perhaps even more central role.

aphereto ("ascent")[62] in verse 51 and *analambanein* ("take up") in Acts 1:2, 11, 22 and Luke 9:51 as evidence of an Elijah motif. Dillon (pp. 177n.) sees more parallels with 2 Kings 2:9f.: "taken up from" in 2 Kings 2:9 is like Acts 1:11; "ascended into heaven" in 2 Kings 2:11 is like Acts 1:11; "and they did not see him" in 2 Kings 2:12 sounds like Acts 1:9; and "returned" in 2 Kings 2:13 is like Acts 1:12 and Luke 24:52. Although these linguistic similarities show the Elijah motif is primarily present in Acts 1, they may also suggest it appears in Luke's account of the ascension as well.

Still, how much Elijah imagery is suggested in Luke 24:50 – 53? Certainly the transfiguration pericope in 9:31 with Elijah and Moses "appearing in glorious splendor" with Christ and speaking of his "departure" prefigures Jesus' ascension, as does verse 54's "fire called down from heaven." Jesus' miracles which deal with raising the dead (Luke 7:11f.) are a kind of parallel to Elijah's miracles in 1 Kings 17:17f. and 2 Kings 4:18f., and Jesus himself makes the theme explicit in 4:24f. when he compares his ministry to Elijah's work with the widow of Zarephath.[63]

Jesus may also be seen as a kind of new Moses; Manek says ("New Exodus," pp. 208f.) *exagein* ("lead out") describes Moses in

62. Like "worshiped him" in verse 52, the phrase "ascended into heaven" is a western non-interpolation. For the same reasons argued there and elsewhere in chapter 24 (see comments above) we believe that it is authentic.

63. The major problem is the extent of Elijah imagery in the Gospel. Its presence in 9:51 is debated; since the passage relates more to the passion, van Stempvoort (pp. 32f.) believes that the ascension is not meant there, but rather his death. Dupont (*"Ana-lemphthe,"* pp. 154f.), however, presents cogent arguments for an ascension interpretation, and there is a good possibility that Elijah typology is intended in 9:31 (*exodos*, "departure"), 52 ("before his face"), 54 ("fire . . . to come down from heaven . . . and consume"). The connected miracles dealing with raising the dead (Luke 7:11f. = Acts 9:36f.) may also parallel the Elijah/Elisha chronicles (cf. 1 Kings 17:17f. and 2 Kings 4:18f.). The theme becomes explicit, of course, in 4:24f., and this has led Hinnebusch and Conzelmann (*Luke*, pp. 22f.) to conclude that for Luke the Baptist's role as the Elijah-prophet virtually disappears. Danker (*Luke*, pp. 26f.) adds that this separation of John from Elijah allowed Luke to replace the Baptist with Jesus, who comes in the "power of the highest" (1:35). He does omit Mark 1:6, 9:9f. on John as Elijah, but in 1:17, 76 it is stated that John would "prepare the way" "in the spirit and power of Elijah." It is also true that many traditional Elijah emphases (the conversation at the transfiguration, the taunt at the cross) are missing. It seems therefore, that both the Baptist and Jesus are related to Elijah, yet that relationship in both cases is muted. For Luke, John was indeed a person like "Elijah" and Jesus does have a prophetic role; indeed, one could say (*contra* Conzelmann and Danker) that the Baptist remains the forerunner and Jesus the prophet with power. However, there is no "new Elijah" motif and the prophetic role transcends that theme.

Acts 7:36, and is also used to describe Jesus in 24:50. The forty-day theme and cloud in Acts 1:3, 9 thus become symbols of a "new Exodus" in which Jesus leads his people out of the land of oppression (each into the promised land—heaven). Yet this may be stretching the point a bit far, although both Moses and Elijah do appear with Christ at the transfiguration and speak about Jesus' *exodos*. Perhaps both prophetic figures are a part of ascension imagery, Jesus fulfilling the messianic hopes which center upon both and ascending triumphant in his prophetic role.

Luke's ascension scene then is a kind of link between heaven and earth, the climax of God's redemptive plan, yet an event which initiates a new phase of salvation-history in the age of universal mission. Franklin ("Ascension," pp. 191f.) states that the eschatological power of God according to Luke is more evident in the ascension than in the parousia. While this goes too far (the two are linked in Acts 1), it is true that this demonstrates that Christ reigns within history but is also transcendent over it; he is absent from the world yet is present via the Spirit in the world.[64] This present lordship exists in dynamic tension with his transcendent glory, and both aspects meet in the living presence of the Risen Lord in the community. The ascension is the visible promise of the future glory of the parousia (Acts 1:11).

Conclusion

All the evangelists sum up their theological messages in their resurrection narratives, and Luke is no exception. His major theme in his Gospel is the revelation and accomplishment of salvation in the person and passion of Jesus Christ. This is seen in the Lukan addition of the soteriological significance of the resurrection. In 24:7, 26, and 46 he demonstrates the relation of the passion to a proper understanding of the resurrection. This is also a car-

64. Conzelmann's de-eschatology theory, whereby he claims Luke changes the eschatological tradition of Jesus to a salvation-history, has come under increasing attack. Talbert, "Lukan Theology," pp. 171f., says Luke was not writing under the impetus of a parousia delay but rather was combating the belief that the parousia had already occurred: Luke stresses its nearness. Ellis, "Eschatology," pp. 27f., and Wilson, pp. 330f., both argue for future elements and imminency in Lukan eschatology, along with the present emphasis.

dinal doctrine of Acts (see chap. 3). For Luke, then, the resurrection is more than vindication of Jesus' death; it is also an integral part of the redemptive thrust of the passion which signifies the new life that results from it.

Luke also focuses on the reality of the resurrection. The first half of his narrative climaxes in the recognition scene of verses 30–31. The angelic message, centering on "He has arisen" rather than the Galilee command (so Matthew and Mark) is anticlimactic, and curiously unsatisfying in light of the doubt scene in verses 9–11. Peter's puzzlement adds to this suspense, and the blindness of the followers in verses 16f. provides a tension which demands release. This release comes in verses 30–31, from which all other events flow. The threefold doubt is answered by the threefold proof (vv. 36–43), stressing the authenticity of the resurrection, and all of Jesus' teaching centers on the power of resurrection witness. The ascension is the capstone of this reality, Jesus' eschatological glory resulting in genuine adoration and worship from the emerging church.

Luke also stresses ecclesiology, with each resurrection pericope a kind of transition to the church age. He stresses a witness theme which, in the last chapter authenticates the reality of the resurrection message. And his worship motif provides a good transition to his soteriological emphasis which would culminate in the church's universal message of salvation. The resurrection in Luke thus is a transition rather than culmination of God's power in Jesus Christ and becomes the impetus for the mission outreach of the church.

The final chapter of Luke also focuses on the messianic nature of Jesus, proven not necessarily by the ressurection so much as the passion (vv. 7, 26, 46), yet not fully understood except through the resurrection. Jesus the Messiah is also Jesus as Lord in death (v. 3) as well as ascendency over death (vv. 5, 25, 50f.). Matthew and Mark may stress the vindication of Jesus' death, but Luke stresses his lordship over it. Jesus' messianic authority provides the doctrinal foundation for the future mission of Acts.

Luke also emphasizes sovereignty and divine necessity in passages which explain how Christ fulfilled Old Testament prophecy (vv. 7, 26, 46) as well as how the Emmaus disciples failed to recognize their Risen Lord (v. 16), building his theology not on the words of men but on the causative power of God. God is the one

who created the redemptive plan which was fulfilled in history by
his Son. God also is the one who will complete the universal
mission through the work of his Holy Spirit. Eschatologically Luke
is like other New Testament writers who indicate both present
and future aspects of the passion-resurrection, yet his work stresses
the "now" more than Mark or Matthew. This emphasis links the
resurrection closely with the passion and stresses the living presence of Jesus in the community.

Luke's *Sitz im Leben* (life-situation) becomes apparent through
his theology; he probably wrote this Gospel after the early church
was established when eyewitnesses were beginning to die and the
church (was) left without a valid witness.[65] Luke wrote not only
to prove the validity of past testimony but also to tell about the
continuing witness of the Risen One through the presence and
work of the Holy Spirit. He also wrote about the increasing influence of gentiles in the church and the impact of universal mission,
adding to Mark's concept of universalism that of God's continuing
efforts to reach out to the Jews.[66] Though they had rejected the
Messiah, they were still offered salvation on an individual basis.

65. This is also seen in the strong doubt motif of Luke's narrative, which sems particularly relevant to his own day. The refusal of the disciples to believe in verse 11, Peter's
puzzlement in verse 12, the blindness of the followers in verses 16f., and the threefold
doubt motif of verses 36–43 are all seen as natural reactions to the unexplainable mystery of the resurrection. Yet they can be overcome by the realization of the living presence
of Jesus (vv. 30–31), the proclaimed truth of the Word (vv. 25f., 44f., 48) and the witness
of the Spirit (vv. 48f.).

66. Wilson, *Mission*, pp. 248–49, follows Jervell, p. 187f., in positing that Luke's
Jewish-Gentile tension reflects the later situation, with the church ostracized by the
Jews as an "illegitimate offspring of Judaism." Therefore, Luke answered by stressing
Jewish responsibility for rejecting Christianity and the legitimacy of the church's roots.
However, though this has some truth regarding the Jews, Luke does show the continuing
place in the church, for two reasons: (1) to the church he shows the continuing need of
a Jewish mission; (2) to Jews he says that the doors remain open though the nation had
rejected salvation. In the context of Acts 28:25f. (at the center of the "final rejection"
theory) Paul spoke to Jewish leaders (vv. 17f.), with the result that "some were convinced
... while others disbelieved" (v. 24). The emphasis is on corporate responsibility, not
rejection. See also Jervell, *passim*.

5

John's Resurrection Narrative

John's resurrection account is divided into two sections, the conclusion (chap. 20) and appendix (chap. 21). The conclusion includes two emphases, one of which is based on its structure. This structure carefully weaves together four episodes[1] (the race to the tomb, the visit of Mary, the appearance to the Twelve, and to doubting Thomas) and presents four types of faith which illustrate John's view of faith as a personal encounter with Jesus, a decision which does not necessarily demand empirical proof (v. 29). John moves beyond Luke in this emphasis, presenting his evidence in a kind of descending spiral from the highest type of faith to the lowest or most meager kind of faith. He thus presents the "beloved disciple" who comes to faith apart from empirical proof (or from "understanding," v. 9) on the basis of love, to the lowest type, or cynical Thomas who demands physical proof. Somewhere between these extremes is Mary who did not recognize the truth without the "call" of the Good Shepherd (cp. 10:3−4), and the Twelve, who needed to see the Risen Lord to overcome their fear. The Gospel of John emphasizes that Christ encounters each person at the level of his faith, since faith, whether great or small, is still valid for belief.

1. I agree with Schnackenburg (pp. 354−55) who says (vs. Brown, p. 965) that the four should be separate. Brown reads too much into the relationship between the morning appearances and the evening appearances when he argues for two scenes (vv. 1−18 as grave scenes and vv. 19−29 as appearance scenes). He tends to miss the thematic development from scene to scene.

147

John's second emphasis in chapter 20 is, as Haenchen says, based on his understanding of the Easter tradition as "a code for the coming of the Spirit" (p. 580). This emphasis fits in nicely with Jesus' farewell discourse (chaps. 14−16), especially the middle episodes stressing Jesus' ascension (v. 17) which leads to the gift of the Spirit to the disciples who then become "sent ones" (vv. 21−22). Because this theme does not continue throughout the episodes, however, Haenchen's assertion that it is primary is probably faulty. Nonetheless, John does make an important connection between the meaning of faith and its significance for the believer. The apostle carefully presents a series of episodes which show how the presence of the Risen Lord becomes the significant factor in faith-encounter, regardless of the condition of the individual. Then John goes on to present the results of such an encounter in a twofold stress on mission (vv. 18, 21−23) and Christology (vv. 17, 21, 28).

The appendix of John's resurrection account (chap. 21) has a different emphasis. Perhaps this change came about because John wrote this section much later than the conclusion of chapter 20, but at any rate its meaning is clear. Since almost all the eye-witnesses of the resurrection were dead the church was forced into the position of relying on the secondhand testimony of creeds or written-down accounts. John thus stresses here the importance of obedience and discipleship within the context of universal mission. The interplay between the "beloved disciple" and Peter is a unifying stylistic device as the episodes progress from mission (dependent on the presence of the Risen Lord, 1−14) to pastoral responsibility which results from love for Jesus (15−17), and then to radical discipleship in life and in death (18−23).

The Conclusion: Soteriology, Chapter 20

Introduction: The Visit to the Tomb, 20:1

Maloney (pp. 202−12) does an extensive linguistic comparison between verse 1 and the synoptic time notes, concluding that verse 1 "has its origin in a synoptic-like narrative not far from Mark and in a developed stage close to Luke" (p. 212). This relationship is especially evident in the time note *tē de mia tōn sabbatōn* ("on the first day of the week") which sounds like Luke 24:12, and *prōi . . . erchetai* ("came early") which is like Mark 16:2. John's focus on Mary here, which is typical of his own style (cp. his focus on Nicodemus, Thomas, and Pilate), is nonetheless different from other Gospel accounts. John uses this in order to center on his themes rather than on the interplay of characters. Still, his awareness of tradition comes through with the use of the plural "we don't know" in verse 2 as he centers on Mary, the individual expression of his theme. Although it could be an editorial "we" (e.g., Grass, Bode), the plural probably reflects the tradition behind the verse while John's preoccupation with Mary is redactional.

Benoit says ("Marie-Madeleine," pp. 141–42) verse 1 is an introduction to the next pericope, binding together the two sections of verses 1–18. This is especially evident in John's use of the phrase "while it was yet dark." At first these words seem to contradict the other Gospels (Luke says "at early dawn," Mark "when the sun had risen," and Matthew "toward the dawn"), but further study should prove the event took place just before dawn. John stresses darkness undoubtedly for thematic purposes.[2] Brown and Schnackenburg also note a "symbolic sense" here, John focusing on darkness as a symbol of Mary and the other disciples' lack of understanding or spiritual blindness (vv. 1f., 9). Mahoney adds still another emphasis, "the gradual dawning that is to take place in the following verses, culminating in the self-revelation of Jesus in 20:17" (p. 238).

John condenses the trip to the tomb into even fewer words than Luke, rushing the narrative to the empty tomb where he lingers longer than any other evangelist. In fact, the apologetic use of the empty tomb reaches fullest expression here where faith actually results from the empty tomb rather than from Jesus' post-resurrection appearances. Peripheral data such as the motive[3] and doubt of the women and disciples is omitted here so that the

---

2. Westcott (II, p. 337) and Wenham, ("Easter") try to reconcile these differences by suggesting two groups visited the tomb; Mary arriving in darkness and the others coming at sunrise. Yet, see the fuller explanation in Wenham (*Enigma*, 83–89). We will argue below that for all the problems this is a viable theory.

3. Several scholars (Bultmann, Bernard, Brown, Lindars, Rigaux) say John omitted the anointing motif because he had already included it in the passage about Joseph of Arimathea (19:38f.). This may be a valid assumption yet perhaps the primary reason here is that John did not wish to dwell on secondary details. Only two facts are important: they came, and they saw.

reader can focus on *to mnēmeion* ("tomb") in each clause and the center of the verse.

The verse reminds us of Jesus' raising of Lazarus. In that account (11:38, 39) Jesus "came to the tomb" and ordered the Jewish mourners to "take away the stone." *Airo* ("take away") is the key word here, one which also appears frequently (vv. 1, 2, 13, 15), always within the context of Mary's questions regarding the fate of Jesus' body. John thus creates a parallel between Jesus' greatest miracle and his own resurrection; the miracle anticipates the resurrection and both demonstrate Jesus' lordship over death.

The Race to the Tomb, 20:2−10

The tradition behind this section is suggested by its parallel account in Luke 24:12, especially its use of pre-Johannine language and style (cf. Fortna, Hartmann) in words such as *soudarion*, the adverbs *chōris, entulissō, anastēnai*, and the embryonic presence of verses 9−10 in Luke 24:12. Redactional elements, on the other hand, are John's focus on the "beloved disciple" as well as the belief motif. This section of John is perhaps best analyzed by a thematic outline rather than verse-by-verse approach.

The Beloved Disciple and Peter

Mahoney says (p. 278), "The general opinion of exegetes that the point of the pericope lies to a great extent in the relationship between the two disciples and the manner of their respective precedence is not lightly to be set aside." We should therefore examine the role of the "beloved disciple" in the fourth Gospel and his relationship to Peter before we can fully understand this passage. Since so much has been written on this topic perhaps a few highlights of current discussion will suffice. "Beloved disciple" is a key to the authorship of this Gospel (cf. 21:24) as well as a theological term within the Gospel itself (chaps. 20−21 being a major source of material). The issue is whether this disciple was an actual person or a symbol of the archetypal disciple.[4] Most critics today

---

4. Kragerud believes the "beloved" symbolizes the early church's prophetic activity which was responsible for the Gospel.

believe he was an actual person[5] but one who was idealized by the evangelist (and the church, cf. 21:24).

The question, of course, is who exactly was he? Was he John the Apostle,[6] John Mark,[7] Lazarus,[8] Matthias,[9] an anonymous figure from the Twelve,[10] or a separate disciple whose teachings were authoritative for the church?[11] Although this last category is attaining some consensus in modern Johannine scholarship (see Kysar, pp. 98−101),[12] one wonders if scholars are splitting theological hairs in order to avoid accepting the traditional view of John the Apostle as the "beloved," a view which still seems to be most reasonable. John 21:2 suggests he was either a son of Zebedee or one of the two unnamed disciples who was present at the Last Supper and the cross. Brown (John, scvi-scvii) argues that John, the son of Zebedee, is the only one who fits the requirements. He was one of the Twelve, had a special relationship with Jesus and with Peter, and had special memories to write down.

A brief look at passages which feature the "beloved disciple" should clarify his theological role: (1) 13:23−25 shows him interceding for Simon Peter as he asks who is to betray him, (2) 19:26−27 tells how Jesus places Mary under his care, (3) 20:2−10 describes how he and Peter raced to the tomb where the "beloved"

5. Schnackenburg argues that the constant juxtaposition of Peter with the "beloved" definitely indicates that the unnamed disicple is a historical person.

6. Morris and Brown (John, I, xcii−xcviii) say the "beloved" is the apostle, but Brown separates him from the evangelist who used John's tradition in composing the Gospel.

7. Johnson ("Beloved Disciples," pp. 157−58) and Parker ("John Mark," pp. 97f.). Although John Mark was from the priestly class, grew up in Jerusalem, and knew Peter, he was not one of the apostles.

8. Filson, "Beloved Disciple," pp. 83−88, and Brownlee, "John," pp. 191−94. Sanders ("Those Whom Jesus Loved," pp. 29−41) believes Lazarus was the "beloved" whose memoirs were edited by John Mark the evangelist (the "other disciples" in 1:37f. and 18:15f.). Brown says (xcv), however, this would only be relevant if the readers did not know the identity of the author. Subtle euphemisms would not be necessary in John's circle.

9. Titus, "Beloved Disciple," pp. 323−38. This view has even more problems than Filson's and Brownlee's work.

10. Lindars, John, pp. 31−34. Why would anyone want to accept another member of the Twelve and yet deny John? As a disciple he should at least be a viable candidate.

11. Schnackenburg, "Origin," pp. 231, 239; and Johannesevangelium, III, pp. 450−56; as well as Lorenzen, pp. 74−82.

12. Culpepper (pp. 266−69), for instance, believes that the Johannine community stood in the same relation to the "beloved" as the "beloved" to Jesus and Jesus to the Father. Therefore, the "beloved" parallels the Paraclete (the technical term for the Holy Spirit in chaps. 14−16) in function and performs the work of the Paraclete for the community, i.e., as the final revealer of Jesus' teachings.

both "saw and believed," (4) 21:7 shows how he recognized the man standing on the shore as "the Lord," (5) 21:20−23 tells about Peter questioning Jesus about whether "the disciple whom Jesus loved" would live to see the parousia, and (6) 21:24 testifies to the "true witness" of the "beloved."[13] Note how all these references come from the last half of the Gospel, its passion and resurrection sections. Then look at John's stress on the intimacy between the "beloved" and Jesus ("whom Jesus loved," "leaning on Jesus' breast"), how that intimacy is linked to revelational ministry (explicit in 21:24 and 19:35 [if that is a "beloved" passage] and implicit in 13:23f.; 21:7), and then how this affects the relationship between the "beloved" and Peter.

Does the author of John present a deliberate contrast between these two prominent figures? Kragerud and Lorenzen see a definite rivalry between the "beloved" and Peter which seems to be a symbol of conflict in the community itself. Kragerud (pp. 147−48) identifies this as conflict between the ecclesiastical hierarchy (represented by Peter) and the prophetic element (the "beloved"), while Lorenzen (pp. 89−96) sees it as conflict between Jewish Christianity (Peter) and the Johannine community. The argument pales somewhat, however, in light of the extremely positive portrait of Peter in this Gospel, especially in chapter 21.[14] In fact, never does the evangelist view Peter as less worthy than the "beloved," even in 18:15f. Therefore, we theorize a positive role of both as paradigms for discipleship.

In John 20:2−10 some question exists about the separate use of "the other disciple" (1:37f.; 18:15f.) and "the disciple whom Jesus loved" (13:23f.; 19:25f.). Boismard thinks ("Saint Luc," p. 202) two traditions are combined here and that Luke was the editor who combined them, but this theory is based on slim linguistic evidence. It seems far more likely that the two phrases were combined by John himself. Consider, for example, 19:26 and 35[15] which

13. Passages which imply the "beloved disciple" but do not explicitly mention him are omitted here (1:41; 18:15−16; 19:35).

14. See Brown, in *New Testament*, pp. 133−47. The conclusion here is that the "beloved's" authority is highlighted by his interaction with Simon Peter. See pp. 130−33 for the picture of Peter, which they conclude was not significantly different from the synoptic portrayal.

15. See Brown, p. 936, for an analysis of 19:35 which Brown says is "parenthetical, probably editorial, but completely Johannine." See also Morris, p. 822n *contra* Lindars, p. 589, who says "it is an interpolation by the later redactor."

say that the "witness" of the "beloved" is not only "true" but based on his certainty that he is telling the truth. These verses which connect the motifs of witness and the "beloved" are supported by 21:20 and 24 which attest to the fact that the first-century Johannine church accepted this man's witness as authentic.

The linking of witness with the "beloved" may also have theological implications. John describes this "disciple whom Jesus loved" as a person who interacts with Peter, the disciples, and Jesus' mother in juxtaposition with both witness (19:35; 21:24) and belief (1:37f., 18:16, 20:2f.). He thus represents both the apostolic authority behind the resurrection claims (witness) and the evangelistic intent of those claims (belief). In this regard many critics believe that Peter is a foil to the "beloved one,"[16] failing Jesus by betraying him (18:15f.; 20:2f.), whereas "the disciple whom Jesus loved" (in 21:7) is the first disciple to recognize the Risen Christ and inform Peter of that fact. This view may be stretching the facts somewhat; chapters 19 and 20 include no suggestions of Peter's failure. Mahoney's assessment of Peter's role as a positive one seems more likely, "to anchor each stage in Jesus' going to the Father in tangible, earthly reality" (p. 282). Peter thus works with the "authentic witness" of the "beloved disciple"; together they offer the proper reaction of the church to its Risen Lord.

Belief (Faith)

Included in the working relationship of the "beloved" and Peter is a progressive development within each role. John 20:2 − 10, for instance, moves toward the "other disciple's" faith and insight in two ways: (1) The running imagery suggests that the "beloved" is more anxious than Peter to see the empty tomb for himself. Mahoney says (p. 245f.) one should not read too much into the race scene, yet the description seems indicative of more than just local color. In fact, the words which vividly describe how the "other disciple outran Peter" to arrive first at the tomb, then pausing while Peter impetuously pushed past to enter the tomb beautifully set the scene for the denouement of verses 8 and 9. The disciple who arrives first at the tomb reminds us of the priority of faith,

16. Schnackenburg, "Junger," pp. 104 − 05, and *Johannesevangelium*, IV, pp. 365 − 67, says the evangelist builds on Peter's reputation and uses him as a foil to establish the authority and prestige of the "beloved."

while the disciple who actually enters the tomb first sets us up for the apologetic motif of verse 9. (2) Mary's statement in verse 2 prepares us for what happens in verse 8 where the "other disciple" "saw and believed." Her words are obviously important; they are repeated twice more (vv. 13 and 15) and serve both to establish the parameters of dawning belief as well as a foil to it. This is especially evident in the use of the word *oida* ("know") in verses 2 and 13 which includes an inherent double meaning (it is used elsewhere in the fourth Gospel in conjunction with *horaō*, "see," and *pisteuō*, "believe" [v. 8], both salvific terms). Mary's lack of knowledge and faith thus prepare the reader for the role of the empty tomb in producing faith in the Risen Lord.

Brown says (p. 1006f.) the key element in this scene is love, since that is what provides the bridge to faith and understanding. The special "love" relationship gave a greater insight into spiritual truth. Faith, sight, and knowledge are all closely connected in John; as Dodd says (*Interpretation*, pp. 185−86) this passage clearly illustrates how faith becomes "knowledge." Several key passages (6:36, 46−47; 11:40, 45; 20:25−29) demonstrate the deepening of religious commitment when faith accompanies vision. Gaffney (p. 215f.) sees christological significance in the believing/knowing theme; Jesus is not the subject of believing (especially regarding the Father) as much as knowing, and he is the object of both as the revelation of God.

Faith is a primary motif in John. *Pisteuō* appears ninety-eight times in the Gospel (fourteen in Mark, eleven in Matthew, and nine in Luke). Yet its noun form (used more than its verb form in the New Testament) never appears in John. John uses only the verb form; faith to this writer is a dynamic process. Schnackenburg ("Glaube," pp. 165f.) illustrates this difference between John and other Gospel writers. While Mark describes faith in operation only after the revelation of the Risen Christ, John describes those who respond to Jesus' self-disclosures without complete understanding (10:24f.; 16:15) yet often with recognition. In John revelation comes through Jesus' teaching and signs and is the result of seeing, then knowing. It is a personal response to the authority of the earthly Jesus, not just the Risen Christ. In John's resurrection narrative we see the consummation of true faith (cf. 20:29). Although the "seeing" motif is used (especially in v. 29), literal "seeing" or

faith in the Risen Christ is not. The "beloved" disciple thus "sees" the empty tomb but not the resurrected Jesus.

This tension between seeing and knowing is also crucial to Johannine theology. Mahoney notes (pp. 264–70) how both seeing and knowing are involved in partial discipleship (see 2:23–25 and 6:30, 36) and how "seeing" can occur without "believing." The important thing then is to identify the earth-heaven dualism in the act of seeing. True sight which leads to faith occurs on the heavenly plane as the "eye of faith." This is the kind of sight the "beloved" exhibits, while Thomas and the other disciples in 20:29 reveal another kind of sight which is dependent on earthly evidence.

Initially verse 9 seems to contradict the faith motif of verse 8 when it says, "For they as yet did not know (*oida*) the scripture, that he must rise from the dead." Here "knowing" is contrasted with faith, yet at the same time serves as the basis (*gar*) for that faith. Some critics (Bultmann, Hartmann, Benoit) think this verse was a late addition to the narrative. They may not be wrong; the material here is probably redactional on the part of the evangelist (*contra* Mahoney). John probably repeated the synoptic fulfillment tradition (perhaps from the angelic message, cp. Luke 24:6–7), then applied it here to strengthen his "faith without seeing" motif (or to show how the "beloved" believed without knowing that scriptural fulfillment demanded it.)[17] Any seeming contradiction disappears when one sees how John used the fulfillment theme to accent the centrality of true faith and to show how belief arose despite incomplete understanding of Old Testament prophecies or Jesus' predictions.[18] Faith thus rises from the empty tomb, not just in response to the resurrection appearances.

Apologetic Motif

The mention of "signs" in verse 30f. suggests that chapter 20's

---

17. The Lukan language in this verse shows the presence of tradition: Graphē (24:27, 32, 45), dei (24:7, 26, 44), ek nekrōn anastēnai (24:46). Bode, pp. 81–82, notes that anastēnai is never used of the resurrection in John, nor is dei employed in a fulfillment context.

18. Brown, pp. 987–88, finds no reference to Jesus' predictions which are not recorded, even though he sees Johannine parallels in the Son of man sayings. If John knew Luke though, he could have retained that thrust, changing the traditional graphas to his own singular collective graphē which refers to both Old Testament and Jesus' predictions.

narrative is a "sign" written down to inspire belief in Jesus Christ.[19] Mahoney says (p. 269), "It is the essence of a *sēmeion* ("sign") that it points beyond itself to a great reality, that it prods to believing something physical eyes cannot have seen." The apologetic element in this pericope appears primarily in verses 7 – 9, especially in verse 7 where John describes the condition of Jesus' burial clothes inside the tomb. How did Jesus rise from the dead? Did he pass through the napkins (Duparc and Salvoni) or did he take off the burial clothing, then fold it neatly (Reiser)? Or was John simply making the point here that thieves did not steal the body of Jesus since they would not have bothered to undress the body (Léon-Dufour)? These solutions are speculative at best, with Léon-Dufour's apologetic approach the most likely.

John's "sign" here contains both a negative as well as positive inducement to faith: (1) negatively it counters the rumor that Jesus' body was stolen,[20] and (2) positively, it shows how faith came into being as a response to the empty tomb (connected to John's "signs" theology). Grundmann says ("Verständnis," pp. 131f.) this apologetic motif is even more than that and is, in fact, a major theme of the book which expresses itself in four ways: (Peter and the "beloved"), the word (Mary), the new life (the disciples), and persevering faith (Thomas). Thomas's faith is somewhat like awakening faith (2:11; 4:50) but in itself is insufficient; only the interpreting word leading to a persevering faith (8:50) can suffice. Riga says ("Signs," pp. 402f.) John enlarges the synoptic parable theme here by applying the enigmatic parable to Jesus' miracles. His purpose is to force the crowd to decision and the result is two groups: those who seek further understanding and those who only ask for more signs. The signs thereby have christological force, stressing Jesus' sonship and the Father's approval, and are based

19. It is difficult to know whether or not chapter 20 was originally part of any "signs source." Recently, Fortna and Nicol have reopened Bultmann's original thesis (*John*, pp. 6 – 7), and this has influenced many (e.g., Robinson, *Trajectories*, chap. 7; Schnackenburg, I, pp. 64 – 67). However, Schnackenburg doubts that the resurrection narratives can rightly be labeled "signs" at all, since they have no function with respect to the world but relate only to the disciples' faith. Nevertheless, we agree with Brown (pp. 1058f.) and Mahoney (pp. 268f.) as stated here.

20. See Campenhausen, *Tradition*, pp. 66 – 67, who says the "gardener" of verse 15 is evidence of an early Jewish polemic. A later story of "Judah and the gardener," for instance, says Judah removed the body. Although that story is too late to be used as evidence of an early origin for the polemic, we would agree with Campenhausen that its presence in Matthew and John indicate it was well known by the apostles.

on the soteriological decision of the individual. In this passage then, these two sides of the theme unite as the "sign" of the empty tomb brings faith. Feuillet adds (p. 197) that this "sign" goes beyond the empty tomb to the resurrection event itself, becoming an apostolic witness to the significance of the empty tomb.

Peter is the focal point of the apology,[21] the one who enters and verifies the reality of the empty tomb. Then the narrative becomes rich with detail as John impresses on the reader the full impact of Jesus' resurrection. We now arrive at the final stage of the development in the apologetic value of the empty tomb for faith in Mark to its greater place in Matthew and Luke, and finally to the primacy of the empty tomb in John. The details in verses 6b—7 are particularly important in this regard. "Strips of linen" and the "burial cloth" lying "folded up by itself, separate from the linen" are more than just local color;[22] they are vivid reminders of the reality of the resurrection event.

The Appearance to Mary, 20:11—18

Fortna (pp. 138—39) and Hartmann (pp. 204—206) believe that this pericope about Mary and the "gardener" at the tomb comes from tradition because of pre-Johannine elements such as *pros* ("to") with the dative (v. 11b), and similar descriptions such as Mary's "stooping" (v. 11b) and the angels' white garments. Still, the account includes redactional elements too such as Mary's remaining "outside" *(exō)* the tomb (in Mark 16:5 and Luke 24:3 she and the others enter), her weeping, and her conversing with a man she does not recognize.

John more than likely wanted his readers to remember that Mary followed the two disciples to the tomb, evidenced by his use of the pluperfect *eistēkei* ("had stood") in verse 11 which forms a bridge between Mary's encounter with the disciples and her en-

21. Mahoney sees the use of Peter's full name in verse 6 as significant here. Normally in John "Simon Peter" appears first while "Peter" comes later. The reversal of the pattern here indicates the apologetic importance of "Simon Peter."

22. Feullet (p. 1977) says John reports the linen cloths as remaining spread out while the cloth band (which passed over the head and under the chin to keep the mouth of the corpse closed) was rolled up in a separate place.

counter with Jesus. The use of the pluperfect verb here suggest an intervening time between the two episodes.[23]

Mary's Sorrow, 11–13

Vellanickal thinks the first two pericopes in chapter 20 emphasize two aspects of resurrection theology: verses 3–10 teach the continuity between the earthly and the Risen Jesus while verses 11–18 show the difference between his earthly ministry and risen status. This view, however, places too much emphasis on verse 17. The continuity of faith seems rather to be the main issue. Mary's reaction has distinct theological overtones, her confusion and sorrow symbolic of the struggling disciple who cannot comprehend the fact or significance of the resurrection. She simply does not understand.

Some critics note John's failure to write much about the angels at the tomb, saying they are no more than "stage furniture of no significance" (Bultmann, *HST*, p. 287) or "superfluous relics" (Fuller, *Resurrection*, p. 137) who "serve no real purpose" (Benoit, *Passion*, p. 257). This explanation is unnecessary; synoptic tradition included the angels as heavenly witnesses to the resurrection, and John does make mention of "two angels" in the second pericope where Mary stoops to look into the tomb. Schnackenburg (IV, pp. 371–72) stresses the continuity between the angels here and Peter in the previous scene as witnesses to the empty tomb. In this account the heavenly messengers help to prepare Mary for the final removal of her sorrow. "Weeping," which is mentioned three times (vv. 11, 13, 15), is the major focus of this section. It is an expression of doubt and spiritual ignorance,[24] especially in contrast to the faith of the "beloved one."

23. When Lindars (p. 603) and Benoit (pp. 256f.) say that Mary has been forgotten due to an "imperfect interweaving of two traditions," they give too little attention to the pluperfect here, which is out of place if the race narrative is removed. This verb indicated an intervening time and presupposes Mary's return previous to this episode.

24. Léon-Dufour (pp. 229–30) calls this weeping "eschatological activity," citing the "weeping and gnashing of teeth" motif in Jewish apocalyptic literature. Although some trace of this may be present, judgment as a theme is absent from this scene. It is far more likely that this scene continues the theme of misunderstanding and prepares for the victory of one who follows Christ rather than the defeat of one who does not.

Mary and the Risen Jesus, 14–18

Although many scholars see parallels between this pericope and Matthew 28:9–10, a lack of linguistic evidence proves there was less literary dependence than the sharing of common tradition (such as Mark). The only words common to both narratives are *adelphos* ("brother," but note the difference of style) and *anggellein* ("announce"), while words which differ from account to account are in abundance. John's touch is all too evident in passages such as the ascension theme, which makes use of phrases like *anabainō* (16 in John vs. 9 each in the others), *oupō* (12 vs. a total of 7 in the others), and *patēr* (137 vs. 18 in Mark, 64 in Matthew, 56 in Luke). Yet even here there is tradition; "go and tell my brothers" may reflect the Matthean tradition since "brothers" is found only in these two (see the chart of the parallels in Fuller, p. 138). Further, the *oupō* here seems to contradict the earlier *oupō* motif (2:4, 7:3–8, 30; 8:20) which pointed to Jesus' death. Therefore John probably redacted earlier material here.

John's pericope about Mary and Jesus includes many important theological motifs. Schnackenburg notes (IV, p. 371) the "dramatic effect" produced by the author's description of Mary's grief in comparison to Jesus' calm response. The faith motif (cf. chaps. 1, 4, 9) is expressed in a recognition scene which proceeds from ignorance to full-blown faith, but in a way which is distinctively peculiar to John. A weeping woman turns from the questions of two angels to the inquiring eyes of a stranger. He asks her the same question the angels asked and she responds with emotion as strong as her lack of understanding: "Sir, if you have carried him away, tell me where you have put him and I will get him."

The enigmatic pause here is a stylistic device which sets us up for the climax. In two brief words, "Mary" and "Rabboni," recognition takes place and faith is born. Why is the evangelist so dramatic here? Brown (*John*, p. 1009) sees three reasons for it: (1) apologetically it shows how the disciples were totally unprepared to see a Risen Christ, (2) it clearly describes Jesus' transformed condition in contrast to those who still doubted, and (3) the "misunderstanding" of Mary which parallels Luke's nonrecognition theme shows how those who "see" Jesus still may fail to recognize him. In fact, Mary's faith here is a direct contrast to that of the "beloved disciple"; Mary's could only come through the spoken word.

The high drama of this scene also includes christological force. Some scholars (Evans, Brown, Hartmann) think John used the word "Lord" in verses 2 and 13 because of the influence of the later church, but most critics believe Mary used the term as a simple title of respect which, through dawning understanding, later became "Rabboni,"

It is doubtful however that John would have used Mary to express deeper insight in the non-recognition scene than in the moment of understanding. Perhaps "Lord" is, instead, an example of Johannine "double-meaning" (see Wead, pp. 20−46) in which the prior *kyrios* anticipates the later and fuller use in verse 18. Note the progression from respect (vv. 2, 13), to the first stage of recognition (v. 16),[25] then to full-fledged faith in Christ's lordship (v. 18), all within the context of a dramatic contrast between misunderstanding (vv. 2, 13) and faith (v. 18). The evangelist uses the common Semitism[26] (*rabbouni ... didaskale*) in the final development of this recognition scene, yet holds back from saying any more. The story is not finished yet; John wants to move further into other portraits of faith before the most complete expression of faith (v. 29) is given.

John's primary thrust here is soteriological. Faith is prompted by the living presence of the Christ, the keynote of John's Gospel which is explicitly stated in 20:31. Although this theme is evident already in chapters about Jesus' signs and wonders, it is also a great part of discourse sections in chapters such as 6, 8, and 10. In chapter 6, for instance, the "bread of life" discourse (6:25−59) presents Jesus as the eschatological "manna" who gives eternal "food" or life to those who believe (note the close relationship between "believe" [6:29, 30, 35−36, 46, 47] and "life" [6:27, 33, 35, 40, 47−48, 51−54]). The "light of the world" discourse in chapter 8 (vv. 12−20), on the other hand, stresses the antithesis between light

25. Brown (p. 1010) says the vocabulary here is similar to 1:38 where Jesus asks the Baptist's followers, "What are you looking for?" and is answered, "Rabbi" ("teacher"). He concludes "Rabbi" is "a title that is characteristic of the beginning of faith." We see another parallel here with chapter 1 which offers a progression of titles from "rabbi" (v. 38), to "Messiah" (v. 41), to "Son of God," and "king of Israel" (v. 49).

26. This element is so strange that several Western texts fail to catch John's point, amplifying *didaskale* to *kyrie* or *kyrie didaskale*.

and darkness in matters of salvation, and focuses on Jesus as the one true "witness" (vv. 13, 17—19). The shepherd discourse in chapter 10 (vv. 1—21) portrays Jesus as both "shepherd" (vv. 11, 14) and "sheepgate" (vv. 7, 9) who gives "life" to the sheep (vv. 9—10) by "leading them" (vv. 3—4) and "laying down his life" for them (vv. 11, 15, 17—18). Nearly every section stresses Christology within the context of soteriology.

The same emphasis is evident in chapter 20 as Mary hears her name from the lips of the "gardener." He does not say *"Maria"* (the common Greek form[27]) but "Mariam" (the intimate Aramaic form). Mary's grief thus far has caused confusion and the inability to recognize Jesus, yet unlike the "beloved" who needed only to see the empty tomb to believe, Mary needed more. Like the sheep of the Good Shepherd Mary had to "hear his voice," be "called by name," and be "led forth" into faith. Still, the Risen Lord met her where she was in terms of faith, and called her to himself. Like a lost sheep her recognition could come only when her shepherd called her to himself.

Verse 16 may be the climax of dramatic action in this pericope, but verse 17 is definitely its theological high point. In it Jesus warns Mary, "stop touching me" as he explains he must "return to the Father." Why does Jesus say no to Mary here, yet encourage Thomas a little while later to feel the nailprints in his hands and the gash in his side? Brown summarizes (pp. 992—93) discussion on this question: (1) Some say Jesus demands only Mary should respect his glorified body by not touching him; the Twelve are not placed under this restriction. (2) Some interpret *mē haptou* ("stop touching me") as "do not fear" (Bernard) or even the positive "touch me." (3) Others (Lagrange, Barrett, Léon-Dufour) translate the verse, "Do not insist on touching me; it is true that I have not yet ascended to the Father, but I am about to do so."

The discussion does not end with Brown's summary; there are even more opinions: (4) Rigaux says (pp. 235—36) the emphasis in this expression is that Mary must "stop clinging" to Christ prior to his ascension since his glorification is outside the boundaries

27. See Brown (pp. 990—91) for a discussion of *Maria* (Alexandrinus, Bezae) or *Mariam* (Vaticanus, Sinaiticus). He doubts we can make much of the latter reading (clearly preferable on manuscript grounds) since evidence in five passages where the name appears (19:25; 10:1, 11, 16, 19) is inconclusive (the Aramaic form occurs in the latter two). We believe, however, that the change here is deliberate.

of time. (5) Marxsen (p. 61) says the phrase means something like, "you could still touch me but at this particular moment I want you to do something else—like go and tell the disciples that I will be leaving soon." The point here is that Jesus is tangible until he ascends to the Father. Hoskyns (p. 647) agrees with Marxsen but adds a eucharistic emphasis; no one can touch Jesus now but after the ascension they will "touch" him via the eucharistic celebration (cf. 6:51—58). (6) Many critics (Sanders, Lindars, Morris, Brown) favor Dodd's translation (*Interpretation*, p. 443n) which is, "do not cling to me." Dodd says Mary is being warned not to "cling to" old relationships and concepts. Charbel adds a little to Dodd's translation by making Jesus' words a question rather than a statement: "Do not cling; have not I ascended to my Father?" Jesus is asking Mary to give up her desire for an earthly relationship in favor of a spiritual one.

Charbel's analysis certainly offers a good solution to the problem of verse 17; suggesting that the Risen Christ is about to usher in a new kind of God-man relationship which Mary must not fight by clinging to old ideas. As Forestell says (p. 98), "The entire movement of Jesus' life in John is *pros ton patera*" ("to the Father," 7:33; 13:3; 14:12, 18). His exaltation to the Father is not complete so long as earthly relationships continue.[28]

John's concept of the ascension is also significant in this passage. Benoit suggests ("Ascension") John combines two distinct promitive traditions in this concept: (1) an invisible glorification which took place on Easter contiguous with the resurrection, and (2) a visible ascension after forty days. Many others (Brown, Mahoney, de Jong, *contra* Lohfink) agree: Mary can "not yet" know Jesus' permanent presence which depends on his final "ascension" to the Father and the corresponding gift of the Spirit. The ascension in John is thus a timeless event in which "I am ascending" does not refer either to Jesus' state before or after the event. Brown adds, "It is a theological statement contrasting the passing

---

28. There are two key terms: *oupō* and *anabainein*. The former is found frequently in John (eleven times) often in passages regarding "the hour" (2:9; 7:6, 8, 30; 8:20), always as a basic negation. As Olssen asserts (pp. 43—44) regarding the possibility that 2:9c is a question, *oupō* is never used thusly in John and only four times in the synoptics (Mark 4:40; 8:17, 21; Matt. 16:9). Therefore it is likely that here as well it is a statement rather than a question (*contra* Charbel).

nature of Jesus' presence in his post-resurrection appearances to the pertinent nature of his presence in the Spirit." This makes sense especially in light of the connection in John (especially in the Farewell Discourse, chaps. 13 – 17) between the departure of Christ and the coming of the Spirit.

The timeless quality of the ascension is especially evident in verse 17's juxtaposition of "not yet" with "have ascended" (perfect tense) and "am ascending" (present tense). To understand this seeming contradiction one must understand the verse within the context of John's eschatology. He often uses "not yet" in connection with the "hour" of Jesus' glory; and in 7:39 for instance, Jesus was "not yet" glorified because "the Spirit had not been given" (cf. 12:23, 27, 31f.; 13:31.; 17:1f.). The "hour of glory" in John refers to Christ's passion in soteriological terms; its true significance would become only evident after Christ's ascension when the Holy Spirit could make it all clear to Jesus' followers.

Mahoney (p. 276) believes three verses in John (3:13; 6:62; 20:17) which include the imagery of Christ's "going to" the Father are linked to the Son of man imagery of Daniel 7:13 and the glorification theme of Psalm 110:1. In John the crucifixion itself signifies "glory" or "ascent" (cp. 1:51; 12:32, 53) and is intimately connected with the ascension and "hour" (7:8; 17:1) or "glory" (13:31f; 17:23, 32) of Jesus. The point is particularly relevant for a complete understanding of verse 17 where "not yet" might seem inappropriate after the crucifixion. Obviously here the phrase refers to the completed work of salvation in history, a process which includes the death, resurrection, *and* appearances.[29] Thus "I am ascending" becomes progressive tense rather than futuristic present (as also Brown, p. 994; Schnackenburg, IV, p. 377).

Jesus is telling Mary that she must not cling to her earthly relationship with him since the messianic age is about to begin. In that age she will have a new relationship with him which will be intense, more personal, and focused through the presence of

29. Fuller's attempt (*Resurrection*, 138 – 39) here to replace *theios-anēr* Christology with a *katabasis-anabasis* thrust is wrong since it teaches that Mary can no longer cling to the "God-man" Jesus but only as the Ascended One. Such a concept does not fit John's balance between the divine Christ and the earthly Jesus. John does not oppose synoptic Christology; he supplements it.

the paraclete.[30] Forestell states it well (p. 98): "Raised upon the cross and through the cross exalted to the Father, he (Christ) draws all men to himself, i.e., into communion of life with himself and the Father. . . . The prophecies of the Old Testament have been fulfilled and a new family or people of God has been formed."

The Appearance to the Disciples, 20:19–23

The next section is very similar to Luke 24, with: the same day theme, *tē mia sabbatōn* ("first day of the week"), "stood in the midst," "Peace to you," "showed them his hands and his side," commission, gift of the Spirit, and the power to forgive sins. The passage, in fact, seems to combine several sources, the major borrowing coming from Luke. Added to this is some redaction by John.

Verse 19 presents some problems in time notes which are partly solved by their parallels in Luke. Still, they are not completely solved; the use of such complex time notes surely indicates more than just an editorial connective with the preceding pericope. More likely "on the evening of that first day of the week, when the disciples were together" prepares for the next time note in verse 26, "eight days later," which reminds us of the "first day of the week" in verses 1 and 26. Bultmann (p. 691) says "that day" refers to the eschatological day of individual decision which is such a clear theme in this Gospel and throughout the New Testament.[31]

30. This interpretation is favored by two additional factors: (1) The caption "brothers," as Grundmann says ("*Zur Rede Jesu*"), culminates the discipleship motif in John by giving them a new post-resurrection status analogous to the Father-Son relationship. In this light Dodd adds (p. 442), "It is not the resurrection as Christ's resumption of heavenly glory that needs to be emphasized, but the resurrection as the renewal of personal relations with the disciples" and even more to a new sphere of fellowship in the Spirit. (2) The phrases, "my Father and your Father . . . my God and your God," with the deliberate *mou . . . hymōn* ("my" . . . "our") accent in both, elevate the disciples to a position alongside the Son and further cement this new relationship with the Father. Yet the singular-plural contrast is also deliberate rather than stylistic. He is "the unique Son" (1:14, 18; 3:16, 18) while they "become sons of God" (1:12) through his redemptive activity (see further de Jonge, chap. 6). Yet as Moule says (*Worship*, p. 77) the stress here is on identity, "my Father, who is also your Father."

31. This is seen in "peace" and "joy," Jewish eschatological themes. He has a point, for "that day" is Johannine (1:39; 11:53; especially 14:20; 16:23, 26) and in fact is a common New Testament apocalyptic concept (e.g., Mark 13:11f; Luke 24:32; Acts 2:18; 2 Tim. 1:12f., 4:8; Rev. 9:6). It would be appropriate here to note a partial fulfillment of the kingdom

Many critics[32] link the three time notes in verse 19 with the Sunday worship motif of Revelation 1:10, saying John presents a liturgical or sacramental motif here which presupposes the living presence of Jesus in the eucharistic celebration.[33] They support this by quoting Mark 16:14 which also presents a post-resurrection appearance of Christ at the time when the disciples "sat at meat." Although this eucharistic emphasis may be true of the last (questionable) section of Mark, it is probably less true of John who, nonetheless, may well include some liturgical material.

The Scene, 19–20

Although the "closed" or "locked" doors of verse 19 have often been used to prove Jesus already had a glorified body, nowhere in the verse is any mention made of his passing through those doors. More than likely the real point of John's detail about these locked doors was to continue the theme of surprise which is a part of the doubt motif in the preceding pericope, or to stress how the "fear of the Jews" had forced Jesus' followers into extreme precautions. *Hoi Ioudaioi* ("the Jews," found seventy-one times in John) is a kind of all-inclusive term which John uses to describe many Jewish sects without differentiating between them. Some critics think John shows an anti-Semitic bias here as well as elsewhere in his book (he links "the Jews" with "the world"). There is a definite polemic. Nearly every Jewish institution is superseded by "the Christ." Ritual purification, the temple, Jerusalem-worship, and feasts (chaps. 5–10) are all replaced by Jesus who is the ser-

via the resurrection. However, we must correct Bultmann's existential hermeneutic; it is not specifically "decision" here but rather the entrance of the last days and presence of the kingdom blessings.

32. Lindars, p. 609; Brown, pp. 1019f.; Léon-Dufour, p. 181; and Barrett, p. 477, see liturgy in verses 19–29: assembling on the Lord's day, the blessing, the descent of the Spirit, the absolution (v. 23), the eucharistic presence, the confession, and the application (v. 29).

33. The debate on the presence of sacramental overtones in John is too extensive to put into a brief footnote. For a good (although somewhat negative) overview, see Kysar, pp. 49–59, although we would not be so negative as he in our conclusions. It seems clear that John wishes to theologize the eucharistic words, especially with the important 6:51–58 following the liturgical tone of the entire chapter (see Borgen's important work on this). However, reading this into other pericopae, as here and 21:11–14, is not so simple. We are quite pessimistic about eucharistic overtones here, but as we will state below, more open to it in 21:11f.

vant of God (1:29, 34), lamb (1:29), King (1:49), and Holy One (6:69). "Jews" are hostile to this servant in contrast to others who may be Jewish (such as the parents of the blind man in 9:22) but are not opposed to him and also "fear the Jews."

Although John does have a polemical thrust here, the "anti-Judaism" charge does not hold up if we recognize that he uses "Jews" to typify unbelievers in general. In fact, the motif stands for the general hostility of the world against Jesus even though he is the fulfillment of Jewish (or all the world's) hopes more than the harbinger of judgment (see also Michaelis and Schnackenburg). The links between Christianity and Judaism are so clear that the "fear" motif of verse 19 should be viewed only within the context of a scene of victory. "Fear" becomes "joy" (v. 20) as Christ, the Risen Lord, reveals himself.

Jesus' greeting, "Peace to you," is the antidote to fear as well as the eschatological result of God's activity in the last days. Jesus says it three times (vv. 19, 21, 26), proving it is more than just a greeting. Obviously John too[34] considers it an expression of theological truth. In fact, the statement reminds us of Jesus' promises (14:27, 16:33) which have not been fulfilled.[35] "Peace" is closely linked with "that day" or the fulfillment of the Old Testament promise of messianic salvation (cf. Ps. 29:11; Isa. 9:6; 52:7; 55:7; Ezek. 37:26; Zech. 9:10) in the "Day of the Lord."

"Joy" is also found with "peace" in the farewell discourse (14:27; 15:11), and is associated with the gift of salvation (14:28; 15:11; 16:20f.; 17:13; cf. 3:29; 4:36; 8:56; 11:15). Jesus' saving work has brought with it the peace and joy of the Eschaton; yet this joy is incomplete since today it comes through suffering (cf. 16:20f.) while one day when the Kingdom is fully ushered in it will be complete.[36]

---

34. Brown, p. 1029; and Lindars, p. 611, argue for Johannine style vs. Bultmann and Hartmann who say this duplication is a sign of late editorial expansion.

35. Note W. C. van Unnik's *New Testament Essays in Honor of T. W. Manson*, pp. 207 – 305, on a similar formula, "The Lord is with you." Van Unnik says (p. 283) when the verb is used here the phrase stresses certainty, but when it is not the phrase becomes a command. Brown applies this distinction to "peace be with you," and says this phrase minus the verb also becomes a command: "Peace to you."

36. Johannine eschatology is a massive subject in which discussion has moved well beyond Dodd and Bultmann's presentation of a "realized" thrust. Kysar says (p. 208) modern discussion stresses the subordination of eschatology to Christology as well as the presence of a futuristic aspect in the Gospel. Howard, however, (*Christianity*, p. 106f.) says John includes no antithesis between eschatology and mysticism. The vertical ele-

The apologetic element of Jesus "showing them (the disciples) his hands and feet" which prompts their "joy," is important in verse 20,[37] yet the stress is not so much on physical proof as on recognition. Proof leads to victory over fear as seeing leads to believing (v. 20, cf. vv. 8, 25f.). Jesus "showed" and they "saw," which then produced "joy." This follows John's natural progression from the first three episodes; the "beloved" needed only the empty tomb to believe; Mary required the voice of her Good Shepherd in addition to the tomb; and the disciples (who were afraid) had to experience the specific sight of Jesus' hands and side in order to believe.

The Missionary Commission, v. 21

Jesus begins this section with "Peace be with you," a message which roots the "sending forth" of the disciples in the kind of eschatological peace which Christ has ushered in by his suffering, death, and resurrection. The commission itself is the final statement of the "sent one" and a kind of "chain of revelation" or key to the whole concept of mission in John: Jesus, who is sent from the Father, sends the Spirit to disciples, who then are sent out into the world. This process, says Schnackenburg (IV, p. 384), is like the one indirectly expressed in 4:38: "I sent you to reap what you have not worked for. Others have done the hard work, and you have reaped the benefits of their labor" (NIV). Each member of the chain builds on the previous person's work. Kysar says (p. 244), "Each continues the mission of the former and depends on the former."

The commission also parallels 17:18 which reads, "As you sent me into the world, so I have sent them." John does change verb tenses, but as Van Hoff notes, the perfect tense is a usage typical

ment itself demands a future fulfillment. Therefore we would follow Cullmann ("L'evangile Johannique," pp. 111f.) and Ladd (*Theology*, p. 298f.) in asserting an inaugurated thrust, with the primary emphasis on the vertical, itself part of the horizontal present, yet recognizing the futuristic. "Judgment," for instance, is a future event in 5:28f. and 12:48, yet actualized in faith-encounter (3:18f.) and thereby a spiritual reality in the present.

37. Léon-Dufour (pp. 182–83) says that the Lukan apologetic is eliminated along with the doubt motif and that John stresses only triumph over fear. However, he overextends John's emphasis. Rigaux (pp. 237–38) is more correct when he notes the dramatization of the doubt in the belief-unbelief antithesis. The apologetic element is present but subservient to soteriology. John, in fact, echoes Luke, replacing "feet" with "side" in light of verses 25b and 27b and because of the spear thrust in 19:34.

of John to stress present relevance. Jesus now commissions the disciples on the basis of the passion events. He sends them forth in two ways: (1) in the full authority of the Son given to him by the Father with whom he is united in thought and action; (2) in the authority of disciples who are sent forth by the Son and therefore are also grounded in the Father. The Son passes on his authority to his followers who carry on his work.

The Sending of the Spirit, v. 22

Haenchen ("Der Vater") says Jesus' "sending" his disciples forth is closely linked with the sending of the Spirit who provides the impetus and reveals the true meaning of Jesus' words. The power for mission is bestowed as the "witness," or spirit of truth (15:26), guarantees the witness of the disciples. The gift here matches the expectations of earlier passages (1:33; 7:39; 14:16f., 26; 15:26; 16:7) in which the coming of the Spirit is seen both as the act of the Father and of the Son. Now Jesus fulfills those expectations when he "breathes" (*emphusēsen:* a *hapax legomenon*) his Spirit on the disciples. Since he has already been "glorified" (cp. 7:39) he can now impart the Spirit. In John the outpouring of the Spirit begins with the resurrection which publicly proclaims the "glory" of the Messiah.[38]

In John the Spirit also has a special relationship to Jesus who is the bearer of the Spirit (1:32, 34) and so bestows the Spirit. The evangelist does not mention the unique relationship between the Spirit and Jesus' miracles, perhaps because here the Spirit is more personal than charismatic and so is the "ambassador" or "representative" of Jesus (as A. Johnston and Brown). Perhaps this is the

---

38. John's preference for *doxa* matches Luke's, but John gives it a unique twist. He makes glory visible in the acts of the earthly Jesus (2:11; 11:40; 17:4) who personifies divine glory (1:14), and links it to the praise of the Father (7:18; 12:43) rather than men (5:41; 7:18). In fact, the term does not appear after the resurrection but was manifest in the passion (12:23f.; 13:31f.; 17:1f.). Thüsing (*Erhohung*, pp. 201–204) asserts that John has united the earthly and the glorified Christ. While we admit that this accords somewhat with the picture, he goes too far when he declares that John read back the post-resurrection theology into the earthly ministry. Rather, we note a proleptic "glory" which accords with the "signs" theology. The acts and words of the earthly Jesus point to the glorified Christ, but it is not the glorified Christ who speaks in the earthly Jesus. Wead, pp. 1–11, is more correct when he discusses the "post-resurrection point of view" in which John provides glimpses of the "glory to come" in the words and acts of Jesus.

best description of the true function of the Paraclete, since his work so closely parallels that of Christ's. In 14:16, for instance, he is, like Jesus, "another Paraclete" whose mission (15:26, 16:27) and function are the same (teacher, 7:14 = 14:26; witness, 8:14 = 15:26; judge, 3:18f. = 16:8f.). He thus serves the eschatological function of continuing the kingdom work begun by Jesus as he works through the preaching and witness of the church. Thus this "Johannine Pentecost" has a definite empowering function: positively, to proclaim Jesus' message through the church; negatively, to judge the sinful world (both themes relate to v. 23).

Not everyone agress with this analysis. Some scholars (Windisch, Hartmann, Holwerda, Schulz) argue that no connection should be made between this passage and other Paraclete passages, since this passage simply portrays "the giving of life to believers and the formation of the Christian community" with abolutely no suggestion of empowering (Forestell, p. 100).

This verse presents essentially a rebirth theme which may include echos of Genesis 2:7 ("God breathed into man's nostril the breath of life") as well as Ezekiel 37 (the vision of dry bones coming to life with God's "breath"). Forestell thinks John may originally have written this verse to describe Christ's simple gift of life to his disciples but that later an editor reworked it (influenced by Luke and Paul) to include implications of Spirit-indwelling as well as forgiveness of sins. Perhaps the best way to interpret this verse is not to force an either/or position between ecclesiology and soteriology. In fact, perhaps both are elements here; ecclesiology providing the conclusion to a soteriological pericope (as in verse 17 of the previous section). Moreover, this is not a purely "Pauline" theme but as stated above is part of a crucial Johannine theme.

The Promise of Authority, v. 23

The power to forgive or retain sins introduced in verse 23 has been a divisive issue in Catholic-Protestant dialogue; Catholics traditionally defining it in terms of penance, and Protestants in terms of kerygmatic proclamation. Although initially Jesus' announcement is both surprising and abrupt (causing Forestell and others to doubt its authenticity), good reasons exist for believing its source is tradition. Lindars (p. 612) and Dodd (*Tradition*, pp. 348f.) find evidence of this in its Semitic style and *hapax legomena* (non-

Johannine terms like "forgive," "sins," and "grasp"). Fuller (p. 141) sees evidence such as: the two-part style with the first related to man and the second to God; antithetical parallelism; and the use of the reverential passive for God's activity.

Another problem with this verse is its connection with Matthew 16:19 and 18:18. Many critics think John adapted Matthean tradition here, but Dodd (*Tradition*, pp. 348f.; " 'Herrenwort,' " pp. 85f.) says *kratein* ("grasp") in John does not correspond at all with *dein* in Matthew. John must have therefore adapted a variant form with an independent origin. Thus the criterion of "multiple attestation" would further support the authenticity of this saying. J. A. Emerton says ("Binding and Loosing," pp. 325f.) both of these terms come from a common Aramaic saying which is based on Isaiah 22:22 (also Lindars, Sanders, Brown).

Perhaps both penance and kerygma are suggested in verse 23. Lindars says (p. 613) the verse cannot refer to a "rigid penitential discipline, comparable to that of the Qumran sect, when Jesus' preaching to the tax-collectors and sinners was so open." Yet Brown maintains (p. 1041) that John never connects forgiveness with preaching the gospel. The solution here is the context, where the power to forgive is based on the presence of the Spirit (v. 22) within the framework of mission (v. 21). Through mission Jesus' disciples (the generic use of *tines* suggests the followers of Jesus in general) convict men of sin and lead them to decision, which in turn leads to forgiveness. With their decision, "forgiveness" or "retaining their sins" occurs. Thus the proclamation of the kerygma has a judging function, parallelling Jesus' activity.

Jesus' function as judge is interesting here in light of the author's careful efforts prior to this to distinguish between Jesus' ontological character as judge (which is denied, 3:17) and his function as judge (which is accepted, 5:22; 9:39). The key passage is 8:15, 16, which brings the two sides together; Christ is not eschatological judge, yet his presence in the world reveals the Father and forces man to a decision which brings judgment. Jesus' works here are now passed on to his followers as is the convicting activity of the Spirit (16:8 – 11).

Although many critics (e.g., Hoskyns, Barrett, Dodd, Grass, Evans) argue that both church discipline and proclamation are suggested here, the element of penitence is definitely subdued.[39] In fact, little or no basis for it exists in this context or anywhere else in the Gospel. Léon-Dufour says simply (p. 187), "Here John is reproducing a Jewish tradition, of which a trace can still be seen in the Qumran writings, according to which the Messiah will cleanse men from all sin." The Messiah's work as well as authority is passed on to the disciples in the mission of proclamation.

The Doubting Thomas Episode, 20:24–29

The story of Jesus' confrontation with Thomas is the climax of John's faith motif. Although the "beloved" is the epitome of faith, that lesson is not clear until this episode. The one who simply "saw and believed" in verse 8 is a direct contrast to the complex doubt of Thomas here, and in between is the faith of Mary through recognition and that of the Twelve through physical evidence. Although John does not make the doubt theme explicit in earlier episodes, he does so here, as Jesus dramatically removes it from his disciple.

Forestell says (p. 101) that verses 24–29 are a rewrite of 19–23 "for an entirely different theological purpose," yet it is doubtful that the resulting blend of harmonious and disharmonious elements proves this is so. Rather the two should be seen as separate episodes linked redactionally to the soteriological purpose of the chapter. All themes in this passage build up to the seeing-believing motif and faith-statement of verse 29.

The Doubt Motif

Both Thomas's cynicism and Jesus' response to it are taken from tradition, although some details are added such as Thomas's stubborn refusal to believe without physical proof, and his request not only to "see" but also to "touch" that proof.

We know Luke wrote his episode (24:36f.) in response to some

---

39. For the Catholic debate regarding sins committed before and after conversion see Brown, Léon-Dufour, and Schnackenburg. All conclude that such a distinction is foreign to John.

kind of gnostic group which denied the reality of Jesus' resurrection body, but how much this group also influenced John is highly debatable. Bultmann thinks (*John*, 7—9) John was influenced through a "revelation discourse" source which was gnostic in its dualism, three-stage world view, preexistence, and redeemer myth (paralleled in the Odes of Solomon and Mandean writings). However, Schnackenburg (I, pp. 135—52), Braun (*Jean*, pp. 111—21), and Colpe (*Schule*, pp. 39f., 50f.) believe that Christian gnostic circles were influenced by John rather than had an influence on him.[40]

John more often seems to be anti-gnostic rather than proto-gnostic (note the incarnation theme of 1:14; 6:51—58, 63; 19:34); the anti-docetic element in this account of Thomas is as responsible as tradition for the emphasis on physical proof.

Thomas is the focal point of John's doubt motif.[41] He is the hardheaded realist and stubborn skeptic who exemplifies the disciples' lack of understanding (11:16) as well as honest confusion (14:5). Both episodes include some evidence of soteriology ("believe" in 11:15 and "know" in 14:5) and prepare for the climax of doubt in chapter 20.

John's Christology

Thomas's cry, "My Lord and my God," is the apex of Christology in the fourth Gospel. Barrett says (p. 58), "what John perceived with far greater clarity than any of his predecessors was that Jesus *is* the Gospel, and that the Gospel *is* Jesus." What is crucial here

---

40. Käsemann (*Testament of Jesus, passim*) has taken the theory beyond Bultmann and states that the fourth evangelist was a Christian gnostic who argued for a heavenly redeemer rather than the historical Jesus, on the following grounds: (1) John's Christology, dominated by the "glory" motif, overwhelms the incarnate Jesus with a divine Christ; (2) his ecclesiology, dominated by the "Logos" motif, places the individual over the community (e.g., the de-emphasis of the Twelve); (3) his soteriology, dominated by dualism, stresses the unity of the believer with Jesus as a microcosm of the Father-Son relation. However, Käsemann has presented a one-sided picture of John; in each area there is a counterbalance: (1) The divine Christ is balanced by the incarnate Jesus (*not* "overwhelmed"! See further the next section.). (2) The "Word" becomes part of the mission, and the "disciples" typify the later church (much the same as in Matthew); there is no "de-emphasis" (see Schnackenburg, I, pp. 162—63). (3) The unity of the believer with Christ is based on Jewish, not gnostic, parallels. As Schnackenburg states (p. 141), a realization of the Jewish background behind key parables like the shepherd and the vine was instrumental in changing Edward Schweizer's earlier Mandean oriented position.

41. This tendency is not theological (*contra* Käsemann) but stylistic, a literary method used to centralize the drama.

is not Jesus' messianic office; the messianic misunderstanding which is so central to Mark changes emphasis in John. John's christological key to understanding who Jesus really is is the special sonship (20:31) which clarifies his messianic office. He thus is virtually equal to the Father (10:30) yet obedient to the Father (5:19f.; 15:10; cf. 14:10; 17:8). M. I. Appold goes one step further, *(Oneness Motif)* saying this "oneness" is the unifying theme in John's theology as it translates the unity between Father and Son into the relationship between Jesus and his followers. Their oneness is both relational (union of purpose and essence) and revelational (Father revealed through the Son).

John also includes some incarnational theology here (1:14a) in which Jesus is truly man (1:30; 4:29; 8:40; 9:11f.; 10:33) with full humanity expressed in emotional awareness (11:33; 12:27; 13:27), exhaustion, and thirst (4:6f.; 19:28). John's interest in the historical Jesus offers a balanced portrait of incarnation in its presentation of "the indivisibility of flesh and glory" (Kysar, pp. 195f.).

Thomas's statement though, in verse 28, primarily focuses on Jesus' glory. As B. A. Mastin observes ("Neglected Feature"), the fact that Jesus as "God" appears specifically at the beginning (1:1, 14) and close of John's Gospel (20:26), as well as generally throughout (3:18; 8:58; 10:30f.; 12:45; 14:9; 17:11), shows how important high Christology is. The same Jesus who reveals God is God himself, yet is one who has a personal relationship with his followers (note the stress on "my" in both phrases). Lindars (p. 616) states that this personal emphasis shows Thomas's cry was not an argument against emperor worship (contra *Evans*, pp. 125f.) as much as an expression of true faith. Brown (p. 1048) and Léon-Dufour (p. 189) even see a covenant thrust here; verse 17 promising God would be a Father to the disciples, and verse 28 the ratification of that covenant by his people (cf. Hos. 2:25).

The Faith Motif

Verse 29 is the finale in John's resurrection drama. Through each of the previous episodes he has presented a different kind of faith, all the while progressing toward Jesus' final description of the highest form which is the kind that "has not seen and yet has believed." What specifically does Jesus mean by this? Bultmann says (p. 695f.) John is providing a critique concerning the value of the Easter stories which "can never produce faith but only have kerygmatic value." He thinks Jesus' statement is the culmination of John's "signs" theology which is directed specifically against those who are weak in faith (4:48). On the other hand, H. Wenz says (pp. 17f.) the emphasis here is Jesus' warning against those who do not believe because they cannot see; only those who "believe" (with or without signs) can truly see Jesus. Several critics such as Fuller, Brown, Lindars, and Schnackenburg agree with Wenz, saying Thomas does have a valid faith, yet far better is the faith that trusts without external proof (or seeing). Clearly John's emphasis here is the juxtaposition of seeing and believing within the context of soteriology.

The *Sitz im Leben* of this passage is interesting. Benoit comments (*Passion*, p. 287) that the past tense (aorist) of the verbs *idontes* ("see") and *pisteusantes* ("believe") probably are indications of redaction, since Jesus' original saying must have looked to the future (in the present tense). Although Benoit assesses the grammar incorrectly,[42] he does have a point theologically. The verse seems to reflect John's own time in which eyewitnesses were beginning to die off and people increasingly were forced to rely on second-hand testimony. Jesus presents here a beatitude which contrast two kinds of "blessedness," in effect saying, "Blessed are the eyes that, by faith, see what you see" (Dodd in *Tradition*, pp. 354f.) Thomas represents the generation which still depends on first-hand testimony, while the later generation of John's time is even "more blessed" because it believes based on the witness of others.

The First Conclusion, 20:30—31

Although some critics[43] say verses 30 and 31 are simply the conclusion of chapter 20, most believe they finish the entire Book of John. "Many other signs" in verse 30 thus refers to all the other signs or miracles that Jesus did and that John knew about but

---

42. Aorist participles in such a situation can refer to future action (cf. John 11:2). Here it is probably meant to have the same time sense as the main verbs, which are perfect tenses having present force. Again, there is a timeless sense—"at any time blessed are those who...."

43. See Hoskyns, pp. 655f. and Morris, p. 859, who refer to 1 John 5:13 as a similar verse which does not conclude a book. The similarity is only external, however.

could not include in his Gospel. The verse is the capstone to the "signs" theology in *John,* linking it unalterably to faith in "the Christ, the Son of God." As de Jonge says (p. 119), "Signs give *life* to those who are willing and able to believe it Him who presents life through these signs."

The verb *pisteusate* ("believe") in its aorist tense has prompted some extensive debate. If John uses his tenses strictly, the use of the indeterminate past tense here suggests a missionary purpose (come to believe) and the present a didactic or catechetical thrust (continue to believe).[44] Risenfeld says (*"hina*-satzen," pp. 213f.) John does use his tenses strictly, thereby calling believers to perseverance in faith. But other critics such as Morris, Barrett, and Schnackenburg refuse to assume too much from these tenses since such a strict limitation of John's purpose seems unrealistic. Kysar, in fact, says (p. 148) the problem is "further complicated by the evangelist's irregular use of verb tense so that only by drawing inferences from portions of the Gospel concerning the concrete situation of the evangelist and his purpose can the precise meaning of 20:31 be ascertained."[45] In fact, John's soteriology prohibits any narrow definition of purpose since didactic, evangelistic, and polemical elements are all present. The author, for instance, often utilizes dualism which contrasts elements such as light and darkness, life and death, spirit and flesh, thus presenting two alternative destinies.

This multipurpose thrust is also a part of the two-sided description of Jesus in verse 31. He is both "the Christ" and "the Son of God": "Messiah" in the sense of having provided for "life," and "Son of God" in his intimate connection with the Father. Further, the second term clarifies the former, and his messiahship in the fourth Gospel is primarily royal, as illustrated in the triumphal entry and the entire passion narrative which follows. The terms are neither synonymous nor separable; rather, they refer to the

44. The textual evidence is evenly divided with א C A C D K L W et al reading the aorist but p[66vid] א * B et al the present. Most believe the latter is preferable, since John favors it in *hina* clauses.

45. He goes on to discuss four major theories—the dialogue with the synagogue, an anti-docetic polemic, a Samaritan mission, and a universal appeal to Christians—and concludes that while the first is uppermost, there are minor subpurposes which may embrace aspects of the others.

horizontal (for man) and vertical (to God) aspects of Jesus' person and work.

John's concept of zaō ("life") is also crucial to the meaning of this verse. He uses it often in his writings, linking it with aiōnios ("eternal") to mean that life which belongs to the Father (5:26, 6:57) and the Son (11:25, 14:6), and is offered to men through Jesus' words (6:63; 10:10) and death (3:16; 7:39) on the basis of faith (3:16; 5:24; 20:31). Bultmann thinks this concept originated in Gnosticism, and Brown thinks it came from Judaism, but Dodd probably is most correct when he says John borrowed from both, though primarily from Judaism (cp. Dan. 12:2; 2 Macc. 12:43f.; 1 Qs 4:7, etc.). The concepts relate to both groups.

Note the interesting paradox in *John* between grace and free will (see Carson, *Sovereignty*). The evangelist often includes a strong predestination thrust; only those chosen by the Father are able to come to faith (6:37f., 65f.; 8:47; 15:16; 18:37). Still, man is personally responsible for rejection which is deliberate (9:39f.) and caused by a self-seeking nature (5:44) under the influence of sin (3:19) and the devil (8:44). Life and judgment walk side-by-side through the Gospel.

Ecclesiology, Chapter 21

Since 20:30−31 seems to be the natural conclusion of this Gospel, chapter 21 becomes a real problem. Most early manuscripts include it as a part of the book even though internal evidence[46] seems to argue against that. Most critics believe it was an appendix or "epilogue" (Brown) attached to the book at a later time. Whoever added it remains questionable even though John's authorship of its seems likely. Whatever the conclusion about authorship, it clearly stands thematically within the mainstream of Johannine ideology.

Appearance to the Fishing Disciples, 21:1−14

The first episode in chapter 21 sounds much like the account in Luke 5:1−11, causing most scholars to assume a common origin

46. Brown, p. 1078, adds that the beatitude of verse 29 makes any more stories of appearances very unlikely.

for the two. Which is the more primitive account? The answer to that question is not relevant at this point, but the problem itself is intriguing since a comparison of the two accounts highlights so much redactional material. Clearly both authors utilize tradition in their own way to present their own unique message.

Pesch says (*Fischfang*, pp. 53f., 148f.) John 21 is the combination of two traditions, a "miraculous catch of fish" (vv. 2, 3, 4a, 6, 11) and an appearance tradition (vv. 4b, 7, 8, 9, 12, 13) which are woven together by other verses such as 1, 5, 10, and 14. Fortna, on the other hand, argues (*Signs*, pp. 87f.) that the story as a whole was the third miracle in the "signs" source. Although Pesch's theory is too complex to be plausible, Fortna's explanation seems far too simplistic.[47] Perhaps the most reasonable view here is that John took the basic appearance tradition and worked with it on the basis of his own theological interests.

Schnackenburg sees (IV, p. 408) five basic themes in chapter 21: (1) the person, ecclesiastical purpose, and fate of Peter; (2) the person and purpose of the "beloved" and his relationship to Peter; (3) Jesus' continued fellowship with the disciples and the church; (4) Jesus' work in the church through the ministry of Peter and the "beloved"; and (5) the mission and unity of the church. Schnackenburg probably places too much importance on the role of Peter and the "beloved"; they are perhaps better viewed as a means to an end within the primary motif of ecclesiology. As chapter 20 stressed soteriology, so the epilogue stresses the church. The opening section includes the following emphases:

Recognition Motif

The bridge from chapter 20 to chapter 21 is the recognition theme[48] which also, says Dodd, is the central element in this per-

47. For the redactor to have combined his sources as woodenly as Pesch maintains is difficult to accept. Brown (*Resurrexit*, p. 260) notes three weaknesses with Pesch's theory: (1) The appearance story is truncated, for too much of it is missing to make it coherent; in fact, part of the setting Pesch postulates is found in the catch of fish. (2) The appearance story is inconsistent itself, e.g., the twofold recognition in verses 7 and 12. (3) The method of the redactor is virtually inexplicable and raises more problems than it solves. In the same way, it is unlikely that the evangelist would merely have incorporated a source wholesale, as Fortna claims.

48. John Alsup, *The Post-Resurrection Appearance Stories of the Gospel-Tradition* (London: SPCK, 1975, pp. 211–13), believes they all have the same *Gattung*, or desire to restate the church's experience of the Risen Lord in Old Testament terms. All three terms, however, are grouped together on dogmatic grounds and any formal similarities are insufficient to prove common origin.

icope ("Appearances," p. 109). One of its key phrases is *ephanerō-sen heauton* ("he manifested himself"); John uses the verb often in his writings.[49] In 1 John[50] the term refers to Jesus' earthly ministry (1:2; 3:5), parousia (2:28; 3:2), life, and resurrection within the context of soteriology (3:8; 4:9), while in the Gospel of John the term refers to the progressive "revelation" of Jesus through his works (9:3; 17:6). In the miracle at Cana, for instance, John says Jesus "revealed his glory," a clear post-resurrectional reflection on the significance of his first "sign" which resulted in "belief." Hence, it is reasonable for the evangelist to use this term three times (twice in v. 1, v. 14) for the final, ultimate "revelation" of God's "glory" in Jesus. Brown comments (pp. 1095 – 96) that "the task of the Baptist proclaimed in the first chapter of the Gospel has been brought to completion in the last: Jesus has been fully revealed to Israel, that is, to the community of believers represented by the disciple." The phrase is redactional, an expression of the evangelist's reflection on the significance of Jesus.

Verses 4–7 sound much like the narratives of Mary and the disciples on the Emmaus road, the early part of all three stressing how people failed to recognize Jesus. After his death and resurrection the disciples return to their former occupation, but their inadequacy is clearly reflected by their failure to catch any fish. Only after they obey the instructions of the "man on the shore" do they achieve success and recognize him. The message in this story is simple; without Jesus his disciples can do nothing. Recognition and success are closely linked; in an ecclesiastical motif the disciples represent the church's encounter with Jesus' lordship as they obey his commands and experience his blessings. John makes good use of editorial selection here, structuring tradition in such a way that it provides theological meaning.

The "beloved" is the first to recognize Jesus as he shouts, "It is the Lord!" In chapter 20 Mary's recognition of Jesus is a part of

---

49. Lindars (p. 624) says that its absence in chapter 20 shows that it is not characteristic of John in a resurrection context, and Alsup argues further (p. 203; cf. Pesch, p. 88 and Schnackenburg, IV, p. 418) that it is found only in late redactional strata and is evidence of a later "editorial seam." However, these arguments are obviated by John's constant practice of providing a gradual unveiling of Jesus' true nature to his followers, culminating in the resurrection itself.

50. Cf. W. G. Wilson, "An Examination of the Linguistic Evidence Adduced against the Unity of Authorship of the First Epistle of John and the Fourth Gospel," JTS 49 (1948), pp. 147 – 56; Kümmel, Introduction, pp. 442 – 45, et al.

soteriology as faith provides the key to true perception of the Risen Jesus (cp. 20:8), but in chapter 21 recognition is a part of John's ecclesiastical purpose as the disciples who had been experiencing failure now find prosperity through obedience to the command of the Risen Lord. They may have hesitated to ask the question "Who are you?" (21:12) but not because they didn't recognize Jesus. Rather John makes that comment to stress the fact that "they knew it was the Lord."[51] The exalted lordship of Jesus has, in fact, produced awe on the part of the disciples who recognize that he is Lord but are being assured that lordship includes fellowship.

The Beloved and Peter

The relationship between the "beloved" and Peter is similar in this scene to that of the race scene in 20:2–10. Peter is the impetuous one on both accounts who prepares for the role of the "beloved" and who provides insight into the true significance of the scene. It is Peter who jumps into the water to get to Jesus (even after he recognizes him) in this account even as it is Peter who enters the tomb first in 20:6f., yet in both scenes Peter's impulsive action is motivated by a real love for the Master. In this scene Peter has an even greater role than that of the "other" disciple as he prompts the other disciples to fish, jumps in the water to swim toward Jesus, and hauls the bulging net of fish to shore. These last two actions however, are prompted by the "beloved" who first recognizes "the Lord."

The role of the "beloved," on the other hand, includes both witness (13:23; 19:35; 21:24) as well as perception or faith (18:16; 20:8), and his special intimacy with Jesus qualifies him as the one who reveals the actual meaning of the scene. Peter's ministry is more that of the foundation-stone; he is the disciple who acts in serving Jesus.

Mission Motif

The first part of chapter 21 contains no overt mission thrust as other group appearance passages do (Mark 16:7; Matt. 28:19; Luke

---

51. Note the use of similar language to describe both the Baptist in 1:19 and Jesus in 8:25. Barrett says that since Jesus has "manifested" himself totally to his disciples and they now recognize him, such questions are no longer necessary. This view, however, seems much too simplistic, especially in light of the disciples' hesitancy.

24:44f.; John 20:21), yet its symbolism may suggest such an emphasis. Luke 5:1–11's strong teaching about fishermen symbolizing "fishers of men" dependent on the Lord for success must have influenced the early church's understanding of John's passage; the great catch, an obvious symbol of mission, results. If Marshall is correct (*Luke*, p. 200) when he says Luke's passage influenced John, a mission thrust in this passage is definite.

The number of fish (153) in this account is peculiar, a number which is repeated nowhere else in Scripture. Although John might simply have used the figure recorded in tradition,[52] the primitive church might also have included the number here because it was significant to them. Is the number an indication of both tradition and redaction? Although many scholars today believe the number is evidence of redaction, the problem of narrowing down all possible interpretations of the figure[53] has led many (e.g., Smalley, "Sign," p. 284; Schnackenburg, IV, pp. 426f.) to adopt a more general interpretation; the number is universal in character and suggests the results of church mission.

Linguistic evidence may support such a conclusion. The term for "hauling in" the burdened net of fish in verse 6 (*helkuein*, vv. 6, 11) also appears in 12:32: "But I, when I am lifted up from the earth, will draw (*helkusō*) all men to myself" (NIV). The term for "torn" in 11b ("the net was not torn," *schizein*) is also used in 19:24 to describe the decision of the soldiers at the cross not to "tear up" Jesus' robe, and is related to *schisma* in John 7:43, 9:16, and 10:19 where it means the "dividing up" or "tearing apart" of people because of differing responses to Jesus. The term for "breaking" in Luke's account (5:1–10), however, differs considerably from John's; Luke says the nets were so full of fish that they were "breaking," while John (v. 11) specifically says "the net was not torn."

Schnackenburg says (IV, p. 427) this difference adds to the mission symbolism of 21:11 since it alludes to the unity of the church, yet the net which "was not torn" may also simply be a term used to highlight the miracle in this scene. One must ask whether all terms with *helkuein* and *schizein* roots are actually parallel and

---

52. Morris, *John*, p. 866, says "love for exactness and a readiness to supply numerical detail can be documented elsewhere in this Gospel." Brown, *John*, pp. 1075–76, says the exact number comes from an emphasis on authentic eyewitness tradition (cp. 20:7).

53. For more complete coverage, see Grant, "Large Fish," pp. 273–75; Emerton, "Fishes," pp. 86–89; McEleney, "Great Fishes," pp. 411–17; Brown, pp. 1074–76; and Lindars, pp. 629–31.

whether some critics are guilty of drawing false theological conclusions by equating widely divergent semantic meanings (cf. Barr,
Semantics, chap. 3). Still, if John knew about Luke's account or at
least the tradition behind Luke when he wrote his own account,
then good reason exists for believing he included a mission stress
here. The very fact that *helkuein* is repeated both in Luke 5 and in
John 21 indicates more than just historical fact, especially if the
catch of fish is a theological symbol. At least the semantic meanings of these terms in both accounts are parallel.

John's passage suggests the unity of the church in mission.
Smalley says ("Sign," pp. 278–84) this mission theme is closely
linked with John's theology of "signs" and Christology. John uses
"signs" to show "the manifestation of the Word to the world" (chaps.
1–12) as well as "the glorification of the Word for the world" (chaps.
20–21). Flesh is the carrier of spirit in John's twofold Christology
where the Word (divine) becomes incarnate in the flesh (human).
Mission is grounded in Christology where the revelation of the
Word is an integral part of the human mission (building on 20:21–
23).

Eucharistic Motif

The meal scene in verses 12 and 13 is commonly believed (e.g.,
Alsup, Pesch) to be a separate story from Jesus' appearance to his
disciples, but one which was added to the account by redaction.
Several reasons are given for this view including: (1) verse 12's
phraseology which is so unlike John's; (2) close similarities between verse 13 and 6:11; and (3) the apparent contradiction between Jesus' request in verse 10 to "bring some fish" to shore and
verse 13's statement that breakfast was already prepared when the
disciples came to shore. Critics who espouse the view that this
meal scene is a separate story say verses 12b and 14 are the editorial links which bring two stories together.

Perhaps the critics are right; almost all the evangelists arrange
historical episodes thematically rather than chronologically, and
elements of a primitive tradition exist in both of these accounts.
Still, does the narrative really demand that verses 12 and 13 are a
separate scene, or are critics reading more into the differences in
these accounts than is necessary? Barrett says (p. 582), for instance, verse 12's "no one dared to ask" is *not* a clear indication
that two separate accounts are being combined. Furthermore, the

seeming contradiction between verses 5, 10, and 13 might easily be due to the brief nature of the scenes without demanding separate sources.

How much better, it would seem, to view all the verses in this account (1−14) as a single event in which the fire (v. 9) and Jesus' request for fish (v. 10) prepare for the meal scene where the fish that is served (v. 13) is both fish that Jesus has already prepared as well as that which the disciples caught. Such a view brings all the elements of this section together into a unified whole. The disciples share in the miracle and its results.

The theological issue in this scene is whether the meal scene of verses 12 and 13 is primarily sacramental or liturgical. Although sacramentalism in the fourth Gospel has been the subject of innumerable studies, no definite consensus has been reached.[54] Perhaps a middle position which allows for some liturgical thrust here is the best approach, with John stressing the spiritual significance of the sacraments (table fellowship here) without ever including an explicit reference to a sacrament.

In the meal scene itself, verse 13 sounds much like 6:11; in both Jesus takes bread and distributes it to the disciples. Still, in chapter 6 the suggestion of Eucharist is much stronger than in 21. Sanders (pp. 448f.) and Morris (p. 868) caution against seeing liturgy in chapter 21, yet other critics (Barrett, p. 484; Rigaux, p. 243) persist in finding it in: (1) an early connection between Jesus' appearances and the table fellowship of the church (cf. Luke 24:13−35; Acts 10:40f.), and (2) the use of fish (ancient Christian symbol) in the Eucharist. Yet there are questions as to whether table fellowship was always viewed sacramentally, and even greater doubts as to whether fish had eucharistic significance in the first century. Despite this somewhat debatable evidence John 21 avoids any specific reference to Eucharist, yet possibly represents an early "table fellowship" motif much like that in the Emmaus account (cf. Luke 24:30f.). The use of such a motif was probably John's way of reminding his readers of Jesus' living presence through table fellowship with possible hints of eucharistic fellowship.

The primary focus of this section is ecclesiology, the success of the church dependent on the reality and recognition of the Risen Christ in her midst. Church unity and mission is thus rooted in

54. While more scholars than previously note some sacramental interest (e.g., 6:51−58), Kysar has sided with the anti-sacramental school, taking 6:51−58 as a late insertion into a non-sacramental passage.

Christology, since Christ is glorified through the ministry of the church in the world.

The Reinstatement of Peter, 21:15–17

As in previous episodes, we believe that the text has been carefully chosen and colored to fit into the theological development of the chapter. John's account of Jesus and Peter includes two basic emphases: the question of love and the imagery of a shepherd. Jesus' hard questions to Peter about love include a complex interplay between the two Greek terms for love, *agapan* and *philein*. Jesus asks *"agapas me"* twice of Peter who responds with *"philo se."* The third time Jesus questions Peter he modifies his question to include *philein* (Peter's former response) instead of *agapas*, and Peter changes his response to include *ginōskō* instead of *oida* (two terms for "know"). Why does John include all these variations on words?

Some critics believe John's word changes are theologically significant,[55] but more recently commentators have seen these as stylistic variations. Indeed it is difficult to explain how the terminological switch would be meaningful if Peter were assenting to Jesus' question while at the same time giving that question a different definition. Thereby Jesus would finally agree to a lower definition of love when he finally accepts Peter's usage. Perhaps the real truth lies somewhat in between, John using different terms to avoid monotony within a rigid three-part formula, yet at the same time suggesting the complex nature of the love-relation between Jesus and Peter. Lindars says (pp. 634–35) John uses two terms for love so that this exchange can relate to other passages on love such as 15:13, where *agapē* (love) lays down one's life for one's *philōn* (friends). The account here thus includes a kind of Jewish synonymous parallelism which compares more than one account, emphasizing the complex nature of the truth stated.

Still, John 21:15–17 makes use of more variations on words than can be explained stylistically. Theology is also suggested, perhaps a stress on the universal nature of love. This whole exchange between Jesus and Peter forces us to look at the question of Peter's

---

55. Westcott, pp. 366f; Evans, "Agapao," pp. 64f.; and Spicq, "la charite," pp. 358f. believe that *agapan* is the higher form of love, while Trench, pp. 42f., says *philein* is higher.

leadership in the church[56] which some critics say is reinstated here. Evidence for this position includes:

1. The neuter *pleon toutōn* ("more than these") in verse 15 could be a masculine "Do you love me more than these (love me)?" The grammar in this passage, however, is so debatable that other translations are possible such as "Do you love me more than these?" or even "Do you love me more than you love these things?" Of all these possibilities the second sounds most likely since it best fits the context.[57] Jesus is asking Peter to let go of his relationships with other people in order to follow Christ. Some (Arvedson in Brown, pp. 1113−14) note a connection between this pericope and Mark 8:34: "If anyone wishes to come after me, let him deny himself." The self-denial is seen in the love question, the cross in the coming martyrdom, and the command in verses 19 and 22. It is indeed possible that the application of this tradition to personal attachments (cf. Luke 14:25−27) is reflected in the question, "Do you love me more than these?" This would remove the major objection to this interpretation, that it sets up a rivalry of love between the apostles and thus has no place in the resurrection narratives.

2. Shepherd imagery in the account is stressed by Jesus' varying responses to Peter's answers which include *Boske ta arnia mou* ("feed my lambs"), *poimaine ta probata mou* ("take care of my sheep"), and *boske ta probata mou* ("feed my sheep"). Although the two words for "feed" here come from the same root word in Aramaic *(r'h)*, John very possibly used both to suggest the complex nature of pastoral care which includes both feeding and tending. The imagery here also beautifully parallels the shepherd analogy in chapter 10[58] which differentiates between the kinds of work a shepherd does as well as the all-inclusive nature of the "flock."

56. So Benoit, pp. 303f.; Schnackenburg, III, p. 430. Brown and Lindars agree with this view but say this is a redactional insert.

57. The phrase would read *mallon ē* if it were neuter (cf. 3:19; 12:43) and the verb would be repeated in such a construction (Lindars, p. 635; Brown, pp. 1103f., on the grounds of Johannine style). The first of the two alternatives remains quite possible and, I believe, best fits the context.

58. *Arnia* ("sheep") is clearly the term in verse 15, but it is difficult to decide between *probata* and *probatia* ("sheep") in verses 16−17. Perhaps the first term is best, although *probatia* might be used on the basis of *difficilior lectio*. *Probatia* does not appear in the New Testament and it is doubtful that a scribe would introduce it here; it may have been inserted in the interest of variation.

Peter's role is unquestionably significant in this pericope. Some scholars (Gaechter, *"Lämmer,"* pp. 328f.; Schnackenburg, IV, p. 435) believe John uses a formal three-part structure here to suggest the solemn, authoritative nature of this confrontation, and others (Bultmann, Cullmann, Cassian, Benoit) simply interpret this passage as the restoration of Peter to leadership among the disciples. This, in fact, must be an intent of the story since John usually presents the "beloved" as the favored one among the disciples and here he does not. Yet this is not the primary thrust, for again eccesiology is predominant.

Jesus' response is the focal point of the whole passage. Sheehan (p. 218) and Brown (pp. 1113f.) believe Jesus, the Good Shepherd, is the primary emphasis, but most critics disagree. The "sheep," in fact, are central here. While the emphasis is how they are to be cared for, the stress also is on responsibility rather than authority; the pastoral duty first a matter of obedience to Jesus' command and second a matter of love.[59] Some scholars (e.g., Spicq, Morris, Schnackenburg, Stählin) see "love" as the primary accent here, however the text itself indicates that love is implied in terms of "tending" the flock. Love stems out of a vertical relationship with Christ and expresses itself in horizontal relationships of "tending" the flock such as pastoring or deeds of mercy and provides the foundation for the horizontal (i.e., Christian service). First Peter 5:2–4 builds on this and may well be a midrash on it, showing that this horizontal ecclesiology is indeed the central purpose of the pericope.

The Prophecy Regarding Peter, 21:18–19

Jesus' description of Peter's old age and death has prompted much discussion. Bultmann thinks (p. 713) the Master's words came from an old proverb which said, "In youth a man is free to go where he will; in old age a man must let himself be taken where he does not will," and that John used the saying in this passage

---

59. The emphasis thus is on "shepherding," and there is more an air of responsibility than of authority. The "shepherd" image in the early church had been applied to the office of "pastor" (Eph. 4:11), and it is doubtful that John's readers would have seen as much authority as some intimate.

to describe what he already knew about Peter's death.[60] Jesus' words probably *were* based on an ancient proverb, yet verse 19's editorial comment provides some evidence that John accepted the words as an original prophecy about Peter.

Does the prophetic statement also suggest Peter's martyrdom, even his crucifixion?[61] John himself sees it this way; verse 19a's "signifying what kind of death" seems to be a deliberate allusion to 12:33 and 18:32 where Jesus predicted his own way of death. Jesus' words, based on an ancient proverb, are used in such a way that they tell the disciples and Peter how Peter is to "glorify God" in his death. This may well have been done by the Risen One himself, who changed the verbs in the second clause to the future tense and added the negative in the *hopou* clause[62] so as to apply it figuratively to Peter's death. It was probably interpreted in the primitive church as a discipleship saying before Peter's death (i.e., applied to believers generally rather than to Peter specifically); to this extent Lindar's isolation of discipleship in the saying may be correct. John evidently had to correct a misinterpretation on the part of the early church. The mysterious air of the saying would certainly fit the parabolic style of the Lord, and the tradition-development above seems indicated by the text.

The verses about Peter's death are structurally connected to the pericope about love and pastoral ministry; both an integral part of a strong love-relationship with the Lord. Some scholars view this passage as a clear statement on martyrdom, but that really is not the focus here. Instead, Peter's death is presented as a kind of participation in Jesus' death (see Cassian, pp. 132f.; and

60. Lindars believes (p. 636) that the proverb is a redaction of an original discipleship saying "similar to Matthew 8:18–22/Luke 9:57–62, where the key word is 'follow' (*akolouthein*), and each of the sayings embodies a proverb." However, this is too speculative and fails because of the ambiguity of verse 18. Brown, however, disputes this, saying (p. 1118), "In our judgment, while the redactor may be responsible for the joining of the sayings, the sayings themselves are old, for neither lends itself easily to the interpretation that has been given to it. . . . Certainly, if the statement had been fashioned in the light of Peter's death, the wording would not have been so ambiguous."

61. Bultmann, pp. 713–14, believes John misunderstood the original saying about Peter. Most others, however, believe his understanding is accurate even though the ambiguous language does not really assert more than Peter's martyrdom. A reference to crucifixion is debatable, depending on a prior decision regarding "stretching out your hands" which is an ancient expression for crucifixion. See Barrett, p. 585.

62. It seems likely that the negative was not in the original proverb, which said, "in old age a man is taken where he wishes."

Schnackenburg, IV. p. 437) which results in "glorifying God" (see also 12:23 and 15:8).

Discipleship is the most important issue here; in verse 19 Jesus says most emphatically, "Follow me!" The literal sense is seen in verse 20; and a theological thrust, in which one becomes a follower via faith-decision, is part of the "double meaning" of the passage (see Wead, p. 40). The words echo the Master's original calling of his disciples (1:43) and bring to mind other imagery such as light ("whoever follows me will never walk in darkness" in 8:12), the Good Shepherd ("His sheep follow him because they know his voice" in 10:4–5, 27), and discipleship itself. The words also bring to mind chapter 13:36–38 where Peter swore he would "follow" Jesus even if it meant death, only to be corrected by Jesus' predictions about Peter's denial. Within the context of chapter 21 then, "Follow me" clearly refers to Peter's present pastoral duties as well as any future suffering, pain, or martyrdom that might result from it.[63]

The Prophecy Regarding the "Beloved," 21:20–23

Jesus' seemingly harsh words to Peter about the future of the "beloved" (vv. 22, 23) are believed by many to show John's particular interest in squelching rumors about his own immortality. The saying in verse 22, its misunderstanding in verse 23a, and the correction in verse 23b have led to various problems:

1. The use of the word *ean* ("if") in verse 22. Should it be translated in the classical sense meaning "if, as is expected"? Verse 23a seems to confirm this translation, thereby affirming the early church's belief that Peter would die but that the "beloved" would live to see Jesus' return. John, however, uses the Koine sense of *ean* in verse 23b, indicating "if, as may or may not be true." Clearly he is saying here that Jesus never meant what he said in verse 22 to be taken as literal prophecy.

2. Was the "beloved" alive or dead when this chapter was added to the Gospel of John? Some scholars believe he was already dead,

---

63. See Cullmann, *Peter,* pp. 71–157 for an in-depth discussion of the problems of Peter's death. The presence of "follow" in both the shepherd passages and the previous prophecy of Peter's death lends credence to the view above that John stressed the connection between this and the "shepherd" imagery of verses 15–17.

thereby explaining why his immortality was the subject of so much controversy (cf. Barrett, p. 485; Sanders, p. 457). Still, the wording is so tricky here that it might also mean the "beloved" was simply approaching death (cf. Bernard, p. 771; Morris, pp. 878f.) Lindars (p. 640) makes a crucial point in this regard, saying the interpretation depends on one's decision regarding the identity of the "beloved." Was he John the Evangelist? Fuller says (p. 153) this pericope "must have been added by the redactor to identify the 'beloved' as the author of the Gospel." The wording of verse 24 seems to support this; the present participle *martyrōn*[64] ("the disciple who testifies these things") implies this disciple was still alive. The words become even more meaningful if we accept John as the "beloved" and see verse 24 as an indication of his own uneasiness about readers who might not accept his impending death.

3. This leads to the problem of the delay of the parousia. John's Gospel was probably written a long time after Jesus' promise that he would return, thus forcing the evangelist to focus on realized eschatology where kingdom promises applied to the present spiritual life of the believer, rather than Jesus' return. Yet this focus does not exclude any future expectations, rather, both are important in John[65] as they are in 21:22f. Critics who dismiss this section as the work of a redactor certainly ought to realize that what is included here repeats other emphases in the Gospel and indeed functions very well as a summary of the author's expectations.

4. Peter's motivation for asking the question about the "beloved" adds further difficulties. Was Peter curious because he considered the "beloved" to be a rival? Some critics think so, reading into Peter's question a hint of jealousy which prompted Jesus' curt response, and citing later efforts of John's followers to promote him above Peter (see Brown, pp. 1120f.; Bultmann, pp. 715f.).

Peter's question, however, wasn't necessarily impudent; it might just as easily have been prompted by an honest interest in the

64. Note the deliberate contrast with the next *grapsas*, which probably implies he still is witnessing but has completed his writing.

65. Dodd's judgment that "the naive conception of Christ's Second Advent in 21:22f. is unlike anything else in the Fourth Gospel" (*Interpretation*, p. 431) is certainly untrue in light of such passages as 5:27f., 14:3f. Both realized (the place of the believer now in the community of believers) and final (the future place of the believer in heaven) eschatology have a place in John. See R. H. Gundry, "In My Father's House are Many *Monai*" (John 14:2), *ZNW* 58 (1967), as well as Paola Ricca, *Die Eschatologie des vierten Evangeliums* (Zurich: Gotthelf, 1966), *passim*.

welfare of the "beloved." In this light Jesus' reply suggests a double purpose: to prepare the church for the time when all "eye-witnesses" would be dead, and to stress the importance of true discipleship. Consider, for example, the repeated use of *su* ("you") in verse 22b as well as 19, which is also the key phrase of verses 18 — 23. Peter and the "beloved" are symbols of the church as a whole where obedience as well as discipleship remain critical regardless of how long it takes Jesus to return. One of the major purposes for adding chapter 21 to the Gospel is undoubtedly seen here.

The Second Conclusion, 21:24 — 25

Some critics who believe John wrote verses 24 and 25 argue that these verses are the only true ending to the book. They say "we" in verse 24 is editorial rather than literal (Bernard, p. 713; Chapman, pp. 379f.). Brown objects (pp. 1124f.), however, saying the writer refers to himself both in the third person singular (v. 24a) and the first person plural (v. 24b). Brown believes "we" in verse 24 means the author of chapter 21 in conjunction with other members of the early church. C. H. Dodd seems to have the best solution to this problem ("Note," pp. 212f.), arguing for a more indefinite meaning like "as is well known" (cf. 9:31). "We" thus means the community as distinct from the author of the epilogue.

The passage includes other problems such as: (1) John's failure anywhere else in his Gospel to write in the first person, (2) a seeming duplication of other verses such as 19:35 and 20:31. Was 21:24 and 25 added to John because without them the Gospel would have no conclusion, or were they tacked on to an epilogue which really needed no conclusion (20:30, 31 being the proper conclusion)? Finally, (3) both *houtos* in verse 24a and *oidamen* in 24b indicate that verses 24 and 25 represent the approval of the early church. Is this because the Gospel of John has such an anonymous nature that overt affirmation is necessary?

Verses 24 and 25 include some important information about the "beloved" as well as author of *John*, however. *Grapsas* in verse 24 can be interpreted either literally (the "beloved" was also the writer of this Gospel: Westcott, Lindars, Morris), or in a more figurative sense as "he had these things written" by someone else, like an amanuensis (Bernard, Braun). The term might even suggest this special disciple was merely the source of the original tradition which lay behind this work (Bultmann, Brown, Barrett). Although the second usage seems to parallel John 19:19 where Pilate "caused the words to be written" on the cross, and Romans 16:22 where Tertius is named as Paul's amanuensis, the passages are really not similar. The parallel with *martyrōn* would favor the view that it refers to the "beloved's" previous composition of the Gospel (option one above).

How valid is the role of this passage as imprimatur (sanction or approval of that which is published) of the Gospel of John? It would seem that function is a natural part of the evangelist's eyewitness motif, suggested by the terms *martyrōn* and *autou hē martyria*. The passage sounds so much like 19:35 that Bultmann believes (pp. 678f.) both are later additions to the text. There are, however, significant differences in the verses which prove they are not parallel. Verse 24 of chapter 21 is most likely a repetition of 19:35 in which the author of this Gospel affirms the truth of his own testimony.[66]

The verses themselves also provide internal evidence for their authenticity in conjunction with external evidence such as the Dead Sea Scrolls and archeological discoveries which have affirmed the accuracy of John's historical asides (see Brown, "Problem," pp. 1f.; Smalley, *John*, pp. 30f., 162f.; Robinson, *Redating*, pp. 254f.). Finally, the large volume of detail and personal reminiscence in John's Gospel also supports the soundness of this passage.

Are verses 24 and 25 then the work of a first-rate storyteller who knew how to weave in authentic-sounding details, or the statement of an eyewitness reflecting on his experiences? D. E. Nineham says ("Eyewitness") that the "eyewitness" motif which was used as authenticating proof of the resurrection (1 Cor. 15:3f.), did not really apply to Jesus' earthly life until later New Testament works. Form criticism argues that Gospel pericopes developed apart from eyewitness testimony and are theological reflections rather than historical reminiscences. Morris, on the other hand, believes (*Studies*, pp. 139f.) that the vast amount of detail in the

---

66. John took great pains to establish this, evidenced by the term *alēthēs* which appears fourteen times in the Gospel. R. Bultmann, 'ἀληθής,' *TDNT*, I, pp. 238f., 245f.; and Dodd, *Interpretation*, p. 177 argue for a hellenistic provenance, (reality vs. appearance), while Brown, pp. 499f.; and Morris, *John*, pp. 293–296, see a greater connection with Old Tesament views of faithfulness. A. C. Thiselton argues for a view that sees both aspects.

Gospels such as time notes must be seriously considered as evidence for a historically accurate document.

Truth probably lies somewhere between both these views; surely John functions both as historian and theologian. A definite eyewitness emphasis appears throughout his work which is surely more than just a theological note. *Martyreō* is found 33 times in John's Gospel, and *martyria* fourteen times, both in application to the person and work of Jesus (Strathmann). The term applies somewhat to historical events (as here), but even more so to the validity of the evangelist's interpretation of these events. It thus lends credence to John's theological interpretations by providing a historically accurate foundation for it.

This solid historical foundation gives John the freedom then to draw out from it what he considers significant. All his redactional nuances should be carefully studied since event and interpretation so often mesh together. The study of John 20 and 21, for instance, reveals a great amount of redaction causing us to ask how the claim of this Gospel's eyewitness influences its historicity. We have attempted to demonstrate that it does, indeed that it is crucial to a proper understanding of the relationship between history and theology in the fourth Gospel. Brown says (p. 1129) we must separate ourselves from "modern historical preoccupations" and accept a basically non-historical interpretation of "true witness" in this Gospel, but we believe the interpretation of the eyewitness here is accurate, even crucial to a proper understanding of the relationship between history and theology. On this basis the use of an imprimatur in verse 24 is justified.

Verse 25 also seems to be a later addition although its style is different from 24. The difference is probably due to imitation of different sources rather than different authorship (*contra* Schnackenburg, III, p. 448). The use of hyperbole was common in ancient writings so the reference in verse 25 that "even the whole world would not have room for the books that would be written" about Jesus is historically acceptable. The Gospel ends on a note of universal glory.

Conclusion

John's resurrection narrative forms a kind of harmonious unity that is not as evident in the other synoptic accounts. This unity is largely due to John's post-resurrection viewpoint which he uses as a framework for Jesus' life and ministry as it anticipates his post-resurrection "glory." Chapter 20 is, of course, a natural part of this with its soteriological emphasis, but so is chapter 21's ecclesiological message.

Chapter 21's basic structure may form a chiasmus (a favorite style device in John[67]), a structure which focuses on the "beloved's" authority in recognizing the Lord as well as Peter's pastoral responsibility. Here the AB:BA would center on the "beloved" and Peter, with A = "beloved" centered passages and B = Peter-centered passages. The two "beloved" passages (21:1–14; 20–23) center on his authority in recognizing the Lord and providing authentic witness. The two Peter passages (21:15–17, 18–19) center on pastoral responsibility.

John's resurrection narratives are also unified in the way they develop into ecclesiology; the first two accounts focus on responsibility and success in mission, and the later ones on discipleship and the ultimate witness of martyrdom. While the sections are of quite different length, it is only verses 1–14 which are significantly longer, and a balance is nevertheless achieved on the thematic level.

The *Sitz im Leben* of chapter 21 is probably late in the life of John, its purpose probably to make the church aware of its responsibilities in mission now that the last eyewitnesses were about to die. The written imprimatur of John's testimony in verse 24 thus becomes vitally important since John would no longer be alive to affirm this Gospel's authenticity.

Although Robinson argues (*Redating*, pp. 278–282) that verses 20–23 in John 21 emphasize the return of Christ more than the "beloved's" death, he tends to read more into "wait until I come" in 23b than the text warrants. Nonetheless, no internal evidence exists for believing John was written after the death of Peter. "Follow me" is the crucial command here, regardless of time or place.

---

67. See Brown, cxxxv; and Léon-Dufour, "Trois chiasmes," pp. 249f. They made chiasm in 5:19–30, 6:35–40, 12:23–32, 15:7–17, 16:16–33, 18:23–19:42.

Part Three

Tradition Study

6

The Empty Tomb Narratives

Bruce Chilton ("Announcement," pp. 149f.) says a proper approach to redaction criticism should consider redactional elements first and traditions after that, since sources can be determined only after a writer's style is known. This is not necessarily true since both redaction and tradition are interdependent. The ideal approach is to consider both redaction and tradition simultaneously. Chilton's approach, however, is used here only because it best fits the natural transition from the Gospels' theological messages to the traditions behind them.

J. B. Tyson ("Source Criticism") calls for a holistic approach which treats the Gospel as an "intentional unity." This method seems to be the best approach, seeking a proper blend of redaction criticism and tradition criticism (see my "Redaction Criticism: Critique and Methology"). We must walk carefully through the labyrinth of tradition-critical criteria, recognizing the pitfalls noted by Barbour, Hooker, Stein, and others.

What is the best possible approach to the historical data? The "hermeneutics of suspicion," characteristic of many scholars, should first of all be avoided in favor of a more balanced approach. A more optimistic use of critical tools would provide a more serious analysis of the claims of the Gospel writers. In this light Stewart Goetz and Craig Blomberg discuss the "burden of proof," arguing that assumptions which place that burden on the person affirming authenticity are unwarranted since they include a skep-

tical approach to historiography. Such an approach to history ignores the "direction of causal lines," or the natural progression
forward from historical cause to effects within a text. Working
backward from effects to cause necessarily involves forcing one's
presuppositions on the study. Goetz and Blomberg's positive tests
of correspondence and coherence are much better, and the burden of proof falls on the one who denies historicity.

Ben Meyer (*Aims*, pp. 76 – 94) notes a positive interaction between the intention of the author and the historical data with
which he works. The methodology involves both interpretation
and explanation. As such Meyer challenges the supposition that
the early church created data wholesale, asserting that the issues
are more complex and that one must allow the data to speak.
Then one can infer from the evidence the likelihood of an event
or saying. One constructs hypotheses and then verifies them on
the basis of coherence with the data. In the next chapter (pp. 95 –
113) Meyer views his results from the perspective of "history and
faith." Since the historian cannot deny his/her own presuppositions or "faith," he/she must work positively within that framework. I might add that it is good to identify the link between the
historian's framework and that of the text itself. On the basis of
the interpretation in this book, I would argue that the text demands to be taken seriously as historical data. France ("Jewish
Historiography") denies that the evangelists produced "creative
midrash"; their historical methodology was much more closely
aligned with the original events (see also my "Redaction Criticism";
and Banks, "Quest").

Kenneth Grayston ("Empty Tomb," p. 267) lists seven possible
explanations for the empty tomb narrative:

1. God brought Jesus up from the underworld to appear on
earth (like Samuel).

2. Jesus was raised from the grave to heaven (cf. Phil. 2:8 – 9)
with no hint as to what actually happened to the body.

3. Elaborating #2, Jesus appeared from heaven, again with no
necessity of an empty tomb.

4. God led his followers to establish a memorial to Jesus, leading to "tomb reverence" and requiring a tomb with bones.

5. "God caused him to live again in the cultic meal of his people," again with no requirement of an empty tomb.

6. God revived the body of Jesus and created the empty tomb
as a sign for faith.

7. God revived the body of Jesus in order to prove that the Risen One was indeed the same person as the Crucified One.

Grayston argues that the tomb was empty but that in the final analysis it did not matter. We would agree with the first statement but not the second. On the basis of the narratives themselves, we believe that the evangelists would have accepted both of the last two possibilities.

The most important consideration in this study is the intent of the Gospel writers themselves. Were they writing history, saga, myth, or creative midrash? Or was it a combination of these methods (e.g., Gundry's commentary on Matthew)? Or do the Gospels themselves provide substantial evidence of historically accurate tradition enriched by redactional emphases?

A basic problem with any approach is how to consider the Gospel presentation of Jesus' paradoxical nature as both human and divine. Martin (*Mark*, pp. 138–39) asserts that in Mark this counterbalance between the two aspects shows that Mark was not writing "myth" in the classical sense but rather sought to present the human Jesus both as he appeared and as he was, his "messianic misunderstanding" motif providing the redactional tool to illustrate the difference. Luke and John did somewhat the same. In his prologue (1:1–4), for instance, Luke explains how he will provide an "orderly account" of events which have been "passed down" (*paredosan*) by "eyewitnesses and ministers of the word," so that Theolphilus may "know the truth (*asphaleia*) concerning the things of which you have been informed." Marshall says (*Luke— Historian*, pp. 37–41, cf. 53–76) the prologue is evidence of Luke's desire for historical accuracy, but Cadbury believes (*Beginnings*, II, pp. 489f.; *Making*, pp. 344f., 358f.) the prologue is apologetic rather than didactic, its real purpose being to defend the Christian message by "authenticating" it. The Book of Luke as a whole, however, indicates it is much more than apology. Fitzmeyer says (*Luke*, p. 301) Luke writes to anchor a series of catechetical teachings in an "accurate" and "orderly" presentation of Jesus' life for the new convert Theophilus, in order to provide "assurance of the matters about which you have been instructed" (v. 4).[1] Luke's in-

---

1. S. Brown ("Prologues") argues that Luke 1:1–4 is probably an introduction to both volumes, serving evangelistically to characterize Christianity "as an intellectual movement capable of holding its own in competition" (p. 108). Tiede (pp. 13, 31) states, "an appeal to the *literary integrity* of the work in its historical setting has required the recent reconsideration of the redaction critical contributions of the 1950s."

tent is to provide historically accurate tradition as well as apology. John's intent includes the role of the "true witness" (19:35; 21:24), a theme which may or may not refer specifically to historically "authentic" material, but one which in context combines redaction and historically authentic tradition without tension or disharmony.[2] This kind of redaction does not mean ahistorical creative midrash; this kind is based on historical events and does not deviate from them. The burden of proof then is on the critic who denies the historical basis of the Gospels, not the one who accepts that historical basis and approaches Gospel data from a positive perspective. Each Gospel narrative should be accepted in a positive sense as authentic unless good evidence is provided against it.

On the Way to the Tomb

The Time Notes

When did the women in the Gospel narratives actually arrive at Jesus' tomb? Matthew and Luke say they came "at dawn," John "while it was still dark," and Mark "just after sunrise." The apparent contradiction in time notes has already been discussed in previous chapters as was its resolution: that the women probably arrived just at dawn, any stress on lightness or darkness being a matter of interpretation.[3] Marshall says in this regard that "possibly two varying traditions of the story were extant" (Luke, p. 884); some witnesses remembered the darkness when they set out, others the early light.

Each Gospel writer was free to stress whatever best fit his ac-

2. Since I have already treated this elsewhere ("John 21," pp. 176f.) I will summarize data here. While the theme may refer only to the tradition-substratum behind the Gospel (i.e., only to a small part, with the rest later additions) or it may refer to existentially rather than historically "authentic" material, we believe that the context plus the Gospel itself combines redaction and history.

3. Some (Black, Taylor, Grintz) state that Matthew and Mark place the visit the evening before Easter morn, thus harmonizing with John's "while it was dark." However, John's *proi* echoes Mark 16:2 and agrees with the sense of Luke 24:1, "at early dawn." We prefer to place the event at dawn itself; therefore it was a matter of interpretation as to which side was stressed, darkness or light.

count; John emphasizing darkness,[4] Matthew and Luke the coming of "light," and Mark the progression from darkness to light. John's account is linked with both Mark's and Luke's, perhaps indicating an awareness of both (so Mahoney). The evangelists themselves saw no contradiction in these time notes which came directly from resurrection tradition (cf. 1 Cor. 15:4, "on the third day") and were all linked together by the phrase *tē mia tōn sabbatōn* ("on the first day of the week," found in all four Gospels). The conclusion is that no true discrepancy exists in the redactional choices of the evangelists regarding the time notes.

The Names of the Women

Which women were actually present at the tomb? Mark says three women were there, Mary Magdalene, Mary the mother of James, and Salome; Matthew says there were two (excluding Salome). Luke says Joanna, Mary Magdalene, Mary the mother of James; and "the other women," and John has Mary only, but who speaks as "we." Marxsen says (*Resurrection*, pp. 41f., 43f., 48f., 56) these differences are irreconcilable, and Broer states ("*Diskussion*," pp. 40f.; Grab, pp. 87f., 280f.) the differences prove the burial and empty tomb stories are independent traditions with little historical accuracy. Other critics (e.g., Craig, Cranfield, Ellis, Lindars), however, are unwilling to draw such drastic conclusions from surface contradictions and, in an effort to reconcile the different Gospel accounts, suggest a group of at least five women (cf. Luke's "others" and John's "we"[5]). Mark probably received his list from tradition (made the three lists in 15:40, 47; 16:1) while Luke, who wrote "Joanna and others," drew from special sources (cf. 8:1–3). Matthew, then, simply omitted "Salome" from Mark's account, and John, for editorial purposes, chose to focus only on Mary. Taylor's belief (*Mark*, pp. 603f.) that these names were written on the basis of regional interests (each evangelist choosing names his audience knew) is difficult to prove.

All these differences cannot diminish the fact that all four Gos-

---

4. See John 3:2; 6:17; 8:12; 9:4; 11:10; 12:35, 46; 13:30; 19:39.
5. R. E. Brown, *John*, p. 984 asks: if Bultmann is correct (that John 20:2 uses the editorial "we"), why does Mary switch to "I" in verse 13? (See also Alsup, p. 96).

pels feature these women as witnesses of the truth of the resurrection. Several have pointed out that women in the ancient world could not legally serve as witnesses.[6] Neither Jew nor hellenist would have invented such a tale. The anomaly itself makes it likely that the role of the women was an integral part of early tradition as well as the event itself.

The Motive of the Women

Why did the women rush to the tomb that Easter Sunday? Mark and Luke say they went "taking spices they had prepared," Mark adding they went "to anoint Jesus' body." Matthew, however, says the women went only to "look at the tomb," and John includes no reason at all. Is there a contradiction here evidencing redaction rather than tradition? Some critics believe so, questioning even the need for anointing Jesus' entombed and possibly decaying body (see notes on Mark 16:2).[7]

Another problem is that Mark says the women purchased spices "when the Sabbath was over" (16:1) while Luke says they prepared them prior to the Sabbath (23:56). Creed concludes (*Luke*, p. 292) that Luke follows "literary convention" rather than "historical exactness." Grundmann adds (p. 436) that different sources caused these different accounts. Geldenhuys even suggests (p. 619) that the women did not buy enough spices prior to the Sabbath so they had to go back for more after the Sabbath. This seems somewhat fanciful, since an "exact amount" was hardly demanded.

Perhaps Strack-Billerbeck's note (S-B, II, p. 53) is the best explanation. He explains that in Bible times a body might be embalmed on the Sabbath but with spices purchased and prepared on a day other than the Sabbath. Mark then included the information from tradition about spices purchased on a day other than the Sabbath, while Luke, who did not stress this spice motif, simply bypassed the time note. Marshall argues (*Luke*, p. 881) that Luke 23:56 is a

---

6. See Cranfield, *Mark*, p. 464; Schweitzer, *Mark*, pp. 369f.; Falk, p. 508; Stagg, pp. 47f., 53; and Jansen, pp. 42f.

7. Craig says the anointing was not an attempt to correct a job poorly done but was simply an act of devotion which could have been done even if the body had started to decay. Longstaff ("Women," pp. 277f.) adds that Jewish tradition demanded that tombs be visited for three days to make certain that the deceased was truly dead.

transition to the empty tomb narrative providing a thematic rather than chronological link. Verse 56a concludes the burial narrative while verse 56b begins the tomb episode. Literary considerations thus prompt the description of events even though they remain true to history. The evangelists do not intend to present an exact progression of events but rather to portray the impact of the event itself.

Why did the women go to the tomb, and are the differing Gospel accounts in opposition with each other? Does Matthew's statement that the women came to "look at the tomb" (also implied by John) conflict with Mark and Luke's statement that they came to "anoint Jesus' body"? Probably not, especially if one assumes that Matthew (rather than Mark) redacted tradition in order to fit it into the context of a theme. John's silence here also is indicative of his own style which focuses on theology rather than peripheral details even though earlier (19:39, 40) he did describe the embalming of Jesus' body.

No real conflict exists either between Jesus' first embalming and the women's intent to embalm his already entombed body. Craig cites (p. 184) a Jewish precedent, for instance, (Semachoth 8, Ebel Rabbath; 4:11) that permitted tombs to be opened for late visitors. The women's act of devotion would not be unusual, and hardly the basis for rejecting Mark and Luke's accounts as invalid.

The Guards at the Tomb

Is Matthew 28:4's description of the guards at the tomb who were so afraid of the angel of the Lord that they "shook and became like dead men" actually based on tradition? Consider, for example, the use of terms like *epaurion, paraskeuē, planos/planē, koustōdia, asphalizo,* and *sphragizō,* non-Matthean language that Broer says (*Grab,* pp. 67f.) proves that Matthew borrowed from tradition (Mark or Q) and wove into a new composition. McNeile (p. 428) and Kratz (*Auferweckung,* pp. 72f.), however, say this is evidence of oral or written tradition which Matthew reworked, a view which seems much more likely in light of the importance of the hapax terms in the narrative. *Aurion,* for instance, appears in 6:30 and 34 (a Q passage) as well as here, a highly unlikely choice unless Matthew was following tradition. Furthermore, only here out of all the Gospels, is *planos/planē* used; such strong language unlikely even on the lips of Jesus' enemies unless it were traditional. Fuller also notes (*Resurrection*, p. 72) that Matthew 27:63 appears to combine Mark's "after three days" with the independent middle *egeiromai* ("raise"—Mark has *anastēsomai* and Matthew *egerthēsomai*), suggesting that Matthew probably made use of a non-Matthean tradition as his source.

Matthew's episode about the guards at the tomb is full of seeming inconsistencies however, prompting many critics to feel that his apologetic intent overcomes any historical basis. Campenhausen, for instance, says (*Tradition*, p. 63; also McNeile, Hill, Evans, Broer, Alsup) "As is generally the case when such a specific intention is dominant, the narrator has chiefly in view his special apologetic aim, and so fails to see the absurdities that follow right and left from his account."

The problems in the narrative prompt questions such as: Why were Jewish leaders willing to defile themselves on the Sabbath by pleading that Pilate (a Gentile) "secure" Jesus' tomb? Why did the priests believe Jesus' prediction about rising on the third day and understand what it meant even though the disciples could not? On such slim evidence, why were they convinced of the necessity to propose such an elaborate scheme to Pilate? Why did Pilate agree to such an outlandish idea despite the innocence and helplessness of Jesus' disciples who had already scattered in all directions? Was this whole episode at best an apologetic reaction of the early church and Matthew as well?[8]

Most of the inconsistencies in Matthew's account are not as real as they appear. Were the Jewish leaders, for instance, breaking the Sabbath when they came to Pilate? Recent research into Sabbath exceptions during Jesus' day may indicate not (see Jeremias, *EW*, pp. 75f.; Filson, p. 299; Lee, p. 172; Wenham, "Resurrection," pp. 49f.); Fuller concludes (pp. 72f.), "We should not attach too much weight to these apparent breaches of the Sabbath."[9]

---

8. Many critics (e.g., Kratz, pp. 72f.) agree that Matthew was developing some tradition but say it happened much later. Ramsey (*Resurrection*, p. 60) says many conservatives accept legendary accretions here, labelling the whole process "Christian midrash rather than history."

9. He denies authenticity on the grounds of such "post-Easter" elements as the middle *eigeiromai* rather than passive *egerthēsomai* (the stress on Jesus' active role was a product of the later church), the third-day motif, the mention of Jesus' claim to be Messiah, the

What about the unlikelihood of Jewish leaders as well as Pilate believing the stories about Jesus rising again; is that a basis for proving it never happened? Filson says the story is unbelievable since the leaders seemed to be so aware of Jesus' resurrection predictions which were given only privately to his disciples. He suggests two possible explanations: Judas may have told the priests and scribes (v. 63), and verses such as 12:40 suggest Jesus' public predictions of his own resurrection (the sign of Jonah). Still, why did the rulers understand predictions Jesus' own disciples did not? Perhaps the emotional distance of the leaders enabled them to see the significance of Jesus' predictions while the intimacy of his disciples prevented them from doing so. Wenham (p. 50n) and Craig say that the disciples' misunderstanding was due to their own stubbornness. The leaders who listened to Jesus' teachings understood but refused to believe, yet with a twist; they did not fear the fulfillment of Jesus' predictions about his own resurrection as much as the disciples' possible attempt to fabricate one. The disciples misunderstood because of their application of Jewish messianism to Jesus' statements. This is hardly impossible; the actual difficulty lies not so much with the leaders as with the disciples themselves.

Other problems such as the elaborate scheme to guard the tomb and Pilate's willingness to do so are fairly easy to explain. The need for guards is quite understandable in light of the rulers' perceived threat of a stolen body, and Pilate probably agreed because he was tired of the whole business. Why was Matthew,[10] however, the only Gospel writer to include this? Perhaps he was the only one who was interested in the Jewish controversy. Historians are not overly skeptical of single witnesses to an event. Neither Mark nor Luke, in fact, was concerned with this problem, and John dealt with it indirectly through Mary in 20:2, 13, and 15.

Markan form of the empty tomb narrative, and the Jewish polemic against it (cf. 28:11 – 15). However, these do not prove later origin. The middle voice is simply a redactional change which hardly affects the veracity of the narrative; none of the other elements is inherently post-Easter, not even in terms of probability.

10 Craig shows how the parallel in the Gospel of Peter actually shows the restraint of Matthew. There the tradition has been altered to present an airtight case: the leaders go on Friday to Pilate, who gives them a Roman guard. Therefore there is no period (such as Friday PM to Saturday morning) when the tomb is left unguarded. Matthew's narration makes the guard almost an afterthought, which would favor the original event rather than polemical fiction.

The guard episode would thus have been redundant in John, and unnecessary in Luke and Mark.

The *Sitz im Leben* Kirche of this passage does not suggest late composition as much as selection and coloring. If the rumor of Jesus' disciples stealing his body was actually circulating at the time of his death, the priests would have done exactly what Matthew said they did. Why should Matthew make up a story to counteract another story? An apologetic composed out of nothing would all too easily be dismissed.[11] In short, the "burden of proof" is on the skeptic who does not accept this account as true, and his arguments lack substance.

The account of the guards is somewhat of an enigma to the critic, providing little evidence to disprove its authenticity, yet at the same time little to prove its authenticity. The story appears in only one Gospel where it is intimately connected to the purpose of that book. Its language strongly suggests tradition yet does not prove authenticity. Still, most of the evidence in the account itself favors authenticity, and other subtle shades of meaning suggest an earlier origin which was grounded in historical fact. In fact, a good argument can be made for its technical placement at the end of the Jewish-Christian phase of the primitive church, when the anti-Christian polemic began.

The Stone Before the Tomb

How did the women who went to the tomb that resurrection morning expect to get into that tomb? Mark says they were deeply concerned about the stone that sealed the entrance to the tomb and asked each other, "Who will roll the stone away from the entrance to the tomb?" Luke and John, on the other hand, exclude that question, implying the women never thought about that problem before it was solved for them. Matthew shows the stone actually being moved by the angel of the Lord in front of women who stood silent. Is there a real discrepancy here between the Gospel accounts? Some critics (Taylor, Grundmann, Evans, Fuller,

---

11. Critics who say this is Matthew's "clumsy" attempt to confute rumor should reevaluate their opinion of the author, one who Wenham describes (p. 48) as "a man of considerable literary and theological ability." Would he make such an awkward attempt? If the story were true, however, the validity of the argument is obvious.

Alsup) think so; noting particularly the women's ignorance about the soldiers at the tomb, their casual attitude toward the problem of the stone that sealed the tomb, their desire to embalm an already embalmed body, and the hint that they realized their problem only on the way to the tomb.

Perhaps the problems are not so difficult, however. Women in mourning might naturally overlook practical problems such as how to enter a sealed tomb. Their ignorance of the soldiers is also quite understandable; guards were not placed at the tomb until the second night (Matt. 27:62f.), a fact the women knew nothing about. And, the question in Mark's account ("Who will roll the stone away from the entrance to the tomb?") expresses the mental confusion of the women and it strongly suggests an eyewitness account. Perhaps it is a kind of "unintentional" historical sign which proves authenticity (see my "Tradition Criticism," p. 123). Taylor says (*Mark*, p. 605) the question is a direct reflection of the women's motive which was "to anoint Jesus' body." Although this question and motive appear only in Mark, any discrepancies between it and other Gospel accounts are minor; for the most part Mark's account meshes with the others thereby making it probable that it was a part of the original event.

The Earthquake and Tomb Events

Why does Matthew alone record the earthquake at the tomb? Perhaps the event was part of his strong emphasis on supernatural powers at work in the resurrection (cp. 27:51–54). Still, it is difficult to prove the earthquake has a basis in tradition since the language in the account is Matthean and the subject matter belongs only to him. Some elements in the story, however, parallel Mark, such as the presence of the angel of the Lord, his position (sitting), and his clothing (white), as well as the fear motif which is transferred here to the soldiers.

Evans thinks (pp. 48, 82) Matthew's story includes a legendary development of Mark's account inserted here to link the empty tomb with the resurrection itself. Walter says ("Schilderung," pp. 418f.) verses 2–7 in Matthew are based on an early legend which included an "opening of doors" motif (similar to liberation legends in ancient mythology as well as Acts 5, 16). He says this section is a "third type of resurrection narrative," the first being the empty tomb and the second, Jesus' appearance.[12] Matthew thus altered the original story to fit in with Mark's account, and added an apologetic emphasis. Walter says the apocalyptic flavor of Matthew's account comes from the original legend, while the earthquake and descent of the angel came from later additions. Walter's thesis is doubtful however. The earthquake in chapter 28 does parallel other scenes in Matthew, and the descent of the angel is much like Mark's account.

Several elements in the account however do differ with Mark. In Matthew the women seem to be actual witnesses of the stone being rolled away from the tomb, while in Mark they arrive at the tomb after the stone has been moved. Is this a serious discrepancy? Several scholars (Plummer, Tasker, Gaechter) think not, saying the aorist verbs in Matthew's account (*katabas*, *proselthōn*, *apekulisen*), contrast with the imperfect *ekathēto* in verse 2 implying that the stone was moved prior to the women's arrival. They came to the tomb only to witness an empty tomb and an angel sitting on the moved rock.

When did the angel sit on the stone? Mark seems to indicate that happened after the women entered the tomb, while Matthew says the women saw the angel first and he led them into the tomb. Are these differences due to the somewhat emotional (and therefore less accurate) testimony of several witnesses? Perhaps that rationalization is not necessary at all. Consider, for instance, Matthew's specific lack of geographical data. In light of this the angel's invitation to "come and see" in verse 6 might well have been phenomenological language, uttered when the women were already inside the tomb. They were simply invited to view the place where Jesus had laid.

The supernatural elements in this scene probably cause more problems than anything else, since these appear only in Matthew's account. The theological significance of the earthquake, for example, is often cited as evidence of a late origin (Grass, Benoit, Evans, McNeile, Campenhausen). However, Wenham asserts ("Resurrection," p. 42) earthquakes were common in Matthew's day and that the temple lay on a geological fault. Wenham also says that

---

12. Walter links this with the Gospel of Peter. However, in an appendix (pp. 426–29) he differentiates the two versions. Though both are dependent on the same tradition, they are developed differently by the two authors.

the explicit supernaturalism in Matthew is implicit in the other Gospels and that Matthew himself wrote about the earthquake as a historic rather than symbolic event. Such extraordinary phenomena would not rise out of a historical vacuum either, lest they be too easily disproved.

Once again, the skeptic's viewpoint does not provide enough data to disprove the historic basis of the earthquake in Matthew, and until it does the account should be accepted as historically valid.

The Race to the Tomb

The discrepancy between Luke 24:12 and John 20:2−10 which was discussed in chapters 4 and 5 includes the resolution that Luke used a later tradition in his narrative in order to provide more evidence for the relevance of the empty tomb. John took this tradition and personalized it in order to give it more of a salvation emphasis.

Much disagreement exists, however, about the composition of John 20:1−18:[13]

1. Wellhausen and Schweitzer believe verses 2−10 and possibly 11 are interpolations.

2. Hartmann believes that the original story is found in some verses (1−3, 5, 7−11, 14−18) on which John expanded (Bultmann says verses 1, 6, 11, 12, 13 are original).

3. Benoit says a synoptic story (20:11a, 14b−18) is joined to a non-synoptic story (1−10) as well as John's version of synoptic tradition (11b−14a).

4. Lindars says John rearranged synoptic tradition by placing the women's report prior to the angel's message and added the race to the tomb to expand the former with a Christophany.

5. Brown and Léon-Dufour say John combines three narratives (two visits to the empty tomb and the appearance to Mary).

6. Mahoney believes John uses two traditions: the story of women at the tomb taken from Mark but told in a way similar to Luke, and the appearance of Jesus at the tomb. The race story

---

13. See Lindars ("Composition," pp. 142−47), Hartmann (pp. 202f.), Bultmann (pp. 681f.), Benoit ("Marie-Madeleine," pp. 141f.), Brown (p. 998), Léon-Dufour (pp. 223f.), and Mahoney (pp. 171f.)

thus developed independently but was written in its final form by John who inserted it into the story about the women at the tomb.

Perhaps the best way to view this empty tomb narrative is as a kind of three-stage synoptic development: First, Mark and Matthew stress the women's visit and the angel's message. Second, Luke adds the story of Peter's race to the tomb, placing it after the angel's message as a transition to the Emmaus pericope. Finally, John adds the "beloved" to Luke's account of the race to the tomb and places the event prior to the angel's message to fit his own structure.[14] It is also quite possible that two separate incidents are combined in these accounts with two different angel appearances merging into one. While attempts to harmonize often cloud rather than clarify issues, and though I admit separate angelophanies are impossible to prove, such a theory is not only viable but coheres with the evidence.

John 20:1f., despite its controversial composition, does contain many eyewitness events. The issue then is not, for instance, whether Peter ran alone or with a companion to the tomb, but whether John's naming the "beloved" as the companion is valid. Since the "beloved," however, is the one whose testimony is written down here, he is undoubtedly a historical, real person (see Craig, *Historicity*).

The race scene presents several other discrepancies in various Gospel accounts. John is the only writer, for instance, who mentions Jesus' burial clothing (the "strips of linen" and "burial cloth" that had been around Jesus' head). John's rich detail reveals his obvious emphasis on the tangible proof of Christ's resurrection, but is this information taken from history? If this proof was so obvious, why did only the "beloved" believe? Why did Peter fail to note the clothes?

Craig answers all these questions by proposing that the clothes did not look like an "unbroken cocoon" in a conspicuous place but instead were folded so neatly on the bench that only the "beloved" realized what they were. Mahoney adds to this (p. 260f.) that John simply was concentrating here on the "beloved's" "impulse to faith," not "Peter as Peter" or even Peter in comparison with the "beloved." Therefore, this becomes invalid as an argument

14. The combined views of Hartmann and Lindars seem to be the best solution to the problem. Linguistic similarities between verses 3–10 and Luke 24:12 suggest John used Luke, and verses 1 and 11–18 seem to be John's redaction of Mark's narrative.

against historicity. Once again, the eyewitness tone of the narrative favors a positive verdict on this issue. I. T. Ramsey (*Christian Discourse* 2, in Mahoney, pp. 261f.), for instance, shows how John uses three verbs for "seeing" in verses 5–8 which lead us to the climax of belief in verse 8.[15] Brown warns (*John*, pp. 501f.) that the terms for "seeing" in John are not consistent and therefore we should not attempt to read too much into them. But John 20's verbs include two which specifically refer to physical sight and one which means spiritual perception. In this context then, the verbs specifically produce an eyewitness tone which lends historical credence to the whole scene.

Another problem with this scene is the "beloved's" belief which seems to contradict what is said in verse 9. Was this "other disciple" included with "they" who "still did not understand that Jesus had to rise from the dead"? If so, why did not the believer share his faith with Peter, Mary, or the others?

Some critics answer these questions by suggesting the whole account was either a free composition (Fuller) or a clumsy insertion (Marxsen, Evans, Alsup). The clumsiness, however, is more apparent than real. Hooke says (*Resurrection*, p. 84) John purposely did not include a strong thematic connection between the episodes. Each instead is a complete entity which reflects in its own way a single aspect of the resurrection.

Hooke's point is good but he misses the strong theological continuity of the episodes. Perhaps the best way to evaluate the discrepancies in this account is to recognize they are more apparent than real. Perhaps the "beloved" believed but without total understanding of the consequences of that belief; why should not he walk away from the tomb with some questions about what it meant? And, even though John did not mention it, why could not he have attempted to tell the others about his new belief?

In conclusion, the best way to approach this account is to accept the trip to the tomb as historical fact. Even though Luke's more straightforward account seems more verifiable than John's redacted one, the basic story behind both of them is authentic, even suggestive of Jesus' "first appearance to Peter" in 1 Corinthians 15:5.

15. While he is correct when he connects the "seeing" with spiritual discernment (though see the remarks of Brown, *John*, p. 986), we do not believe that this obviates the eyewitness impact which the wording was meant to have on the reader.

At the Tomb

The Angels

How many angels were present at the tomb? Mark says one "young man," Matthew an "angel of the Lord," Luke "two men in clothes that gleamed like lightning," and John "two angels in white." Benoit calls (p. 247) these differences variations in tradition, Bultmann (*HST*, pp. 314f.) secondary mythological accretions, and Lightfoot (*Mark*, pp. 23f.) a redactional gloss from the early church which wanted to make the resurrection an eschatological event. Most critics, however, agree on this point, that all the Gospels refer to angels despite Mark and Luke's anthropomorphic language. Swete, in fact, says (*Mark*, p. 374) these differences prove that the evangelists were not mechanically repeating tradition but instead were making honest, creative attempts to tell the truth.

Cranfield (*Mark*, pp. 428f.) believes the angels serve as mediators of the resurrection event which human eyes were not permitted to see, thereby providing the link between man and incomprehensible glory. Despite the individual differences in description each evangelist does report at least one angel at the tomb, so there seems little reason to doubt the historical reality of the event itself. Some critics (Grass, Marxsen, Fuller, Evans, Koch, Alsup) argue that the bodily form and speech of the angel proves the event was legendary. Yet, Craig maintains that the angel's appearance is the focal point of each Gospel account and therefore of the empty tomb tradition. If Kremer is correct (pp. 148f.) that we have here a literary device intended only to highlight the divine origin of the message, then we ask with Craig why John has them without any stress on a divine message; there they merely ask why Mary is weeping. Although Matthew most frequently stresses the supernatural, the others agree with him on this essential.

How many angels were at the tomb, and why the differing numbers in the Gospels? Perhaps John followed Luke, changing the number to two in accordance with the legal requirement for witnesses. Some critics see this number as redactional (Fuller, Alsup), while others believe it is traditional (Lagrange, Lohfink). Still others think the difference in numbers might be due to different traditions, however, any attempts that have been made to harmonize the accounts (Wescott, Hodges, Wenham) by projecting two different angel appearances (one to the women followed by one to Mary) certainly may lead to improbable results. Similarities in language and style between John and the synoptics do indicate a common tradition, yet verbal similarities are minimal ("white," "sitting"). The mood of each scene is also so different that a common origin is questionable. Good reason does seem to exist for separating the visits. Although Catchpole says ("Tradition," p. 15) the timing shows they are one event, that relates only to John 20:1 and of the visits in Mark 16 and John 20, not to John 20:11f. Perhaps a moderate attempt at harmonization here is the best solution; one which Plummer agrees with by saying, "Where out of two or more only one is spokesman, he is necessarily remembered. The other or others may be easily ignored or forgotten. It is an exaggeration to call such differences absolute discrepancies." The presence of one or two angels at the tomb is too important to this account to be a late addition; although Luke and John may have stressed "two" angels for redactional emphasis, this redaction was not necessarily ahistorical.

The Angels' Message

What was the message of the angels at the tomb? Matthew and Mark basically agree on what was said, but Luke differs significantly from those accounts, and John records a question instead of a statement. Matthew and Mark's angel speaks basically about the command to go to Galilee to wait for Jesus. Luke's angels speak about the fulfillment of Jesus' predictions in Galilee, and John's angels simply ask Mary why she is weeping. Bernard concludes (p. 664), "What really happened is not possible now to determine." Total reconstruction of the basic tradition is practically impossible, yet neither Luke nor John were ignorant of what Matthew and Mark had written. The language and style of all the resurrection narratives show too many similarities to suggest an intellectual vacuum in which all the writers worked with little or no knowledge of traditions. They selected portions and redacted (edited) them according to their own theological purposes, but this does not mean that they freely created them, nor does it mean that there is no historical basis for them.

Marshall believes the angels' command is a literary device used to "provide a commentary on the situation" ("Resurrection," p. 73; also Cranfield, pp. 465f.). He sees two major problems with this, however. First, the evangelists' accounts change according to individual literary purposes, and second, if the command is historical, why did the disciples remain in Jerusalem so long (the Thomas episode was "one week later"), and why did Jesus first appear to them there instead of in Galilee? Perhaps these differences are exaggerated; although it is difficult to come up with a detailed harmonization with any degree of accuracy, one can detect a distinct core of historical tradition here.

The command to go directly to Galilee is a problem in light of Jesus' appearances to the disciples in Jerusalem recorded in Luke and John. The problem can be resolved in three possible ways: (1) The command to go "to Galilee" might be a redaction to stress the appearance in Gaililee (Marshall) and to add more authority to the witness of the empty tomb tradition (Alsup). (2) The command might be historical (Tasker) especially if we understand the verb in Matthew 28:7 as the prophetic present, "he is going to precede you" (as a promise and not a command). (3) Luke and John might have omitted Jesus' Galilean appearances which occurred prior to the Jerusalem appearances. This might also explain the enigmatic character of John 21:1−14 which may have described an early appearance. All of these explanations make sense, especially the last two. Luke might have emphasized the angel's prediction in order to avoid the command without denying its historical basis for literary purposes. And John might have omitted the entire message for literary reasons, but even more likely because he recorded a completely different angelophany.

Conclusive evidence against the authenticity of the angel's message is simply not to be found. The message ("Jesus has risen") as well as fulfillment motif ("as he told you") probably come directly from tradition, and since they both agree with Jesus' own predictions are therefore historical.

Galilee vs. Jerusalem

Where did Jesus' appearances take place, Galilee or Jerusalem? The problem is that the Gospel writers focus on different areas;

Matthew[16] and Mark on Galilee, and Luke and John on Jerusalem. John 21 moves from Jerusalem to Galilee, but the whole chapter is a supplement to the book and was probably added after John's church learned about the Galilean tradition (Lohmeyer, Fuller). Earlier critics believed that the oldest tradition centered on Jerusalem appearances (the origin of the church's mission),[17] but more recently scholars (Lake, Grass, Gardner-Smith) have begun to believe that the Galilean appearances were first. Their line of reasoning asserts that: First, the empty tomb tradition came late and led to the development of a Jerusalem appearance tradition. Therefore the Galilee tradition is more historically valid, especially since the Galilee appearances sound more like first appearances (e.g., John 21:1f.). Second, placing the Galilean appearances first would better fit the premise that the disciples fled to Galilee after the crucifixion (cf. Mark 14:27, 50). Third, the appearance to the women in Matthew 28:9f. did not happen until the disciples returned to Jerusalem and heard Mary's story (Marxsen, pp. 96f., cf. 79–97). And fourth, the Jerusalem tradition rose "through a tendentious desire on the part of the Jerusalem church to locate Christian origins there" (O'Collins, *Resurrection*, p. 23).

Perhaps here, as in the discussion about the number of angels, one ought to consider that each Gospel writer might be expressing theology rather than ignorance or disapproval of tradition. O'Collins admits such motives were operative both in developing tradition and in writing it down in the Gospels. Each episode thus became a vehicle of theology as it fit into the development of the writer's Gospel as a whole. At the same time passages such as Matthew 28:9–10 seem to indicate the writer used more than one tradition. And if Matthew uses Mark in verses 9–10 (see chap. 2), both Gos-

16. Matthew does record an appearance to the women in Jerusalem (28:9–10) but this is usually dismissed as a secondary addition from the Galilean tradition on the basis of 28:5–7.

17. Creed (p. 316f.) summarizes the arguments of Weiss and Burkitt: (1) Mark 14:27 should read "lead you into Galilee." Luke turned the statement into prophecy because Jesus never fulfilled it. (2) The crucial role of Jerusalem in the New Testament favors Jerusalem as the older tradition. Creed argues against this, citing the evidence in Mark (16:7) which makes the adding of a Jerusalem tradition more likely than adding a Galilean tradition. More recently, Steinseifer argues that Matthew 28:16–17 and Mark 16:7 are redactional and that John 21:1–14 is not an Easter message, contra Lorenzen ("Galilee"), who counters that the disciples fled from Jerusalem (they had no part in the burial or empty tomb stories) and therefore that the earliest appearance tradition centered on Galilee.

pel writers must be aware of more than one tradition. No good reason seems to exist for denying the possibility of two appearance traditions either, even though an exact harmonization of them would be difficult. No one knows for sure why the Gospel writers chose to include some appearances and omit others, even though all were valid.

Taylor says (*Formation*, pp. 59f.) the resurrection tradition does not follow the same form as the passion tradition. The passion necessarily takes a fixed chronological form, each episode naturally flowing into the next. The resurrection, however, is a series of isolated vignettes, each of which encourages faith in the Risen Christ. Early Christian preachers could choose from these vignettes exactly the ones which met the needs of their audience. The same kind of selection process was probably used by the Gospel writers themselves, both in the resurrection narratives as well as elsewhere in their books. The normal selection process thus is the primary reason for the seemingly haphazard presentation of resurrection appearances.

The best answer to the Galilee-Jerusalem question may be Moule's theory ("Festival," pp. 58f.) that the disciples' geographic movement may have followed that of festival pilgrims who remained in Jerusalem for Passover, went home to Galilee, then returned for Pentecost. This combined with the second or third possibilities mentioned with regard to the angel's command (see above) makes it very possible that the appearances in Jerusalem (Matt. 28:9–10; Luke 24:9–54; John 20:11–23) preceded the appearances in Galilee (Mark 16:7; Matt. 28:7, 16–20; John 21; 1 Cor. 15:6f.?), which then were followed by some final appearances in Jerusalem (Luke 24:44?–53; Acts 1:1).[18]

The Deception by the Priests, Matthew 28:11–15

Several problems in this account have prompted some scholars (Campenhausen, McNeile, Hill, Grundmann, Alsup) to suggest that

18. Verses 44–49 illustrate why reconstruction cannot account for all the problems. These verses are linked to verses 36–43, yet belong in time to verses 50–53 since the disciples are commanded to "stay in the city." Perhaps Luke combined two or more traditions here.

Matthew's particular story about the priests' deception is an apologetic creation. They cite several reasons for this theory:

1. The soldiers should have reported to Pilate rather than the high priest.

2. Sleeping is a capital offense; it is doubtful that the guards would have agreed to incriminate themselves to this extent.

3. Pilate could never have overlooked such a breach of discipline on the part of the soldiers (in the Gospel of Peter he commands them to say nothing).

4. The guards' and officials' acceptance of the empty tomb as fact seems to suggest a late apologetic creation.

5. The irony of priests spreading the very rumor they had previously tried to stop (27:62–66) suggests composition. Some critics, to be sure, say composition happened early in tradition (Walter, Kratz), yet the real question is whether Matthew reworked an earlier tradition or created his own account. Most critics say he created his own, citing 27:51f. as another example of Matthean redaction.

Certain historical facts, however, should explain away many of these discrepancies. First, Matthew 27:62–67 is not necessarily evidence of a late redaction. Some critics (e.g., Tasker, Filson, Albright, Wenham) call attention to the fact that Pilate's guards were voluntarily placed in subjection to the Jewish leaders; they would therefore report back to the Jews rather than Pilate. Wenham adds (p. 50), "the soldiers may have regarded it wiser to report the loss of the body they were supposed to be guarding to the Jews than to the governor." Also, Matthew does not describe what the soldiers' reaction to the empty tomb was. Why should he? The evidence was convincing enough for anyone. The irony of priests spreading the very rumor they had formerly tried to suppress is also historically possible, the rumor being the handiest explanation available in a time-pressured situation. Perhaps the rulers even believed the lie themselves.

Some problems in this account are less easy to solve. Consider, for instance, the problem of the soldiers sleeping on the job. Why did Pilate overlook this serious offense? Orr says (p. 106) that "the breach of discipline had already been committed in the soldiers' flight from the tomb," and that they might already have given Pilate the information he needed to excuse their behavior. On the other hand, Lee states (pp. 173–75) that the soldiers were accountable

only to the priests who probably believed their story of the empty
tomb. Pilate probably did not become involved in the soldiers'
breach of conduct at all since he considered the whole thing a
Jewish matter. Perhaps the guards also agreed to the lie to the
priests because they simply had no other choice; they were pawns
in the hands of the Jews.

Matthew 28:11–15 is a difficult section; like 26:62–66 it produces few arguments against authenticity, yet little evidence for
authenticity. The account appears only in Matthew where it clearly
is a part of its theology. It probably was written late in the Jewish-
Christian phase of the early church, yet is authentic. Its apologetic
overtones, however, reveal a certain amount of tradition-development, (e.g., the stress on the deceit of the priests) particular to
the time when Jewish-Christian relationships were declining. Perhaps Matthew's polemical use of the empty tomb was not a late
development though; 1 Corinthians 15:3–5 uses the same technique to counter false teaching. The resurrection was an intimate
part of every bit of Christian teaching as well as polemics. For
instance, it is utilized in baptism (Rom. 6:2f., Col. 2:12), in the Eucharist (Luke 24:13f.), and in Jewish and Gentile polemics (the
speeches in Acts). Thus there is no reason at all why this section
must be a "late creation" of the early church.

Conclusion: The Empty Tomb

Many scholars (Taylor, Marxsen, Fuller, Clark) agree with Bultmann who says that the empty tomb tradition is the byproduct
of Judaic views on the unity of body and soul. They say Paul knew
nothing about the empty tomb story, and that Acts even treats it
as a secondary theme. This line of reasoning is shortsighted; the
empty tomb tradition is not subordinate at all. Instead it is a basic
presupposition of the resurrection tradition.[19] Many details in the
account, in fact, provide evidence of great antiquity such as the
Semitic terminology of Mark 16:2 (echoed in Luke 24:1 and John
20:1), the unity of the basic tradition, and the role of the women

19. See also Shaw (Resurrection, pp. 21f.), Menck ("Empty Tomb," p. 276), and Brown
(pp. 976–77) who mention verses like Romans 6:4; 8:29; Colossians 2:12; and Acts 2:29–
32; 13:36–37. Campenhausen (pp. 43f.) says 1 Corinthians 15:3f. provides strong evidence
for authenticity.

(which would hardly be a part of a free composition). Moule and Filson suggest that none of the empty tomb statements would have stood the test of time if they had been false, and Wilckens (in Moule, *Significance*, pp. 72–74) even proposes that the empty tomb traditions *preceded* the stories of Jesus' appearances. It therefore seems quite unnecessary to deny the authenticity of the empty tomb tradition.

Tradition-development does occur within the resurrection narrative as a whole, however, as well as in the empty tomb tradition. Yet like the passion story, the empty tomb tradition seems to have circulated as a basic whole from the very beginning. The nucleus is found in all four Gospels (redacted somewhat by John) and includes this basic story line: several women went to the tomb and found it empty. While they were there they met an angel who told them Jesus had risen from the dead.

Several peripheral traditions were added to this basic story as need arose. The first was probably the fulfillment motif in connection with the church's growing concern with that problem (cf. 1 Cor. 15:3–5 et al.), although this might also have been an early part of the tradition. The second addition might have been the witness motif included in Luke's "two angels" as well as the witness theme in Acts. The supernatural evidence recorded in Matthew may have come from this same time period, when the power of God over nature became more and more an integral part of tradition (as evidenced in Acts). Finally, an apologetic emphasis was added when Jewish-Christian relationships became fractured, although it was offered only to readers who might be influenced by the problem (Matthew and also John).

What is the probable *Traditionsgeschichte* ("tradition-history") of the empty tomb narrative as a whole? Catchpole[20] notes two possible ways it might have developed: (1) John 20:3–10 was not originally part of the narrative; John 20:1f. and 11f. were originally one unit taken from the Mark 16:1f. tradition. Mark took his material from another pre-Markan unit. The order of development thus could be pre-Mark to Mark to John and the other Gospels. (2) John 20:11–13 might be an editorial bridge (based on the Synoptics) which leads to the appearance to Mary, the original form

---

20. D. Catchpole, "Tradition Criticism," pp. 16–17. This section is taken from his unpublished paper, "Matthew's Resurrection Narrative," delivered to the Tyndale Conference, Cambridge, July, 1972, which was unavailable to me.

of Matthew 28:9f. John 20:1f. might also be a separate unit which developed even earlier than Mark 16 (Benoit, Alsup). The order here would be John to pre-Mark to Mark and then to Matthew and Luke.

A third order is also possible, however; one which probably fits the evidence better. Many of the differences in these accounts might be due to editorial revision rather than tradition development, reflecting selection rather than a further stage in the development of tradition. The evangelists chose pericopes and emphases from a common "pool" of stories in the early church. The "basic" pre-Markan story was thus in a fluid rather than fixed state and included many emphases which could be added or subtracted by a preacher at will. A "pre-Mark" tradition thus cannot be clearly identified, even though a basic nucleus can. From this basic story came Mark's finished account which combined more than one tradition with redactional highlights. The other three Gospels were then separate spinoffs from Mark, with the exception of John who wove Mark and Luke together. Each had access to and made use of separate sources, although John shows the greatest amount of redaction.[21]

In conclusion, a limited amount of tradition-development does exist, however, all of it takes place within pericopes rather than in the empty tomb tradition as a whole. A clear line of progression from one form to another cannot be drawn; rather several parallel lines for different sources must be sketched in, and to these can be added additional pericopes and theological purposes. Episodes thus can have a traditional base and yet exhibit redactional characteristics which have been added to speak to the specific needs of their readers. This is evidenced in the empty tomb narratives, especially in such parts as the guard episode or the race to the tomb. Both are based on tradition but formed in such a way that they present a message to meet the current needs of the church.

The empty tomb is most definitely a historical event. Many details of the story are debatable, of course, and many problems in the account will never be fully resolved. Taken as a whole, however, the evidence is overwhelmingly supportive. Craig lists eight rea-

---

21. Tradition-development is indicated here, although due perhaps more to redaction than tradition. Progression here moves from the Markan nucleus to Mark to Luke and then to John, each presupposing the one before. Matthew would follow a separate line from pre-Mark to Mark to Matthew.

sons why the empty tomb narratives are historically valid ("Empty Tomb," pp. 189–94):

1. Paul's testimony (1 Cor. 15:3–5) implies it. Since he lived in Jerusalem within six years of the event and says it really happened, why should anyone later in time doubt its validity?

2. The pre-Markan passion tradition's use of the empty tomb narrative proves it was not written later than AD 37. Furthermore, how could all the so-called "legendary" elements come together so quickly without a historical nucleus?

3. The absence of the "third day" motif from the Gospel accounts makes it likely that the tradition behind them is even older than AD 37 (cf. 1 Cor. 15:3–5), and if *tē mia tōn sabbatōn* is a Semitism it lends even greater credence to a very primitive tradition (see Bode, p. 161).

4. The lack of apologetic motifs in the basic narrative plus the lack of dramatic, legendary features (such as the description of the resurrection itself) suggests its primitive nature.

5. The women's discovery of the tomb would not have been added by later scribes since women could not serve as legal witnesses. This feature is a major element in favor of historicity.

6. The investigation of the tomb by the disciples is historically credible since it is unlikely they had already fled to Galilee.

7. The resurrection would not have been proclaimed in Jerusalem if the tomb had not been empty. The Jews would never have accepted a resurrection of the spirit without the body.

8. The Jewish-Christian controversy of Matthew 27:62f. and 28:11f. presupposes the empty tomb. Jews never denied the fact of the empty tomb; they only sought to explain it away.[22]

---

22. They could have answered the proclamation simply by pointing to the tomb if it had not been empty (*contra* Mahoney, p. 159).

The Appearance Narratives

The appearance narratives should be approached somewhat differently than the empty tomb narratives, since the empty tomb narratives have parallel accounts in the Gospels, while the appearance narratives are basically independent, selected from a large collection of stories. This does not mean that the appearance narratives have no parallels at all; however, the majority of them do not. The Gospel writers selectively chose only those events which best fit the theological purposes of their respective works. Each appearance should thus be evaluated as an independent unit and tradition-critical data will become a crucial part of this analysis.

Many critics believe the appearances began as credal statements which later developed into full-length stories. Dodd says, however, that the form of the appearance stories does not prove that less-developed narratives originated prior to more-developed ones ("Essay," p. 10). In fact, many signs point to the real possibility that the appearances were well-developed stories right from the start. 1 Corinthians 15:5f., for instance, is part of a credal passage that contains an official list of witnesses which were obviously familiar to the writer's audience. The list also presupposes stories which were more developed and circulating at that time.

1 Corinthians 15:5—8

The earliest verification of the resurrection is probably 1 Corinthians 15:3—5, possibly the oldest fragment of a New Testament creed. Verses 5—8 of this passage, in particular, represent the earliest appearance tradition and thus can be used as a contrast to the more developed Gospel accounts.

Certain problems immediately become apparent. Except for the second appearance in the Corinthians account, none of the others clearly parallel appearances in the Gospels. The appearance to Peter, for instance, is only casually referred to in Luke 24:34, and the appearance to James is not found in the Gospels at all. Could many of the stories have been lost? In spite of this, however, the passage remains a proving ground for theories regarding the nature, means, and historicity of the resurrection itself.

Most scholars believe the Corinthians passage is the oldest tradition in the New Testament, citing as evidence: (1) the use of the two introductory words in verse 3, *paredōka* ("delivered") and *parelabon* ("received"); (2) the use of parallelism with four *hoti* ("that") clauses divided into two major sections, one on the death and the other on the resurrection; (3) the use of non-Pauline elements such as "for our sins," "according to the Scriptures," "has been raised," "on the third day," "was seen," and "to the Twelve."

Critics differ, however, on the exact origin of this tradition:

1. Some say (Jeremias, Klappert, Delling) it came from an Aramaic original, noting such factors as synthetic parallelism in the four strophes; the origin of *hyper ... graphas* ("according to the Scriptures") in the Hebrew text of Isaiah 53 (*hyper* is not in the LXX); the adversative *kai* ("and") in line 3; the word order of *tē hēmera tē tritē* ("the third day"); the lack of particles apart from *apo* ("from"); the presence of *ōphthē* rather than the more common *ephanē* ("appeared"); and the use of the dative rather than *hypo* after the passive verb.

2. Others argue (Conzelmann, Vielhauer) that it came from the LXX because of its imagery and hellenistic Christology.

3. Some compromise, saying (Fuller, Kloppenberg, Wilckens, Craig) the tradition had a Palestinian origin but came to Paul via hellenistic Judaism. The formula itself began in the earliest Palestinian church.

Most of the evidence seems to support the third view. Although the tradition probably took final form in a Greek-speaking environment (*kata tas graphas* ("according to the Scriptures") and *egēgertai* ("risen") cannot have an Aramaic origin since there is no equivalent phrase). The core of the kerygma thus "did not originate with Paul or the later church but came from the earliest apostolic community" (Jeremias, *EW*, p. 103). The historical context of this passage is probably Paul's first visit to James and Peter in Jerusalem after his conversion (Gal. 1:18, 19); note how the lists in verses 5 and 7 single out James and Peter (Grass, p. 95). If the tradition behind this account was developed by the time of Paul's visit (about AD 40), then it probably began shortly after Jesus' death.

The form of the original credal statement is difficult to determine since it contains four *hoti* ("that") clauses (vv. 3 – 5) followed by two *epeita* ("then") clauses (vv. 6 – 7) and a personal reminiscence (v. 8), verse 5 being a problem because it seems to fit in with both sections. Several theories have risen regarding the basic structure of the original:

1. Harnack ("I Cor. 15,3f," pp. 62f. described in Fuller, pp. 12f.) was one of the first to suggest different origins for the lists. He followed the Tübingen approach and proposed a combination of two rival lists, one from Peter's followers (v. 5) and one from James' followers. Harnack, however, failed to account for the other appearances, and his thesis was too speculative.

2. Michaelis (*Erscheinungen,* pp. 12f.) revived Harnack's basic theory that the original credal statement ended with "he appeared" and that Paul added to this three groups of two appearances each naming an individual and a group. He also believed Paul considered his list to be complete in its catalogue of witnesses.

3. Although few critics accept this threefold pattern, most (Bammel, Winter, Wilckens, Kloppenberg) agree that Paul's list of appearances (vv. 6f.) was added separately. He combined two separate lists which were not necessarily rival groups.

4. Fuller says all these theories fail to note the careful use of chronological words such as "then" and "afterward" which mark the time sequence in the list. They also clearly indicate three lists (vv. 5, 6, 7) which Paul combined. Fuller believes the first and third were compiled after Paul's visit to Jerusalem (Gal. 1:18f.) where he visited both Peter and James, the same event which also produced verses 3 – 5.

5. Evans says the original formula ended at verse 5, Paul adding verses 6 and 7 later because of the changed *Sitz im Leben* of the epistle. Paul also added verse 8, a very personal testimony written possibly because of constant challenges to his apostolic authority.

The best way to evaluate this passage probably is to see verses

3 — 5 as the original formula, with verses 6 — 8 added by Paul later because of changes in the developing church. James and Peter were named specifically because they had become leaders in the church and thus qualified as "official" witnesses. Hence the original tradition was the four *hoti* clauses of verses 3 — 5 with their AB:AB style:[1]

A[1]. That Christ died for our sins in accordance with the Scriptures

B[1]. That he was buried

A[2]. That he was raised on the third day in accordance with the Scriptures and

B[2]. That he appeared to Cephas, then to the Twelve.

Paul inserted the formula here to provide an official statement of belief which could correct the false teachers of Corinth. It thus had a polemical function. The formula itself, however, as an independent unit had a purpose prior to Paul; it must have been used by the early church both kerygmatically and catechetically to authenticate the basic message of Christianity. Barth argues that the list consists of witnesses to the resurrection, not proof of it, thus providing, says Wilckens, "legitimation formulae" stressing the authority of the apostles. The phrase "most of whom are still alive" (v. 5), however, seems to suggest an apologetic purpose. It is difficult to believe first-century Christians could detect any difference between evidence for the appearances and proof of the resurrection. Too often scholars read the data with modern presuppositions rather than from a first-century perspective.

The passage includes three basic purposes: (1) a didactic purpose to correct the false views of the Corinthians about the resurrection of the dead; (2) an apologetic purpose to prove beyond a doubt the truth of Paul's teachings even to skeptics (v. 6);[2] (3) an authentication purpose to establish Paul's own apostolic authority

1. Although many critics such as Grass, Jeremias, and Rengstorf believe that the first and third lines are primary while the second and fourth are secondary, Mussner, Schmitt, and Craig are more believeable when they say the lines are parallel and have equal weight. The sequence is chronological rather than topical.

2. Sider even says Paul wanted to prove Jesus' resurrection really happened to Corinthian sectarians who denied it ("Nature," pp. 124f.). While this fits the strong use of the details, it goes beyond the evidence, which does not demand that the opponents denied Jesus' resurrection itself. It is better to see this with Pannenberg, (*Jesus*, p. 89) as a stress on the facticity to add greater force to Paul's argument.

to correct false teachings (v. 8). The three purposes are complementary, not contradictory.

Much discussion regarding Paul's use of the verb ōphthē ("appeared") in this passage has taken place through the years;[3] however, Léon-Dufour's approach (p. 95f.) seems to be best. He says
Paul's use of the verb suggests what actually happened in front of
the witnesses rather than how that happened.[4] The mode, he says
(a vision, divine revelation, or actual event), cannot be determined
simply on the basis of a single verb. That can be determined only
on the basis of the major claims of the New Testament itself.

The Appearances to Peter and the Twelve (v. 5)

The list of witnesses in the Corinthians passage divides naturally into four grammatical groups, each major section marked by
ōphthē and epeita, and each minor section by eita. Parallelism is
evident in a comparison of phrases; one and three have similar
structures (each contain two appearances) as do two and four
(each has a single appearance). Jesus' appearance to Peter in this
account is not specifically described anywhere else, although Luke
24:34 and Mark 16:7 possibly refer to it.

Why isn't Peter's experience described more fully somewhere
else? Perhaps Paul's attitude toward his own Damascus experi-

3. There are several approaches: (1) Marxsen (pp. 84f.) says we can know only that
the followers had "visions" which led them to believe Jesus rose from the dead. Seidensticker (pp. 31f.) calls it a "revelatory situation" like Old Testament visions. However, this
"irreducible minimum" is unsatisfactory. (2) Michaelis (TDNT, V, pp. 357f.) removes it from
the physical realm but still calls it a valid vision. However, as Delling states (pp. 84–85)
1 Corinthians 9:1 and Galatians 1:16 point to the Damascus experience, which Paul
clearly differentiated from a "vision" (cp. 2 Cor. 12:1). (3) Fuller argues (pp. 30f.) more
strongly for the transcendent reality of the revelatory event but states the subject (Christ)
rather than the object (Cephas et al) has stress. However, I do not find this dichotomy
necessary. (4) Delling (pp. 84f.) correctly demonstrates that ōpthēnai ("see" or "reveal")
means not merely to reveal as present but includes the idea of a bodily resurrection in
the context. Luke's use of this in Acts 16:9 is editorial and only serves to distinguish it
in salvation-history from the other appearances. The eyewitness aspect of horaō ("see")
is present in 1 Corinthians 15:8, especially in the polemical nature of the creed here (cp.
Col. 2:1; 1 Tim. 3:16).

4. Alsup says, "One cannot say more than the following: ōphthē reflects Old Testament
(LXX) terminology by which an encounter of theophanic dimension is intended and
further information about the descriptive nature of that encounter cannot be won from
the terminus alone but must be arrived at through an analysis of the form following the
superscription" (pp. 53–54).

ence is a clue here, since in his epistles he never mentions his experience except as proof of his apostleship (cf. 1 Cor. 15:8; Gal. 1:16), Luke is the one who describes the full event. Was Paul's reluctance here prompted by humility or a desire not to elevate his experience to the level of "works"?[5] Or was it due to the intensely private nature of the experience itself? Only late in his ministry (Acts 26) was he even willing to talk about it. In much the same way perhaps Jesus' appearance to Peter (confronting the effects of his denial) was so personal that the Gospel writers simply left it alone.

Some scholars propose other reasons for the silence: (1) Käsemann believes (Essays, p. 49) "more detailed narratives which were available were suppressed on dogmatic grounds, because they had ceased to correspond to the views of the second and third generation of Christians." (2) E. L. Allen (p. 349) says earlier accounts were lost probably because of human frailty and a primitive Christian emphasis on God's deeds rather than man's experiences. (3) Wilckens says (Significance, pp. 73f.) no primitive account of the appearances ever existed apart from the empty tomb narrative. Statements which later developed into a group of traditions probably provided the impetus for Paul's statements in 1 Corinthians 15.

Wilcken's view seems highly unlikely; Paul would hardly have used a developed account in a credal list. That list instead presupposes a more developed account. Perhaps a combination of Käsemann and Allen's view is the best approach here,[6] more detailed accounts of the appearances are not available, particularly the ones concerning Peter and James, either because they were never known in detail, or the terminology changed to the point where the stories became oblique references in the Gospels.

Alsup (pp. 55–58), after an extensive consideration of the possibilities, concludes that the solution may lie in the difference between kerygma and Gospel. Individual appearances were important in the kerygma, especially in such a list as 1 Corinthians 15:5–8, but were not important in the Gospel tradition.

Cullmann (Peter, pp. 192f.) and Brown (John, p. 1085) believe that

---

5. Hansen says Paul avoids writing about the call because it would conflict with his doctrine of justification by making the call a "meritorious achievement of his own."

6. Käsemann's theory is a rehash of Harnack's which fails to provide enough concrete evidence. Allen's theory also fails to provide a solution since "human frailty" is too general a term and can include any number of possible reasons.

Jesus' appearance to Peter, for instance, is a part of the keys-to-the-kingdom narrative in Matthew 16:17–19[7] as well as the re-instatement of the Peter scene in John 21:15–17. In fact, virtually all the major stories about Peter (such as the miraculous catch of fish in Luke 5:1–11 or transfiguration in Mark 9:2–8), they say, include elements which link it to Jesus' appearance to Peter. Alsup disagrees, however, saying (pp. 55f., 139f.) the stories themselves are such strong, independent traditions that they should not be viewed as part of an entirely different historical situation.

Does verse 5b of 1 Corinthians 15 refer to specific Gospel appearances, and if so, which ones—Matthew 28:16f.; Luke 24:33; or John 21:1f.? Since we know Jesus appeared several times to the Twelve (Acts 1:3), perhaps the best way to narrow down any specific appearance mentioned in verse 5b is to first of all limit it to ones which happened on the "third day" and in which specific mention was made of the appearance to Peter. Luke 24:33f. best fits this description, even though Luke uses the term "Eleven" here instead of "Twelve," a choice which reflects historical accuracy rather than a different appearance. There were undoubtedly several appearances to the Twelve (cf. Acts 1:3) This would best fit that which occurred on the "third day" according to Luke and John.

Fuller says (p. 35) these first appearances are vital, "the foundation of the eschatological community" since they are " 'church-founding appearances.' " As such, they must be distinguished from the later appearances, whose function is the call and sending of apostles to fulfill a mission." There is, however, no dichotomy between the two functions; they are synonymous (as noted in the Gospel accounts). The early appearances were the foundation of the church which from the beginning had mission as its purpose.

The Appearance to the Five Hundred (v. 6)

Paul's reference to Jesus' appearance to five hundred, "most of whom are still living," calls attention to their witness function but also causes some critics like Grass (p. 96n) to say that Paul does

7. Fuller says the use of "Cephas" rather than Peter indicates authority and reminds us of the authentication ceremony of Matthew 16:17–19 (p. 35). Conzelmann believes the name was given to Peter in this appearance. Both say Matthew 16 is a post-resurrection passage. With respect to the two pairs (vv. 5, 7), Wilckens (*Significance*, pp. 59f.) and Fuller (p. 35) assert that the individual (Peter, James) is here emphasized as being in authority over the group (the Twelve, the apostles). Yet this may read too much into the intent; the lists are not primarily "legitimation formulae" (see above) and the whole is probably more chronological and representative than hierarchical.

not present "historical proof in the modern sense." Perhaps he does not, choosing not to present events simply as they occurred but rather to combine event with interpretation. Nevertheless, he was vitally interested in the historical event.

Since this appearance cannot be clearly identified in the Gospel accounts, it has provoked a number of speculations:

1. Some (Robertson and Plummer) say Matthew 28:16f. is the source here since the phrase "some doubted" seems to include the five hundred. Seidensticker (pp. 286f.) believes this account is the only authentic resurrection appearance and that Luke's and John's appearances are merely later developments of it. The Emmaus and fishing appearances are separate legendary creations on the basis of later missionary needs. This attempt, however, to select one of many traditions and arbitrarily assign it a place of preeminence is presumptuous, arising more out of dogmatic interests than tradition-critical criteria (see Alsup, pp. 40 – 95).

2. Von Dobschütz, Gilmour, and Jeremias say verse 6 refers to Pentecost; however, Goguel disagrees. He says Acts 2 describes a pneumatic experience of the early church rather than a Christophany (La foi, pp. 255 – 61).

3. Gilmour, Jeremias, and Fuller believe the verse refers to John 20:22; somewhere along the line the tradition changed from Christophany to an ecstatic experience of the Spirit. As time passed this pneumatic element became so important that in Acts 2, for instance, it lost its original setting. This thesis presents some problems: (a) the connection between John 20:22 and Acts 2 is debatable, and (b) since glossolalia (speaking in tongues) was an integral part of the Acts 2 account, why was it not also a part of John 20? It seems far more likely that all three (1 Cor. 15:6, John 20:22, Acts 2) were separate events.

4. Kearney says the number 500 is symbolic, and on the basis of Paul's eschatological use of *epanō* and *ephapax* refers to the glorious nature of the appearances rather than to a specific event. He believes the original account was a two-part formula, verse 7b saying, "He appeared above to 500 brothers, once for all to all the apostles." If Kearney is right, why did Paul separate the two parts into separate appearances? Kearney provides no convincing evidence for the two steps and so the thesis remains unlikely. He admits that his thesis and Paul's usage are "to some degree antithetical" stylistic parallelism.

Perhaps the best conclusion here is that verse 7's appearance is not described in the Gospels. Allen (pp. 349f.) believes the Gospel writers omit it since "brothers" in verse 7 refers to rank-and-file Christians who witnessed this appearance while the Twelve did not.[8] Perhaps Paul mentions the appearance for apologetic purposes, to include laypeople as witnesses who could testify from an unbiased viewpoint. The evangelists, on the other hand, centered on the eyewitness account of the disciples. Yet Paul also includes "official witnesses" on his list; if the disciples were present at the appearance he probably would have added "and to the disciples."

Where did all these appearances take place? Some critics say Galilee, some Jerusalem, and some both places, but Paul's list here is so sketchy that geographic location cannot be determined unless each appearance is clearly identified.[9]

The Appearance to James and "All the Apostles" (v. 7)

Who is "James" in verse 7? Is he James, the son of Alpheus, and one of the Twelve? Although this James is mentioned by name in Mark 3:18 and Acts 1:13, he is not referred to elsewhere as one with sufficient authority to qualify for Paul's reference. Is he James, the brother of John, and therefore one of the inner circle? This James was an early martyr (Acts 12:2) who was known to the Corinthians only through tradition. Was he James, the brother of Christ, who was not a believer during Jesus' earthly life (Mark 3:21f.; John 7:5), yet later became the leader of the Jerusalem Church (Acts 15:13; Gal. 2:1f.)? This James is most likely Paul's reference

8. This is supported by the fact that Paul could easily have added "and to the disciples." Allen believes, however, that they were forgotten because it occurred in Galilee and went unknown (Galilee was forgotten by the early church). This fits neither the growth of the church nor Paul's use of the tradition. He assumes the witnesses were present in Corinth. It therefore may have been included by Paul simply for apologetic purposes.

9. Galilee vs. Jerusalem is, of course, due to the debate regarding which was the setting of the earliest appearances. Actually, the list here can be made to favor either location, as can be seen by comparing the adherents of each. Unless we can truly identify the appearances here, we cannot make such decisions; this one and the appearance to James, for instance, could have occurred in either place. Scholars will always read their own decisons into this, and therefore 1 Corinthians 15:5f. cannot have any bearing on the Galilee-Jerusalem debate.

here; the James whose conversion and affinity to Christ led him into an important position in the church.[10]

Winter believes (pp. 142f.) verse 7b reads in the original, "then to the apostles and all the brethren," and is the same appearance as that recorded in verses 5 and 6, the only exception being the substitution at the beginning of "James" for "Cephas." Winter says the two names appear as the result of a split between the gentile church and Jewish Christians, the Jews making James their primary figure after the split. The Gospel to the Hebrews makes the appearance to James first (see Jerome's *De viris illustribus*, p. 2). There seems to be no historical basis, however, for such an assumption. Moreover, at this time Peter was still a force in the Jewish church, and it is conjecture to posit a split.

The appearance to James is not mentioned in the Gospels. Winter says it is omitted because of the antagonism between the gentile church and Jewish Christians; however, this is unlikely, especially since both Matthew and John include such a strong Jewish emphasis that they could easily have included the appearance. The appearance to James is more likely omitted for editorial purposes; it simply did not blend into the development of the resurrection narratives.

Perhaps the Gospel writers were not totally aware of this appearance (similar to Harnack), yet this seems unlikely. Craig says the chronological setting of this appearance depends somewhat on the truth of Acts 1:14 which lists the people who met in the upper room to wait for Christ's return. James is specifically mentioned here "with the brethren," an inclusion which suggests Jesus must have appeared to him prior to this time in the forty days of the appearances. Moreover, the Gospels and Acts restrict the appearances to this early period. Paul clearly separates his experience both in kind and in time.

"All the apostles" probably means more than "the Twelve" in verse 5 since James is named as the leader of "all the apostles." Since "apostles" in Acts includes Jews as well as gentiles (Andronicus and Junias, Rom. 16:7), Fuller suggests (pp. 40, 41) that Paul

---

10. Fuller says, "If there were no record of an appearance to James the Lord's brother in the New Testament we should have to invent one in order to account for his post-resurrection conversion and rapid advance" (p. 37).

stresses that both Jews and Gentiles are involved in church leadership.[11] There is no inherent reason why this could not be so.

When did this appearance to "all the apostles" take place; was it at the ascension recorded in Luke 24:50f. and Acts 1:1f.? Perhaps this is the best suggestion; "all the apostles" present on that occasion which also took place in time between the appearances to James and Paul. Primarily however, Paul adds this to verse 5 to show that all the leaders, both in the beginning (v. 5) and now (v. 7) saw the Risen Lord.

The Appearance to Paul (vv. 8–10)

This appearance is the only one we can definitely identify elsewhere in Scripture; Paul's Damascus experience is described three different times in Acts 9:1f.; 22:3f.; and 26:1f.; and is alluded to in Galatians 1:12f. and 1 Corinthians 9:1. The experience is Paul's primary proof of apostleship, a fact he describes (like all the other appearances) with the use of the term *ōphthē*. Bruce says, (*Corinthians*, pp. 54f.), "If Paul uses the same language of his own experience and of the experience of Peter and of the others, it is to suggest not that their experience was as "visionary" as his but that his was as objective as theirs." Paul thus does not consider his experience to be a vision in the strict sense. He did not mean that his "seeing" (9:1) was the same as the others, but rather that it meant the same to him; the Risen Lord had "appeared" to him as he had to the others in his call to apostleship. Furthermore, as Grass maintains (pp. 189f.), the term *ōphthē* does not of itself indicate a visionary experience; in fact, vocabulary by itself cannot demonstrate the nature of an appearance. The rich variety of terminology in Paul and the Gospels shows the diversity of meanings any term carries.

Fuller (pp. 45–47) says Luke (in Acts) contradicts Paul's attitude to the Damascus experience. He is not an apostle in the true sense, but one who stands in apostolic succession. He says Luke omits Paul as a true apostle since qualifications of this office demanded

11. Fuller (pp. 40–41) states that the presence of Jewish and Greek names proves this. However, his statement that verse 7 details a mission-inaugurating rather than church-founding function is dubious. There is no reason to suppose Jesus would have had no followers among diasporate Jews during his ministry. Of course, it is also possible the Greek names are redactional, in the same way as Saul became Paul.

such a person had to have accompanied the earthly Jesus as well as witnessed the Risen Christ (Acts 1:21–22). Since Jesus appeared to Paul in a "vision" (26:19) rather than in person, Paul was not an original apostle but a second-generation apostle. Rigaux, however, says the dichotomy is more apparent than real, a theory of contradictions that "brings back a fallacious historical method which interprets silences as denials."

Paul's statements in Galatians 1:1b and 1 Corinthians 9:1 are polemical supporting his authority by aligning himself with the apostolic tradition. While *ektrōma* in 1 Corinthians 15:8 could be a Corinthian derogatory term borrowed by Paul (Bruce, Léon-Dufour), or refer to a violent upheaval (Barrett), or Paul's unworthiness (Grass, Michaelis), it most likely is temporal, referring to a "misplaced birth." Paul's experience was "out of time," distinct yet of the same order as the others. Moreover, the very fact that Luke repeats the Damascus experience three times (Acts 9, 22, 26) shows how important it was to him. This is not the act of one who minimizes Paul's vision or "apostolic commission." Paul is a "witness" (22:15, 26:16), a term with apostolic connotations (cf. 2:32, 3:15, 5:32).[12] Luke relates the commission as coming via Ananias (9:15), a vision in the temple (22:17–21) and in the Damascus vision itself (26:17–18). These very "inconsistencies" are deliberate on Luke's part to stress the centrality of Paul's commission as "apostle to the Gentiles."

In fact, neither Paul nor Luke contradicts each other. Both view the Damascus event as the sovereign conversion of Saul as well as apostolic commission of Paul. Luke does not denigrate Paul's apostolic calling to a "second-generation" status,[13] nor does Paul

---

12. Rengstorf (*TDNT,* VIII, pp. 542f.) says, "Once again there stands in the background a recollection of his appointment as an apostle. . . . The emphasis, then, . . . is on the task which the *kyrios* has laid upon him. It is quite logical that the task of the new apostle as a witness should be defined in terms of an adoption and continuation of Jesus' own task, cf. v. 18 with Luke 2:30ff."

13. Wilckens (*Missionsreden,* pp. 72–100) argues that the witness accounts in the speeches of Acts have different origins, since they have distinct purposes and do not cohere in their details (the only parallels being the appearance to Peter, Luke 24:34, and the phrase "on the third day," Acts 10:40). Wilckens believes that the Pauline speeches of Acts are Luke's own composition and cannot support the reliability of the 1 Corinthians 15:3–8 tradition. However, as Craig states, these distinctions are "exaggerated and artificial." The historicity of the speeches in Acts has been well defended by Bruce, Marshall, Longenecker, and others. We will not dwell on it here, except to say that there are no contradictions. Potential differences, such as the absence of a stress on substitutionary

elevate himself to equal status with the Twelve; he is an "abortion" chosen by divine will to usher in the Gentile mission era. Luke echoes Paul's distinction (2 Cor. 12:2f.; 1 Cor. 15:8) in Acts 22:17f. where Paul's temple "vision" is differentiated from his Damascus road experience.

Luke and Acts also support the historical basis of the kerygmatic traditions in 1 Corinthians 15:3 – 8 as a valid account of resurrection appearances in which Jesus revealed himself bodily to his followers. These followers then became "witnesses" and proclaimers (Acts 10:41 – 42) of the reality and meaning of the resurrection.

The Appearance to the Women, Matthew 28:9 – 10; John 20:14 – 18

The fact that Matthew and John (possibly also Mark) chose to write about women discovering the empty tomb as well as witnessing Jesus' first appearance is truly remarkable. Although the details of this appearance differ as to circumstances, setting, and message, the similarities are sufficient enough for many scholars to believe the accounts are parallel developments of the same tradition (see Schnackenburg, III, p. 360).

The appearance of the angel is the first parallel element in Mark 16:5 – 7 and Matthew 28:3 – 7. Some critics (McNeile, Wilckens) say Matthew's account of Jesus meeting the women is a "double," that is, the same account as Mark's angel meeting the women, a later tradition in which the "young man" becomes the Lord himself. Other critics (Hill, Brown, Alsup) extend this thinking to include the possibility that John 20's account of Mary and the "gardener" is an independent form of the story, perhaps even the earliest form of the story. This thinking has led to the suggestion that tomb Christophanies developed out of angelophany traditions, originally to provide an apologetic reinforcement but gradually coming

atonement (cp. "for our sins," 1 Cor. 15:3), can be seen in the apologetic purpose of the speeches. Moreover, as Craig demonstrates, Acts 20:28 is a clear statement of vicarious sacrifice (admitted even by Haenchen, *Acts*, p. 92), and the offer of forgiveness of sins is constant (Acts 2:38; 3:19; 4:12; 5:31; 10:43; 13:38 – 39). In fact, Wilckens undermines his own position when he admits (*Missionsreden*, pp. 193f.) that the Jewish speeches in Acts stem from the tradition behind 1 Corinthians 15. It is difficult to see then why the same basic material in the Pauline speeches is Lukan.

to replace them. Fuller, for instance, (pp. 77f., 136f.) notes the later *Epistula Apostolorum* 9 in which Christophany entirely replaces angelophany. He adds that the Gospel accounts are all independent developments of that tradition.[14]

Did Christophany in the Gospels develop from angelophany? Matthew's account, for instance, is extremely clumsy with its use of Christophany in conjunction with angelophany. Still, any repetition in the message seems more indicative of authenticity than composition. Matthew is a good storyteller; if he were creating an event here he surely would have avoided repeating the message to the women twice. If the women were running home in terrified silence after the angel's appearance, however, the Risen Christ who met them would have to repeat the message, especially "Do not be afraid." Grundmann notes here that changes in the message show it is meant to reinforce the earlier one.

Campenhausen (*Tradition*, p. 61) and Schnackenburg (*Johannesevangelium*, III, p. 380), however, interpret this repetition differently, saying Luke denies an appearance to the women when he specifically writes (24:24) that the women saw the empty tomb and a "vision of angels" who told them Christ was alive, but "him they did not see." Was Luke simply unaware of the tradition that Christ met the women? Perhaps the explanation is less extreme. Luke's concentration on the angel's message in chapter 24, for instance, might be due to his editorial decision to center on Jerusalem appearances. He thus alters the Galilean segment of those appearances even though he is fully aware of Mark's account of them. Perhaps he exercises the same kind of editorial judgment in the account about the women, choosing to omit an appearance which might interrupt his theme which calls for a recognition scene much later at Emmaus.

What is the specific connection between Matthew 28:9–10 and John 20:14–18? Examinations of the scenes which include the race to the tomb and angel appearances have already suggested that although attempts to harmonize the accounts fail to deal with

14. Matthew, according to Fuller, composed his to link the empty tomb with the appearances. Lohmeyer (*Matthäus*, pp. 408f.) asserts that there is an inner connection between the three; Matthew stands in a line of development from Mark's angel-tradition to the later tradition in John. He notes the presence of (1) one young man in Mark, the Risen One in Matthew, and further development in John to an appearance to Mary alone; and (2) of three women in Mark, two in Matthew, and one in John. However, these changes are more redactional than traditional (the emphasis on a solitary figure, e.g., is a Johannine trait), and the thesis is unlikely.

all the redactional elements in the narratives, differences in the accounts themselves strongly suggest separate incidents as a historical basis. Perhaps Matthew's and John's accounts of Jesus' appearance at the tomb are also separate incidents, with differences outweighing any similarities. Jesus' appearance to the women was thus different from his encounter with Mary. We feel this better coheres with the evidence.

Still, how many of these differences are due to tradition and how many to redaction? Matthew seems to deviate very little from Mark's account, except in his mixture of fear and joy (Mark uses the fear motif later in v. 8). John's account, on the other hand, is a heavy mixture of redaction and tradition. His setting is dramatic, the fear of Mark's rendering vividly personified in Mary's weeping and the reversal of that fear powerfully achieved in the recognition scene with the Risen Christ.[15] The "beloved's" account is rooted in history here, but his memories are written down by a masterful storyteller who also teaches the theological significance of those events.

Although the second part of John's account includes even more terminology and theology that is distinctively his, Benoit's observation that this account is based on a primitive tradition which connects the ascension and the resurrection seems plausible. John was doing more here than presenting his own theology; he was writing down one of the earliest traditions or even one of the earliest eyewitness accounts.

Jesus' appearance to the women probably happened in conjunction with the angel's appearance rather than after it, and little change occurred in the tradition of that event. The two Gospel accounts written prior to John do show a gradual linking of the appearances with the empty tomb narratives as well as the ascension theme. However, redaction is also evident in both Matthew and John who used that tradition within their own editorial framework.

The Emmaus Pericope, Luke 24:13−35

Wanke and Dillon have compiled a tremendous amount of research on theories regarding the development of Luke's account

15. In addition, the probability exists that Jesus was indeed grasped by Mary (John 20:17) and commanded to tell "my brothers." The two probably came from the same tradition which was Mark's.

of the two disciples on the way to Emmaus. A summary of all this data includes: (1) early studies which center on a historical reconstruction, (2) history-of-religion studies which focus on numerous parallels with other religious myths, (3) form-critical analyses which try to separate tradition and redaction in order to identify a *Sitz im Leben* and corresponding development of traditions, (4) redaction criticism which tries to consider the story as a whole as it isolates Lukan additions, and (5) structural analysis which tries to evaluate the pattern of the narrative as the key to its message.

The use of many terms as well as motifs in this passage which are clearly Luke's has caused many scholars to doubt its historical validity.[16] They especially question the authenticity of the Emmaus travelers' dialogue (vv. 14–15a, 17–27), saying Luke wrote it to present his own beliefs by blending creedal material (vv. 19a–20; cf. Acts 2:22f.; 10:37f.) with references to tradition (vv. 22–24). They say, for instance, that the question in verse 32 ("were not our hearts burning within us while he talked with us on the road and opened the Scriptures to us?") is Luke's indirect statement of his fulfillment theme, and verses 33–35 ("the Lord has risen and has appeared to Simon") are an accommodation to the tradition of Jesus' appearance to Peter.[17]

This evidence, however, is not conclusive; most of it, in fact, leads to the opposite conclusion, that Luke consistently uses traditional material and writes it down according to his own style. A close study of the so-called "Lukanisms" in the passage, for instance, shows that most of them are used by the other Gospels as

16. Terms such as the periphrastic imperfect (vv. 13, 32), "it came to pass" (15, 30), *sun*-compound verbs, and *Hierousalēm* (13, 18, 32). Motifs like the closing of the disciples' eyes, the Jerusalem location, proof from Scripture, meal setting, and redemption emphasis.

17. Few modern scholars deny the traditional source of this episode; even if doubtful passages are removed a strong nucleus remains. For a chart of opinions with respect to Luke's additions:

Alsup	14-15a	17-27	32-35
Dibelius		21b (22)-24	
Dillon	14-16	17-27	32-35
Fuller	14-15a	17-27	32-35
Grundmann		21b-24	33-35
Hahn	14-15a	17-27	32-35
Léon-Dufour	14-15a	17-27	32-35
Rigaux	14-15a	17-27	33b-34
Schubert	14-15a	17-27	32-35
Wilckens	14-15a	17-27	32b, 33b-34

well as Luke.[18] Furthermore, the use of these "Lukanisms" seems to be evident less in the questionable sections.

Luke's dialogue does not express purely Lukan theology, either. Marshall says, (p. 65), in fact, that it reveals strong traditional elements. The traveler's discussion, for instance, presents Jesus as *ho Nazarēnos* and a prophet; Luke usually prefers *Nazaraios*. Jesus is "handed over," identified as the one who was "going to redeem Israel," and three days have lapsed since his death; all strong parallels of Mark's theology as well as the third-day theme of 1 Corinthians 15:4. Jesus' reply indicative of fulfillment theology also stresses more than Luke's theology.

In short, no internal reason demands free Lukan composition, and most evidence favors the probability that Luke took this account from tradition and presented it in his own style.[19]

How did the tradition develop from the original? Was it based on an actual event or did it originate in the kerygma? Why is this appearance mentioned elsewhere only in the pseudo-Markan ending (16:12−13)? Many scholars believe the story is basically a legend. Betz calls it a "cult legend" from hellenistic myths because of elements such as the manifestation of the divine in human form, the appearance of the dead to the living, the presentation of gods as "wanderers," and the opened eyes of the travelers.

Some scholars believe the story is a unique creation of the early church. Schubert (p. 170) and Marxsen (p. 160) say it started because of the church's desire to link the Eucharist with the Risen Christ. Grass (pp. 35f.) believes the pre-Lukan traditions were interwoven into the story by him. However, Fuller (pp. 107f.) sees a

18. Many of the words noted by Taylor are not truly Lukan: *existēmi* occurs four times in Mark vs. three in Luke (eight in Acts); *apechō apo* is found in Luke 7:6, 24:13 but also in Mark 7:68; Matt. 14:24, 15:8; *diermeneuō* is more frequent in 1 Corinthians 12 and 14 (four times) than in Luke and Acts (twice); *athroizō* and *orthinos* are *hapax legomena; kai idou* is also Matthean. The Septuagintalisms were characteristic of the early church and can scarcely be called "Lukanisms." Moreover, when one studies the incidence of these in the various sections, some interesting facts emerge: e.g., the rate of occurrence is lightest in the sections regarded to be most doubtful, (vv. 22−24, etc.) and more in those passages that are not questioned.

19. Lukan elements are the travel setting (the meeting on the road was traditional, but Luke added the "from-to" stress and expanded the trip back), the recognition motif (especially the emphasis on divine sovereignty), the place of the word and bread (given ecclesiastical force), and the fulfillment motif (the presence in each segment [vv. 7, 26, 46] shows it is Lukan). Alsup, pp. 208n and 549, reports the conclusion of Winter et al. that verses 13−21a, 25−35 are taken from an Aramaic original.

historical nucleus in the account which may correspond with Jesus' appearance to "all the apostles" in 1 Corinthians 15:7, but which also developed in the context of a Syrian-Christian community which added the divine-man element as well as mythological overtones.

Still, a closer look at the evidence should reveal that much of Luke's Emmaus story is historical. The geographic details of the trip, for instance, were probably part of earliest tradition as is the place-name "Emmaus" which appears in historical records of this era. Where precisely this city was located is not clear (see Liefeld, *Luke*), but that it existed is unquestionable. And a literal place speaks much in favor of a reliable tradition. If it were a place with theological connections it would be questionable; but the obscurity of this village favors authenticity. Hence the basic travel setting seems traditional rather than a legendary element.

Jesus' joining up with the travelers in verses 15 and 16 seemingly suggests two legendary elements, the hidden guise of the divine wanderer and the blinded eyes of the participants. The first element, however, is essential to the episode and may simply mean that the travelers met Jesus on the road. The episode at this point contains no miraculous or legendary elements. Later on the opened eyes of the travelers are hardly miraculous either. Rather it is Luke's editorial note that explains why spiritual blindness existed in the first place (cp. 9:45; 18:34; 19:42).

Is the dialogue itself a purely Lukan creation? Probably not; a hard look at the entire pericope reveals more Lukanisms outside the dialogue than in it. Benoit says[20] Luke sought as much accuracy as possible. He suggests that Luke was perhaps more than a prominent Christian of that time, and might, in fact, have been the source of the story.[21] Benoit may be right; the story does have a strong flavor of authenticity.

What if the original story did not contain dialogue as such but

20. Benoit (*Passion*, pp. 277–78). He adds, "in order to describe a real conversation, but one of which there was no shorthand record and which took place perhaps thirty years earlier." Luke describes only what was probably said and used the exact terms of catechesis.

21. First suggested by Plummer (*Luke*, p. 551). Luke may have avoided mentioning either because he did not know it or else because he wanted to name only Cleopas as his source. Some critics have suggested the companion was Peter, Cleopas' wife, or his son. Grundmann (*Lucas*, p. 443) and Fuller (pp. 107f.) think he was Clopas (John 19:25), the brother of Joseph and father of Simon, second bishop of Jerusalem.

only elements suggestive of dialogue? Although this theory might be true, it does not have to be. Why could not early stories have also contained dialogue? Some evidence of development in the dialogue form does exist, but not in the content itself. Perhaps as time passed conversational elements condensed into the wording of verses like 19b, 20, 21b, and 25b–26 as well as the summation of events in verses 22–24.

Fuller says that verse 21a "recaptures precisely the historical mood of the disciples during the hours before Easter" and probably reflects pre-Lukan tradition. Betz says (p. 67) verses 21–24 are "secondary pre-Lukan" redactions since the narrative flows from verse 21a to verse 25 if the middle verses are omitted. Betz misses the impact of verse 26 which speaks of the resurrection and provides a natural capstone to verses 21b–24. Also, the travelers hardly would have discussed the crucifixion apart from the empty tomb. The conclusion here is that Luke's dialogue in this pericope is based on tradition but presented within the framework of Luke's style.[22]

The Eucharist story in verses 28–31 is most likely traditional. Betz (pp. 39f.) says it is the very heart of the Emmaus story, and Dillon says it is the only authentic part. The motif is also present in other resurrection narratives. Cullmann (*Worship*, pp. 14f.) believes this Eucharist element was an important part of earliest tradition since in it was the fulfillment of the promise of the Last Supper. Marshall says (p. 44), "If Luke were creating freely, there is nothing in this story that could not have been included in the following scene where the features of a meal and the exposition of the Old Testament are again found."

Perhaps both the breaking of bread and teaching of the word were linked already in earliest tradition, since it was common for the head of a household to give an exposition at the meal. Recognition might then have come as the result of both elements. It seems unlikely they would not have known him as he "interpreted to them in all the scriptures the things concerning himself" (v. 27b.). At any rate, verse 31's "opened eyes" are undoubtedly Luke's editorial capstone to the "unrecognizing eyes" of verse 16; "Burning hearts" in verse 32, on the other hand, seems to be redactional but

22. Verse 26 is a Lukan emphasis (cp. vv. 7, 46) and may therefore be a redactional emphasis. It is also, however, a natural part of Jesus' explanation of the significance of the resurrection event. The verse is probably a blend of tradition and redaction.

is more likely an honest reflection of the original scene. The phrase also clearly links the Eucharist with the sacramental word and is an integral part of the recognition motif.[23]

Some critics omit verses 33–35 because they say they only are transitional to verses 36f. Marshall says, however (p. 46), "the story is incomplete without the hasty return to Jerusalem." Perhaps the original version of this story read, "They returned to Jerusalem in joy," but the travel emphasis here is distinctively Lukan and leads into the next pericope. Verse 34 seems so strange in this context that it is almost unquestionably authentic ("The Lord has risen and has appeared to Simon"), as is Luke's use of the term *Eleven*. If he were trying to add a footnote to verse 12, he would have given it a greater place in his narrative. He may have included it in verse 34 because the tradition had it. This would also indicate that the report of "the Eleven" was a pre-Lukan addition, though not a part of the original. In the development of the tradition the report to the Eleven was added first, followed by the appearance to Peter.

In conclusion, the Emmaus pericope came from eyewitness testimony, (perhaps from Cleopas himself) and told about two disciples on their way to Emmaus who met a mysterious traveler who talked with them about recent events in Jerusalem. When they stopped to eat with him at Emmaus, the stranger broke bread and taught them from the Scriptures; the result being that they recognized him as the Risen Christ. Jesus disappeared and the travelers returned to Jerusalem with the good news. From this basic eyewitness account gradually emerged a kind of credal dialogue as the church used the story to teach its beliefs regarding the Risen Christ. Luke then took the story and expanded it to include his themes of blindness (vv. 16, 31), fulfillment (v. 26), and geographic movement.

The Great Commission, Matthew 28:16–20

Matthew's section on the Great Commission shows some evidence of tradition within the context of much distinctively Mat-

23. Marshall (p. 46) says the two *hōs* clauses of verse 32 are awkward and that thereby the second may be a Lukan addition, to interpret further the significance of the Word-event. This would provide further evidence for the balance of redaction and tradition in the dialogue.

thean terminology and redactional themes. The setting for this event, for instance, uses the phrase "to which Jesus had appointed them" which is not Matthean and therefore offers some basis for tradition.[24] The message itself seems to be a Matthean composition because of the large number of Matthean words in it. However, other words such as *give, authority,* and *heaven and earth,* are used by other Gospel writers as well as Matthew. Jesus' command to "disciple" the nations is typical of Matthew's style yet may also reflect tradition; consider its parallels in other resurrection narratives such as Mark 16:9f., Luke 24:47, and John 20:21. Wenham says (*TB,* pp. 40f., 51f.) the combination of mission and authority in this passage also occurs in Luke and John and is hardly a Matthean peculiarity. He notes that in Luke the mission is linked with the sovereign power of God and the authority of Scripture, and in John the disciples are sent out with authority. This is not a free composition but a Matthean version of the tradition.

Jesus' command to baptize sounds like an original teaching; no other explanation can account for the widespread practice among early Christians. "Teach" sounds more like Mark and Luke than Matthew, and "keep" more like John and Acts. Many scholars (Barth, Bornkamm) believe verse 20b is a Matthean composition because of its vocabulary and themes; however, the theology of this verse appears elsewhere in John as well as Paul (cf. John 14:8f, 15:1f, 16:25f.; Paul's "in Christ" motif; and numerous passages on the Paraclete or Spirit of Christ).

In conclusion, good evidence exists for asserting this pericope is based on tradition even though it is expressed in predominantly Matthean language. Perhaps Matthew even borrowed the basic event from Mark. Still, some critics (Bornkamm, Michel, Barth) persist in questioning the historicity of the account, saying Matthew's mountain is theological not geographical and Jesus' appearance presupposed rather than stated. Luck (pp. 494f.) believes Matthew wrote this out of the *Sitz im Leben* of the Gentile mission which focused on Jesus' and the church's work to bring all nations to conversion. Seidensticker (pp. 286f.) believes this account is the

---

24. *Tassō* is not Matthean (it occurs elsewhere only in Matthew 8:9 and Luke 7:8) and may be taken from tradition, where it speaks of an event not recorded in the Gospels. The use of "worshiped" may have been duplicated in the original Markan ending (see chap. 2), where it would have stood in contrast with the mocking "homage" of the soldiers in 15:19 (see also on Matt. 28:9 in chap. 6).

only authentic resurrection appearance (verified by 1 Cor. 15:6) and that the appearances in Luke and John are later developments of this one. This attempt to select arbitrarily one tradition out of many, however, is unjustified, stemming more out of dogmatic interest than tradition criteria (see Alsup, pp. 90 — 95).

An early origin for this account seems likely for many reasons. Malina believes (pp. 97f.) many of the ideas come out of a Jewish context, and Klostermann says (pp. 231f.) many of them come from the eyewitness testimony of the evangelist himself. Geography and theology go hand in hand in Matthew; he uses Galilee as well as Jerusalem to express both ideas. Matthew does stress certain elements in order to make his Gospel relevant to the church's needs, but never without a firm basis in reality.[25]

When did the various parts of this episode orginate? Did it begin with the early church or at a later time? Despite some obvious redactional elements in the prologue (vv. 16 — 17), there are also definite indications of tradition. The original tradition may have said simply that the disciples went to Galilee and were met by the Risen Christ on a mountain top. At first some doubted what they were seeing, but when they accepted the physical reality of the Risen Lord, fell down, and worshiped him. Matthew's term for worship here is probably traditional and may also have been a part of Mark's account. In Matthew it occurs in verses 9 and 17 both of which were borrowed from Mark.

Verse 18 at first seems to be a Matthean composition because of its terminology, yet Strecker believes (*Der Weg*, pp. 209f.) the verse has a pre-Matthean source. The sweeping power of verse 18's assertion, in fact, goes far beyond Matthew's imagination. Its aura of divine power can only have originated from Jesus himself, or at best those who lived in the era which emphasized Jesus' divinity (1 Cor. 12:3; 16:22; Phil. 2:6f.; Rom. 10:9). The original tradition may have contained *dynamis* rather than *exousia*, and Matthew may also have added "in heaven and earth" to express his themes.

25. Further, it is not true that the early church would fail to neglect and then bicker over universal evangelization if the Risen One had really said this. It would be natural for the followers to misinterpret this in a Jewish proselyte sense, in light of their background; they probably felt they were fulfilling this command. The Gentiles were to come to them (as at Pentecost) and embrace Christianity in a Jewish context. This was the real debate at the Jerusalem council (Acts 15) rather than the fact of Gentile converts.

The command of verses 19 and 20 also combines tradition and redaction. *Mathēteuō* ("disciple") is Matthean and probably a derivative of the original word meaning "preach the Gospel" or "witness to." Fuller (p. 83f.) says this idea was a later composition of the early church and was modeled after the missionary mandate of the earthly Jesus (Matt. 10:5). Bornkamm says ("Risen," pp. 209f.) the word is like the one used in Mark 13:10 and Matthew 24:14 and is used here in the context of the Gentile mission to enlarge the theme of the evangelization of the nations. Once that evangelization was a part of the apocalyptic Son of man theme, but now it becomes subordinate to the exaltation motif. Bornkamm concludes by saying Matthew's usage here is interpretation rather than valid inference.

Bornkamm's thesis, however, depends on the presupposition that sayings of the Risen Lord are not authentic when they parallel themes in the life of the early church, an assumption which simply is not compatible with an objective view of the resurrection. The mission to preach to "all nations" did not begin with the gentile movement but with the proselyte theology of Jewish Christianity. The combination of mission and authority Matthew uses here also appears in Luke and John; therefore the command itself goes back to earliest tradition and most likely to the event itself.

Jesus' injunction to baptize in this account, however, has no parallels in the other Gospels. It seems to be a late addition; most scholars are convinced it resulted from later church tradition which was read back into the resurrection events. Yet it may have come from an original tradition which is expressed here for the first time.

Baptism can be connected with the resurrection, and the command of Christ to the disciples in Matthew 28:19 is a logical place for its institution (Flemington, Beasley-Murray, Cullmann). Although baptism was originally practiced by Jesus' disciples, it had become somewhat rare by the time of his early ministry (John 3:22f.; 4:2). Probably this "ceremonial washing" would have disappeared altogether had not Jesus reinstituted it with his command in Matthew 28:19.[26] Here baptism is infused with new

26. Beasley-Murray (pp. 68−71) believes it disappeared from Jesus' ministry because his was a different type than John's. Jesus' message was eschatological and personal, centered in ontological, not functional, concepts. It is unlikely that the early church would revive such a ministry.

meaning through the act of Christ's death and resurrection; it is qualitatively different from Jewish antecedents such as the Qumran rite,[27] Jewish proselyte baptism,[28] the ceremonial washing of John the Baptist,[29] or even similar rites from the Greek mysteries.[30] Although this new baptism may have been influenced by other rites, its real origin probably began with the command of Jesus Christ to "baptize" all the nations "into the name of the Father and of the Son and of the Holy Spirit." As such its theology is rooted in Christology. This is evidenced in the presence of this theme in the earliest creeds (cf. 2 Tim. 2:11; 1 Peter 3:19f.; and Acts 2:30f., 8:36f.).

Matthew uses the term *baptizo* seven times but the problem is that the baptism formula elsewhere (Acts 2:38; 8:16; 10:48; 19:5) includes only one member ("in the name of Jesus") whereas here it includes three (Father, Son, and Holy Spirit). Why should this Trinitarian formula appear only here in the New Testament? Some scholars believe Matthew should be amended here to read, "Go make disciples of all nations in my name" (Eusebius) implying that neither baptism nor the trinitarian formula were original. However, the trinitarian formula is used prior to Eusebius (Justin's Dial. 39:2; cp. Apol 61:3; Did. 7:1). So most scholars today believe it is a Matthean addition, due perhaps to his own *Sitz im Leben*, but probably taken from a late tradition and inserted here (cf. 1 Cor. 12:4 – 6; 2 Cor. 13:14; Gal. 4:6; Eph. 5:5 – 6, 1 Pet. 1:2), especially since the concept is prepared for in Matthew's approach, as in Jesus' baptism (3:11, 16 – 17) and the Father-Son antithesis (11:27 = Mark 13:32; 24:36; cf. 12:32 for the Son of man-Spirit). Schaberg's basic thesis is that Matthew's formula is a traditional midrash of Dan-

27. The daily lustrations of Qumran, called the "waters of purification," were sacramental and ethical. They were daily acts rather than rites of admission, private rather than public, and indicative of ritual purity rather than repentance (see Rowley, "Baptism," *New Testament Essays*, ed. Higgin, pp. 219f.).

28. Rowley says this proselyte baptism is a better antecedent since it was an initiatory, once-for-all act. Others, however, disagree, saying Jewish baptism is intimately connected with circumcision whereas the New Testament church views baptism as union with the Messiah at the dawn of a new age.

29. This transcended Qumran and proselyte baptism. It was eschatological and soteriological: a new rite which included yet moved beyond the others. Still, it too is an insufficient antecedent for the church's rite which transcended even John's practice.

30. The "dying and rising myth" of Greek mysteries has often been repudiated as an antecedent for Christianity (Colpe); the same holds true for baptism.

iel 7, which she believes originated in the liturgy of baptism. She assumes, however, that it originated in the early church.

Perhaps the best way to evaluate this passage is to see it as a Matthean redaction of a monadic formula which was the condensed version of a much longer speech in the original (see my "Redaction Criticism," p. 206). Luke and John may well show that Matthew's account is part of early tradition. Several critics (Wenham, Fuller, Brown), for instance, see a suggestion of baptism in the forgiveness passages of Luke 24:47, and John 20:23. Linguistic evidence also seems to support this, since *baptizō* is not Matthean and neither is the theme. It probably is based on tradition, and the presence of its theme in early credal formulae favors a very early date for its origin. There is no adequate foundation for the practice apart from the command of the Risen One and therefore I would argue that the origin is Jesus himself rather than the early church.

The command to teach in verse 20a also combines tradition and redaction. *Didaskō* ("teach") is Matthean, but the word itself is found more frequently in Mark and Luke. *Tēreo* ("keep") appears six times in Matthew, but eighteen times in John. Its basic idea of keeping the commandments is used elsewhere in Matthew 19:17, but also in John 8:51f.; 14:15, 21f.; 15:10, 20; 17:6; and 1 Timothy 6:14. Although the command reflects Matthew's theology, it may also have a basis in tradition, possibly the same *Sitz im Leben* as John's Gospel. The criterion of multiple attestation would show that it was common in early church tradition.

Jesus' promise in verse 20b is distinctively Matthean, its terminology richly indicative of his style. Most critics believe therefore that this is a Matthean composition. The theology of the verse, however, is not distinctively Matthew's; it is repeated elsewhere in John's Gospel, Paul's epistles, and the church's early creeds (Col. 1:15f.; 2:12f.; Rom. 6:2f.; Heb. 7:25). Perhaps Matthew's words come from early tradition on the basis of multiple sources, the credal connection showing it originated as early as the emphasis on the lordship of Christ, and the connection with independent traditions favoring its basic authenticity.

In conclusion, Matthew's passage on the Great Commission seems to indicate he redacted an actual tradition (perhaps from Mark) of a threefold statement made by the Risen Christ on a mountain top in Galilee. The statement itself makes a claim of authority, issues a command to evangelize, and offers a promise of help in Matthean terms such as *authority, discipling, teach,* and *I am with you.* While we cannot prove it goes back to Jesus himself, there is no compelling evidence to demand otherwise.

The Appearance to the Twelve, Luke 24:36–49; John 20:19–23

The setting of Luke's and John's pericopes about Jesus' appearance to the Twelve is significantly different from Matthew's. So is the subject matter.[31] Although the commission to evangelize sounds like it might have come from the same tradition, it is more likely that Luke's and John's account is a separate tradition from Matthew's with parallels, if any, only between these two.

Most scholars admit a common oral tradition between the Synoptics and John, but perhaps even a more direct connection exists (even though John used more than one source and redacted them). The double time note in John 20:19, for instance, seems to suggest a separate source, yet *apsia* which appears only one other place in John is used five times in Mark and seven times in Matthew. On the other hand, the joy motif which is so subdued in Luke is emphasized in John. Clearly John used several traditions in this account.

He also used redaction in the time notes, the phrase "for fear of the Jews", the joy motif, the wording of the commission, the "breathing" of the Spirit in verse 22, and the authority motif of verse 23.

Alsup (pp. 171–77) believes that Luke's rendering of this appearance parallels the "walking on water" miracle story of Mark 6:45–52, Matthew 14:22–33, and John 6:16–21. He see linguistic parallels in the use of *pneuma* ("spirit"), *dokeō* ("seem"), the fear motif, and Jesus' words. Alsup concludes that the basic core of each story (the approach of Jesus, fear of the disciples, and the dispelling of those fears by Jesus) has a common tradition origin. He says Luke probably took this story from Galilean tradition and

31. Alsup groups these appearance together and says the Galilee and Jerusalem locations are redactional rather than historical (pp. 162–63). Fuller says the Jerusalem location is only hinted at and therefore is inconclusive (p. 114).

changed it into an appearance story. Alsup's parallels are more apparent than real, however, and the differences far greater than the similarities. He is forced to remove speculatively such ingredients as the miracle itself in the synoptic story and the proofs motif, etc., in the appearance version, in order to make them parallel.

Several elements are included in both Luke and John such as:

1. Jesus' physical proof of his resurrected body. Many critics believe this emphasis on his hands, feet, and side comes from a later apologetic representing the noncorporeal resurrection of 1 Corinthians 15, Mark, and Matthew. Perhaps this emphasis does reflect later needs, yet it should properly be seen as selection rather than composition. If indeed the resurrection was physical, any objection to physical proof of it disappears. It becomes difficult to explain why the evangelists were not more explicit, in light of their Jewish monism, if it were not a physical resurrection (cp. Paul's own differentiation in our discussion of 1 Cor. 15:8f.). Luke most likely wrote this account based on tradition, its strong emphasis on physical proof suggestive at least of the early stages of the gentile mission era. Nothing in this section disproves an authentic tradition, although its three-part proof may be a Lukan redaction.

2. The doubt motif. John does not overtly refer to this motif here (perhaps wishing to save it for the next pericope), yet his "fear of the Jews" is a subtle reminder of his awareness of it. Grass says (p. 41) the disciples would not have been afraid if they already knew about Jesus' first appearance; thus the doubt motif is a late redaction to Luke's account.

It should not be difficult, however, to understand how men of that era would experience doubt and fear in the midst of such an event.[32] Luke's doubt motif is therefore acceptable as tradition even though he may have expanded the original story in conjunction with his witness theme; his account includes two statements of doubt (vv. 39, 41) as well as three physical proofs of the resurrection.

The questions and answers in his account, however, have a clear basis in tradition. Although Luke utilizes such rhetorical

32. See Morrison (pp. 251f.) for a discussion of the psychological problem. Marshall ("Resurrection," pp. 92f.) agrees that Grass correctly denies Acts 12:14 as a parallel but notes that Livy 39:49.5 provides a sufficient example of such a phenomenon.

questions elsewhere (24:26), they are not peculiar to him. John also uses this stylistic device (20:13, 29; 21:15f., 20f.) even though the parallel scene to this one describes what Jesus does rather than what he says. Critics have usually suspected Luke's three-part physical proof is redactional since it obviously connects with his witness theme (note the three fulfillment quotations in vv. 7, 26, 46). They conclude that John's account is therefore more original than Luke's. This reasoning, however, is based on the form-critical assumption that a more complex account usually comes later in time than a simpler one. Literary critics have proved this assumption wrong, saying the reverse of it is more often true; time often simplifies legends rather than embellishes them (see Travis, "Form," p. 159).

Luke's stress on this three-part witness does not mean a departure from tradition either. The device is probably redactional, yet not necessarily ahistorical. Most critics (e.g., Dillon, p. 162) assume that John was aware of this multiple proof but shifted his use of it to the Thomas scene; a selection which does not disprove the historic accuracy of either scene.[33]

Neither do John and Luke's redactions of doubt and physical proof prove the evangelists used them to combat docetic tendencies; Marshall says the fact that both Luke and John included them demonstrates a broader origin. The origin of this in the event itself is more plausible than theories demanding a later creation by the church. Dillon, in fact, (pp. 193f.) believes Luke's message is the specific identification of the Risen Lord with the earthly Jesus. Luke's narrative thus has a very close connection with tradition. The same may be said of John's narrative; Mahoney says (pp. 280f.) John too is concerned about relating the events of the empty tomb and appearances in "tangible, earthly reality." Any parallels with a later docetic problem are analogical, not genealogical. Neither Luke nor John is combating false teaching; both are presenting theological truth (see also O'Collins, *Resurrection*, pp. 83f.)

---

33. Dillon (pp. 185f.) follows Michaelis (*Erscheinungen*, p. 120) in asserting that Luke here accommodates the angelophany form to a Christology situation (*contra* Martini, pp. 236f.). Although Jesus' greeting and words of reassurance in Luke's account here sound much like the angel's words in 1:28−30, that is no basis for believing Dillon's theory that Luke turns an angelophany into a Christophany. Both elements follow the Old Testament commission form, and the nucleus of both is traditional.

The meal scene in Luke 24:41–43 could be a Lukan addition due to his frequent use of such. Yet while John omits this element (probably does not fit his needs, so Dillon, p. 192). The fact that John includes a similar scene in 21:11–14 is some indication that it was a vital part of the resurrection appearance tradition.

The missionary command in Luke 24:47 and John 20:21b clearly reflects the theological interests of each writer even though both are probably different versions of the original command (independent from Matthew's account). Alsup says (pp. 197–98) verses 44–48 are non-Lukan because of linguistic grounds. He and Wilckens (*Auferstehung*, pp. 88f.) believe Jesus' mission command is the key to the validity of the group appearances, Luke's account of it so closely following his third fulfillment statement (vv. 44–46) that it becomes a part of it. While Jesus' use of promise fulfillment is probable (the tradition is too widespread to be inauthentic), and while it is also likely that the Risen One used this theme (it is paralleled in the oldest creeds—Rom. 8:34, 1 Peter 3:22, Acts 2:33, etc.), it is also clear that Luke uses the promise-fulfillment theme theologically, combining it with the mission motif and Jesus' consciousness of that mission.[34] Luke probably inserted it here though on the basis of tradition. The missionary command, though once probably independent from the fulfillment motif, is combined with it here in an obviously Lukan structure. John's account of the mission command also includes a lot of redaction. "Peace to you" (in verse 21) may be traditional since it is strongly Semitic and integral to the scene. Forestell (p. 99), however, suggests it is a late addition since it represents the fulfillment of the preach-prophecy in 14:27 and 16:33 in much the same way that the joy of the disciples in 20:20b fulfills 16:21–22.

Forestell's view is insufficient, however, to deny the strong possibility that both "joy" and "peace" stem from tradition even though the repetition of the peace-promise (vv. 19, 21, 26) does reveal some theological redaction. The joy theme is quite predominant in the resurrection appearance traditions as a whole (see Matt. 28:8; Luke 24:41, 52) and "peace" may simply have been omitted in the parallel

---

34. Matthew includes a greater fulfillment emphasis in his Gospel as a whole but a more subdued use of it in his resurrection narrative. Fuller says Jesus never spoke of this theme himself; it was an emphasis of the later church (p. 116). New Testament data, however, strongly supports Jesus' sense of fulfillment in its portrait of one who reinterprets the Law and considers himself the authoritative teacher.

Luke 24:36.[35] The mission command is clearly written in John's own style (see 17:8), and expresses the significance of Jesus' world mission in terms of the Father-Son relationship. The command has a traditional origin even though its form is John's.

The promise of the Spirit in both Luke and John has caused some debate. Many critics see here a kind of "Pentecost" which is such a personalized account in John that it can hardly be reconciled with Luke's account (Bultmann, Marxsen, Lindars, Brown). Others believe John represents the earliest account which proves that from the start the church linked together the resurrection and Pentecost (Sanders, Barrett, Fuller). Benoit says this is a false assumption, however, since John emphasizes the inner, sanctifying work of the Spirit while Luke writes about the outward, charismatic work of the Spirit. The accounts are supplementary, not contradictory.

Westcott notes (II, pp. 350f.) the absence of the article in John's account of the Spirit (*pneuma hagion*) and calls it "a gift of the Spirit" (cf. 7:39) or quickening power rather than the personal presence of the Holy Spirit. This point is difficult to prove, however, since the article is also omitted in texts such as Acts 2:4. Still, differences in tone here have led many critics to suggest that John hints at two probable outpourings of the Spirit, an inward and an outward one, an invisible and a visible one, and a private and a public one.

Other critics (Windisch, Hartmann, Forestell) say this description of the Spirit is neither a Johannine Pentecost nor a fulfillment of the Paraclete promise but a redaction peculiar to this scene which stresses the life-infused beginning of the Christian community in the imagery of Ezekiel's dry bones vision. Dry bones imagery may indeed be valid here, yet it does not invalidate either the traditional origin of this pericope, or its allusion to a kind of "Johannine Pentecost."

Although attempts to harmonize parallel passages often prove to be too speculative, elements in both Luke's and John's account give strong indications that the two accounts might represent two halves of a single whole. It would be logical, for instance, for the

---

35. The further reading *kai legei autois, Eirēnē hymin* in Luke 24:36 is attested in all the ancient manuscripts, except D. In spite of the widespread attestation, however, nearly all editors assume that it is assimilated from John 20:19 (it is bracketed in WH, UBS). If it is original to Luke (which the manuscript evidence at least would support), it would add force to our argument here.

Risen Christ to "breathe out" the power of the Spirit on his disciples, then promise them a public outpouring in the near future. Dodd[36] says this promise of the Spirit and Christ's glorification (7:39; 20:22) are so unrelated to Jesus' farewell discourse in chapters 14−17 that they must have come from different traditions, a theory which sounds logical especially in light of John's "breathing out" scene which does not naturally develop from other Johannine emphases. Luke's account is even more redactional and provides good theological preparation for the Book of Acts. Still, both John and Luke's accounts are based on tradition.

Jesus' promise of authority to forgive sins in John 20:23 is also suggested in passages such as Matthew 16:19 and 18:18; thus it is not clear whether this is a pre-Easter or post-Easter saying. Fuller believes (p. 141) Jesus' statement has a primitive origin although he also says, "it is impossible to assign it with certainty to the earthly Jesus." His problem lies in his demand for certainty. When we approach it on the basis of probability theory, the arguments carry much more weight. Therefore, this most likely has a primitive origin. Fuller assigns it to "primitive Christian prophecy" on the grounds of its apocalyptic overtones; we believe it may well go back to Jesus himself.

The original tradition probably developed in the context of a Jerusalem tradition; from the beginning this appearance story focused on the overcoming of doubt through Jesus' physical presence. Luke expanded it to a scenario which consisted of a kerygmatic development of tradition (vv. 44−46, 48) with Lukan redaction (the *dei* motif and greater emphasis on the witness theme), a rendition of the missionary charge (v. 47), and his own version of the Spirit tradition (v. 49). John took Luke's version and edited it to smooth over the break between the original tradition and the added parts. To this somewhat abbreviated form he added, most likely from his own reminiscence, a final emphasis on Jesus' transmission of authority to the disciples (20:23).

The Thomas Pericope, John 20:24−29

John's story about Thomas is unique to this Gospel; a fact which has led many critics to believe John created the episode both to

---

36. Dodd, *Interpretation*, p. 430. In his later *Tradition*, p. 144, he notes the connection with "wind" (3:8) and flowing water (7:38−39) but still maintains his thesis, *contra* Brown, p. 1030, who mistakenly believes Dodd changed his view.

bring his doubt theme to a climax as well as illustrate the possibility of true faith. This passage does seem to be a composition, attached as it is to the previous episode by verse 24's somewhat elaborate explanation, verse 26's time note, and the entire message of the passage which seems to be an expanded version of the earlier story. Forestell says (p. 101) verses 24–29 are a repetition of verses 19–23 which John adds for theological emphasis. Still, the story does show some signs of tradition. Bultmann believes (*HST*, p. 693f.) John took the account from a source which showed a special interest in Thomas (11:16; 14:5), and says *heis ek tōn dōdeka* ("and of the Twelve") confirms it since "the Twelve" are seldom mentioned anywhere else in John. Benoit says (*Passion*, p. 286) the realism in the scene reveals a traditional origin (*contra* Dodd).

The passage includes other elements which indicate a traditional source. Hartmann says this pericope's physical proof, doubt motif, and description of skepticism are taken from the previous story and simply transferred to Thomas. Yet the motifs are not the same. The Thomas story expresses skepticism rather than doubt. Hartmann's theory about the traditional origin of Thomas' faith-cry, however, seems valid; "My Lord and my God" provides a natural conclusion to other messianic titles in this Gospel such as *Messias*, Christ, Son of man, Son of God, prophet, and Holy One of God. Jesus as "God," although a definite title of interest to John (see Prologue, 10:30f.), is hardly his own creation. The use of "Lord" by Thomas is also unusual in John's post-resurrection setting. Other phrases such as *ōde, pistos, apistos*, and *makarios* are also atypical of John. Dodd (*Tradition*, pp. 354–55) notes a synoptic background for the "makarism" (v. 29, cf. Matt. 13:16; Luke 10:23) and for the "belief-unbelief" antithesis (v. 27, cf. Matt. 24:43f., Luke 21:42f.), with 20:27 the "moral" of the parable, *contra* his previous position.

Rigauz (p. 238) calls Dodd's arguments here "unconvincing" but bases his critique on dogmatic rather than linguistic grounds. Stylistic criteria also show a traditional course.

Nicol (pp. 17–18, 23–24) lists the stylistic characteristics of Schweitzer and Ruckstuhl and adds 32 of his own, 82 in all. Of these only four are found here—no. 2, *oun* historicum (v. 25); no. 6, asyndeton (v. 26); no. 16, *apekrithē kai eipen* (v. 28); no. 75, conditional parataxis in a subordinate clause (v. 29). This results in an average of 0.67 characteristics per verse, well within the limit for non-Johannine material (0.58 average, ranging from 0.30 to 0.75) set by Nicol. Also, two of the examples (nos. 6, 75) are Semitic in nature, and the other two (nos. 2, 16) occur in transitional material, which is naturally editorial. Finally, two other characteristics— no. 8, the article + *emos* (cf. vv. 25, 28) and no. 42; *pisteuein eis* (cf. vv. 25, 29)—could easily have been written into the passage, but John chose the other way of saying it, probably because he followed his source.[37] This fits the other evidence adduced above for an origin in tradition.

In conclusion, John did not create the story of Thomas but took it from tradition and shaped it through editorial styling. Although the pericope's connection with verses 19−23 is redactional, its basic nucleus is traditional. To this John added highlights such as the emphasis on physical proof[38] and the seeing-believing antithesis. Dodd (*Tradition*, pp. 354f.) says the doubt-faith contrast of verse 27 and the beatitude-like saying of verse 29 were drawn from synoptic tradition, so John even in redaction added what was already a part of tradition.

How much of this story goes back to the original event? Answers to that question must take into consideration the low-key nature of this account. John, for instance, implies that Thomas never reached out to touch Jesus' nail-marked hands or sword-pierced side; yet later legendary accounts of this story imply that he did. John also focuses on Thomas who must have been a part of tradition for John to have used him. He was, after all, "one of the Twelve," says John, and his presence goes back as far as the tradition.

The historical truth of this account depends on two factors: (1)

37. Carson, "Source," pp. 414f. argues against the validity of these tools. By comparing seven source critical scholars—Bultmann, Becker, Schnackenburg, Nicol, Fortna, Teeple, and Temple—he shows the methodological disarray of the school. With regard to the linguistic approach of Nicol et al he rightly argues (pp. 425f.) that the repetitive words and the variations tend to cancel one another out and that the type of material determines the presence of stylistic and semantic repetitions. We agree with this assessment and utilize the tool only to demonstrate that even on the basis of the criteria adduced by Nicol, Fortna, et al this must stem from tradition. For a more detailed discussion of Johannine critical scholarship, see Carson's "Historical Tradition."

38. Hartmann believes John took this physical evidence from the previous episode, yet differences in the two accounts do favor the probability of a second occurrence. Luke uses the evidence as a group demonstration, while John views it as a personal confrontation even though the disciples are present. This fits John's style, but it also may indicate that John is developing an existing tradition.

a decision regarding the evangelist's desire to be historically trust-worthy, and (2) the value of the eyewitness motif itself. Both of these factors should be affirmed as trustworthy, for John as well as the early Christian community. Even though traditions devel-oped in different *Sitzen in Leben* and showed different *Tendenzen*, they always retained a basic historical core. They were thus not free creations of a church with little concern for history. Any rea-sons for denying authenticity such as corporeality or links with previous episodes dissolve if presuppositions change. The New Testament fails to support a noncorporeal resurrection anyway, and linguistic data emphatically supports a traditional origin; hence the historical core is trustworthy. Thomas's doubt was real and probably rose from a Jewish belief in a single general resur-rection rather than individual ones. Jesus had to convince him that he had indeed risen. Thomas responded to that reality with worship and awe. Any redaction in this account, such as the expansion of doubt and physical proof, merely emphasizes what happened rather than adds to it.

Thomas's cry is dramatic; how could a man who was so skep-tical make such a leap of faith not only to Jesus' messianic signif-icance but also to his lordship and divinity? Perhaps all the clues Jesus gave prior to this about his divinity finally made sense to Thomas (Taylor, *Person*, pp. 156f.). Undoubtedly the disciples would often discuss these matters in light of the resurrection, and now the emotional high of Jesus' appearance probably prompted his cry of awakening faith. Although this remains conjecture, it seems far more reasonable than skepticism about the historical reality of Thomas's experience.

John 21

The major debate concerning John 21 centers on its authorship. Who wrote it, and who added it to the Gospel of John; the evan-gelist himself or a later redactor?[39] The answer, for the most part,

39. Westcott, Ruckstuhl, Cassian, Schlatter, and Smalley favor John's authorship, while Boismard, Bultmann, Lightfoot, Dodd, Marxsen, Brown, Schnackenburg, Alsup, and de Jonge do not.

can be derived only by a comparison of this chapter and the rest of the Gospel (see Brown, Boismard, Cassian).

Similarities in both include:

the use of "Sea of Tiberias," the characters Simon Peter, Thomas, and Nathaniel, the linking of the "beloved disciple" with Peter, the term *opsarion*, the charcoal fire, the question "who are you?", the breaking of bread and fish, the numbering of appearances, the name of Simon's father, the partitive *ek*, sheep imagery and variation, the twofold "Amen," the symbolism of verse 18, explanatory notes and parenthesis in verse 19, the witness theme, and the reference to "other deeds" in verse 25.

Differences in both include:

the use of *epi* instead of *hypo*, *phaneroun* (v. 1), *hypagō* plus infinitive (v. 3), *prōia* for *prōi* (v. 4), *ischyō* for *dynamai* and causal *apo* (v. 6), *ou makran* for *engys* (v. 8), *tolman* and *exetazō* for *erōtaō* (v. 12), *pleon* for *mallon* (v. 15), *epistrephō* for *strephō* (v. 20), *heōs* (v. 22), and *adelphos* (v. 23), and 28 terms found only here.

Few critics, of course, are willing to make an evaluation on the basis of terminology and style alone, yet most agree that the differences between the accounts are not numerous enough to prove John 21 was written by another author. Instead, most critics reject John's authorship of chapter 21 because of the clumsy transition between the Gospel and chapter 21, and theories of editorial revision which take into account other evidence from the Gospel itself.

The first objection seems to ignore the basic structure of the Gospel itself where structure often is sacrificed because of theological considerations. In fact, the Gospel's basic lack of cohesion seems to be a major stylistic trait of the evangelist. Lindars says (*John*, pp. 621f.) this form and structure are typical of John, "a synoptic-type episode of further dialogue." He adds, "Really important differences are not sufficiently numerous to be decisive against Johannine authorship." Transition terms in chapter 21 thus may indicate a later addition, but they do not demand a separate author. The second criticism is more difficult to deal with since much of it is based on the growing belief among scholars that in spite of stylistic unity throughout the Gospel, John also reveals a basic disunity in his handling of sources. Several sections such as 1:1–18, 6:51–58, 15–17, and 21 seemingly are out of place. Indeed, most recent Johannine commentators have been preoccupied with questions of source criticism (e.g., Schnackenburg, Smalley).

Yet source criticism may be unnecessary here. Robert Kysar says, for instance (p. 54), that even after all the theories are discussed, the "Johannine puzzle" remains. Efforts to smooth out the narrative have succeeded only in creating more breaks and incongruities in the book. Carson says ("Source Criticism," p. 428) a "probing agnosticism" is needed to deal with all these problems. Would it not be easy and more judicious in the long run to accept any so-called inconsistencies as deliberate traits of John rather than clumsy editing on the part of another redactor? John may have used more than one source for his Gospel,[40] and the late addition of chapter 21 does suggest some stages in the composition of the book; perhaps these factors in part account for inconsistencies without sacrificing his authorship of chapter 21.

B. de Solages has done an excellent study on John which includes an extensive linguistic comparison between John 21 and the first twenty chapters of the Gospel, between John 20 and John 1—19, and also between John 21 and the Gospel of Luke. The study which takes into consideration text, vocabulary, and expressions, makes some interesting conclusions: that John 21 is more closely linked to chapters 1—19 than John 20, and that chapter 21 also shows more affinity to the rest of John than it does to Luke. De Solages argues that it is not possible to attribute this chapter to any other than the writer of the Gospel of John (p. 234).

John's work thus is best explained as a unity, with any so-called aporias, displaced pericopae, and theological incongruities deliberate efforts on the part of the evangelist in working with his own sources. Chapter 21, although a later addition to the Gospel, still remains a part of it, since evidence simply does not warrant a separate author. Further examination of this chapter should help strengthen this conclusion. Differences in chapter 21 can better be explained by redactional activity on the part of the evangelist himself.

40. Most argue for John's independence from the others. However, see Barrett (John, pp. 42f.), for the view that John used Luke. Dodd (Tradition, pp. 366—87), posits that the connection occurred at the preliterary stage; and Blinzler (Johannes, pp. 58—59), believes that John quoted Mark (and perhaps Luke) from memory.

The Fishing Appearance, 21:1–14

Numerous parallels between John 21:1–4 and Luke 5:1–11 have led many critics to suggest both accounts utilized the same source. The details in both are strikingly similar.

1. The disciples fish all night but catch nothing.
2. Jesus commands the fishermen to throw their nets in again, promising them this time they will catch fish.
3. Other disciples are present.
4. The disciples obey Jesus and catch fish.
5. Peter's impulsive act singles him out from among the disciples.
6. Jesus reveals himself as Lord.
7. The story ends with a mission motif.

Even though the accounts have similarities, they also include many differences. These seem so convincing to the majority of scholars that discussion today centers on which represents the more primitive tradition.[41] Yet there are also notable differences: most significantly, the pericope is marked by distinctive Johannine style. In addition, within each similarity we find the following differences (keyed to the categories above):

1. John says seven disciples were present; Luke says three.
2. Luke says the nets were so full of fish they were breaking; John says "the net was not torn."
3. Luke stresses the confession of Peter; John the confession of the "beloved."
4. John emphasizes the nonrecognition motif; Luke does not.
5. John makes the "beloved" the central figure; Luke stresses Peter.
6. Peter swims to shore in John; he arrived there by boat in Luke.
7. John's account concludes with meal fellowship; Luke's with Jesus' command to become "fishers of men."

Are these differences simply due to redactions of the same account? Sanders says no; "It is fairly clear from the limited amount

41. Those who argue for Lukan priority include Goguel, Dodd, the early Bultmann (*HST*), Benoit, Fuller, and Pesch. Those who accept Johannine priority would include the later Bultmann (John commentary), Brown, Grass, Klein, and Bailey.

of common material that the one narrative cannot be an edited
version of the other" (pp. 449f.). Could the two represent separate
events? Brown states that it is highly unlikely that Peter would
have experienced two such similar situations without recognizing
Jesus in John's later account (p. 1090). He says both accounts are
a combination of Jesus' appearances to Peter and to the Twelve
(1 Cor. 15:5).

Brown's theory, however, ignores human fallibility. Peter, who
was frustrated after a night of unsuccessful fishing, might easily
have been so tired and discouraged that he failed to recognize
Jesus who had helped the fishermen before. Marshall says the
only real similarity between these accounts is Jesus' command to
let down the nets, a suggestion hardly striking enough to jog Peter's memory. Marshall suggests the traditions might have influenced each other, especially since John probably knew about Luke's
account before he wrote his own. Both accounts probably represent separate traditions about two different historical events.[42]

What is the original source of John's story? Bultmann says (John,
pp. 705f.) this was "the first (and only) appearance," which
may explain why the disciples were so uncertain. John's list of
disciples is probably a combination of tradition and redaction
since John only names those who are prominent in his Gospel,
then adds simply "two others."

Regardless of Bultmann's theories, John's partial list may indicate a very early tradition, as does the fishing eipsode itself. Brown,
in fact, suggests this episode may be the very first Galilean appearance. Perhaps the doubt motif was part of the original story
then, since this account shows the most restrained usage of all.
The core of the story in verses 5 and 6 was probably part of the
original tradition, but the rest of this pericope was redacted to fit
into John's mission theme. The exact number of fish (153) in
verse 11 may be a combination of tradition and redaction, since
originally it should have been used in verse 6's description of the

42. In fact, if John did know Luke's Gospel, he could easily have consciously drawn
parallels between the first "call" and the final "recommissioning" of the disciples. Further,
many scholars have noted the fact that Luke's scene shows no formal signs of a resurrection story. Pesch, pp. 126–30, argues against its historicity, but his points are based
on tradition critical assumptions which themselves are highly disputed. The so-called
"legendary accretions" do not disprove authenticity. For a good discussion of this, see
Barbour, Tradition-historical Criticism, passim. It is therefore probable that these are separate traditions which reflect distinct historical incidents.

big catch. John, however, puts this number after the recognition scene and mission imagery for theological emphasis. Brown says the number indicates an eyewitness source but is "not a solution to the problem of historicity."

The recognition scene itself may have appeared last in the original, but John uses it in the middle of his story to lead into the mission motif. The disciples' long trip to shore is full of mission imagery, yet many of the symbols do not seem Johannine since they are too subtle for his overt imagery. The net, for instance, as a symbol of the church sounds like Luke; perhaps John borrowed the association here. The role of the "beloved" is also redactional since it is based on personal reminiscence (contra Pesch). The central role of Peter, however, was undoubtedly part of the primitive tradition since his impulsive act matches his synoptic portrayal.

The so-called "eucharistic scene" in verses 11–14 should not be separated from the major story, even though tradition-critics consistently find fault with the transition to, and differences between, it and the main account. Any discrepancy between verses 5, 10, and 13 can be explained by John's abbreviated version of the event rather than accepting the theory that he combined two separate sources. Further, the fire in verse 9 and the command in verse 10 prepare for just such a scene, and it seems likely that the fish in verse 13 is the same fish caught in the previous scene. "No one dared to ask" is not a second "recognition" and verses 12b and 14 are not thereby artificial editorial attempts to link the two episodes. The story is a compact whole.

In conclusion, the fishing appearance pericope of John 21: (1) is an integrated whole which does not combine two or more separate traditions, (2) is based on a distinct historical tradition, and (3) includes some redaction in word choice and structural development. All of this, however—redaction, tradition, history, and theology—are not at odds with each other in this account but instead complement and enrich each other.[43]

43. One of the major proofs of a primitive source occurs in verse 3; the disciples seem to be without a plan and expect nothing. This is highly unlikely in a later resurrection narrative and is quite similar to Mark's discipleship motif, i.e., an accent on their failure. In fact, Brown (p. 1087) uses this as further evidence for his thesis that verses 1–17 reflect the first appearance to Peter of 1 Corinthians 15:5. Moreover, while we do not believe that Luke 5 is the same event, the "criterion of multiple attestation" would still

Our reasons for asserting that redaction in this case does not demand an ahistorical provenance are: First, the criteria noted point to a primitive tradition and possibly to a basis in history. Second, the theological stress is not restricted to those points unique to the evangelists; the structure and indeed the very choice of one tradition over another gives it theological import. John's tendency to focus on individuals in the tradition, here the "beloved" and Peter, is a case in point. That is likely a personal reminiscence and therefore redaction, yet it is at the same time authentic history. Personal reminiscence bridges the gap between history and redaction, yet it is at the same time authentic history. Further, the link via verses 9 and 10, which some find clumsy and artificial, is a deliberate redactional ploy to stress the connection between the miraculous catch and the meal fellowship; and the wording of verse 13, if a purposeful allusion back to 6:11, adds a sacramental flavor to the episode. Finally redaction and tradition, history and theology (note the deliberate chiasm) co-exist and supplement one another in 21:1–14.

The Reinstatement of Peter, 21:15–17

Two basic problems in this account include John's use of the time note in verse 15 and his three-part question-and-answer structure in 15–17. Is John's use of *hote oun ēristēsan* ("when they had finished eating") such an artificial attempt at linkage that it proves the entire scene was added to John 21 at a much later date? Many critics think so, although Von Wahlde thinks *hote oun* is a "repetitive resumptive" which marks a return to tradition after the redactional insertion of verses 11–14. The parallel in verse 9 (*hōs oun*), however, argues against this theory.

apply. While this is normally used of sayings, the principle would also apply to events, applicable here on the basis of our previous thesis that the language of Luke 5 influenced the nature of the John 21 episode. The miracle of a great catch of fish was so important to the early church that two divergent episodes are recounted (cf. the feedings of the 4,000 and 5,000). Finally, of those criteria which point to a later or nontraditional pericope (see Westerholm, pp. 6–7) only one may apply at all to verses 1–14, the criterion of derivative speech/elements, i.e., signs of later reflection or creation. However, this shows only redaction not inauthenticity.

Actually, John's time note is neither vague nor clumsy and serves as a natural part of the narrative. *Touton* ("they") in verse 15 probably refers to the "disciples" of verse 14, and the seashore setting is the same in both accounts (it would be superfluous to mention it in a dialogue scene). Peter's presence in both scenes also enhances their cohesiveness and suggests they were linked together early in tradition, possibly at the time of the original event itself. At the same time, all three (with vv. 18–19) may have belonged to an early Peter-centered tradition which employed rabbinic "pearl-stringing" techniques in collecting and joining the episodes. In this case they would have circulated independently at first. However, this latter supposition is speculative, and the unity of verses 1–17 may be the more viable solution.

How much redaction is evident in John's three-part question-and-answer structure in verses 15–17?[44] The basic structure may come from early tradition, but its three-part formula strongly suggests redaction since: (1) the threefold pattern is not natural and may serve here as a symbolic parallel of Peter's original three-part denial (Westcott, Cassian), and (2) this stylistic device so typical of John's writing (see Freed, pp. 192f.) is hardly the way Jesus and Peter must originally have interacted.[45] Perhaps John specifically used the structure both to remind his readers of Peter's three-part denial, as well as the threefold witness that was necessary to seal a legal contract (see Gaechter, pp. 328f.). Schnackenburg, (III, p. 435) calls this "the language of commission" which "installs" Peter into the pastoral office.

Yet is John's use of the structure necessarily a redaction? Could not Jesus himself have used the three-part structure to awaken Peter to reinstatement and mission? Perhaps only the variation in terminology in this episode is redactional, while the structure is traditional. Some might argue that we cannot separate the variation in terms from the threefold pattern. However, Peter's obvious

44. The presence of *agapan* here is not Johannine. If it were redactional, one would expect *pisteuein*. While the sheep imagery is Johannine, it is also attached to Peter in the tradition (cf. 1 Peter 5:2–4). Fuller (p. 153) believes that the Galilean location, the meal motif, and the Petrine imagery show evidence of a very primitive tradition. Alsup (pp. 62, 202n) goes so far as to suggest that this is the lost Markan ending entailing the appearance to Peter. Schnackenburg (III, pp. 429–31) however, takes it as primarily Johannine and thus redactional.

45. Although several Aramaic verbs mean "I love," no Hebrew or Aramaic equivalents exist for *agapan* and *philein*.

frustration in the third instance would better fit a situation in which Christ used the same terms. If there was variation originally, one would expect Peter to understand more than he does.

In conclusion, the pericope of 21:15−17 includes both tradition and redaction.[46] Several methods such as the "criterion of unintentional signs of history"[47] as well as the "criterion of multiple attestation"[48] suggest the story has a traditional origin, despite the efforts of some critics to prove it was a much later addition. Tradition is indicated by John's use of the threefold formula and its question-response pattern, although redaction is a part of its linguistic variation.

The Prophecy Regarding Peter, 21:18−19

Bultmann says verses 18 and 19 were added much later to chapter 21, an example of the early church's attempts to lump various events into a single story. This compilation, however, does not necessarily mean the pericope is a later creation. Linders, in fact, says (p. 636) "Previous experience has shown that this (double Amen formula) is often an authentic saying of Jesus." Ambiguity in the passage itself also seems to indicate authenticity; obviously it went through a developing interpretive tradition before John clarified its meaning.

Bultmann (p. 713) correctly demonstrates that verse 18 comes from an ancient proverb which reads: "In youth a man is free to go where he will; in old age a man must let himself be taken where he does not will." John's use of the saying shows it was well known during his time. Lindars believes (p. 636) the proverb is a redaction

46. Form critical theory often concludes that pericopes floated independently during the oral period, and therefore this connection could be discounted on an a priori basis (but see Travis, "Form Criticism," pp. 153−54). While various elements could have been used independently, there is no reason to doubt that these episodes were at all times connected chronologically as, for instance, the passion narrative or Mark 4:21−43.

47. The elevation of Peter is below the surface of the text and is not characteristic of the evangelist and so probably came to him from the tradition.

48. If 1 Peter 5:2 builds on an independent version of this tradition, it may very well point to a historical event; at the least, it is evidence that this was indeed a much-used tradition. Again, the negative criteria (e.g., the "criterion of the tendencies of the developing tradition") point to redaction but do not truly negate the authenticity of the pericope. These could argue against the threefold form, but as we stated above stronger evidence exists for the validity of this as well.

of an original discipleship saying like Matthew 8:18–22 or Luke 9:57–62 where the key word is "follow" (*akolouthein*). Each of these sayings "embodies a proverb," he says. The ambiguity of verse 18, however, speaks against that theory[49] which might also mean that John redacted the proverb in light of Peter's death. The editorial aside in verse 19a provides evidence that the evangelist accepted this as originally a prophecy of Peter's death.

The fact that this saying probably came from an ancient proverb does not prevent its imagery from suggesting Peter's martyrdom and possibly even his crucifixion. Bultmann (pp. 731–34) believes John misunderstood this intent of Jesus' saying, but most critics accept it as a prophetic statement about Peter's death. Although "stretching out your hands," was a common expression for crucifixion at this time, Jesus' use of the words to suggest Peter's crucifixion is debatable (see Barrett, p. 585). Still, "signifying what kind of death" in verse 19 probably is a deliberate allusion to 12:33 and 18:32.

Originally the proverb behind this saying spoke about the helplessness of old age, but in the second part of verse 18 Jesus changed the verbs to future tense and added the negative *hopou* ("but") clause so that it applied figuratively to Peter's death. Perhaps originally Jesus' statement was quoted outside its context of discipleship. That is why John adds the editorial commentary of verse 19f. to correct any misinterpretation on the part of the early church.[50]

The tradition behind this passage seems certain in light of the obvious primitive source of Jesus' saying. Perhaps the historical progression of the passage started with Jesus' use of an ancient proverb to prophesy how Peter would die. The early church seemingly misunderstood Jesus' words, however, so John had to put that statement back into context so they could understand what

49. Brown says, "In our judgment, while the redactor may be responsible for the joining of the sayings, the sayings themselves are old, for neither lends itself easily to the interpretation that has been given to it." He adds, "Certainly, if the statement had been fashioned in the light of Peter's death, the wording would not have been so ambiguous."

50. It was probably interpreted in the primitive church as a discipleship saying before Peter's death (i.e., applied to believers generally rather than to Peter specifically); to this extent Lindar's isolation of discipleship in the saying may be correct. John corrects the misinterpretation and takes his readers back to Jesus' original intention. Here, then, is the extent of the redaction. It is John alone who uses this primitive tradition to make his point, i.e., that discipleship for Peter meant martyrdom. Moreover, John adds this to his united tradition in verses 1–17, thereby further developing his central ecclesiological message.

Jesus really meant it to say, that discipleship for Peter meant martyrdom.

The Prophecy Regarding the Beloved Disciple, 21:20—23

Does this next section about the "beloved" belong with the preceding one about Peter? Some critics doubt it, saying the connecting words of 19b and 20a are insufficient to put the two episodes together, and the subject matter switches to the future of the "beloved." John may not have felt a need for a formal transition here, however, presupposing a logical connection between them. Although he might have added verses 20—23 because of his own pending death, the transition itself and the tone of the two (Peter's death in vv. 18—19 and the "beloved's" here) fit together too well.

Verse 22, like verse 19, comes from primitive tradition, and as Brown says, "The very fact that the writer claims the saying has been misunderstood makes it incredible that the saying had been recently invented, for then it would simply have been denied" (p. 1118). Jesus' words, "If I want him to remain alive until I return," are probably repeated exactly from tradition, while verses 20 and 23 come from John's own reminiscence. "Follow me" in verse 22b may also be authentic since it so beautifully fits the development of thought here. It is a favorite phrase in John yet not exclusive to him as an author. Perhaps the phrase was a part of tradition which John used to connect both his theme and the two stories of Peter and the "beloved." At any rate, the central emphasis here is the prophecy about the "beloved" which is repeated twice (vv. 22, 23), perhaps because John was so concerned to combat rumors about his own immortality.

Verses 18—23 altogether are a section of tradition-material which centers on the deaths of Peter and the "beloved." Prophetic statements about both deaths were misunderstood by the early church, and both "rumors" are confronted here by John who shows how Jesus' statements about the disciples were more concerned about discipleship than death.

Ecclesiology, such as in the symbolism of Peter and the "beloved" and the emphatic "follow me," is present but subservient to John's major theme about his own inevitable death.

John's Second Conclusion, 21:24 – 25

Critics who say John wrote verses 24 and 25[51] say they are the only true ending to his Gospel. The "we" of verse 24, they say, is editorial rather than literal. This view, however, prompts some problems. First of all, nowhere else but in these verses does John use "we" or "I" except for some controversial examples in 1 John 1:1 – 5. Second, verses 24 and 25 seem to duplicate 19:35 and 20:31; if chapter 21 is an epilogue why would a conclusion which duplicates an already sufficient ending be necessary? Finally, both *houtos* ("this") in verse 24a and *oidamen* ("we know") in verse 24b seem to indicate that verses 24 – 25 are the joint testimony of the early church which was added here probably because of the anonymous nature of John's Gospel.

The verses also include an important link between the "beloved" and the author of this Gospel; *grapsas* in this context meaning: (1) literally, that the "beloved" was the author of the entire Gospel, (2) in a causative sense, that "he had these things written" either by an amanuensis or someone else, or (3) figuratively, that he was the source of the original tradition which lay behind this work. John 19:19 seems to support the causative meaning; the same word translates "Pilate *caused* the words to be written on the cross" (cp. Rom. 15:15). Still, most parallels at best are mere suggestions for the proper meaning of *grapsas*.

Are verses 24 and 25 valid as an imprimatur then? That function depends for the most part on John's eyewitness motif, stressed in words such as *martyrōn* ("witnessing") and *autou hē martyria* ("his witness"). Since verse 24 is such an obvious parallel with 19:35, Bultmann believes both are late additions to the text. Significant differences between the two, however, prove they are not parallel but that 21:24 imitates 19:35. Internal evidence in the text seems to support this as well as evidence such as the Dead Sea Scrolls and archeological discoveries which have undergirded the accuracy of John's historical and theological situation in first-century Palestine. Finally, the great amount of insignificant detail and personal reminiscence in the Fourth Gospel also support this conclusion.

51. Bernard (pp. 12f.), Hoskyns (p. 669), and Sanders, (pp. 47 – 48). Schnackenburg believes the verses are important to the Gospel yet they were still written by the final redactor.

Either these verses are the work of a first-rate storyteller who knew how to weave in authentic-sounding details, or they are the written-down version of an eyewitness account. Nineham says the "eyewitness" motif, though a definitive part of the resurrection (1 Cor. 15:3f.), is not applied to Jesus' earthly life until later New Testament works such as John and Acts. Form criticism demonstrates that the Gospel pericopes developed apart from eyewitness testimony and are theological reflections rather than historical reminiscences. Morris, on the other hand, believes that the vast amount of insignificant detail in the Gospels such as time notes must be seriously considered as evidence of a historically accurate document.

The Ascension, Luke 24:50–53; Acts 1:9–11

A comparison of Luke's accounts of Jesus' ascension in his Gospel as well as Acts prompts some important questions. Did Luke write them or were they added by a later redactor? Several scholars such as Lake, Wilder, Menoud, Conzelmann, and Evans say the ascension passages, especially Acts 1:1–5, were late, second-century additions. Reasons for this theory include: (1) the Bethany setting of Luke 24 which conflicts with the Jerusalem location of Acts 1, (2) the same-day theme in Luke which conflicts with the forty-day theme in Acts 1, and (3) the phrase "lifting up of the hands" in Luke which is a second-century phrase found only here in the New Testament. Luke seems to be a paraphrase of Acts. Other commentators such as van Stempoort, Flender, Fuller, and Anderson, however, disagree with this analysis, saying that Luke's Gospel pericope in verses 50–53 is essential to Luke's purpose as well as based on the theology of the Gospel rather than on Acts 1. It also provides a satisfactory conclusion to the Gospel, seems to be based on tradition, and by virtue of its differences from the Acts account is not a paraphrase of it. Dillon goes so far as to call this latter view a "consensus" (pp. 170ff.) and at least one of the above (Menoud) has since altered his position.

Is Luke 24:50–53 a creation of Luke or a passage taken from tradition? Some critics say Luke wrote it on his own[52] since no-

52. See Lohfink (pp. 147–51, 163–75) as well as Marxsen (*Resurrection*, p. 172) and Fuller (pp. 122–23).

where else in the New Testament is mention made of a separate ascension. The account also fails to harmonize with Acts 1. Lohfink adds that anywhere else the ascension is mentioned[53] it appears tangential to the resurrection as a heavenly, invisible event (pp. 81—98). Luke's account, on the other hand, describes an earthly, visible event which takes place apart from the resurrection. Lohfink suggests Luke wrote this account as a transition from the appearances to Pentecost.

Lohfink's theory is not necessarily true, however. Although the language and style of this passage is distinctively Luke's, this might simply indicate he told the event in his own words. Logically, it is also doubtful that he would have failed to clear up any conflict with Acts 1 if he thought there was any.[54]

What specifically are the discrepancies between Luke 24:50—53 and Acts 1:9—11? First of all, any contradictions are more apparent than real. The mission time note, for instance, in verse 50, and the implication of the same-day theme is only a part of Luke's theological emphasis, hardly concrete evidence of a conflict. Bethany is also a suburb of Jerusalem; no conflict exists between the Gospel's mention of Bethany and Act's use of Jerusalem. The difference is simply theological. Van Stempvoort says that the Gospel account is doxological (with its priestly blessing and worship) while Acts is ecclesiastical, historical, and preparational for the development of the church (pp. 37, 39). Luke 24 is thus an appropriate conclusion to the Gospel and especially the appearances while Acts 1 serves as an introductory christological foundation for the rest of the book. The ascension serves two functions for the author; it is both an end and a beginning.

What are the discrepancies between Luke's ascension passages and the rest of the New Testament? Lohfink is correct when he says the New Testament for the most part links together the ascension and resurrection. His analysis, however, is based on a too-

53. See 1 Thessalonians 1:9f.; 1 Corinthians 15:3f.; Romans 1:3f., 8:34, 14:9; Philippians 2:6f.; Colossians 3:1; Ephesians 1:19f., 2:5f., 4:8f.; 1 Timothy 3:16; 1 Peter 1:20f., 3:18f., 21f.; Hebrews 1:3, 5:5; the endings of Matthew and Mark.

54. Fuller (p. 123) correctly notes a Palestinian tradition behind this. However, he is wrong in his formulation of the tradition into an ascension theology. He calls this phrase Jesus' "assumption" into heaven, which was concurrent with the resurrection (originally) and was separate from his exaltation. Then, with the "progressive materialization of the appearances," it was necessary to conclude the appearances with a physical, distinct ascension event. However, this is speculative at best.

literal look at the data. Theological identification does not necessarily mean historical or chronological identification; the epistles were doctrinal rather than historical. In them the ascension meant Jesus' glorification which naturally extended to the resurrection as a whole. Except for 1 Corinthians 15, Jesus' post-resurrection appearances are not mentioned apart from the resurrection since "resurrection" was an all-embracing term in the kerygma of the early church which generally stood for all the events in Jesus' glorification.

Matthew and Mark's failure to mention any ascension, however, is more of a problem. Still, John 20:17 is evidence of an independent tradition which also separated the resurrection and ascension.[55] Perhaps Matthew and Mark chose not to end their Gospels with an ascension scene, using instead Jesus' command to "Go and baptize the nations" in order to conclude with a strong missionary emphasis. Since Luke was already planning to write a full account of the church's mission efforts in Acts, that ending was not as necessary to his Gospel.

Finally, it is not true that Luke was separating the resurrection and the exaltation of the Lord, as Lohfink argues. While the exaltation is more evident in this passage, it is not absent from the earlier narrative. Luke, in fact, adds to Mark's description of the angels at the empty tomb, replacing "white robe" with "dazzling apparel," thereby linking the "dazzling" glory of Jesus on the Mount of Transfiguration in 9:29 with the resurrection event. Verse 26, which specifically mentions Jesus entering "into his glory," is directly linked to the resurrection. Luke's theology then does not differ appreciably from the rest of the New Testament.[56]

Luke's ascension accounts probably come from tradition but are written down in his Gospel and Acts in his particular style. It is difficult though to separate tradition from redaction in these accounts since this particular tradition only appears here. Perhaps the Gospel represents the historical core while Acts expands on it with prophetic imagery and apocalyptic symbols. Editorial em-

---

55. Perhaps, as Dillon (p. 174) states, Barn. 15:9 provides a further independent tradition.

56. We may also note Haenchen's remark (Acts, p. 138n) regarding "as far as Bethany," v. 50; "Why should Jesus take them to Bethany if his absence from them was merely temporary? This detail is in itself evidence that Luke was reproducing an ascension-tradition." There is no reason for such a detail apart from a traditional source, for Bethany has no place in "Lukan" theology (only 19:29 elsewhere).

phasis in the Gospel as well as imagery (such as the forty-day theme)[57] in Acts, however, might also represent historical developments in the tradition itself.

Luke's accounts seem to be a mixture of historical fact, tradition—development, and historical expansion. Redaction in the Gospel includes the time note "then" in verse 50 and the emphasis on worship in the terms *blessed, great joy, worshiped*, and *in the temple blessing God.* Verses 50 and 51 probably are the traditional core of this passage, although Jesus' twofold "blessing" is emphasized here as part of the priestly act which is part of Luke's liturgical emphasis.

Much of the Acts account seems to be editorial rather than traditional. The conversation between Jesus and the disciples in verses 6—8, for instance, is so full of Lukan expressions that many critics think the whole passage is a free composition. This is especially evident in verse 8 in words such as *power, Holy Spirit, come upon,* and *witness.* Verses 6 and 7 on the other hand, contain such non-Lukan phrases as *restore the kingdom, times or seasons,* and *the Father has set by his own authority,* indicating Luke may also have borrowed from tradition. The original version especially of verse 8 (which forms a "table of contents" for Acts), cannot be recovered. Since Luke has already produced a version of the commission (24:47), it is probable that the tradition behind this was separate from that and belonged to the ascension story itself.

Many critics such as Haenchen and Lohfink believe verses 9—11 are Luke's own composition, but others such as Hahn and Fuller believe the verses have a basis in tradition. They say the verses express a primitive Christian eschatology (a passive assumption into heaven rather than active exaltation to a glorious role) which is evidence of an early, possibly Palestinian, origin. They say the apocalyptic imagery which comes from Daniel 7:13f. and 2 Kings 2:11 may also indicate early origin.[58]

---

57. Benoit (p. 342) and Moule ("Festival," pp. 58f.) assert that the time note is perfectly plausible in light of the difference between Passover and Pentecost and the probable movements of the disciples during that time.

58. Fuller (p. 129) however, goes on to posit that the tradition was originally coincidental with the resurrection and originated before the empty tomb tradition. The original tradition (cp. Gospel of Peter 13:57) was a "primitive kerygmatic" part of the resurrection tradition later expanded into an apocalyptic narrative which included the apostles as witnesses and was placed after the appearances (cp. Ep. Barn. 15:9). Finally, Luke's farewell scene looked forward to the coming of the Spirit at Pentecost. Fuller's evi-

No real contradiction exists between an invisible ascension after the resurrection (John) and a visible one at the end of the appearances (Luke). If John knew Luke's work, he probably worked to supplement rather than argue with it.

The original tradition, behind this account in Acts, is probably the final appearance of Jesus to the disciples at Bethany (the place name an "unintentional" sign of authenticity). This appearance included a farewell address (vv. 6–7 and a primitive form of v. 8) as well as a worship scene (vv. 50–51). This traditional core was passed along by the early church which probably expanded it to include apocalyptic imagery from the Old Testament in order to symbolize the eschatological glory of the event. Luke then added some final touches to it by (1) using part of it in two scenes in keeping with his theological purposes, (2) developing a liturgical emphasis out of worship elements, (3) redacting verse 8 into an outline for his second book, (4) expanding the angel-tradition, and (5) adding more color to the ascension scene itself by the use of terms such as *men of Galilee* in verse 11 to express his Jerusalem-Galilee theme.

Conclusion

The appearance pericopes do not neatly align themselves chronologically; neither do they suggest one basic tradition which includes all of them. Nonetheless, a basic historical core of each episode can be suggested along with certain conclusions about its

dence from the apocryphal Gospels, however, is inconclusive, since they represent, on the whole, later developments of the resurrection narratives. Fuller's decision, in the end, is made on dogmatic grounds rather than the actual evidence. There is no real evidence for Fuller's first step and we would replace it with a simplified version, minus the apocalyptic imagery (added a little later in the tradition-development, in relation to the emphasis on the exaltation of Jesus by the community, cp. Phil. 2:9f., 1 Cor. 16:22, etc.). This does not demand an unhistorical origin for the cloud, etc. There is every reason why God would have utilized this imagery to link these key events of salvation-history, i.e., the resurrection and ascension. Again, dogmatic considerations determine the denial of historicity. It is likely also that the parousia reference in verse 11 (cf. vv. 6–7) was expanded from an original statement that the Lord would soon return. The role of the "two men in white robes" may be editorial (cf. Luke 9:30, 24:4) but may also be based on an original angel-tradition (as with 24:4). We would opt for the latter (criterion of coherence).

use and development. The search for these traditions leads to other conclusions such as:

1. The appearance stories circulated in the primitive church as independent units which were in a fluid rather than fixed state. Preachers felt free to emphasize certain parts and omit others as they considered the needs of their audience. Luke's and John's application of the mission theme in their Gospels is a good example of this.

2. These independent units eventually took the form of either concise narratives or more detailed circumstantial plots, not because of tradition-development or theological emphases as much as the purposes of individual redactors themselves (compare Luke 24:12 and John 20:3–10, or Luke 24:50–53 and Acts 1:1–11).

3. Each writer felt free to select and use tradition as he saw fit, a fact which makes it difficult to trace development or to separate tradition from redaction. No one can suggest a pattern of development from tradition to final Gospel form with absolute certainty; all at best are reasonable possibilities.

Some reasonable assumptions might include:

1. Mark's and Matthew's appearance narratives are quite similar. Matthew added little to Mark's probable theme when Jesus appeared to the women. He did give verses 9 and 10 a slightly different thrust, however, and expressed Jesus' Galilean appearance in his words and according to his own particular theology.

2. Luke wrote an account different from Matthew's and Mark's because of this decision to focus on the Jerusalem appearances. He used other sources and redacted them according to his needs. His major stress is the recognition of the living Christ through the "word" and the "bread" (24:30–31) in an ecclesiastical motif. The historical core was probably somewhat simpler, the first (vv. 13–35) being a recognition scene without as strong a liturgical atmosphere and the second (vv. 36–49) another recognition scene with the physical proof aspect receiving more and more attention as a result of community needs. His ascension scene comes from an extensive tradition which Luke divided, then redacted in accordance with his theological use of the ascension as both a doxological end to the appearances and a liturgical beginning for the church.

3. John redacted the traditions used by Mark and Luke. In verses 14–18, for instance, he borrowed from and redacted Mark in his

essay on faith, and in verses 19—23 he redacted Luke. Verses 24—29 were taken from a separate tradition and redacted to make a special statement about faith, culminating in the strong Johannine statement of verse 29 (although the beautitude is traditonal). Chapter 21 employs a Peter-sermon (vv. 1—11, 15—19) with other traditions possibly inserted (vv. 12—13) and added (vv. 21—22) but more likely connected from the beginning. Verses 14, 20, and 23 were added by the evangelist and verse 24 by the community.

Despite all these independent units, a basic historical picture emerges: the Risen Jesus appeared to his disciples first in Jerusalem. There he appeared to the women, to Peter, the men on the way to Emmaus, and to the Twelve. He then went to Galilee where he appeared again to the Eleven and the fishing disciples. Finally he returned to Jerusalem where he ascended into heaven.

Part Four

Conclusion

8

History and Interpretation in the Resurrection Narratives

The resurrection narratives are a mixture of tradition and redaction, and what that combination suggests about the historical event and its theological interpretation is the final focus of this study. The analysis begins with the historical basis of the resurrection accounts in a search for the probable nucleus of events behind any interpretation. It then proceeds to trace the development of interpretation through preliterary creeds and hymns, then through the epistles, and finally in the Gospel narratives themselves. Then answers can be formulated in response to these questions: Do the events merit the developing traditions? How valid are they both historically and theologically? What does the resurrection mean for faith today?

The Mode of the Resurrection

What are some of the major interpretations of the resurrection event, and which ones best match the New Testament accounts in light of historical research? Basically Bible scholars have considered six possible explanations for the resurrection, theories which necessarily distinguish between what the New Testament writers thought they were describing (a corporeal or spiritual resurrection), and what modern scholars believe lies behind their reports. The theories include: political theory, the swoon theory, the myth theory, the subjective vision theory, the objective vision theory, and the physical resurrection theory. The first two views are old arguments;[1] the last four are current today.

The Political Theory

Reimarus believed the disciples made up the entire resurrection story in order to gain notoriety and recognition for themselves. He said that when Jesus died he simply ceased to exist. His disciples who wanted to start a new religion had to steal his body. Then they could preach the messianic message Jesus himself never believed. This theory never gained much support; it is highly unlikely that unethical men would have produced the morality and ethics of Christianity. It is also improbable that such men would have been willing to die for their beliefs.

The Swoon Theory

Paulus, Schleiermacher, and Hase proposed this theory which said that Jesus merely fainted on the cross and was later revived in the tomb.[2] Strauss, however, clearly showed how illogical this view was; how could Jesus have recovered so fast and so completely in such a short time? Why did not the Romans who were experts on crucifixion notice that Jesus had swooned instead of died? How could a man who had endured both a crucifixion and a sword-thrust deceive his disciples into thinking he had risen from the dead? Hase and Schleiermacher's theory seems more like a miracle than the resurrection itself.

The Mythical View

Strauss first proposed this theory in combination with the subjective vision theory. Bousset, Loisy, Bultmann, and Tillich support him, saying that the resurrection narratives are simply myths cre-

1. The political theory, however, has made a recent comeback in the work of H. Schonfeld who theorizes that Jesus hatched the resurrection plot with his disciples in order to become Messiah.
2. The Ahmiddiya sect of Islam also advocate this theory, saying Jesus survived to preach forty more years in the Middle East, then was buried in Kashmir where he remains to this day.

ated by the early church to portray the significance of Jesus' message and death,[3] even though Jesus simply ceased to exist after that death. The theory is difficult to believe; how could all the resurrection accounts be myths? Evidence against the view has prompted several arguments:

1. There was insufficient time for such mythology to appear, especially since 1 Corinthians 15:3f. proves the stories began within a few years of Jesus' death. Myths do not normally develop while eyewitnesses are still alive.

2. Why would the disciples have been willing to die on the basis of a myth? People do not jeopardize their lives or heritage for half-truths.

3. The resurrection stories are vastly different from pagan myths. Pagan myths are cultic celebrations of nonhistorical events, while the resurrection narratives are based on eyewitness experiences of an actual event in history.

4. The New Testament records actually "demythologize" hellenistic myths by "historicizing" them. The evangelists presented what they knew to be historical events/miracles in a mythical format in order to tell pagans that their religious longings had now come true in Jesus the Christ.

The Subjective Vision Theory

Strauss, Renan, Marxsen, and Fuller propose this view which says that the disciples had a series of dreams in which they saw Jesus; these became the basis of the resurrection narratives even though Jesus, in fact, was dead. Many scholars argue against this view, saying Jesus appeared to people who were not expecting to see him rather than to those who were psychologically prepared (see Wilckens, Goppelt, Moule, Schweizer). The disciples were a defeated, discouraged group after the crucifixion; mere dreams or visions about Jesus would hardly have been enough to effect Paul's

---

3. Norman Perrin (Resurrection, passim), for instance, believes that the synoptic accounts present "primordial myth" (Mark) as well as "foundation myth" (Matthew and Luke). Mark makes the resurrection a daily experience of the believer in such a way that the individual is transformed via endurance in discipleship. Matthew and Luke stress the resurrection as the origin of the church and the common experience of all believers. Perrin's discussion of "what really happened" (Resurrection, p. 83) concerns entirely "the impact of Jesus upon their lives" rather than the facticity of the event.

turnabout, James' conversion, or even Peter's restoration. Niebuhr says it is possible to explain the resurrection appearances psychologically but highly improbable to do so. The theory does not explain either why Jesus' appearances continued for a short time and then ceased, or how Jesus could have "appeared" (in a dream) to five hundred people at the same time.

The Objective Vision Theory

Lampe, Davies, Schweizer, Bornkamm, Grass, Wilckens, and Moule all believe the appearances were visions rather than physical events, but visions that were sent from God to teach Jesus' followers that his resurrection was a spiritual reality.[4] This view is somewhat dependent on the meaning of ōphthē (see also chap. 7) in 1 Corinthians 15:5f., a word which can mean either "seeing" literally or else "seeing" as in a vision. The rest of 1 Corinthians 15 contradicts this thesis, however; Caird says Paul compares Christ's resurrection body to the believer's "spiritual body" which is not incorporeal but the product of a literal transformation of the physical body. The disciples did not "see" a disembodied Jesus, they saw the transformed Risen Christ.

Paul's efforts to distinguish between visions and real experiences in 2 Corinthians 12 also makes it difficult to believe that the early church taught a visionary rather than literal resurrection. Nothing in the Gospel accounts or New Testament as a whole indicates the earliest witnesses did not believe in a corporeal resurrection.

The Corporeal View

Barth, Brunner, Creed, Marshall, and Wenham all subscribe to this view which alone seems to mesh with New Testament evidence. Yet arguments against the theory abound: (1) the corporeal theory appears only in later, probably secondary New Testament works such as Luke and John. (2) Paul equated the appearances to James and the apostles with his vision in 1 Corinthians 15:8. (3)

---

4. Edward Schillebeeckx (Jesus, pp. 380–97) calls the resurrection a "conversion vision" which prompted the restoration of the disciples through the experience of forgiveness. In his Interim Report on the Books Jesus and Christ (pp. 74–93), Schillebeeckx says that although the resurrection event is not historically verifiable, the experiences of Jesus' followers are.

The appearances themselves are described in mythological and legendary language. (4) The event has no analogical parallel in history so therefore it is impossible to assimilate it.

All of these arguments have been refuted point by point: (1) the corporeal resurrection is presupposed in passages such as 1 Corinthians 15:3–8. (2) Paul's equating his vision with the appearances does not mean they were the same; only that his experience had the same impact on him that the appearances had on the disciples. (3) Differences between New Testament language and pagan mythology clearly prevent the resurrection appearances from being called myths. (4) There are parallels in history (such as Indonesia today), but they are not believed either.

Why do the earliest Gospel accounts remain silent about the corporeal reality of the resurrection? Was there no such concept at that time, or does their very silence argue *for* physical reality rather than against it? Certainly the context of Jewish monism would make it natural for anyone affirming the "resurrection" to assume it was physical. If Jesus' body had been separated from the spirit, surely someone would have mentioned that. If the appearances were "visions" or "revelations," someone would have mentioned that too. The absence of any such allusion means that most likely the early church wanted the resurrection understood in physical terms.

The empty tomb is also evidence of a corporeal resurrection, its physical nature clearly understood. Why was this physical resurrection so important to the early church? (1) The New Testament documents as well as Gospels are problem-oriented; when "false teaching" arose Jesus' physical nature was emphasized. Docetic gnosticism with its stress on a nonbodily resurrection in particular made this emphasis necessary. (2) The Gospel writers never hesitated to include evidence of Jesus' bodily resurrection when their theology warranted such a stress. The physical resurrection of Jesus Christ thus seems certain in light of New Testament evidence; his body was not resuscitated but transformed from death into new life.

Event and Interpretation

Since the resurrection of Jesus Christ was never directly witnessed by any man, the pure historical fact of that event can never be ascertained.[5] The Gospel accounts tell about disciples who could testify only about seeing Jesus alive after the crucifixion. Any affirmation of the resurrection then necessarily involved interpretation of that event. This does not mean, however, that the historian has no role in this affirmation.[6] Interpretation is the function of the historian who must decide whether data warrants interpretation and whether this interpretation is indeed valid. For instance, when historians investigate the evidence regarding the assassination of President Kennedy, they must decide whether that evidence warrants the charge of "conspiracy" (as many have interpreted it) and, more appropriately, whether or not the assassination sealed his image as martyr and charismatic cult figure. The historian is intimately involved in interpretation.

The probable events of the resurrection begin with the fact of Jesus' death which is accurately described in the Gospel accounts. He died on the cross and was buried in a tomb. What happened next on Easter Sunday is more difficult to determine, since the events have no true analogy in history. Yet the events must first be accepted on their own before any interpretation of them can be evaluated.

The Gospel writers definitely combined tradition and redaction in their accounts, a procedure that was natural as well as valid. Their interpretation of events was not ahistorical but instead a part of history itself. Furthermore, the "burden of proof" argument places responsibility on those who would disprove the historical basis of the resurrection narratives rather than those who approve it. And the negative critics simply have not sufficiently proved their case. Probability thus favors authenticity.

A summary of the evidence follows:

5. Here we must concern ourselves with two things, the probable events as they occurred and the development of the interpreting tradition on the basis of those events. In this way we will work in the opposite order from the paper, isolating the objective basis of the Gospel narratives and then going back to the tradition itself as it developed in the early church. At the outset we agree that the resurrection is not the subject of *pure* history (though this may seem at first a contradiction of previous discussion).

6. O'Collins, *Theology*, p. 62n, goes too far when he quotes L. Geering in *Resurrection: A Symbol of Hope* (1971), pp. 216f., with favor "that we should remove Jesus' resurrection 'from the class of events which are properly called historical and which are open to historical investigation.' *As such* it 'lies outside the scope of historical enquiry' " (italics his). O'Collins differs from Geering in saying the historian must enter into the New Testament interpretation but removes this from the historical role and assigns it to the historian's present faith. I believe he must do so in his very role as historian.

The Empty Tomb

On the basis of 1 Corinthians 15:3f. which seems to assume the reality of the empty tomb as well as the Gospel narratives which describe it, a basic historical nucleus emerges. On the third day[7] several women came to the tomb to perform the rites of mourning and discovered it was empty. Mary apparently ran immediately to tell the disciples and was followed by Peter and John back to the tomb. The women at the tomb meanwhile were confused and afraid, and in that state met someone who later was identified as an angel. The angel said Jesus had risen from the dead and they were to tell that to the disciples. The disciples, however, did not believe their message. At this point Matthew specifically refutes the Jewish rumor about the disciples' supposed plot to steal Jesus' body. John, on the other hand describes the normal reaction to Jesus' missing body; unknown persons must have removed it (20:2, 13f.). The evangelists obviously realized the problems involved here and tried to confront them immediately.

No inner contradiction between the Gospels and the epistles exists, however; the empty tomb is clearly presupposed in 1 Corinthians 15:3f. Grass's contention that the empty tomb was not necessary for faith but rose as a late nonhistorical boost to faith is simply not true; the reality of the empty tomb was empirically verifiable. The fact that any investigation of it proved, rather than disproved its existence, is significant. No real basis exists for denying the empty tomb apart from dogmative reasons.[8] The empty tomb tradition did appear later in New Testament literature, not because of a later origin but rather because it was a part of the appearance stories in the early church and so was not emphasized until later Gospels such as Luke and John.

The Appearances

No real dichotomy exists between the Galilee and Jerusalem appearance stories. The disciples undoubtedly remained in Je-

---

7. The motif is theological but based on the historical event; the empty tomb was discovered on the Sunday following a Friday crucifixion, a period which became three days (two nights and a day) according to Semitic calculations.

8. See O'Collins, "The Empty Tomb in Theological Perspective," (Easter, pp. 90–100). Lampe, (Resurrection, pp. 59, 92–99) says on the basis of incarnational theology that Jesus could not have risen bodily from the empty tomb. When "the Word became flesh," Jesus' body had to decay in the grave just like ours. O'Collins answers we cannot deduce a fact from a preconceived principle which may not be a true basis for comparison. Hordern (Introduction, p. 71) says "The historians have not looked at any evidence, because they 'knew' before they looked that, 'in history,' dead men stay dead, and that therefore, the Easter story cannot be 'historical.' History has been rewritten by definition."

rusalem for the Passover after Jesus' death, which is where he first appeared to them (Luke 24:36−43, John 20:19−29) after he had met the women (Matt. 28:9−10, Mark 16:9f., John 20:14−18), Peter (Luke 24:34, John 21:15−17), and the disciples on the road to Emmaus (Luke 24:13−35). The disciples remained in Jerusalem a few days longer, during which time Jesus appeared to Thomas (John 20:24−29). Then they left for Galilee. The angel's command for them to go to Galilee where they would see Jesus did not necessarily prepare them for his appearance by the Sea of Tiberias, however (John 21:1−14). Their failure to recognize him under the circumstances was understandable. They were expecting Jesus but not at that particular time. The fishing scene also was believable, the disciples returning to the only occupation they knew prior to Jesus' calling. We must remember that Paul continued his profession after his mission had commenced. The disciples were not necessarily despondent or directionless at this point; Jesus simply had not told them what he wanted them to do yet. The "commission" appearance (Matt. 28:16f.) took place in Galilee, as did the appearances to James and the five hundred (1 Cor. 15:5f.).

The disciples returned to Jerusalem for Pentecost where they waited for "power from on High" (Luke 24:49, probably a separate tradition). Perhaps Jesus made other appearances during this time, but Scripture does not record the details. There was probably only a short time, however, for the disciples would hardly have come down too early for Pentecost, and the ascension occurred a few days before Pentecost (Acts 1:9f.).

Does God sometimes act through anthropomorphic symbolism? The ascension seems to indicate that he does. Jesus himself was the living anthropomorphic symbol since in him the "word became flesh" and God's salvation became real to man. He went up into "heaven" in a cloud, knowing his followers would understand the apocalyptic symbolism of the "Son of man" as well as the natural link with the future parousia.

No true harmonization of the appearances is possible since they originally appeared as isolated units in kerygmatic situations; the actual chronology of them is unknown. Where, for instance, does the story of Peter's reinstatement in John 21:15f. fit in, and what about the stories in Luke 24:44−49, John 20:19−29, 21:1−14, 20−23? Each event must be analyzed separately in terms of redaction and tradition; yet each unit itself should be evaluated in terms of historical worth and theological development.

What is the basic outline of resurrection theology? A detailed study of New Testament creeds and hymns, Acts' speeches, and the epistles shows how certain motifs were added to this theology as tradition developed. Three trends become evident: First, although christological development moved from the functional to the ontological, this does not mean the earliest statements had no ontological meaning; a material connection exists between the two. Second, the resurrection was the functional impetus and Jesus' revelation of himself through his teaching provided ontological content for much of early Christian doctrine. Third, the appearance narratives probably first circulated both as credal statements and kerygmatic stories.

The disciples' first response to the resurrection probably was a combination of functional and eschatological motifs. Their apocalyptic mindset led them to interpret it this way, though many scholars believe their insight went no further than that. The earliest creeds (1 Cor. 16:22, 1 Thess. 1:9−10) combine eschatology and lordship;[9] why should not they be connected here as well? Logically this connection makes sense. When the disciples saw the Risen Christ, they naturally must have believed the Kingdom of God had arrived. They thus focused on the person rather than his work, the reason rather than results. They would have assumed the eschatological aspects at first from their Jewish background.

The earliest interpretation of the event undoubtedly included the motif expressed in many of the creeds by the term *Christ* (cf. 1 Cor. 15:3; 2 Cor. 5:15; Rom. 6:4, 9; 7:4; Acts 2:48; Eph. 1:20; Col. 2:12; 1 Peter. 1:21), in Gospel traditions such as Luke 24:26 and 46, the anointing motif of Mark, and the Davidic-Messiah motif (Rom. 1:3f.; 2 Tim. 2:8; Heb. 7:14; Rev. 3:7, 5:5, 22:16). The "Son of God" theme soon joined this; originally it was the royal Davidic title (2 Sam. 7:14, Ps. 2:7) which was used by Jesus to describe himself (Cullmann, Longenecker, Marshall). The two titles are combined in Mark 8:29, 14:61; Luke 4:41; John 11:27, 20:31; Acts 9:20f.; and Romans 1:3f., "Son of God" adding a sense of exaltation to the messianic motif. This is hinted at in the "with power" and "flesh-

---

9. The Emmaus pericope also combines eschatological and ontological motifs. This has led Bultmann to believe this story is a part of the earliest resurrection tradition.

spirit" dualism of Romans 1:3f. In the Epistle to the Hebrews this theme is expanded (cf. 1:2, 8; 3:6; 4:14; 6:6; 7:3, 28; 10:39) so that the "Son" attains cosmic status because of the resurrection. Although this combination probably began in Jesus' own consciousness and teaching, it was not understood until the resurrection had provided the functional basis for the ontological insight. His messianic significance was related to his death, and sonship to his glorification only in the developing creeds of the early church.

Exaltation, which was functionally a separate phenomenon from the resurrection, became an early, dominant theme in the primitive church, seen especially in the fulfillment motif where Psalm 110:1 appropriately described Jesus. The "right hand of God" imagery in the Psalms may have originated with Jesus himself (Mark 12:36, 14:62; Luke 22:69); certainly it appeared early in the developing tradition (Rom. 8:34; 1 Cor. 15:55; Eph. 1:20; Col. 3:1; Heb. 1:3, 13). Here we see the royal enthronement theme applied to Jesus at the earliest stage. The fulfillment motif may also have become important in Gospel traditions at this time; note the third-day and first-day-of-the-week theme in Mark 16:1 and Luke 24:21, as well as the fulfillment theme in Luke 24:7, 26, and 46.

The exaltation motif became significant as it included more of the characteristics of lordship. We might divide the concept into three major areas—personal, cosmic, and creative-sustaining lordship. The concept probably originated early in the post-Easter community and perhaps even during the time of the appearances. Mary's use of *Lord*, for instance, in John 20:2, 13, and 18 may indicate progression from a term of respect to the more exalted title of Jesus. The earliest meaning was probably personal lordship which reflected Jesus' glorification (Acts 2:36; 1 Cor. 6:14; 2 Cor. 4:14; Rom. 4:24), although this also probably included a functional and eschatological thrust (1 Cor. 16:22) which connected lordship with Jesus' function as the Coming One. This latter force evolved rapidly into his personal worth as Lord on the basis of that lordship (Acts 2:36; 1 Cor. 6:14; Rom. 4:24) and then into further functions on the basis of that lordship (intercessor—Rom. 8:34, Heb. 7:25; coming Judge—1 Thess. 1:10; Acts 10:42, 17:31; Heb. 10:13).

Here we enter the area of cosmic lordship, which became fully developed during the gentile mission (see below) but had its origin in Palestinian motifs (cf. Phil. 2:6f. and even the wisdom background behind Col. 1:15f.). Finally, we note the ascription to Him of creative-sustaining lordship, which is closely connected with the divinity motif. In Hebrews 1:3, 1 Corinthians 8:6, Colossians

1:16, John 1:3 this role is applied to him. While the final three belong to the period of the Gentile mission, the first had a Jewish provenance and indicated that the motif may well have originated earlier, in connection with the ascription to Jesus of divine status and Old Testament fulfillment roles.

Theology was changing with all these additions, but so were the appearance traditions themselves. Matthew's Gospel, for instance, emphasized a supernatural emphasis probably in conjunction with the church's growing stress on Jesus' lordship over nature and God's supernatural vindication of his son. This does not mean later creation. The lordship emphasis of Thomas's cry (John 20:28), we have argued, shows that the theme existed from the time of the appearances.

Several peripheral developments also probably happened during this time. The sacramental elements of the resurrection narratives became more important as the early church celebrated the Eucharist (Matt. 28:19; Luke 24:26f.; John 21:12 – 13). Dialogue sections of the Emmaus story started to assume a credal form (Luke 24:17 – 27). The increasing Jewish polemic against the empty tomb provoked answers from the early church (Matt. 27:62f.; 28:11f.), and the witness emphasis began to grow as apologetic needs developed (as in Luke).

Soteriological implications of the resurrection began to emerge from the expanding lordship theme. This soteriology developed quite early (Rom. 4:25, 6:1f.; Acts 3:14f.), perhaps from the "servant" motif and its application to Jesus' death and resurrection as a single event. The concept of suffering servant which probably originated with Jesus himself (Luke 22:37; Mark 10:45)[10] was picked up by the early church and applied to his death and resurrection as a single event in God's redemptive plan. Christ's death was thus the divine means of salvation, while his resurrection was God's vindication of that means.[11] Both Luke and John include

10. Cullmann believes this consciousness came upon Jesus at the time of his baptism (*Christology*, pp. 60 – 69). Longenecker says the New Testament does not make more use of the theme because it might be a "scandal for the Jew" and "foolishness to the Gentiles" (*Christology*, pp. 106 – 109).

11. The title *saviour* was not more common in the New Testament. It appears thrice in Lukan (Luke 2:11; Acts 5:31, 13:23) and twice in Johannine (John 4:42; 1 John 4:14) works and also in Philippians 3:20; Ephesians 5:23; 2 Timothy 1:10; Titus 1:4, 2:13, 3:16. It probably grew out of the combination of lordship with the soteriological force of the passion events and may well have developed from "the already common employment of the expression 'God's salvation' to signal the religious and historical aspects in the salvation Jesus brought" (Longenecker, p. 144).

this soteriological emphasis, John perhaps even more than Luke.

Since Jesus was both personal lord as well as cosmic and life-sustaining lord, New Testament writers easily progressed to the next stage of calling him divine "Lord." This step was natural once the *Kyrios* title was accorded him, for the LXX often connected "Lord" and "God" and the Hebrew term *'dny* and Aramaic term *mar* were commonly substituted for the supreme title *yhwh* in Jewish circles. Barrett says, "This confession (Jesus is Lord) was interpreted in terms of the Old Testament; where *Kyrios* = *theos* the fuller formula was close at hand. The title "Lord," was, in fact, more sacred in Jewish circles than "God." Jesus' divinity then probably was acknowledged very early in the Gospels when the writers called him Lord (see John 20:28 as well as Matt. 28:18, 20).[12]

The divinity theme eventually expanded to include two characteristics: Jesus' preexistence and universal lordship. His preexistence which probably originated in the Jewish period appears in verses such as Philippians 2:5; 1 Corinthians 8:6; Romans 1:3f.; 1 Peter 1:20; Hebrews 1:3; John 1:1. His universal lordship probably developed during the gentile-mission era when theology was freed up from the strictures of Jewish proselyte theology.[13] During this era Christians also began to apply hellenistic titles and concepts to Jesus (see 1 Cor. 12:3; Col. 1:15f.; John 1:18). The latter two especially were forged in the fires of dialogue and sought to portray

12. The name *God* was not given to Jesus until late in the development of the tradition. A list of verses which probably express this includes Hebrews 1:8f.; Romans 9:5; 2 Thessalonians 1:12; Titus 2:13; 2 Peter 1:1; John 1:1, 18. Taylor, Brown, and Longenecker believe this title came late because of the misunderstanding this title would have caused in Jewish circles (with their monotheism) and gentile circles (who would make him just another god). Although many (Dunn, Murphy-O'Connor) argue that Philippians 2:6–11 stems from wisdom concepts and does not include divine categories, we would argue strongly that the latter does not follow from the wisdom background. Rather, it was utilized to proclaim that very divinity.

13. All except the Corinthian and Johannine passages have a Jewish-Christian provenance. The motif probably developed as a result of reflection on both the divinity and the mission of Jesus; if he was "sent" by the Father, and if he himself was divine, then he must have existed "before the foundation of the world." This was paralleled by the descent/ascent theme (1 Peter 3:18f.; Eph. 4:8f.) and the incarnation motif (Phil. 2:6; John 1:14). These themes grew out of the complex progression in the early church from sonship to preexistence, which development included Lordship-divinity concepts and their application to Jesus as the "Sent One."

The idea of Jesus' universal lordship had its basis in the cosmic lordship theme discussed above in connection with Jewish Christianity. However, its complete development did not come until the Gentile mission, when a universalist theology removed the strictures of Jewish proselyte theology from the Christian sense of mission and lordship.

Jesus as universal Lord over all peoples by attributing to him the religious phraseology used in other faiths.

The theology of the resurrection was not closely linked with the church's mission either until the gentile-mission era. Philippians 2:9—11, for instance, which connects the two, universalizes the exaltation motif ("every knee shall bow"), yet states it in Jewish terms which probably originally described the actions of a proselyte. Full expression of the motif appears later in passages such as 1 Corinthians 12:3; 1 Timothy 3:16; and John 1:9, 10, 16 (universal lordship); as well as Acts where the strong sense of mission is directly connected with the resurrection (2:31f., 39; 13:29—39) and linked with the idea of witness (2:32; 3:15; 5:31f.; 10:39f.; 13:30f.). Apostleship was also directly connected with being a witness of the Risen Lord (Gal. 1:1; Acts 1:21f.). The resurrection thus provided the divine impetus for the church's mission to the world.

Gospel traditions also developed during this period as mission nuances began to influence the appearance stories. Matthew 28:18—20, for instance, stressed universal characteristics; Luke 24:47 and the commands of John 20:21 showed more authority. The mission elements of John 21:1—11 also became more important; Luke 24:36f. and possibly John 20:24f.'s corporeality themes acquired new significance. The doubt motif also became more prominent as did the eyewitness theme, especially since eyewitnesses of the resurrection were beginning to die and the event itself was fading in the corporate memory (cf. Matt. 28:17; Luke 24:36f.; John 20:24f.).

Many of these emphases continued in the epistles. The christological emphases, for instance, and the credal teachings were used by other New Testament writers, most of this in its original context. Basically, the only new theological emphasis that was added in this period, however, was the linking of resurrection theology to the relationship between the believer and the Lord.[14]

---

14. This is seen first in the resurrection of the saints (1 Cor. 15:12f.; Rom. 1:4, 6:5; etc.) which was employed both to comfort the persecuted and to correct the misguided. The new life of the believer is also likened to the death-life antithesis embodied in Jesus' death and resurrection (Rom. 6:9f.; 2 Cor. 4:10f.; etc.). In Pauline theology, the believer is made son and heir through Jesus' victory (Rom. 8:15f.; Gal. 4:5f.; etc.). Finally, the Christian has ethical demands made on him by the fact of the resurrection (1 Cor. 15:58; 2 Cor. 5:15; Col. 3:1f.; Heb. 12:1f.). These are also reflected in the developing Gospel traditions. The Spirit-Christ connection probably led to the emphasis noted in Luke 24:49, John 20:22; and the "living presence" aspect of Matthew 28:20 and of the Emmaus story (especially the bread and word motifs) finds impetus in this period.

In fact, the constant application of the theology of the resurrection narratives to the faith-needs of believers (such as in John 20) was the major work of the epistles.

The theology of the resurrection developed as the church added to and expanded the many motifs gleaned from the traditions. Still, what motifs out of all of this did the Gospel writers specifically choose to include in their accounts of the resurrection? We must attempt to separate between motifs in the church as a whole and redactional purposes of the individual writers (which may reflect only the ideas of a single individual). Mark stressed the flesh-spirit dichotomy in the resurrection, choosing to focus on Jesus' exaltation through the glorious affirmation of the empty tomb. The women's failure to understand brought in the misunderstanding motif which also pointed toward the vindication aspect of the resurrection. In all of this Mark chose two aspects of the tradition: Jesus as suffering servant and Jesus as triumphant Son of God. The combination of both of these elements teaches that suffering is a necessary prelude to victory, and victory vindicates any suffering.

This emphasis probably spoke directly to the needs of Mark's readers who may have been confused by conflicting christological views. They needed to know why Jesus first had to suffer as a servant before he could be vindicated as the Son of God. Mark's Gospel also assured persecuted Christians that victory would follow suffering. The resurrection narrative thus is a summary of these truths[15] especially since from the very beginning Mark viewed Jesus' death and resurrection as a single event.

Matthew added the apologetic motif to resurrection tradition, however this was probably not a completely new element. 1 Corinthians 15:5f., for instance, undoubtedly listed the appearances to combat false teaching as well as to vindicate the church's faith. Matthew confronted a specific controversy about the resurrection, namely the question of the empty tomb (27:62f., 28:11f.).

---

15. The ignorant purpose of the women going to the tomb (vv. 1–2) symbolized this constant misunderstanding on the part of Jesus' closest companions. The contrast between the question and its answer (vv. 3–4) pointed to the first glimmer of hope. The simplicity of the empty tomb is all the more vivid in the light of this ignorance. Finally, the contrast between the command (vv. 5–7) and the women's failure (v. 8) provided the final glimpse of the "Messianic misunderstanding," and (according to our theory) led to the final, absolute victory, when their fear was turned to joy by the Risen One himself (cf. Matt. 28:9–10).

Matthew also used the vindication motif to describe the battle as the Risen Lord triumphs over his enemies by means of his authority and teaching. Matthew's mission stress expanded to include the universal mission of the church as well as Jesus' cosmic lordship and omnipotence. This evangelist also stressed the promise-fulfillment motif of the early church and linked the resurrection event with the life and ministry of the earthly Jesus.[16] The exaltation is shown to have greater continuity with the earthly ministry than elsewhere (e.g., Mark seems to stress discontinuity— Jesus is not recognized as Messiah in his pre-resurrection). This continuity has progressively greater stress in Luke and John. Matthew wrote his Gospel during a time of great conflict between the church and synagogue. His resurrection account thus emphasized Christ's glory in the midst of opposition. Highlighted in this narrative are a series of three contrasts which lead ultimately to victory: (1) the posting of the guard at the tomb vs. the women who go to the tomb to anoint Jesus' body (27:62–28:1); (2) the fear of the guards vs. the joy of the women (28:2–10); and (3) the purposeful spreading of lies vs. the confident message of victory (28:11–20). Matthew combines both apologetic and missionary themes to answer critics as well as to evangelize both Jews and Gentiles.

Luke took the soteriological aspect of the resurrection and developed it in his work. He viewed the resurrection as an integral part of Jesus' passion event, in fact, a necessary prelude even for understanding the cross. He also added an ecclesiastical emphasis, showing how Jesus' life and teaching applied to church mission through the authority of the Risen One. Included in this ecclesiastical emphasis were two important elements, witness and worship, which Luke highlighted in a new way for the church which was already concerned about its dying eyewitnesses.

The themes point to the Lukan situation; even if written in the early 60s (a viable possibility in light of the ending of Acts), Luke would have had to deal with the passing of the eyewitnesses. Luke therefore grounded past testimony and the continuing witness of the Lord not in past testimony but in the living presence of the Risen One, in the gift of the Holy Spirit and his witness through

16. This fulfillment theme was an early emphasis and may well have been part of the tradition from the beginning. Matthew, however, expanded Mark's fulfillment theme (cp. Mark 16:7) and gave it greater emphasis.

the community. This is seen in the structure of his work; the setting of his entire chapter in Jerusalem looked to the future importance of Jerusalem as the center of the mission and to the forgiveness of those who opposed Jesus. He also prepared for the recognition motif at Emmaus (vv. 30f.) by a continuing series of doubts and puzzlement on the part of the women, the disciples, Peter, and the two followers.

Luke's Christology emphasized Jesus' messianic nature, especially the sovereign authority behind the suffering Messiah (vv. 7, 26, 46). The resurrection was an event which looked forward to Jesus' continuing message in the church's mission as well as his final glorification in the parousia. Luke's apologetic motif produced two effects: (1) the empty tomb itself became its own kind of proof of the reality of the resurrection (24:12), and (2) Jesus' corporeality was emphasized probably in response to a growing docetic influence in the church (vv. 36f.).

John provided the ultimate expression of soteriology in the resurrection narratives. In his Gospel "belief" and "seeing" became synonymous terms of salvation; both came to full expression in the resurrection. Jesus' earthly "glory" proleptically presupposed his post-resurrection exaltation, and because of this the empty tomb achieved its highest significance. The "beloved," for example, came to faith because of the empty tomb even though he did not yet understand what faith meant (20:8f.).[17]

John's expression of the relationship between doubt and faith is the most complete of all the evangelists. Chapter 20 is structured around that theme and John's entire resurrection discourse centers around the removal of doubt and the awakening of faith which achieves fullest expression in "seeing" not based on visible "proof." (v. 29.)[18]

Christology, apologetics, eschatology, mission, and sacramental elements are all subservient to soteriology in John. Jesus' divine nature and messianic sonship can be perceived only by faith. Any

17. The relation between doubt and faith found dramatic expression in the Thomas episode. Mark stressed the doubt aspect (16:8) and both Matthew and Luke showed how it is removed, Matthew through the physical presence of the Risen One (28:17) and Luke through the physical reality of the Risen One (24:36f.).

18. The "beloved" finds faith without seeing (20:3 – 10); Mary must hear the summons of the Good Shepherd (vv. 11 – 18); the Twelve must see him (vv. 19f.); and Thomas, greatest sceptic of them all, demands to feel his wounds (vv. 24f.).

physical proof of Christ's resurrection simply points the way to victory over unbelief. The present privileges of the kingdom age are God's gifts of salvation. The mission, of course, is a part of God's call to salvation. And finally, any so-called liturgical elements (the time notes in 20:1, 19, 26) are based on the results of a living faith. Many of the themes discussed previously come to their fullest expression in John—the divinity, universal lordship, and exaltation of the Messiah—and all are related to the resurrection. In fact, John more than any other evangelist attempted to show how the post-resurrection "glory" of the Risen Lord was proleptically present in the earthly Jesus; however, it was open only to the eye of faith and could not be understood by those around Jesus. The continuity between the earthly Jesus and the Christ of faith was increasingly stressed as the years went by and the eyewitnesses were no longer present to validate the church's message.

The *Sitz im Leben* of John's resurrection account, especially chapter 21, probably includes the author's desire to prepare his readers for the disappearance of eyewitness authority, as well as to remind them of their own responsibility as witnesses. He thus took the story about Jesus' appearance to the fishermen and applied it to the needs of his day, stressing its call to mission as well as ecclesiology. The fishing scene was given a more extensive mission emphasis (see chap. 7), and the fellowship scene was highlighted (vv. 12 – 13) to emphasize the living presence of the Risen Lord in the community. John then added terminological variation to the threefold scene of verses 15 – 17 to illustrate the all-inclusiveness of the pastoral duties of the church. Finally, the emphasis on "follow me" in the last two pericopes (vv. 19, 20, 22) alluded to the duty of the church in the post-witness era.

Later, during or shortly after the Neronian persecution, there developed the Peter sermon of John 21. This (as mentioned in chap. 5) probably originated shortly after his death, in accordance with his status as the leading disciple/apostle and possibly due to the strange proverb of verses 18 – 19. The original sermon contained three pericopes, John 21:1 – 14, 15 – 17, and 18 – 19 and was connected with the reinstatement of Peter and his part in the missionary movement.

Alsup has done an extensive study of the resurrection narratives which includes parallels in hellenistic, Old Testament, and Jewish literature. His conclusion is that Jewish anthropomorphic stories provide the basic background for the resurrection narratives as well as their *Gattung*. These were used as guidelines for story-development since all the stories contain some of the same elements such as verbs of seeing, encounter, and action; participant reaction, recognition or nonrecognition; Jesus' appearance; his words of address; reaction and rejoinder; and culmination. The stories themselves include both group appearances which feature the commission motif, and other appearances which feature the meal motif (except for the Magdalene pericope), their purpose being to show how Christ's appearances were a part of God's self-disclosure throughout the ages.

Alsup's conclusions are appropriate; however he is not as positive about the historical basis of Gospel development as he should be.[19] Any redaction in the resurrection accounts (as we have sought to demonstrate) should in no way detract from their solid historical nucleus.

History, Interpretation, and Preaching Today

In the final analysis, what is the difference between history and interpretation? History can only affirm, after all, that Jesus who was crucified was seen alive after the event. Various theories can suggest how the tomb where he was buried was found empty three days after the crucifixion, but all these theories are not persuasive enough to warrant dismissing the resurrection accounts of the Gospels themselves.[20]

The evidence in fact, strongly suggests from the beginning a physical resurrection. This historical evidence is sufficient to warrant acceptance of the "witness" of the narratives to the literal appearances of Jesus after his death on the cross. *Resurrection* as a term then, achieves its fullest definition in the New Testament

19. Alsup says his study precludes definite decisions regarding historicity, though he tends to be positive about it.

20. We could postulate that the early disciples stole the body and proclaimed the tomb empty or that Jesus merely swooned on the cross and was later revived. We could also theorize that the appearances were visions rather than physical appearances, either subjective (more dreams) or objective (an actual revelation from God) or that the entire thing was a mythological creation on the part of the early church. However, as we argued at the beginning of this chapter, there is no warrant, on the basis of the New Testament evidence, for such attempts to reinterpret the resurrection.

as "the transformation of the human body of the dead Jesus to the glorified body of the Risen Christ" (cf. 1 Cor. 15).

What about all the theological redaction that was added to these resurrection narratives; does this detract from their historical validity? Did the early church have a right to use the resurrection as a springboard for soteriological interpretations, missionary emphases, messianic motifs, and lordship developments? Here the historian enters his most difficult area and becomes "believer." Here also we note the necessary relation between faith and history.

Any decision about the historical validity of these accounts must first take into consideration Jesus' own evaluation of himself; if he himself provided the basis for interpretive categories they probably are appropriate. He did, of course; thus soteriology in the later church is a reflection of Jesus' own teachings on the suffering servant Messiah.[21] Lordship in church theology likewise reflects the divine-exalted consciousness of the earthly Jesus.

Jesus' mission consciousness also connects with later motifs of the church; even the Gentile mission and its universalism is proselyte theology.[22] This does not invalidate the interpretation of the community that the resurrection led to a universal mission. The leading of the community by God through the Holy Spirit, itself an event in salvation-history (note the argument throughout Acts regarding the role of the Holy Spirit in the genesis of the church and her mission), is sufficient to establish the validity of this theme; and it derives its authority from both the command (Matt. 28:19) and promise (Luke 24:49; John 20:22) of the Risen One.

Even the interpretation of the early church is historically valid then; each step, from messiahship to lordship to divinity to mission proceeds logically from the resurrection in authenticating both the teaching and self-consciousness of the earthly Jesus. Of

21. This, of course, is another area where "faith" must enter the historical decision, although that "faith" has an objective basis in the historical evidence. We have attempted to do this, of course, whenever possible. We have shown, for instance, the continuity between the soteriological interpretation of the later church and the suffering Servant messiology of Jesus.

22. For example, Schweitzer (Jesus, p. 78) asserts that "Jesus ... pictured the expected influx of the gentiles in the imagery of Isaiah 2:2ff.; 66:19ff.; that is, they were expected to pour into Zion and join themselves to Israel." See also Jeremias, Theology, I, pp. 133–34, and Nations, pp. 23 and 212f., where he discounts Mark 13:10, 14:9 as Markan redactions, contra Cranfield, Mark, p. 398; Kummel, Promise, pp. 84f.; Martin, Mark, pp. 223–24. I, of course, would align myself with the latter group.

course, this does bring faith into the arena of risk, but we would argue that this is inherent within the New Testament understanding of faith. It cannot achieve certainty with respect to either past or future, but relies on "trust" with regard to both event and promise.

Many works have been written about the relationship between New Testament language and contemporary preaching.[23] Fuller, in particular, writes about the relationship between the historical resurrection and today by quoting from Schniewind:

> There is another incident which the present writer recalls from his student days at Marburg in 1906. On Ascension Day he went to the service of the Christenberg. Great crowds were flocking thither, attracted by the display of traditional costumes in the procession; most of them were people who had little sympathy with the Christian religion. Would the preacher, one wondered, be able to proclaim the message of "Christ the King" in a way which the crowds could understand? Alas, we were given a naive picture of a literal ascension, such as a non-Christian would dismiss as mere myth. Even Luther poured scorn on such literalism: "Oh that heaven of the charlatans with its golden stool and Christ sitting at the Father's side vested in a choir cope and a golden crown, as the painters love to portray him."
>
> [187,8]

Schniewind's "naive scientism" itself is most likely at fault here since nothing in the New Testament portrayal of the resurrection is intrinsically impossible either scientifically or historically. Modern man tries to fit the biblical picture into a false mold of his own making. In fact, when one notes the growth of interest in the supernatural and the occult today, one realizes that there is nothing in the "secular attitude" which demands the removal of the supernatural element in the New Testament.

The preacher today, however, should not proclaim a rigidly historical resurrection. The event is still the launching pad for the sermon, its true significance evident in its existential implications

23. These include Bultmann's radical demythologization, which removes the resurrection from the scene and replaces it with the significance of the cross; Barth's emphasis on the "mystery" of the transcendent revelation of the historical Jesus; Künneth's exaltation Christology and its ontological implications for man today; and Léon-Dufour's complex discussion of the hermeneutics of resurrection.

for faith today. The preacher must at all times stress the relevance of the resurrection for modern man, and in this I essentially agree with the basic need for interpretation as stressed in Fuller, Künneth, and Léon-Dufour.[24] However, we disagree with Fuller and Léon-Dufour, who combat the "naive" presentation of the pericopes as literal events. Rather, both elements, history and interpretation, are necessary in a presentation of the relevance of the resurrection for modern man in the "secular city." Man needs to know there is a transcendent possibility, an answer to his/her secular dilemma and frustration. One needs to see the applicability of first-century problems and their answer to his/her needs. Jansen, in his discussion of "appropriating the message of the resurrection" (pp. 138 – 50), borrows from Emil Brunner the symbols of faith (Easter as a valid past event), hope (Easter as the promise of divine intervention in our world), and love (Easter as demanding a new communal fellowship).

The empty tomb, for instance, validates both a transcendent reversal of death as well as God's intervention on the human plane. The resurrection is evidence of the "eschatological transformation" (Fuller) of human existence and becomes the basis of Christian hope. The appearances feed into this hope; in Paul's words, "If Christ has not been raised, then our preaching is in vain and your faith is in vain" (1 Cor. 15:14).

Mary's frustration (John 20:2, 11f.) and the disciples' race to the tomb (Luke 24:12 and John 20:3 – 10) become a portrait of modern man's spiritual trauma and search for reality. John's faith in the midst of doubt becomes the hope of people today who must "see" without the physical signs of Jesus' nail-scarred hands or sword-pierced side. The men on the way to Emmaus show how people today can meet Christ in the spoken word and Eucharistic fellowship. The believer is called to "joy" in the midst of table fellowship and our experience of the living presence of Jesus in that event. Likewise, we recognize the transcendent glory of the Risen One in the midst of mission, and his presence and authority in mission are with the church today just as they were with the disciples of

24. See Fuller, pp. 182 – 88; Künneth, chapters 3 – 5. Léon-Dufour, in chapter 11 on the hermeneutics of the early community, attempts to translate the Semitic and hellenistic mythical thought-patterns into the language of this day; his attempt entails his centering on the concepts "resurrection" and "exaltation" and their significance for Jesus' personal lordship in this age.

the first century. To this end we have been given "power from on high" in the presence and activity of the Holy Spirit as we fulfill this task (Luke 24:49, John 20:22 – 23). Our duty is to obey the directions of the Risen One (John 21:1 – 14) and to shed abroad his love to those around us (John 21:15 – 17). Our privilege is to "follow" as he leads (John 21:18 – 23) and to trust his guidance.

The resurrection is relevant today. It is a part of history yet transcends history as it becomes a present experience of joy, power, fellowship, and trust which raises us above the mundane problems of earthly existence. Still, the fact that Jesus lives and dwells among us today does not mean the Christian avoids facing problems in the world because he is "above" them. Rather, it means he meets those problems and deals with them in the strength of Christ's presence. It demands that we build a better world now, not that we ignore this world and concentrate on the next. The social Gospel and evangelistic mission exist side-by-side; they are not mutually incompatible. This is the reality of the resurrection message today.

Bibliography

Primary Sources and Reference Works

The Holy Bible: Revised Standard Version. Glasgow, 1946, 1952.

Blass, F. and Debrunner, A. *A Greek Grammar of the New Testament and Other Early Christian Literature.* Translated by R. W. Funk. Cambridge, 1961.

The Greek New Testament. Edited by K. Aland, M. Black, B. Metzger, A. Wikgren, and C. M. Martini. Stuttgart, 1966.

Hatch, E. and Redpath. H. A. *A Concordance to the Septuagint and the Other Greek Versions of the Old Testament.* 2 vols. Graz, 1954.

Josephus, *Antiquities.* Translated by W. Whiston. Philadelphia, 1957.

Kittel, R., ed. *Biblia Hebraica.* 3d ed. Stuttgart, 1961.

Metzger, B. M. *A Textual Commentary on the Greek New Testament.* London, 1971.

Morgenthaler, R. *Statistik des neutestamentlichen Wortschatzes.* Frankfurt, 1958.

Moulton, J. H. *A Grammar of New Testament Greek,* Vol. 1. Prolegomena. Edinburgh, 1957, orig. 1908.

_____ and Howard, W. F. *A Grammar of New Testament Greek.* Vol. 2. Accidence and Word Formation with an Appendix on Semitisms in the New Testament. Edinburgh, 1956, orig. 1927.

_____ and Turner, N. *A Grammar of New Testament Greek,* Vol. 3. Syntax. Edinburgh, 1963.

_____ . *A Grammar of New Testament Greek,* Vol. 4. Style. Edinburgh, 1976.

Moulton, W. F. and A. S. Geden. *A Concordance to the Greek Testament.* 3d ed. Edinburgh, 1957, orig. 1926.

Novum Testamentum Graece. 26th ed. Edited by E. Nestle and K. Aland. Stuttgart, 1979.

Robertson, A. T. *A Grammar of the Greek New Testament in the Light of Historical Research*. Nashville, 1934.

Synopsis Quattuor Evangeliorum, 10th ed. Edited by K. Aland. Stuttgart, 1978.

Monographs, Commentaries and Articles

Abbott, E. A. *Diatessarica: Notes on New Testament Criticism*. London, 1907.

————. *Diatessarica: The Son of Man*. London, 1910.

Achtemeier, P. J. "Gospel Miracle Tradition and the Divine Man." *Interp* 26(1972): 174—97.

————. " 'He taught them many things': Reflections on Markan Christology." *CBQ* 42(1980): 465—81.

————. "The Lukan Perspective on the Miracles of Jesus: A Preliminary Sketch." In *Perspectives on Luke-Acts*. Edited by C. H. Talbert. Danville, VA, 1978.

Ackroyd, P. R. "The 153 Fishes in John XXI. 11—A Further Note." *JTS* n.s. 10(1959): 94.

Aland, K. "Neue neutestamentlich Papyri II." *NTS* 12(1966): 193—210.

————. "Bemerkungen zum Schluss des Markusevangeliums." In *Neotestamentica et Semitica*. Edited by E. E. Ellis and M. Wilcox. Edinburgh, 1969.

————. "Der wiedergefundene Markusschluss? Eine methodologische Bemerkung zur textkritische Arbeit." *ZTK* 67(1970): 3—13.

Albright, W. F. "Recent Discoveries in Palestine and the Gospel of John." In *The Background of the New Testament and Its Eschatology*. Edited by D. Daube and W. D. Davies. Cambridge, 1956.

————. and Mann, C. S. *Matthew*. AB. New York, 1971.

Allen, E. L. "The Lost Kerygma." *NTS* 3(1957): 349—53.

Allen, W. C. *A Critical and Exegetical Commentary on the Gospel According to Matthew*. 3d ed. ICC, Edinburgh, 1922.

Allworthy. T. B. *Women in the Apostolic Church*. Cambridge, 1917.

Alsup, J. E. *The Post-Resurrection Appearance Stories of the Gospel Tradition: A History-of-Tradition Analysis*. Ph.D. Dissertation. Univ. of Munich, 1973.

Althaus, P. "Fact and Faith in the Kerygma." In *Jesus of Nazareth*, edited by C. F. H. Henry. London, 1966.

————. *Fact and Faith in the Kerygma Today*. Philadelphia, 1959.

Anderson, H. "The Easter Witness of the Evangelists." In *The New Testament in Historical and Contemporary Perspective*. Edited by H. Anderson and W. Barclay. G. H. C. MacGregor Festschrift. Oxford, 1965.

Annand, R. " 'He was seen of Cephas.' A Suggestion about the First Resurrection Appearance of Peter." *SJT* 11(1958): 180—87.

Appold, Mark L. *The Oneness Motif in the Fourth Gospel.* Tübingen, 1976.

Argyle, A. W. "The Heavenly Session of Christ." *Theol* 55(1952): 286—89.

————. "The Ascension." *ET* 66(1954—55): 240—42.

————. *The Gospel According to Matthew.* CBC. Cambridge, 1963.

Armstrong, W. P. "The Resurrection and the Origin of the Church in Jerusalem." *PTR* 5(1907): 1—25.

————. "The Resurrection of Jesus and Historical Criticism." *PTR* 8(1910): 247—70.

Auer, E. G. *Der dritte Tag.* Metzingen, 1970.

Bacon, B. W. *The Story of St. Paul.* London, 1905.

————. *The Fourth Gospel in Research and Debate.* New Haven, 1918.

————. "The Resurrection in the Judean and Galilean Traditions." *JR* 11(1931): 506—16.

Bailey, J. A. *The Traditions Common to the Gospels of Luke and John.* SNT. Leiden, 1963.

Bammel, E. "Herkunft und Funktion der Traditionselemente in I Kor. 15. 1—11." *TZ* 11(1955): 401—19.

Banks, R. J. "Setting 'The Quest for the Historical Jesus' in a Broader Framework." In *Gospel Perspectives II,* edited by R. T. France and D. Wenham. Sheffield, 1981. [61—82].

Barbour, R. S. "Recent Study of the Gospel According to Mark." *ET* 79(1968): 324—29.

————. *Tradition-historical Criticism of the Gospels.* London, 1972.

Barr, James. *The Semantics of Biblical Language.* Oxford, 1961.

Barrett, C. K. *A Commentary on the Epistle to the Romans.* London, 1957.

————. "The Background of Mark 10:45." In *New Testament Essays in Honour of T. W. Manson,* edited by A. J. B. Higgins. Manchester, 1959.

————. *Luke the Historian in Recent Study.* London, 1961.

————. *The Pastoral Epistles.* Oxford, 1963.

————. *New Testament Essays.* London, 1972.

Barth, G. "Matthew's Understanding of the Law." In G. Bornkamm, G. Barth, and H. J. Held, *Tradition and Interpretation in Matthew,* translated by P. Scott. London, 1963.

Barth, K. *The Resurrection from the Dead.* Translated by H. J. Stenning. New York, 1933.

————. *Church Dogmatics.* Edited by G. W. Bromiley and T. F. Torrance. 4 vols. in 12. Edinburgh, 1936—62.

Bartsch, H. W. "Early Christian Eschatology in the Synoptic Gospels." *NTS* 11(1965): 387 – 97.

Beare, F. W. *The First Epistle of Peter.* Oxford, 1961.

Beasley-Murray, G. R. *Baptism in the New Testament.* Exeter, 1962.

Benoit, P. "L'Ascension." *RevB* 56(1949): 161 – 203. Summarized in his "The Ascension of Christ." *ThDig* 8(1960): 105 – 110.

_____. *The Passion and Resurrection of Jesus Christ.* Translated by B. Weatherhead. London, 1969.

_____. "Marie-Madeleine et les Disciples au Tombeau selon Jn. 20:1 – 18." In *Judentum, Urchristentum, Kirche*—Festschrift for Joachim Jeremias. Berlin, 1970.

Berger, K. "Zum traditionsgeschichtlichen Hintergrund christologischen Hoheitstitel." *NTS* 17(1971): 391 – 425.

Berguer, G. *Some Aspects of the Life of Jesus.* London, 1923.

Bernard, J. H. "St. Paul's Doctrine of the Resurrection." *Exp* 5(1908): 403 – 16, 491 – 504.

_____. *The Gospel According to St. John.* ICC. 2 vols. Edinburgh, 1928.

Best, E. *The Temptation and the Passion: The Markan Soteriology.* Cambridge, 1965.

_____. *A Commentary on the First and Second Epistles to the Thessalonians.* BNTC. London, 1970.

_____. *I Peter.* NCB. London, 1971.

_____. "The Role of the Disciples in Mark." *NTS* 23(1977): 377 – 401.

Betz, H. D. "The Origin and Nature of the Christian Faith According to the Emmaus Legend." *Interp* 23(1969): 32 – 46.

Betz, O. *What Do We Know About Jesus?.* Translated by M. Kohl. London, 1968.

Bilezikian, Gilbert C. *The Liberated Gospel: A Comparison of the Gospel of Mark and Greek Tragedy.* Grand Rapids, 1977.

Bishop, E. F. F. "The Risen Christ and the 500 Brethren (I Cor. 15,6)." *CBQ* 18(1956): 341 – 44.

Black, M. *An Aramaic Approach to the Gospels and Acts.* Oxford, 1957.

_____, "The Maranatha Invocation and Jude 14 – 15 (I Enoch 1:9)." In *Christ and Spirit in the New Testament,* edited by B. Lindars and S. Smalley—Festschrift for C. F. D. Moule. Cambridge, 1973.

Blinzler, J. *Johannes und die Synoptiker.* SBS. Stuttgart, 1965.

Bode, E. L. *The First Easter Morning.* Rome, 1970.

Boismard, M. E. "Le chapître XXI de saint Jean. Essai de critique littéraire." *RevB* 54(1947): 473 – 501.

_____. "Saint Luc et la rédaction du Quatrième Évangile." *RevB* 69(1962): 185—211.

Boomershine, T. E. and G. L. Bartholomew. "The Narrative Technique of Mark 16:8." *JBL* 100. no. 2(1981): 213—23.

_____. "Mark 16:8 and the Apostolic Commission." *JBL* 100. no. 2(1981): 225—39.

Bonhoeffer, D. *Christology.* Translated by J. Bowden. London, 1963.

Bornkamm, G. "Des Bekenntnis im Hebräerbrief." *Theologische Blätter* 21(1942): 63—80.

_____. "Zum Verständnis des Christus-Hymnus Phil. 2,6—11." In *Studien zu Antike und Urchristentum, Gesämelte Aufsatze II.* Munich, 1959.

_____. *Jesus of Nazareth.* Translated by I and F. McCluskey. London, 1960.

_____, G. Barth, and H. J. Held. *Tradition and Interpretation in Matthew.* Translated by P. Scott. London, 1963.

_____. *Early Christian Experience.* London, 1969.

_____. "The Risen Lord and the Earthly Jesus—Matthew 28:16—20." In *The Future of Our Religious Past,* edited by J. M. Robinson. London, 1971.

_____. *Paul.* Translated by D. M. G. Stalker, New York, 1971.

Bousset, W. *Kyrios Christos.* 2d ed. Translated by J. E. Steely. Nashville, 1970, orig. 1921.

Bowman, J. "Samaritan Studies." *BJRL* 40(1958): 298—329.

Bratcher, P. G. "*Akouō* in Acts ix. 7 and xxii. 9." *ET* 71(1960): 243—45.

Braun, F. M. *Jean le Theologien et son Evangile dans l'Eglise Ancienne.* Etudes Bibliques, 1959.

_____. *Jean le Theologien et les grandes Traditions d'Israel.* Paris, 1964.

Braun, H. "Die Messianologie in Qumran und in Neuen Testament." In *Qumran und das Neue Testament.* 2 vols. Tübingen, 1966.

Broer, I. "Zur heutigen Diskussion der Grabes geschichte." *BibLeb* 10(1969): 40—52.

_____. *Die Urgemeinde und das Grab Jesu.* StANT. München, 1972.

Brown, E. S. "The Role of the Prologues in Determining the Purpose of Luke-Acts." In *Perspectives on Luke-Acts,* edited by C. H. Talbert. Danville, VA, 1978.

Brown, R. E. The Problem of Historicity in John." *CBQ* 24(1962): 1—14.

_____. "The Johannine Sacramentality Reconsidered." *ThSt* 23(1962): 183—206.

_____. "The Paraclete in the Fourth Gospel." *NTS* 13(1967): 113—32.

_____. "John 21 and the First Appearance to Peter," In *Resurrexit,* edited by E. Dhanis. Rome, 1974.

_____. *The Gospel According to John.* AB. London, 1971.

_____, ed. by *Peter in the New Testament*. New York, 1973.

Brownlee, William H. "Whence the Gospel According to John?" In *John and Qumram*, edited by J. H. Charlesworth. London, 1972.

Bruce, F. F. *The Speeches in the Acts of the Apostles*. London, 1943.

_____. "The End of the Second Gospel." *EQ* 17(1945): 169–81.

_____. *The Spreading Flame*. Grand Rapids, 1953.

_____. *Commentary on the Epistle to the Hebrews*. London, 1964.

_____. *Commentary on the Book of Acts*. 2d ed. London, 1965.

_____. *1 and 2 Corinthians*. NCB. London, 1971.

Bultmann, R. *Theology of the New Testament*. Tr. K. Grobel. 2 vols. London, 1952–55.

_____. *Kerygma and Myth I*. Edited by H. W. Bartsch. Translated by R. H. Fuller. London, 1953.

_____. *Jesus Christ and Mythology*. New York, 1958.

_____. *The History of the Synoptic Tradition*. Translated by J. Marsh. Oxford, 1963.

_____. *The Gospel of John, A Commentary*. Translated by G. R. Beasley-Murray. Oxford, 1971.

Burkitt, F. C. *Christian Beginnings*. London, 1924.

Burney, C. F. "Christ as the ARXH of Creation." *JTS* 27(1926): 160–67.

Cadbury, H. J. "The Titles of Jesus in Acts," and "Commentary on the Preface of Luke." In *The Beginnings of Christianity*, edited by F. J. Foakes-Jackson and K. Lake. 5 vols. London, 1920–33.

_____. "Mark 16.8." *JBL* 46(1927): 344–45.

_____. *The Making of Luke-Acts*. 2d ed. London, 1968.

Caird, G. B. *The Gospel of St. Luke*. 2d ed. London, 1968.

Calvert, R. S. A. "An Examination of the Criteria for Distinguishing the Authentic Words of Jesus." *NTS* 18(1972): 209–19.

von Campenhausen, H. *Tradition and Life in the Church*. Translated by A. V. Littledale. London, 1968.

Carson, D. A. "Current Source Criticism of the Fourth Gospel: Some Methodological Questions." *JBL* 97. no. 3(1978): 411–29.

_____. "Historical Tradition in the Fourth Gospel: After Dodd, What?" In *Gospel Perspectives II*, edited by R. T. France and D. Wenham. Sheffield, 1981.

_____. *Divine Sovereignty and Human Responsibility: Biblical Perspective in Tension*. Atlanta, 1981.

Cassian, S. B. "John XXI." *NTS* 3(1956–57): 132–36.

Catchpole, D. "Tradition Criticism." In *New Testament Interpretation*, edited by I. H. Marshall. Grand Rapids, 1977.

_____. "The Fearful Silence of the Women at the Tomb: A Study in Markan Theology." *JTSA* 18(1977): 3–10.

Chapman, J. "We Know that His Testimony is True." *JTS* 31(1930): 379–87.

Charlesworth, J. H. "A Critical Comparison of the Dualism in 1QS 3:13–4:26 and the 'Dualism' Contained in the Gospel of John." *John and Qumran*, edited by J. H. Charlesworth. London, 1972.

Chavesse, C. "Not on the Mountain Appointed." *Theol* 74(1971): 478.

Chilton, B. "Announcement in Nazara: An Analysis of Luke 4:16–21." In *Gospel Perspectives*, Vol. 2. Edited by R. T. France and D. Wenham. Sheffield, 1981.

Clark, N. *Interpreting the Resurrection.* London, 1967.

Coneybeare, F. C. "The Eusebian Form of the Text, Matt. 28.19." *ZNW* 1(1901): 275–88.

Conzelmann, H. *The Theology of Luke.* Translated by G. Buswell. London, 1960.

_____. "Zur Analyze der Bekenntnisformel I Kor. 15,3–5." *EvTh* 25(1965): 1–10. Translated as "On the Analysis of the Confessional Formula in I Cor. 15.3–5." *Interp* 20(1966): 15–25.

_____. *An Outline of the Theology of the New Testament.* Translated by J. Bowden. London, 1969.

_____. *Der erste Brief an die Korinther.* Göttingen, 1969. ET *I Corinthians.* Translated by J. W. Leitch. Philadelphia, 1975.

Craig, W. L. "The Empty Tomb of Jesus," In *Gospel Perspectives*, Vol. 2. Edited by R. T. France and D. Wenham. Sheffield, 1981.

_____. "The Historicity of the Resurrection of Jesus." Unpublished manuscript. A popular version is his *The Son Rises: The Historical Evidence for the Resurrection of Jesus.* Chicago, 1981.

Crossan, J. D. "Mark and the Relatives of Jesus." *NovT.* 15(1973): 81–113.

Cullmann, O. *Early Christian Worship.* Translated by A. S. Todd and J. B. Torrance. London, 1953.

_____. *Baptism in the New Testament.* Translated by J. K. S. Reid. London, 1950.

_____. *The Christology of the New Testament.* Translated by S. Guthrie and C. Hall. London, 1959.

_____. *Peter: Disciple, Apostle, Martyr.* London, 1962.

_____. "The Breaking of the Bread and the Resurrection Appearances." In *Essays on the Lord's Supper.* Translated by J. G. Davies. Richmond, 1958.

_____. "L'Evangile Johannique et l'Histoire du Salut." *NTS* 11(1965): 111–22.

Culpepper, R. Alan. *The Johannine School.* Missoula, Mont. 1975.

Cupitt, D. and C. F. D. Moule, "The Resurrection: A Disagreement." *Theol* 75(1972): 507 – 19.

Curtis, K. P. G. "Luke xxiv. 12 and John xx. 3 – 10." *JTS* 22(1971): 512 – 15.

Dalman, G. H. *The Words of Jesus.* Translated by D. M. Kay. Edinburgh, 1909.

Dalton, W. J. *Christ's Proclamation to the Spirits: A Study of I Peter 3:18 – 4:6.* Rome, 1965.

Danielou, J. *Theology of Jewish Christianity.* Translated by J. A. Baker. Chicago, 1964.

Danker, F. W. *Jesus and the New Age According to St. Luke.* St. Louis, 1972.

D'Arc, J. "Catechesis on the Road to Emmaus." *LumVit* 32(1977): 143 – 56.

_____"Un grand jeu d'inclusions dans 'les pelerins d'Emmaus,' " *NouRelTh* 99(1977): 62 – 76.

Davies, W. D. *Paul and Rabbinic Judaism.* London, 1948.

_____. *The Setting of the Sermon on the Mount.* Cambridge, 1964.

_____. *Invitation to the New Testament.* London, 1967.

_____. *The Gospel and the Land.* Berkeley, 1979.

Delling, G. "The Significance of the Resurrection of Jesus for Faith in Jesus Christ." In *The Significance of the Message of the Resurrection for Faith in Jesus Christ,* edited by C. F. D. Moule, SBT. London, 1968.

Dibelius, M. *From Tradition to Gospel.* Translated by B. L. Woolf. London, 1934.

_____. *Gospel Criticism and Christology.* London, 1935.

_____. *Studies in the Acts of the Apostles.* Translated by M. Ling. New York, 1956.

Dillon, R. J. *From Eye-Witnesses to Ministers of the Word: Tradition and Composition in Luke 24.* An Bib SL. Rome, 1978.

von Dobschütz, E. *Ostern und Pfingsten.* Leipzig, 1903.

Dodd, C. H. "Note on Jn. 21, 24" *JTS* n.s. 4(1953): 212 – 13.

_____. *The Interpretation of the Fourth Gospel.* Cambridge, 1953.

_____. "The Appearance of the Risen Christ: An Essay in Form Criticism." In *Studies in the Gospels,* edited by D. E. Nineham. Oxford, 1957. Essays in Memory of R. H. Lightfoot. Reprinted in his *More New Testament Studies.* London, 1968.

_____. "Some Johannine 'Herrenworte' with Parallels in the Synoptic Gospels." *NTS* 2(1955 – 56): 75 – 86.

_____. *Historical Tradition in the Fourth Gospel.* Cambridge, 1963.

Driver, G. R. "Two Problems in the New Testament." *JTS* n.s. 16(1965): 327 – 37.

Dunn, J. D. G. "The Messianic Secret in Mark." *TB* 21(1970): 92 – 117.

_____. *Christology in the Making.* Philadelphia, 1980.

Dupont, J. "Le repas d'Emmaus." LumVie 31(1957): 77–92.

―――――. "Anelemphthe (Ac. i. 2)." NTS 8(1962): 154–57.

Ehrhardt, A. A. J. "The Disciples of Emmaus." NTS 10(1963–64): 197–200.

Elliott, J. K. "The Text and Language of the Endings to St. Mark's Gospel." ThZ 27(1971): 255–62.

Ellis, E. E. "Present and Future Eschatology in Luke." NTS 12(1965): 27–41.

―――――. The Gospel of Luke. London, 1966.

Ellis, I. P. "But Some Doubted." NTS 14(1968): 574–80.

Emerton, J. A. "The 153 Fishes in John XXI. 11." JTS n.s. 9(1958): 86–89; and n.s. 11(1960): 335–36.

―――――. "Binding and Loosing—Forgiving and Retaining." JTS n.s. 13(1962): 325–31.

Evans, C. F. "I Will Go Before You into Galilee." JTS n.s. 5(1954), 3–18.

―――――. Resurrection and the New Testament. London, 1970.

Evans, T. E. "The Verb 'Agapao' in the Fourth Gospel." In Studies in the Fourth Gospel, edited by F. L. Cross, London, 1957.

Falk, Z. W. "Private Law." In The Jewish People in the First Century, Vol. 1. Edited by S. Safrai and M. Stern. Philadelphia, 1976, 504–33.

Farrer, A. A Study in St. Mark. London, 1954.

Feuillet, A. "La découverte du tombeau vide en Jean 20, 3–10 et la Foi au Christ ressuscité." EspVie 87. no. 19(1977): 273–84.

―――――. "Le Saint Suaice de Turin et les Evangiles. La Passion et la Résurrection: un unique mystère salvifique." EspVie 89. no. 28(1979): 401–16.

Filson, F. V. "Who Was the Beloved Disciple?" JBL 68(1949): 83–88.

―――――. A Commentary on the Gospel According to St. Matthew BNTC. London, 1960.

―――――. New Testament History. London, 1965.

Finegan, J. The Archeology of the New Testament. Princeton, 1969.

Fitzmyer, J. A. The Gospel According to Luke I–IX. Anchor Bible. Garden City, 1981.

Flemington, W. F. The New Testament Doctrine of Baptism. London, 1964.

Flender, H. Saint Luke: Theologian of Redemptive History. Translated by R. H. and I. Fuller. Philadelphia, 1967.

Flusser, D. "Two Notes on the Midrash on 2 Sam. vii." IFJ 9(1959): 107–9.

Forestell, J. The Word of the Cross: Salvation as Revelation in the Fourth Gospel. AB 57. Rome, 1974.

Fortna, R. T. The Gospel of Signs. NTM. Cambridge, 1970.

_____ "Source and Redaction in the Fourth Gospel's Portrayal of Jesus' Signs." *JBL* 89(1970): 151–66.

France, R. T. *Jesus and the Old Testament*. London, 1971.

_____ "Mark and the Teaching of Jesus." In *Gospel Perspectives*, Vol. 1. Edited by R. T. France and D. Wenham. Sheffield, 1980: 101–36.

_____ . "Jewish Historiography, Midrash, and the Gospels." In *Gospel Perspectives*, Vol. 3. Edited by R. T. France and D. Wenham. Sheffield, 1983: 99–127.

Frankemölle, H. *Jahwebund und Kirche Christ. Studien zur Form- und Traditionsgeschichte des 'Evangeliums' nach Matthäus*. Münster, 1974.

Franklin, E. "The Ascension and the Eschatology of Luke-Acts." *SJT* 23(1970): 191–200.

_____ . *Christ the Lord: A Study in the Purpose & Theology of Luke-Acts*. London, 1975.

Freed, E. D. "Variations in the Language and Thought of John," *ZNW* 55 (1964), 167–97.

Freyne, Seán. *The Twelve: Disciples and Apostles. A Study in the Theology of First Three Gospels*. London: Sheed and Ward, 1968.

Friedrich, G. "Ein Tauflied hellenistischer Judenchristen, 1 Thess. 1, 9f." *ThZ* 21(1965): 502–16.

Frood, R. D. "Variations in the Language and Thought of John." *ZNW* 55(1964): 167–97.

Fuller, D. *Easter Faith and History*. Grand Rapids, 1964.

Fuller, R. H. *The Formation of the Resurrection Narratives*. London, 1972.

_____ , "John 20, 19–23." *Interp* 32(1978): 180–84.

Gaechter, P. "Das dreifache 'Weide meine Lämmer.' " *ZTK* 69(1947): 328–44.

_____ . *Das Matthäus Evangelium*. München, 1963.

Gaffney, J. "Believing and Knowing in the Fourth Gospel." *ThSt* 26(1965): 215–41.

Gardner-Smith, P. *The Narratives of the Resurrection*. London, 1926.

_____ . *St. John and the Synoptic Gospels*. Cambridge, 1938.

Garrard, L. A. "What Happened on the First Easter?" *HJ* 57(1958–59): 213–22.

Geldenhuys, N. *Commentary on the Gospel of Luke*. London, 1965.

Gibbs, J. M. "Luke 24:13–33 and Acts 8:26–39: The Emmaus Incident & the Eunuch's Baptism as Parallel Stories." *Bangalon Theological Forum* 7(1975): 17–30.

Giblin, C. H. "A Note on Doubt and Reassurance in Matt. 28:16–20." *CBQ* 37(1975): 68–75.

Gilmour, S. M. "The Christophany to More Than 500 Brethren." *JBL* 80(1961): 248–52.

————. "Easter and Pentecost." *JBL* 81(1962): 62–66.

Glasson, T. F. "The Kerygma: Is Our Version Correct?" *HJ* 51(1953): 129–43.

Goetz, S. C. and C. L. Blomberg. "The Burden of Proof." *JSNT* 11(1981): 39–63.

Goguel, M. "Did Peter Deny His Lord? A Conjecture." *HTR* 25(1932): 1–27.

————. *La foi à la résurrection de Jésus dans le christianisme primitif.* Paris, 1933.

Goppelt, L. *Apostolic and post-Apostolic Times.* Translated by R. A. Guelich. London, 1970.

van Goudoever, J. "The Place of Israel in Luke's Gospel." *NovT* 8(1966): 111–23.

Goulder, M. D. "Mark xvi. 1–8 and Parallels." *NTS* 24(1978): 235–46.

Grant, R. M. "One Hundred Fifty-three Large Fish, (John 21:11)." *HTR* 42(1949): 273–75.

Grass, H. *Ostergeschehen und Osterberichte.* Göttingen, 1964.

Grässer, E. "Die antijudische Polemik in Johannesevangelium." *NTS* 11(1964): 74–90.

Grassi, J. A. "Emmaus Revisited (Luke 24, 13–35 and Acts 8, 26–40)." *CBQ* 26(1964): 423–29.

Grayston, Kenneth, "The Empty Tomb." *ET* 92. no. 9(1981): 263–67.

Grintz, J. M. "Hebrew in the Days of the Second Temple." *JBL* 79(1960): 32–47.

Grundmann, W. "Verständis und Bewegung des Glaubens im Johannesevangelium." *KD* 6(1960): 131–54.

————. "Zur Rede Jesu vom Vater im Johannes-Evangelium. Eine redaktions- und bekenntnisgeschichtliche Untersuchung zu Joh 20, 17 und seiner Vorbereitung." *ZNW* 52(1961): 213–30.

————. *Das Evangelium nach Markus.* Berlin, 1968.

————. *Das Evangelium nach Matthäus.* Berlin, 1968.

Guelich, R. A. *Not to Annul the Law Rather to Fulfill the Law and the Prophets.* Hamburg, 1967.

Gundry, R. H. *The Use of the Old Testament in St. Matthew's Gospel.* SNT. Leiden, 1967.

————. " 'In My Father's House Are Many Monai' (John 14:2)," *ZNW* 58 (1967), 68–72.

Guthrie, D. *Introduction to the New Testament.* 3 vols. London, 1965.

Haacker, K. "Einige Fälle von 'Erlebter Rede' im Neuen Testament." *NovT* 12(1970): 70–77.

————. "Bemerkungen zum Freer-Logion." *ZNW* 63(1972): 125–29.

Haenchen, E. *The Acts of the Apostles.* Translated by B. Noble and G. Shinn. Oxford, 1971. Ger., 1965.

————. "Johanneischen Probleme." *ZTK* 56(1959): 19−54.

————. "Probleme des johanneischen 'Prologs'." *ZTK* 60(1963): 305−34.

————. "Der Vater, der mich gesandt hat." *NTS* 9(1963): 208−16.

————. *Das Johannesevangelium: Ein Kommentar.* Tübingen, 1980.

Hahn, F. *The Titles of Jesus in Christology.* Translated by H. Knight and G. Ogg. London, 1969. Ger., 1963.

Hamblin, R. L. "Miracles in the Book of Acts." *SWJT* 17(1974): 19−34.

Hamerton-Kelly, R. G. *Pre-existence, Wisdom and the Son of Man.* SNTSMS. Cambridge, 1973.

Harnack, A. *The Acts of the Apostles.* Translated by J. R. Wilkinson. London, 1909.

Harris, M. "Prepositions and Theology in the Greek NT." In *New International Dictionary of New Testament Theology,* Vol. 3. Edited by C. Brown. Grand Rapids, 1978.

Hartmann, G. "Die Vorlage des Osterberichte in Joh. 20." *ZNW* 55(1964): 197−220.

Hartman, L. " 'Into the Name of Jesus.' A Suggestion Concerning the Earliest Meaning of the Phrase." *NTS* 20(1973−74): 432−40.

————. "Baptism 'Into the Name of Jesus' and Early Christology. Some Tentative Considerations." *StTh* 28(1974): 21−48.

Headlam, A. C. *The Miracles of the New Testament.* London, 1914.

Hebert, G. "The Resurrection Narrative in St. Mark's Gospel." *SJT* 15(1962): 66−73.

Hengel, M. "Christologie und neutestamentliche Chronologie." In *Neues Testament und Geschichte,* edited by H. Baltensweiler and B. Reicke—Festschrift for Oscar Cullmann. Zurich, 1972.

Herrmann, W. "Der geschichtliche Christus der Grund unseres Glaubens." *ZTK* 2(1892): 232−73.

Higgins, A. J. B. *Jesus and the Son of Man.* Philadelphia, 1949.

Hill, D. *The Gospel of Matthew.* NCB. London, 1972.

Hindley, J. C. "Witness in the Fourth Gospel." *SJT* 18(1965): 319−37.

Hinnebusch, P. "Jesus, the New Elijah, in St. Luke." *BibTod* 31(1967): 2175−82, and 32(1968): 2237−44.

Hodges, Z. C. "The Women and the Empty Tomb." *BibSac* 123(1966): 301−09.

Hooke, S. H. *The Resurrection of Christ.* London, 1967.

Hooker, M. D. *Jesus and the Servant.* London, 1955.

————. "Christology and Methodology." *NTS* 17(1971): 480−87.

van der Horst, P. W. "Can a Book End with a GAR? A Note on Mark xvi. 8." *JTS* n.s. 23(1972): 121−24.

Hoskyns, E. C. "Adversaria Exegetica." *Theol* 7(1923): 147−55.

Howard, J. K. "Passover and Eucharist in the Fourth Gospel." *SJT* 20(1967): 329−37.

Howard, W. F. *Christianity According to St. John.* London, 1943.

Howe, E. M. "'... But Some Doubted' (Matt. 28:17). A Re-Appraisal of Factors Influencing the Easter Faith of the Early Christian Community." *JETS* 18/3(1975): 173−80.

Hubbard, Benjamin J. *The Matthean Redaction of a Primitive Apostolic Commissioning: An Exegesis of Matthew 28:16−20.* SBLDS, Missoula, MT, 1974.

─────. "Commissioning Stories in Luke-Acts: A Study of their Antecedents, Form, and Content." *Semeia* 8(1977): 103−26.

─────. "The Role of Commissioning Accounts in Acts." In *Perspectives on Luke-Acts,* edited by C. H. Talbert. Danville, VA, 1978.

Hunter, A. M. "Recent Trends in Johannine Studies." *ET* 71(1960): 164−67, 219−22.

van Iersel, B. M. F. "Die Wunderbare Speisung und das Abendmahl in der synoptischen Tradition." *NovT* 7(1965): 167−94.

Ittel, G. W. *Ostern und das leere Grab.* Gütersloh, 1967.

Jansen, J. F. *The Resurrection of Jesus Christ in New Testament Theology.* Philadelphia, 1980.

Jeremias, J. "Die Salbungsgeschichte Mc. 14:3−9." *ZNW* 35(1936): 75−82.

───── and W. Zimmerli. *Servant of God.* Translated by H. Knight. London, 1957.

─────. *Jesus' Promise to the Nations.* Translated by S. H. Hooke. London, 1959.

─────. *The Eucharistic Words of Jesus.* Translated by A. Ehrhardt. London, 1966.

─────. "Artikelloses Χριστός zur Ursprache von I Kor. 15:3b−5." *ZNW* 57(1966): 211−15.

─────. *New Testament Theology.* Translated by J. Bowden. 2 vols. London, 1971.

Jerrell, J. "Paulus—der Lehrer Israel. Zu der apologetisch Paulus in der Apostelgeschichte." *NovT* 10(1968): 164−90.

─────. *Luke and the People of God.* Minneapolis, 1972.

Johnson, Lewis. "Who Was the Beloved Disciple?" *Expt* 77 (1965 − 66) 157−58.

Johnston, G. *The Spirit-Paraclete in the Gospel of John.* NTM. Cambridge, 1970.

de Jonge, Marinus. *Jesus: Stranger from Heaven and Son of God.* SBLSBS 11. Missoula, MT., 1977.

Karnetzki, M. "Die galiläische Redaktion im Markusevangelium." *ZNW* 52(1961): 228−72.

Käsemann, E. *Essays on New Testament Themes.* Translated by W. J. Montague. SBT. London, 1964.

_____. *The Testament of Jesus.* Translated by G. Krodel. London, 1968.

_____. *New Testament Questions of Today.* Translated by W. J. Montague. London, 1969.

_____. *Jesus Means Freedom: A Polemical Survey of the NT.* Translated by F. Clarke. London, 1969.

Kegel, G. *Auferstehung Jesu—Auferstehung der Toten.* Gütersloh, 1970.

Kelber, W. H., ed. *The Passion in Mark: Studies on Mark 14–16.* Philadelphia, 1976.

Kingsbury, J. D. "The Composition and Christology of Matt. 28:16–20." *JBL* 93(1974): 573–84.

_____. *Matthew: Structure, Christology, Kingdom.* Philadelphia, 1975.

Klijn, A. F. "Joden en heidenen in Lukas-Handelingen." *Kerk en Theologie* 13(1962): 16–24.

Knox, W. L. "The Ending of St. Mark's Gospel." *HTR* 35(1942): 13–24.

Koch, G. *Die Auferstehung Jesu Christi.* Tübingen, 1959.

Kodell, J. "Luke's Use of *Laos*, 'People,' Especially in the Jerusalem Narrative: (Luke 19, 18–24, 53)." *CBQ* 31(1969): 327–43.

Kraeling, C. H. "Mark 16.8." *JBL* 45(1925): 357–58.

Kragerud, A. *Der Lieblingsjünger im Johannesevangelium.* Oslo, 1959.

Kramer, J. *Die Osterbotschaft der vier Evangelien.* Stuttgart, 1969.

_____. *Das älteste Zeugnis von der Auferstehung Christi.* SBS. Stuttgart, 1970.

Kratz, R. *Auferweckung als Befreiung.* SBS. Stuttgart, 1973.

Kuhn, K. G. "The Two Messiahs of Aaron and Israel." In *The Scrolls and the New Testament,* edited by K. Stendahl. London, 1958.

Kümmel, W. G. *Introduction to the New Testament.* Translated by A. J. Mattill. London, 1966.

Künneth W. *The Theology of the Resurrection.* Translated by J. W. Leitch. London, 1965.

Kurz, Wm. S. "Hellenistic Rhetoric in the Christological Proof of Luke-Acts." *CBQ* 42(1980): 171–95.

Kwik, R. J. "Some Doubted." *ET* 77(1966): 181.

Kysar, Robert. *The Fourth Evangelist and His Gospel.* Minneapolis: Augsburg, 1975.

Ladd, G. E. *Jesus and the Kingdom.* New York, 1964.

_____. *I Believe in the Resurrection of Jesus.* Grand Rapids, 1975.

Lähnemann, J. *Der Kolosserbrief.* Gütersloh, 1971.

Lake, K. *The Historical Evidence for the Resurrection of Jesus Christ.* London, 1907.

Lampe, G. W. H. "The Holy Spirit in the Writings of St. Luke." In *Studies in the Gospels,* edited by D. E. Nineham. Oxford, 1957.

_____ and MacKinnon, D. M. *The Resurrection.* London, 1966.

Lange, J. *Das Erscheinen des Auferstandenen im Evangelium nach Matthäus.* Würzburg, 1973.

Leaney, A. R. C. "The Resurrection Narrative in Luke (xxiv, 12–53)." *NTS* 2(1955–56): 110–14.

_____. *A Commentary on the Gospel According to Luke.* London, 1958.

Lee, G. M. "The Guard at the Tomb." *Theol* 72(1969): 169–75.

Léon-Dufour, X. *The Gospel and the Jesus of History.* London, 1968.

_____. "Redaktionsgeschichte of Matthew and Literary Criticism." *Persp* 11(1970): 9–35.

_____. *Résurrection de Jésus et message pascal.* Paris, 1971. ET. *Resurrection and the Message of Easter.* Translated by R. N. Wilson, New York, 1974.

Lessing, G. *Lessing's Theological Writings.* Translated and edited by H. Chadwick. Stanford, 1957.

Lewis, C. S. *Miracles* in *The Best of C. S. Lewis.* New York, 1969.

Lightfoot, R. H. *History and Interpretation in the Gospels.* New York, 1934.

_____. *Locality and Doctrine in the Gospels.* London, 1938.

_____. *The Gospel Message of St. Mark.* Oxford, 1950.

_____. *St. John's Gospel: A Commentary.* Oxford, 1956.

Lindars, B. *New Tetament Apologetic.* Philadelphia, 1956.

_____. "The Composition of John xx." *NTS* 7(1960–61): 142–47.

_____. *The Gospel of John.* NCB. London, 1972.

Lindemann, A. "Die Osterbotschaft des Markus. Zur theologischen Interpretation von Mark 16, 1–8." *NTS* 26(1980): 298–317.

Linnemann, E. "Der (wiedergefundene) Markuschluss." *ZTK* 66(1969): 255–87.

Lohfink, G. "Der historische Ansatz der Himmelfahrt Christi." *Catholica* 17(1963): 44–84.

_____. "Die Auferstehung Jesu und die historische Kritik." *BibLeb* 9(1968): 37–53.

_____. "Eine alttestamentliche Darstellungeform für Gotteserscheinungen in den Damaskusberichten (Apg. 9;22;26)." *BZ* 9(1965): 246–57.

_____. *Die Himmelfahrt Jesu.* München, 1971.

Lohmeyer, E. *Kyrios Jesu: Eine Untersuchung zu Phil. 2, 5–11.* 2d ed. Heidelberg, 1961.

_____. *Galiläa und Jerusalem.* Göttingen, 1956.

————. *Das Evangelium des Matthäus*. KKNT. Göttingen, 1962.

————. *Das Evangelium des Markus*. KKNT. Göttingen, 1963.

————. *Die Briefe an die Philipper an die Kolosser und an Philemon*. KKNT. Göttingen, 1964.

Lohse, E. "Wort und Sakrament im Johannesevangelium." *NTS* 7(1961): 110−25.

————. *Colossians and Philemon*. Translated by W. R. Pochlman and R. J. Harris. Philadelphia, 1968.

Loisy, A. *The Birth of the Christian Religion*. Translated by L. P. Jacke. London, 1948.

————. *The Origins of the New Testament*. London, 1950.

Longenecker, R. N. *Paul: Apostle of Liberty*. New York, 1964.

————. *The Christology of Early Jewish Christianity*. SBT. London, 1970.

————. *The Ministry and Message of Paul*. Grand Rapids. 1971.

Lorenzen, T. "Ist der Auferstandene in Galiläa erschienen? Bemerkungen zu einem Aufsatz von B. Steineifer." *ZNW* 64(1973): 209−21.

————. *Der Lieblingsjuner im Johannesevangelium*, SBS 55; Stuttgart, 1971.

Luck, U. "Herrenwort und Geschichte in Matth. 28, 16−20." *EvTh* 27(1967): 494−508.

McCasland, S. V. "The Scriptural Basis of 'On the Third day.'" *JBL* 48(1929): 124−37.

————. "The Basis of the Resurrection Faith." *JBL* 50(1931): 211−26.

McComb, S. "Professor Harnack on the Resurrection of Our Lord." *EXP* 4(1901): 350−63.

McConnell, R. S. *Law and Prophecy in Matthew's Gospel*. Basel, 1969.

McEleney, N. J., "153 Great Fishes (John 21, 11).—Gematriacal Atbash," *Bib* 58 (1977), 411−17.

MacGregor, G. H. C. "The Eucharist in the Fourth Gospel." *NTS* 9(1963): 111−19.

McIndoe, J. H. "The Young Man at the Tomb." *ET* 80(1969): 125.

MacKinnon, D. *Borderlands of Theology*. Edited by G. W. Roberts and D. Smucker. London, 1968.

McKnight, S. "The Role of the Disciples in Mark and Matthew. A Redaction-Critical Comparison." MA Thesis. Trinity Evangelical Divinity School, 1979.

Mackowski, P. M. "Where is Biblical Emmaus?" *SciEsp* 32(1980): 93−103.

M'Neile, A. H. *The Gospel According to Matthew*. London, 1961.

MacQuarrie, J. *Principles of Christian Theology*. London, 1966.

————. *The Scope of Demythologizing*. London, 1960.

Mahoney, R. *The Two Disciples at the Tomb. The Background and Message of John 20.1−10* TUW 6. Frankfurt, 1974.

Major, H. D. A. *The Mission and Message of Jesus.* London, 1937.

Malina, B. J. "The Literary Structure and Form of Matt. xxviii. 16–20." *NTS* 17(1970–71): 87–103.

Manek, J. "The New Exodus in the Books of Luke." *NovT* 2(1957): 208–23; 276–80.

Mann, C. S. "Languages of the Jews." In *The Acts of the Apostles* by J. Munck. New York, 1967.

Manson, T. W. *The Servant Messiah.* Cambridge, 1956.

————. *Studies in the Gospels and Epistles.* Manchester, 1962.

————. *On Paul and John.* London, 1963.

Marrow, S. "Jo 21: Indigatio in Ecclesiologiam Joanneau." *VerbDom* 45(1967): 47–51.

Marshall, I. H. *Eschatology and the Parables.* London, 1963.

————. "The Synoptic Son of Man Sayings in Recent Discussion." *NTS* 12(1966): 327–51.

————. "The Development of Christology in the Early Church." *TB* 18(1967): 77–93.

————. "The Divine Sonship of Jesus." *Interp* 21(1967): 87–103.

————. "The Christ-Hymn in Phil. 2:5–11." *TB* 19(1968): 104–27.

————. *Luke: Historian and Theologian.* Exeter, 1970.

————. *The Work of Christ.* Grand Rapids, 1970.

————. "The Resurrection in the Acts of the Apostles." In *Apostolic History and the Gospel,* edited by W. W. Gasque and R. P. Martin, Festschrift for F. F. Bruce. London, 1970.

————. "Palestinian and Hellenistic Christianity: Some Critical Comments." *NTS* 19(1973): 271–87.

————. "The Resurrection of Jesus in Luke." *TB* 24(1974): 55–98.

————, ed. *New Testament Interpretation.* Grand Rapids, 1977.

Martin, J. P. "Faith as Historical Understanding." In *Jesus of Nazareth,* edited by C. F. Henry. London, 1966.

————. "The Church in Matthew." *Int* 29(1975): 41–56.

————. "The Gospel of Luke." *NIGNTC.* Grand Rapids, 1979.

Martin, R. P. *Worship in the Early Church.* London, 1964.

————. *Carmen Christi.* Cambridge, 1971.

————. *Colossians: The Church's Lord and the Christian's Liberty.* Exeter, 1972.

————. *Mark—Evangelist and Theologian.* Exeter, 1972.

Martini, C. M. "L'apparizione agli Apostoli in Lc 24, 36–43 nel complesso dell'opera lucana." In *Resurrexit,* edited by E. Dhanis. Rome, 1974: 230–42.

Marxsen, W. *Introduction to the New Testament.* Translated by G. Buswell. Oxford, 1968.

_____. *Mark the Evangelist.* Translated by R. A. Harrisville et al. New York, 1969.

_____. *The Resurrection of Jesus of Nazareth.* Translated by M. Kohl. London, 1970.

Masson, C. "A propos de Act. 9. 19b–25. Note sure l'utilisation de Gal. et de 2 Cor. par l'auteur des Actes." *TZ* 18(1962): 161–66.

Mastin, B. "A Neglected Feature of the Christology of the Fourth Gospel." *NTS* 22(1975–76): 32–51.

Meier, J. P. *The Vision of Matthew.* New York, 1978.

_____. *Law and History in Matthew's Gospel.* Analecta Biblica 71. Rome, 1976.

Menoud, P. H., "Rémarque sûr les textes de l'Ascension dans Luc-Actes." In *Neutestamentliche Studien fur Rudolf Bultmann.* Berlin, 1954. ET in *Jesus Christ: A Collection of Studies,* by P. H. Menoud. Translated by E. M. Paul. Pittsburgh, 1978.

_____. "Pendant guarant jours (Actes 1.3)." *Neotestamentica et Patristica.* Leiden, 1962.

_____. "La Pentecote lucannienne et l'Histoire." *RHPR* 42(1962): 141–47.

Metzger, B. "A Suggestion Concerning the Meaning of I Cor. xv. 4b." *JTS* n.s. 8(1957): 118–23.

Meye, R. P. *Jesus and the Twelve: Discipleship & Revelation in Mark's Gospel.* Grand Rapids, 1968.

_____. "Mark 16:8—The Ending of Mark's Gospel." *BR* 14(1969): 33–43.

Meyer, B. F. *The Aims of Jesus.* London, 1979.

Meynet, R. "Comment établir unchiasme. À propos des pelerins d'Emmaus." *NouvRevTh* 100(1978): 233–49.

Michaelis, W. *Die Erscheinungen des Auferstandenen.* Basel, 1944.

Michel, O. "Der Abschluss des Matthäusevangeliums." *EvTh* 10(1950–51): 16–26. *ET,* "The Conclusion of Matthew's Gospel: A Contribution to the History of the Eastern Message." In *The Interpretation of Matthew,* edited by G. Stanton. Philadelphia, 1983.

_____. *Der Brief an die Römer.* KKNT. Göttingen, 1963.

_____. *Der Brief an die Hebräer.* KKNT. Göttingen, 1966.

Moffatt, J. *The Epistle to the Corinthians.* London, 1947.

Moltmann, J. *The Theology of Hope.* Translated by J. W. Leitch. London, 1967.

Montefiore, H. *A Commentary on the Epistle to the Hebrews.* London, 1964.

Montgomery, J. W. "Toward a Christian Philosophy of History." In *Jesus of Nazareth,* edited by C. F. H. Henry. London, 1966.

Moore, A. L. *The Parousia in the New Testament.* Leiden, 1966.

Morgenthaler, R. *Die lukanische Geschichtsschreibung als Zeugnis. Gestalt und Gehalt der Kunst des Lukas.* 2 vols. Zurich, 1948.

Morris, L. "Eyewitness Testimony and the Gospel Tradition." *JTS* n.s. 9(1958): 13 – 25, 243 – 52.

―――――. *Studies in the Fourth Gospel.* London, 1969.

―――――. *The Gospel According to St. John.* London, 1971.

Morris, W. D. "Matt. xxviii. 17." *ET* 77(1966): 181.

Morrison, F. *Who Moved the Stone?* London, 1930.

Moule, C. F. D. "St. Mark xvi. 8 Once More." *NTS* 2(1955 – 56): 58 – 59.

―――――. *The Epistles to the Colossians and Philemon.* Cambridge, 1957.

―――――. "Expository Problem: The Ascension—Acts 1.9." *ET* 68(1956 – 57): 206 – 209.

―――――. "The Post-Resurrection Appearances in the Light of Festival Pilgrimages." *NTS* 4(1957 – 58): 58 – 61.

―――――. "A Reconsideration of the Context of *Maranatha.*" *NTS* 6(1959 – 60): 307 – 10.

―――――. *Worship in the New Testament.* London, n.d.

―――――. *The Phenomenon of the New Testament.* London, 1967.

―――――. "The Christology of Acts." In *Studies in Luke-Acts,* edited by L. E. Keck and J. L. Martyn. London, 1968.

―――――. "Further Reflections on Phil. 2:5 – 11." In *Apostolic History and the Gospel,* edited by W. W. Gasque and R. P. Martin. Festschrift for F. F. Bruce. London, 1970.

―――――. "On Defining the Messianic Secret in Mark." In *Jesus und Paulus,* edited by E. Earle Ellis and E. Grässer. Festschrift for Werner Georg Kümmel. Asttinger, 1978.

Muddiman, J. "A Note on Reading Luke xxiv.12." *EphThLouv* 48(1972): 542 – 48.

Mullins, T. "New Testament Commission Forms, Especially in Luke-Acts." *JBL* 95(1976): 603 – 14.

Munck, J. "Paulus Tanquam Abortivus." In *New Testament Essays,* edited by A. J. B. Higgins. Manchester, 1959. Studies in Memory of T. W. Manson.

Munz, P. *The Problem of Religious Knowledge.* London, 1959.

Murphy-O'Connor, J. "Christological Anthropology in Phil. 2:6 – 11." *RB* 83(1976): 25 – 50.

Mussner, F. *Die Auferstehung Jesu.* München, 1969.

Navone, J. *Themes of St. Luke.* Rome, n.d.

Neill, S. *The Interpretation of the New Testament 1861 – 1961.* London, 1964.

_____. *The Acts of the Apostles*. NCB. London, 1973.

Neirynck, F. "Les femmes au tombeau: Étude de la rédaction Matthéene (Matt. xxviii. 1—10)." *NTS* 15(1968—69): 168—90.

_____. "Parakypsas blepei. Lc 24,12 et Jn 20,5." *EphThLouv* 53. no. 1(1977): 113—152.

_____. "Apēlthen pros heauton. Lc 24,12 et Jn 20,10." *EphThLouv* 53. no. 1(1978): 104—118.

_____. "The Uncorrected Historic Present in Lk. xxiv.12." *EphThLouv* 48(1972): 548—53.

_____. "Marc 16.1—8. Tradition et rédaction." *EphThLouv* 56. no. 1(1980), 56—88.

Neufeld, V. H. *The Earliest Christian Confessions*. Leiden, 1963.

Nicol, W. *The Semeia in the Fourth Gospel*. SNT. Leiden, 1972.

Niebuhr, R. *Resurrection and Historical Reason*. New York, 1957.

Nineham, D. E. "Eyewitness Testimony and the Gospel Tradition." *JTS* n.s. 9(1958): 13—25, 243—52; 11(1960): 253—64.

Nock, A. D. *Early Gentile Christianity and Its Hellenistic Background*. New York, 1964.

Nolloth, C. F. "The Resurrection of Our Lord and Recent Criticism." *HJ* 3(1904—5): 529—42.

Nötscher, F. "Zur Aufserstehung nach drei Tagen." *Biblica* 35(1954): 313—19.

O'Collins, G. *Foundations of Theology*. Chicago, 1971.

_____. *The Easter Jesus*. London, 1973.

_____. "Karl Barth on Christ's Resurrection." *SJT* 26(1973): 85—99.

_____. *The Resurrection of Jesus Christ*. Valley Forge, 1973.

Ogletree, T. W. *Christian Faith and History*. New York, 1965.

Olsson, Birger, *Structure and Meaning in the Fourth Gospel*. CBNTS 6. Lund, 1974.

O'Neill, J. C. "On the Resurrection as an Historical Question." In *Christ, Faith and History*, edited by S. W. Sykes and J. P. Clayton. Cambridge, 1972.

Orlett, R. "An Influence of the Early Liturgy upon the Emmaus Account." *CBQ* 21(1959): 212—19.

Orr, J. *The Resurrection of Jesus*. London, 1908.

Osborne, G. R. "Redaction Criticism and the Great Commission: A Case Study Toward a Biblical Understanding of Inerrancy." *JETS* 19. no. 2(1976): 73—85.

_____. "The Evangelical and *Traditionsgeschichte*." *JETS* 21. no. 2(1978): 117—30.

_____. "The Evangelical and Redaction Criticism: Critique and Methodology." *JETS* 22. no. 4(1979): 305—22.

_____. "John 21: Test Case for History and Redaction in the Resurrection Narratives." In *Gospel Perspectives*, Vol. 2. Edited by R. T. France and D. Wenham. Sheffield, 1981.

O'Toole, R. F. "Luke's Notion of 'Be Imitators of Me as I am of Christ' in Acts 25 − 26." *BTB* 8(1978): 155 −61.

_____. "Luke's Understanding of Jesus' Resurrection-Ascension-Exaltation." *BTB* 9(1979): 106 −14.

Ottley, R. R. "ἐφοβοῦντο γάϱ." *JTS* 27(1926): 407 −09.

Otto, R. *The Idea of the Holy*. Translated by J. W. Harvey. London, 1928.

Palmer, H. *The Logic of Gospel Criticism*. London, 1968.

Pannenberg, W. *Jesus: God and Man*. Translated by L. L. Wilkins and D. A. Priebe. London, 1966.

_____. *Basic Questions in Theology*. Vol. 1. Translated by G. H. Kehm. London, 1970.

Parker, P. "John and John Mark." *JBL* 79(1960): 97 −110.

_____. "John the Son of Zebedee and the Fourth Gospel." *JBL* 81(1962): 35 − 43.

_____. "Luke and the Fourth Evangelist." *NTS* 9(1963): 317 −36.

Patte, D. and A. *Structural Exegesis: From Theory to Practice*. Philadelphia, 1978.

Paulsen, H. "Mk. xvi. 1−8." *NovT* 22(1980): 138 −75.

Payne, D. F. "Semitisms in the Book of Acts." In *Apostolic History and the Gospel*, edited by W. W. Gasque and R. P. Martin. Festschrift for F. F. Bruce. London, 1970.

Perrin, N. *Rediscovering the Teaching of Jesus*. New York, 1967.

_____. *What is Redaction Criticism?* London, 1970.

_____. "(παϱα) διδόναι in connection with the Passion of Jesus." In *Der Ruf Jesu und die Antwort der Gemeinde*, edited by E. Lohse. Göttingen, 1970.

Pesch, R. *The Resurrection According to Matthew, Mark and Luke*. Philadelphia, 1976.

_____. "Eine alttestamentliche Ausfürungsformel." *BZ* 10(1966):220 −245; 11(1967), 79 −95.

Pesch, R. *Der reiche Fischfang*. Düsseldorf, 1969.

_____. "Zur Enstehung des Glaubens an die Auferstehung Jesu. Ein Vorschlag zur Diskussion." *Theologische Quartal schrift* 153(1973): 201 −28.

Peter, J. *Finding the Historical Jesus*. London, 1965.

Petersen, N. B. "When is the End not the End? Literary Reflections on the Ending of Mark's Narrative." *Int* 34(1980): 151 −66.

Pfleiderer, O. *Early Christian Conception of Christ*. London, 1905.

————. *Primitive Christianity.* 4 vols. Translated by W. Montgomery. London, 1906–11.

Pinnock, C. "On the Third Day." In *Jesus of Nazareth,* edited by C. F. H. Henry. London, 1966.

————. *Biblical Revelation—The Foundation of Christian Doctrine.* Chicago, 1971.

Plantinga, A. *Faith and Philosophy.* Grand Rapids, 1964.

Plevnik. " 'The Eleven and Those with Them' According to Luke." *CBQ* 40(1978): 205–11.

Plummer, A. *The Gospel According to Matthew.* London, 1911.

————. *The Gospel According to Luke.* 5th ed. ICC. Edinburgh, 1922.

Pollock, J. L. "Criteria and Our Knowledge of the Material World." *PhRev* 76(1967): 55–60.

de la Potterie, I. "Le titre KYIOΣ applique a Jesus dans l'Evangile de Luc.' In *Melanges bibliques en hommage au R. P. Beda Rigaux,* edited by A. Descamps and A. de Halleux, Gembloux. 1970.

Prentice, W. "St. Paul's Journey to Damascus." *ZNW* 64(1956): 250–55.

Pryke, E. J. *Redactional Style in the Marcan Gospel: A Study of Syntax and Vocabulary as Guides to Redaction in Mark.* Cambridge, 1978.

Ramsey, A. M. *The Resurrection of Christ.* London, 1946.

Ramsey, I. T. *Religious Language.* London, 1957.

————, et al. *The Miracles and the Resurrection.* London, 1964.

Rau, G. "Das Volk in der lukanische Passionsgeschichte: Ein Konjectur zu Lk. 23.13." *ZNW* 56(1965): 41–51.

Rehkopf, F. *Die lukanische Sunderquelle.* Tübingen, 1959.

Reicke, B. "Instruction and Discussion in the Travel Narrative." *StEv* 1(1959): 206–16.

Reicke, B. "The Risen Lord and His Church." *Interp* 13(1959): 157–69.

————. *The Epistles of James, Peter, and Jude.* New York, 1964.

————. *The Gospel of Luke.* Richmond, 1964.

Reimarus, H. S. *The Goal of Jesus and His Disciples.* Translated by G. H. Buchanan. Leiden, 1970.

————. *Reimarus—Fragments.* Translated by R. S. Fraser. London, 1971.

Reitzenstein, R. *Die hellenistischen Mysterienreligionen nach ihren Grundgedanken und Wirkungen.* 3 vols. Leipzig, 1927.

Rengstorf, K. H. "A Formula of the Judean Royal Ritual." *NovT* 5(1961): 229–44.

————. "The Election of Matthias." In *Current Issues in NT Interpretation,* edited by W. Klassen and G. F. Snyder. London, 1962.

————. *Die Auferstehung Jesu*. Witten/Ruhr, 1967.

Renan, E. *The Life of Jesus*. London, 1864.

Reploh, Karl-Georg. *Markus-Lehrer der Gemeinde: Eine redaktionsgeschichtliche Studie zu den Jüngerperikopen des Markus-Evangeliums*. Stuttgart, 1969.

Ricca, Paolo. *Die Eschatologie des vierten Evangeliums*. Zurich, 1966.

Richardson, A. *An Introduction to the Theology of the New Testament*. London, 1961.

Richardson, L. J. D. "St. Mark xvi.8." *JTS* 49(1948): 144−45.

Richardson, P. *Israel in the Apsotolic Church*. Cambridge, 1969.

Riesenfeld, H. "Zu den johanneischen *hina*-Sätzen." *StTh* 19(1965): 213−20.

————. *The Gospel Tradition*. Translated by E. M. Rowley. Oxford, 1970.

Riga, P. "Signs of Glory. The Use of 'Semeion' in John's Gospel." *Interp* 17(1963): 402−24.

Rigaux, B. *Dieu l'a ressuscité*. Duculot, 1973.

Rist, J. M. *On the Independence of Matthew and Mark*. SNTMS 32. Cambridge, 1978.

Robertson, A. and Plummer, A. *Commentary on the First Epistle to the Corinthians*. ICC. Edinburgh, 1911.

Robinson, J. A. "In the Name." *JTS* 7(1905−06): 186−202.

Robinson, J. A. T. "Traces of a Liturgical Sequence in I Cor. 16:20−24." *JTS* n.s. 4(1953): 381−91.

Robinson, J. A. T. "The Most Primitive Christology of All." *JTS* n.s. 7(1956): 177−89. Reprinted in his *Twelve New Testament Studies*. 139−54. London, 1962.

————. Redating the New Testament. London, 1976.

Robinson, J. M. *A New Quest of the Historical Jesus*. London, 1968.

————, and Koester, H. *Trajectories through Early Christianity*. Philadelphia, 1971.

Rohde, J. *Rediscovering the Teaching of the Evangelists*. Translated by J. M. Barton. London, 1968.

Roloff, J. "Der Johanneische 'Lieblingsünger' und der Lehrer der Gerechtigkeit." *NTS* 15(1968−69): 129−51.

Rowley, H. H. "Baptism of John and the Qumran Sect." In *New Testament Essays*, edited by A. J. B. Higgins. Manchester, 1959.

Rowlingson, D. J. "The Moral Context of the Resurrection Faith." In *Christ and the Spirit in the New Testament*, edited by B. Lindars and S. Smalley. Festschrift for C. F. D. Moule. Cambridge, 1973.

Ruckstuhl, E. *Die literarische Einheit des Johannes Evangeliums*. Freiburg, 1951.

Salvoni, F. "The So-Called Jesus Resurrection Proof (John 20:7)." *RestorQuart* 22. no. 1–2 (1979): 72–76.

Sanders, E. P. *Tendencies of the Synoptic Tradition.* SNTSMS 9. Cambridge, 1969.

Sanders, J. N. *The Gospel According to St. John.* Edited by B. A. Mastin. London, 1968.

───────. "Those Whom Jesus Loved." *NTS* 1(1954–55): 29–41.

Sanders. J. T. *The New Testament Christological Hymns.* SNTSMS. Cambridge, 1971.

Sasse, H. "Jesus Christ, the Lord." In *Mysterium Christi.*, edited by G. K. A. Bell and A. Deissman. London, 1930.

Schaberg, J. *The Father, the Son and the Holy Spirit: The Triadic Phrase in Matthew 28:19b.* SDS 61. Chico, CA., 1982.

Schenke, L. *Auferstehungsverkündigung und leeres Grab.* SBS. Stuttgart, 1969.

Schider, F. and Stenger, W. "Beobachtungen zur Struktur der Emmaus perikope (Lk. 24,13–35)." *BZ* 16(1972): 94–114.

Schillebeeckx, Edward. *Jesus: An Experiment in Christology.* Translated by H. Hoskins. New York, 1978.

───────. *Interim Report on the Books Jesus and Christ.* Translated by J. Bowden. New York, 1981.

Schleiermacher, F. *The Christian Faith.* Edited by H. R. MacKintosh and J. S. Stewart. Edinburgh, 1928.

Schlier, H. "Jesus Himmelfahrt nach den lukanischen Schriften." *Geistleb* 34(1961): 91–99.

Schmall, Günther. *Die Zwölf im Markusevangelium.* Trier Theologische Studien 30. Trier, 1974.

Schmiedel, P. W. "Resurrection-and-Ascension Narratives." In *Encyclopedia Biblica,* 4039–87.

Schmitt, J. "Le 'milieu littéraire de la 'tradition' citée dans 1 Cor., xv, 3b–5." In *Resurrexit,* edited by E. Dhanis. 169–81. Rome, 1974.

Schnackenburg, R. "Offenbarung und Glaube in Johannesevangelium." *BL* 7(1966), 165–80.

───────. *The Gospel According to John.* 3 vols. Translated by K. Smyth. London, 1968.

───────. "On the Origin of the Fourth Gospel." In *Jesus and Man's Hope I,* edited by D. G. Buttrick. Pittsburgh, 1970.

Schniewind, J. *Die Parallelperikopen bei Lukas und Johannes.* Darmstadt, 1958.

Schramm, T. *Der Markus-Stoff bei Lukas.* Cambridge, 1971.

Schubert, P. "The Structure and Significance of Luke 24." In *Neutestamentliche Studien für Rudolf Bultmann.* Berlin, 1954.

Schürmann, H. "Die vorösterlichen Anfänge der Logiontradition." In *Traditionsgeschichtliche Untersuchungen zu den synoptischen Evangelien*. Düsseldorf, 1968.

—————. *Das Lukasevangelien I*. Freiburg, 1969.

Schulz, S. "Maranatha and Kyrios Jesus." *ZNW* 53(1962): 125–44.

—————. "Gottes Vorschung bei Lukas." *ZNW* 54(1963): 104–16.

—————. *Die Stunde der Botschaft*. Hamburg, 1967.

Schütz, J. H. "Apostolic Authority and the Control of Tradition: I Cor. xv." *NTS* 15(1969): 439–57.

Schwank, B. " 'Selig, die nicht sehen und doch glauben.' Jo 20, 19–31." *SeinSend* 29(1964): 435–50.

Schweitzer, A. *The Quest of the Historical Jesus*. Translated by W. Montgomery. London, 1910.

Schweizer, E. *Ego Eimi*. Göttingen, 1939.

—————. "Der Menschenson." *ZNW* 50(1959): 197–215.

—————. *Lordship and Discipleship*. London, 1960.

—————. *Neotestamentica*. Zürich, 1963.

—————. "Mark's Contribution to the Quest of the Historical Jesus." *NTS* 10(1964): 421–32.

—————. "The Concept of the Davidic 'Son of God' in Acts and Its Old Testament Background." In *Studies in Luke-Acts*, edited by L. E. Keck and J. L. Martyn. Nashville, 1966.

—————. "Concerning the Speeches in Acts." In *Studies in Luke-Acts*, edited by L. E. Keck and J. L. Martyn. Nashville, 1966.

—————. *Jesus*. Translated by D. E. Green. London, 1971.

—————. *The Good News According to St. Mark*. Translated by D. H. Madvig. London, 1971.

Seidensticker, P. *Die Auferstehung Jesu in der Botschaft der Evangelisten*. SBS. Stuttgart, 1967.

Selwyn, E. G. *The First Epistle of Peter*. London, 1946.

Senior, D. "The Passion Narrative in the Gospel of Matthew." In *L'Évangile selon Matthieu*, edited by M. Dider. Gembloux, 1972.

Shaw, J. M. *The Resurrection of Christ*. Edinburgh, 1920.

Sheehan, J. F. X. "Feed my Lambs." *Scr* 16(1964): 21–27.

Shepherd, M. H. "Paul and the Double Resurrection Tradition." *JBL* 64(1945): 227–40.

Sherwin-White, A. N. *Roman Society and Roman Law in the NT*. Oxford, 1963.

Simpson, P. "The Drama of the City of God, Jerusalem, in St. Luke's Gospel." *Scr* 15(1963): 65 – 80.

Smalley, S. S. "The Johannine Son of Man Sayings." *NTS* 15(1968 – 69): 278 – 301.

————. *John: Evangelist and Interpreter.* Exeter: Paternoster, 1978.

————. "The Sign in John XXI," *NTS* 20 (1974), 275 – 88.

Smith, J. W. D. "The Resurrection of Christ: Myth or History?" *ET* 72(1960 – 61): 370 – 75.

Snodgrass, K. "Western Non-Interpolations." *JBL* 91(1972): 369 – 79.

Solages, B. D. *Jean et les Synoptiques:* Leiden: Brill, 1979.

Sparks, H. F. D. "The Semitisms of Acts." *JTS* n.s. 1(1950): 16 – 28.

Spicq, C. "Notes d'Exegese johannique. La charité est amour manifeste." *RevB* 65(1958): 358 – 70.

Stagg, F. and E. *Women in the World of Jesus.* Philadelphia, 1978.

Stählin, Gustav. *Die Apostelgeschichte.* Göttingen, 1970.

Stanton, G. N. "The Gospel Traditions and Early Christological Reflection." In *Christ, Faith and History,* edited by S. W. Sykes and J. P. Clayton. Cambridge, 1972.

Stauffer, E. *New Testament Theology.* Translated by J. Marsh. London, 1955.

Stein, Robert H. "A Short Note on Mark xiv.28 and xvi.7." *NTS* 20(1974): 445 – 52.

————. "Criteria for Authenticity." In *Gospel Perspectives I,* edited by R. T. France and D. Wenham. Sheffield: JSOT Press, 1980.

Steinseifer, B. "Der Ort der Erscheinungen des Auferstandenen." *ZNW* 62(1971): 232 – 65.

van Stempvoort, P. A. "The Interpretation of the Ascension in Luke and Acts." *NTS* 5(1958 – 59): 30 – 42.

Stenger, W. "Der Christushymnus in I Tim. 3,16." *Trierer Theologische Zeitschrift* 78(1969): 33 – 48.

Stewart, J. S. "The Christ of Faith." In *The New Testament in Historical and Contemporary Perspective,* edited by H. Anderson and W. Barclay. Oxford, 1965.

Stock, K. *Boten aus dem Mit-Ihm-Sein: Das Verhältnis zwischen Jesus und den Zwölf nach Markus.* Analecta Biblica 70. Rome, 1970.

Strack, H. L. and Billerbeck, P. *Kommentar zum Neuen Testament aus Talmud und Midrasch.* 5 vols. München, 1922 – 28, 1956, 1961.

Strauss, D. F. *A New Life of Jesus.* 2d ed. Translated by G. Eliot. New York, 1892.

Strecker, G. "Redaktion und Tradition in Christushymnus Phil. 2." *ZNW* 55(1964): 65 – 78.

————. *Der Weg der Gerechtigkeit—Untersuchung zur Theologie des Matthäus.* Göttingen, 1962.

Streeter, B. H. et al. *Foundations: Christian Beliefs in Terms of Modern Thought*. London, 1912.

Stuhlmacher, P. *Das paulinische Evangelium: I. Vorgeschichte*. Göttingen, 1968.

Styler, G. M. "Stages in Christology in the Synoptic Gospels." *NTS* 10(1963−64): 398−409.

Swete, H. B. *The Gospel According to St. Mark*. London, 1898.

Tagawa, K. "People and Community in the Gospel of Matthew." *NTS* 16(1969−70): 149−62.

Talbert, C. H. "An Anti-Gnostic Tendency in Lucan Christology." *NTS* 14(1967−68): 259−71.

_____. *Luke and the Gnostics*. New York, 1966.

_____. "The Redaction-Quest for Lucan Theology." *Persp* 11(1970): 171−222.

Tannehill, Robert C. "The Disciples in Mark: The Function of a Narrative Role." *JRel* 57(1977): 386−405.

_____. "The Gospel of Mark as Narrative Christology." In *Perspectives on Mark's Gospel*, edited by N. R. Petersen. *Semeia* 16(1980): 57−95.

Tasker, R. V. G. *The Gospel According to Matthew*. London, 1961.

Taylor, V. *The Names of Jesus*. London, 1953.

_____. *The Person of Christ*. London, 1958.

_____. *The Gospel According to Mark*. London, 1959.

_____. *The Passion Narrative of St. Luke*. Cambridge, 1972.

Tenney, M. C. "The Historicity of the Resurrection." In *Jesus of Nazareth*, edited by C. F. H. Henry. London, 1966.

Thévenot, X. "Emmaus, une nouvelle Genèse? Une lecture psychanalytique de Genèse 2−3 et Luc 24, 13−35." *MélSciRel* 37(1980): 3−18.

Thiselton, A. C. "Truth," NIDNTT, III, 874−901.

Thorburn, T. J. *The Resurrection Narratives and Modern Criticism*. London, 1910.

Thrall, M. "The Origin of Pauline Christology." *Apostolic History and the Gospel*, edited by W. W. Gasque and R. P. Martin. London, 1970.

Thüsing, W. *Die Erhöhung und Verherrlichung im Johannesevangelium*. Münster, 1960.

Tillich, P. *Systematic Theology*. 8 vols. Chicago, 1951−64.

Titus, E. L. "The Identity of the Beloved Disciple." *JBL* 69(1950): 323−28.

Tolbert, M. "Leading Ideas of the Gospel of Luke." *RevExp* 64(1967): 441−51.

Travis, S. "Form Criticism." In *New Testament Interpretation*, edited by I. H. Marshall. Grand Rapids, 1977.

Trench, R. C. *Synonyms of the New Testament*. Grand Rapids, 1948.

Trilling, W. *Das Wahre Israel—Studien zur Theologie des Matthäus-Evangeliums*. München, 1964.

Trites, A. "The Prayer Motif in Luke-Acts." In *Perspectives on Luke-Acts*, edited by C. H. Talbert. Danville, VA, 1978.

Troeltsch, E. "Historiography." In *Encyclopedia of Religion and Ethics*, Vol. 4. Edited by J. Hastings. 716–23. New York, 1961.

————. "Uber die historische und dogmatische Methode in der Theologie." In *Gesammelte Schriften*, Vol. 2. 729–53. Tübingen, 1912–25.

Trompf, G. W. "The First Resurrection Appearance and the Ending of Mark's Gospel." *NTS* 18(1972): 308–30.

————. "The *Markusschluss* in Recent Research." *ABR* 21(1973): 15–26.

Turner, H. E. W. *Jesus, Master and Lord*. London, 1953.

Tyson, J. B. "The Blindness of the Disciples in Mark." *JBL* 80(1961): 261–68.

van Unnik, W. C. "The Lord Is With You." In *New Testament Essays in Memory of T. W. Manson*, edited by A. J. B. Higgins. Manchester, 1959.

Van Hoff, A. "It is Made Present." *ET* 81(1970): 377–78.

Vellanickal, Matthew. *The Divine Sonship of Christians in the Johannine Writings*. Rome, 1977.

Vielhauer, P. "Erwägungen zur Christologie des Markusevangeliums." In *Zeit und Geschichte*, edited by E. Dinkler. Tübingen, 1964.

————. "Ein Weg zur neutestamentlichen Christologie." *AufzNT* 31(1965): 145–95.

————. *AufzNT*. München, 1965.

Vögtle, A. "Das christologie und ekklesiologische Anliegen von Mt. 28,18–20." *StEv* 2(1964): 266–94.

von Wahlde, V. C. "A Redactional Technique in the Fourth Gospel." *CBQ* 38(1976): 520–33.

Walker, N. "After Three Days." *NovT* 4(1960): 261–62.

Walker, W. O. "Postcrucifixion Appearances and Christian Origins." *JBL* 88(1969): 157–65.

Walter, N. "Eine vormatthäische Schilderung der Auferstehung Jesu." *NTS* 19(1972–73): 415–29.

Wanke, J. " '. . . wie sie ihn beim Brotbrechen erkannten.' Zur Auslegung der Emmaus Erzählung Lk 24, 13–35." *BibZeit* 18(1974): 180–92.

Ward, R. A. *Hidden Meaning in the New Testament*. London, 1969.

Wead, D. W. *The Literary Devices in John's Gospel*. Basel, 1970.

Webster, C. A. "St. Matthew xxviii. 1–3." *ET* 42(1930–31): 381–82.

Weeden, T. J. "The Heresy That Necessitated Mark's Gospel." *ZNW* 59(1968): 145−58.

_____. *Mark—Traditions in Conflict.* Philadelphia, 1971.

Weiss, J. *The History of Primitive Christianity.* Translated by F. C. Grant et al. London, 1937.

Wellhausen, J. *Das Evangelium Marci.* Berlin, 1909.

Wendland, J. *Miracles and Christianity.* London, 1911.

Wenham, D. "Matthew's Resurrection Narrative." *TB* 24(1974): 20−54.

Wenham, J. W. "The First Easter Morning." Unpublished paper read to the Tyndale Fellowship. Cambridge, July, 1972.

Wenz, H. "Schein und Glauben bei Johannes." *TZ* 17(1961): 17−25.

Werner, M. *The Formation of Christian Dogma.* London, 1957.

Westcott, B. F. *The Gospel According to St. John.* 2 vols. London, 1908.

Westerholm, S. *Jesus and Scribal Authority.* Lund, 1978.

Wilckens, U. *Die Missionsreden in der Apostelgeschichte.* 2d ed. Neukirchen, 1963.

_____. "The Tradition-History of the Resurrection of Jesus." In *The Significance of the Message of the Resurrection for Faith in Jesus Christ,* edited by C. F. D. Moule. SBT. London, 1968.

_____. *Auferstehung.* Berlin, 1970. ET: *Resurrection, Biblical Testimony to the Resurrection.* Atlanta, 1978.

Wilcox, M. *The Semitisms of Acts.* Oxford, 1965.

Wilder, A. N. "Variant Traditions of the Resurrection in Acts." *JBL* 62(1943): 307−18.

Williams, G. S. C. *A Commentary on the Acts of the Apostles.* BNTC. London, 1964.

Wilson, S. G. "Lukan Eschatology." *NTS* 16(1970): 330−47.

_____. *The Gentiles and the Gentile Mission in Luke-Acts.* NTM. Cambridge, 1973.

Wilson, W. G. "An Examination of the Linguistic Evidence Adduced Against the Unity of Authorship of the First Epistle of John and the Fourth Gospel," *JTS* 49 (1948): 147−56.

Wind, A. "The Destination and Purpose of the Gospel of John." *NovT* 14(1972): 26−69.

Windisch, H. *Johannes und die Synoptiker.* Leipzig, 1926.

_____. "Zur Christologie der Pastoralbriefen." *ZNW* 34(1935): 213−34.

Winter, P. "I Corinthians xv 3b−7." *NovT* 2(1958): 142−50.

Wittgenstein, L. *Philosophical Investigations.* Translated by G. E. M. Anscombe. New York, 1964.

Wrede, W. *The Messianic Secret.* Translated by J. O. G. Greig. Cambridge, 1971.

Zahn, T. *Introduction to the New Testament*. Translated by J. M. Trout et al. 3 vols. London, 1965.

Zehnle, R. F. *Peter's Pentecost Discourse*. New York, 1971.

Zelzer, K. "Oude pō gar ēdeisan—'denn bisher hatten sie nicht verstanden.' Zu übersetzung und Kontextbezug von Joh 20,9." *BibLiturg* 53. no. 2(1980): 104–106.

Zumstein, J. "Matthieu 28. 16–20." *RTP* 22(1972):14–33.

Index of Subjects

Amen formula, double, 262
Angelic message, 51–55, 5–11
  community theology in, 53
  fulfillment theme in, 55
  historicity of, 211–12
  mission motif in, 52–53
  misunderstanding motif in, 51, 54
  parousia theme in, 52
  Petrine authority in, 51
  remembering motif in, 107–8
Angel(s). *See also* Angelic message
  anthropomorphic descriptions of,
    49–51
  divine authority of, 80
  earthquake at tomb and, 205–7
  historicity of, 210–11
  lack of, in John, 158
  number of, 106, 210–11
  removal of stone and, 49, 204
  supernatural description of, 77
  as symbol of eschatological glory,
    50–51
  tradition-critical approach to, 234–35
  as witnesses, 106
Anointing of Jesus, 45–47, 200–1, 205.
    See also Women, motive of
  purposelessness of, 52
Anthropomorphic symbolism, 282
Anti-docetic element, in John, 172
Antithetical parallelism, 170
Aphesis, 132
Apocalyptic imagery
  in Ascension accounts, 269–70
  earthquake at tomb, 206
Apocryphal Act of John, 71

Apologetic motif, 155–57, 167, 288–89
  in deception of priests, 215
  historical basis of, 197–98
  in race to tomb, 154
Apostles
  definition of, 112
  faith of, 113
  tradition-critical approach to
    appearance to, 229–31
  women as, 112
Appearance narratives, 221–72. *See also*
    specific narrative
  Alsup on, 35
  event vs. interpretation of, 281–92
  lack of chronology among, 270, 282–83
  1 Corinthians 15:5–8, 221–33
    historical context of, 223
    origin of, 222–23
    purposes of, 224–25
  independent use of, 271
  suggested pattern of development of,
    271–72
Ascension, 136–44
  in appearance to Mary, 159, 162–63
  ecclesiology in, 138
  glorification of Christ and, 138
  preparation of reader for, 104
  priestly emphasis of, 139
  theological themes of, 138–39
  timeless quality of, 162–63
  tradition-critical approach to, 266–70
  typology of, 142–44
  worship emphasis of, 139–42
Ascension accounts
  authorship of, 266

Index of Biblical References